T5-CWK-704

 FINANCIAL

143 Mallard Street, Suite E
Saint Rose, Louisiana 70087
www.kaplanfinancial.com

At press time, this edition contains the most complete and accurate information currently available. Owing to the nature of certification examinations, however, information may have been added recently to the actual test that does not appear in this edition. Please contact the publisher to verify that you have the most current edition.

This publication is designed to provide accurate and authoritative information in regard to the subject matter covered. It is sold with the understanding that the publisher is not engaged in rendering legal, accounting, or other professional services. If legal advice or other expert assistance is required, the services of a competent professional should be sought.

We value your input and suggestions. If you found imperfections in this product, please let us know by sending an email to errata@kaplan.com. Please include the title, edition, and PPN (reorder number) of the material.

KAPLAN REVIEW FOR THE CFP® CERTIFICATION EXAMINATION, VOLUME VII: CASE BOOK, 11TH EDITION ©2007 DF Institute, Inc. All rights reserved.

Published by DF Institute, Inc.

Printed in the United States of America.

ISBN: 1-4195-9952-6

PPN: 4302-4902

07	08	10	9	8	7	6	5	4	3	2	1
J	F	**M**	A	M	J	J	A	S	O	N	D

If found, please notify the following:

Name of CFP® Candidate:_____

Address:_____

City, State, ZIP:_____

Phone:_____

Email: _____

Additional information on review materials and live
instructional review courses near you is available at:

www.kaplanfinancial.com

Please visit our Website regularly
for updates to this and other products.

For answers to your technical questions on the contents of this text, please contact us at:

fpstudent@kaplan.com

PRODUCTS AND SERVICES FOR THE CFP® CERTIFICATION EXAMINATION

KAPLAN FINANCIAL REVIEW COURSES FOR THE CFP® CERTIFICATION EXAMINATION

Kaplan Financial offers several options to meet the diverse needs of candidates—the Live Review Course, which offers both traditional and virtual classrooms, and the Online Review Course.

THE LIVE REVIEW COURSE

Traditional Classroom Program

Kaplan Financial offers the Traditional Classroom Program in over 30 classes in more than 19 states across the country. The Five-Day Review is an intensive program consisting of 38 hours of instruction conducted Wednesdays through Sundays. The Six-Day Review consists of 48 hours of instruction conducted over two (nonconsecutive) weekends, Friday through Sunday. Instruction consists mainly of teaching substantive material and mastering both knowledge and application. The course includes working problems to ensure that the substantive materials taught can be applied to the examlike questions, as well as actual exam-management techniques.

The Virtual Classroom Program

Kaplan Financial's Virtual Review is an instructor-led, Web-based program that provides all the benefits of a classroom review from the convenience of the learner's home or office. This program format is a great option for those who have access to the Web and prefer not to incur the expense of travel. This course is an intensive program consisting of 48 hours of instruction conducted over 17 three-hour sessions held on Mondays, Wednesdays, and Thursdays. Learners receive real-time interaction with the instructor and students and access to a recorded playback option. Playbacks remain active until the first day of the CFP® Certification Examination.

THE ONLINE REVIEW COURSE

For students who have completed the Kaplan University Certificate in Financial Planning, this course provides an extensive review of the concepts covered in our six-course program. The Online Review proceeds through the topics listed by CFP Board, beginning with a detailed outline of each topic to highlight key aspects of the material and concluding with review questions that will help you assess your mastery of each topic.

VOLUMES I–VI

Volumes I–VI contain complete reference outlines that give detailed coverage of the six tested areas of the CFP® Certification Examination. Each volume contains examples, illustrations, and an index. Combined, the six volumes offer over 1,500 multiple-choice problems to prepare you for the exam. The answers and explanations for each multiple-choice problem are also provided. The answers to the multiple-choice problems are identified by topical categories to assist you in focusing your study efforts. The introduction to each volume presents helpful tips on what to expect when taking the exam, tips for studying, sample study plans, and tips for solving both straight and combination-type multiple-choice problems. The introduction also forecasts the number of questions expected in each area of the exam. Each volume has been updated to reflect law and inflation adjustments through January 2007.

VOLUME VII—CASE BOOK

Volume VII—Case Book provides the exam candidate with 16 comprehensive cases, 40 item sets (minicases), and Cognitive Connection questions. The answers and explanations for each multiple-choice question are provided, and the text has been updated to reflect law and inflation adjustments through January 2007. This text prepares you for the three comprehensive cases given on the exam. Your preparation in this area is extremely important because case questions are weighted more heavily than the general multiple-choice questions. Our students who have used the *Case Book* have said that this book is a must if you want to be prepared for the exam.

VOLUME VIII—MOCK EXAM AND SOLUTIONS

Volume VIII—Mock Exam and Solutions simulates the 10-hour comprehensive CFP® exam. The text is broken up into three mock exams, each containing multiple-choice questions, item sets, and a comprehensive case. This text can serve as a diagnostic tool useful in identifying the areas of strength and weakness in a study plan and can be used to create a unique study program to meet your individual needs. This text is also updated to reflect law and inflation adjustments through January 2007.

UNDERSTANDING YOUR FINANCIAL CALCULATOR

Understanding Your Financial Calculator is designed to assist you in gaining proficiency in using and understanding your financial calculator. In addition to helping master the keystrokes for the financial calculator, it is also designed to assist students with the underlying financial theory problems given on the exam. Being familiar with the financial calculations is critical, because mastering these problems is an important step to passing the exam.

All calculations are worked out step by step, showing keystrokes and displays for five of the most popular financial calculators. These include the HP-17bII, HP-12c, HP-10bII, TI-BAII PLUS, and Sharp EL-733A.

Understanding Your Financial Calculator covers the basic operations of the calculators, basic time value of money calculations, fundamental problems (such as mortgages, education needs analysis, and retirement needs analysis), investment planning concepts, calculations (such as IRR, YTM, YTC, Sharpe, Treynor, Jensen, and standard deviation), and more. This text also includes a student workbook with over 200 basic, intermediate, and advanced practice problems and calculations. This text is a great reference for the exam and for practitioners.

FINANCIAL PLANNING FLASHCARDS

Kaplan Financial's Financial Planning Flashcards were created as a study supplement to *Volumes I–VI* study materials. The Flashcards include over 1,000 cards covering topics in each of the areas on the exam and can help you learn basic concepts and definitions. Flashcards provide an excellent way to learn the material by prompting you to recall facts and information quickly. Their portability makes them a valuable study tool for those on the go.

DRILL & PRACTICE SOFTWARE

Our computerized test bank is an interactive software product including over 1,700 questions taken from *Volumes I-VI, Released Cases and Questions,* and additional practice questions written by our authors. The software will allow you to keep score, track your time and progress, and break down your score by sections.

FROM THE PUBLISHER

This text is intended as the basis for preparation for the CFP® Certification Examination (the exam), either as self-study or as part of a review course. The material is organized according to the six functional areas tested on the exam and is presented in an outline format that includes examples with questions and illustrations to help candidates quickly comprehend the material.

We have structured the material into six manageable study units:

- Volume I—*Fundamentals*
- Volume II—*Insurance Planning*
- Volume III—*Investments*
- Volume IV—*Income Tax Planning*
- Volume V—*Retirement Planning*
- Volume VI—*Estate Planning*

The multiple-choice problems and item sets within each volume have been grouped into primary categories that correspond to the major topic headings in the outlines. In addition, the answers also identify more specific topical categories within each study unit.

We are indebted to Certified Financial Planner Board of Standards, Inc. for permission to reproduce and adapt their publications and other materials.

We welcome any comments concerning materials contained in or omitted from this text. Please send your written comments to Kaplan Financial, 143 Mallard Street, Suite E, St. Rose, Louisiana 70087, or fax your comments to us at (504) 461-9860.

Wishing you success on the exam,

Kaplan Financial

ACKNOWLEDGMENTS AND SPECIAL THANKS

We are most appreciative of the tremendous support and encouragement we have received from everyone throughout this project. We are extremely grateful to the users of out texts who were gracious enough to provide us with valuable comments.

We very much appreciate the continued support of the many registered programs who have adopted our Review Materials. We understand that our success is a direct result of that support.

We greatly appreciate the assistance of the following individuals, who reviewed the outlines and problems and solutions for technical accuracy:

- Kathy L. Berlin
- Cindy R. Hart, CLU, ChFC, CFP®
- Lisa Treece Keleher, MS, CFA
- Bobby M. Kosh, AAMS, CFP®
- James J. Pasztor, MS, CFP®
- Joyce Osche Schnur, MBA, CFP®
- Scott A. Wasserman, CPA/PFS, ChFC, RFC, CFP®

We have received so much help from so many people, it is possible that we inadvertently overlooked thanking someone. If so, it is our shortcoming, and we apologize in advance. Please let us know if you are that someone, and we will correct it in our next printing.

We deeply appreciate the cooperation of CFP Board for granting us permission to reproduce and adapt their publications and other materials. CFP Board's Standards of Professional Conduct, copyrighted by CFP Board, is reprinted (or adapted) with permission.

Thanks to John J. Dardis for granting us permission to use material from "Estate & Benefit Planning Symposium" in *Volume VI—Estate Planning*.

INTRODUCTION

Introduction

Volume VII—Case Book is intended for use in preparation for the CFP® Certification Examination and should be used in conjunction with the *Kaplan Financial Review for the CFP® Certification Examination Volumes I–VI*. This text includes 16 comprehensive financial planning cases. These cases cover the six major areas of personal financial planning:

- Fundamentals of Financial Planning
- Insurance Planning
- Investment Planning
- Income Tax Planning
- Retirement and Employee Benefit Planning
- Estate Planning

Each case includes a complete family scenario that represents the information the financial planner obtained from the client. Generally, each case scenario includes information obtained from the client in the following sections and order:

1. Personal Background and Information
2. Personal and Financial Goals
3. Economic Information
4. Insurance Information
5. Investment Information
6. Income Tax Information

7. Retirement Information
8. Gifts, Estates, Trusts, and Will Information
9. Statement of Cash Flows
10. Statement of Financial Position
11. Information Regarding Assets and Liabilities
12. Exhibits

Each case contains 11–31 multiple-choice questions covering the major areas of financial planning. Each case is designed to be completed within 44–124 minutes.

This text contains an appendix for assistance with analysis of the cases and answering the questions.

SOLVING MULTIPLE-CHOICE QUESTIONS

1. **Read the last line (the requirement) first.**

   The last line will generally be the question part of the problem and will identify the types of important information that will be needed to answer the questions.

   Example: "How many personal and dependency exemptions can Mike and Pam claim on their 2005 income tax return?"

   This last sentence of the example identifies the type of information needed from the body of the problem. You can now look for key information while reading through the body of the problem.

2. **Read the question carefully.**

   Underline the concepts, words, and data and make important notes of data or relevant rules to help formulate your answer.

3. **Formulate your answer.**

   Do not look at the answer choices presented on the exam until you have formulated your answer. Looking at the answer choices may distract you or change your thinking.

4. **Select your answer if it is presented.**

5. **Write it or circle it directly on the examination.**

   Watch the clock and enter answers on the answer sheet as you go, or all at once at the end. If at the end, be sure you have enough time. Be consistent.

6. **Review other answer choices for the following:**

   Was your answer sufficiently precise?
   Was your answer complete?

7. **If your answer is not presented.**

   You know you are incorrect. Alternatives:
   - Reread question and requirements.
   - Evaluate answers presented.
   - Skip the question and come back to it later.
   - Guess. (You are not penalized for guessing, so, if time is running out, be sure to fill in all of the open questions.)

HOW TO ANALYZE A CASE

- There is one case in each session.

- Each case answer is worth 3 points.

- Generally, each case contains 10–20 questions.

  - There are 3 cases with 10–20 questions each; the questions will total about 130 points.

- You should practice the cases by working them under time pressure. This text is a great tool for practicing cases and for developing case analysis skills. If you have not practiced working cases, you may find yourself panicking on the exam.

- Our advice is to complete the noncase-specific multiple-choice questions first, then go on to the case.

General Case Approach to the CFP® Certification Examination

Regardless of the age or the family status, there are usually questions concerning insurance deficiencies, asset or property transactions, and the investment portfolio.

1. Every case should present some insurance deficiencies, coverages, exclusions, applications, or taxability of benefits issues.

   Issues should be apparent if you think about four distinct types of families (as provided in #4 below) based on:

   - Age.
   - Marital status (MS).
   - Children and grandchildren (C & GC).
   - Net worth (NW).
   - Income (INC).

2. There are usually questions regarding asset or property transactions, such as:

   - Acquisition (basis) or disposition of assets (capital gain/loss).
   - Acquisition—Basis if received by gift—holding period.
   - Basis if received by inheritance.
   - Disposition—Sale/gift/installment sale/private annuity.
   - GRATs/SCINs/CRATs/CRUTs.

3. There are usually questions regarding investment portfolios.

   - Deficiencies in the current portfolio.
   - Risks associated with the current portfolio including: purchasing power risk, systematic risk, unsystematic risk, lack of diversification, excess liquidity, and insufficient growth.

4. Next there are questions regarding the family that are typically family specific.

	Family #1	Family #2	Family #3	Family #4
Age	25–35	35–45	45–60	60–70
MS	M	M	M	M
C/GC #	2	3	2	4/2
NW	Low	Moderate	High	High
INC	Moderate	Moderate	High	High

Questions Suggested by Each Family			
Family #1	Family #2	Family #3	Family #4
Educational funding	Educational funding	Retirement planning	Estates and probate planning
Home refinancing or buying home	Retirement	Estate planning	Gifts
Debt management Savings and investments	Tax savings	Investments—portfolio analysis	Qualified transfers
Portfolio allocation	Portfolio allocation	Qualified plans	Insurance ownership (life)
	Capital needs analysis	Rollovers, etc.	

5. Obviously there can be strange situations.

   For example: A 70-year-old woman with a high net worth, three children (age 50s), and four grandchildren (age 30s), marries a 17-year-old man. Do not use a QTIP for the 17-year-old spouse if you expect to get the estate to the children and grandchildren; the 17-year-old spouse will most likely outlive the children and grandchildren. You have to think through the objectives and apply your tools for accomplishing the objectives.

Applications of Case Analysis Strategies

- **Approach 1**

  Read the case carefully and slowly making sure that you are involved in the case. Pay particular attention to the age, the marital status, the number of children and grandchildren, the net worth, and the income levels. These variables will give you a good idea of what the case is about. Try to read thoroughly so you do not have to flip back. Anticipate questions and make notes. When a topic comes up, make a mental or written note. When additional information is provided on that topic later in the case, it is a good bet that there will be a question unless the additional information negates the question. Read each question and the answers provided. Answer the easy questions first. Answer the complex questions last. The calculation questions (e.g., probate estate, gross estate, education funding, capital needs analysis, minimum distribution, mortgage qualification) are time users; come back to them later.

- **Approach 2**

  Read questions quickly. Make notes. Answer any questions that do not require reading the case, then read the case only looking for the answers to the questions asked.

  Steps:

  1. Read the questions—last line first.

  2. Make notes.

  3. Answer all questions that are possible without reading the case—mark the answer on the test.

  4. Read the case to answer the specific questions—record the page number of information related to the question.

  5. Make sure all questions are answered and then review the answers.

TOPIC SUMMARY BY CASE

Question #	Case 1 Nicholson	Case 2 Berger	Case 3 Savage	Case 4 Topplemeir	Case 5 Farrell	Case 6 Roth
1.	FUND	FUND	TAX	TAX	INV	EST
2.	TAX	INS	TAX	TAX	RET	EST
3.	TAX	TAX	TAX	FUND	INV	EST
4.	FUND	TAX	RET	INS	INV	TAX
5.	FUND	TAX	RET	INS	INV	EST
6.	INS	INV	RET	INV	EST	RET
7.	INS	INV	INS	INV	EST	INV
8.	INS	EST	INS	INV	EST	INV
9.	INS	EST	INS	INV	FUND	INV
10.	TAX	RET	EST	FUND	EST	INV
11.	TAX	RET	EST	RET	EST	INV
12.	FUND	TAX	EST	TAX	EST	INV
13.	EST	EST	TAX	INS	EST	INS
14.	INS	FUND	EST	EST	INV	TAX
15.	RET	EST	RET	TAX	INV	TAX
16.	TAX	INS	RET	INV	INS	TAX
17.	RET	FUND	INS	INV	FUND	INS
18.	INV	INS	INS	TAX	INV	INV
19.	TAX	INS	INV	FUND	EST	EB
20.	TAX	INS	INV	EST	INS	INV
21.	FUND	INS	INV	EST	TAX	FUND
22.	TAX	FUND	INV	X	TAX	FUND
23.	X	INS	TAX	X	X	INS
24.	X	INV	X	X	X	X
25.	X	INS	X	X	X	X
26.	X	INV	X	X	X	X
27.	X	FUND	X	X	X	X
28.	X	INV	X	X	X	X
29.	X	INV	X	X	X	X
30.	X	EST	X	X	X	X
31.	X	EST	X	X	X	X
Estimated time to complete	88 min	124 min	92 min	84 min	88 min	92 min

TOPIC SUMMARY BY CASE

Question #	Case 7 Ackerman	Case 8 Blocker	Case 9 Klar	Case 10 Hobert	Case 11 Martin	Case 12 Wood
1.	TAX	TAX	RET	FUND	FUND	EST
2.	EB	TAX	RET	INV	FUND	EST
3.	INS	TAX	EST	INS	INS	FUND
4.	INS	TAX	EST	INV	INS	EST
5.	TAX	EST	EST	INV	EST	RET
6.	INS	INS	TAX	TAX	TAX	EST
7.	TAX	RET	FUND	RET	INV	EST
8.	TAX	INV	EST	RET	TAX	EST
9.	INV	FUND	EST	RET	RET	FUND
10.	RET	RET	RET	FUND	INS	INV
11.	RET	EST	RET	EST	RET	INV
12.	RET	EST	RET	FUND	EST	INV
13.	RET	FUND	INV	EST	EST	RET
14.	INS	EST	EST	INV	INV	EST
15.	EST	INS	TAX	TAX	TAX	INS
16.	EST	INV	RET	EST	EST	INS
17.	EST	EST	TAX	INS	EST	TAX
18.	EST	RET	INS	INV	TAX	TAX
19.	EST	EST	INS	INV	INV	FUND
20.	EST	INV	INS	INV	INV	RET
21.	INV	EST	EST	TAX	EST	X
22.	INV	X	X	TAX	X	X
23.	INV	X	X	INV	X	X
24.	TAX	X	X	FUND	X	X
25.	X	X	X	INV	X	X
26.	X	X	X	RET	X	X
27.	X	X	X	EST	X	X
28.	X	X	X	EST	X	X
29.	X	X	X	EST	X	X
Estimated time to complete	96 min	84 min	84 min	116 min	84 min	80 min

TOPIC SUMMARY BY CASE

*Question #	Case 13 Mathews	Case 14 Kincaid	Case 15 Clarke	Case 16 Davis
1.	TAX	FUND	INV	RET
2.	FUND	RET	INV	INS
3.	TAX	EST*	INV	INV
4.	RET	EST	EST	INV
5.	RET*	EST	INV*	RET
6.	EST	FUND	INV	TAX
7.	INS	RET*	INV	INV
8.	TAX	INS	INS	EST
9.	EST	INS	RET	RET*
10.	TAX	INS	EST	TAX
11.	EST	INV	TAX	EST
12.	Deleted	INS	X	TAX
13.	RET	INS	X	X
14.	INV	INV	X	X
15.	EST	TAX	X	X
16.	EST	X	X	X
17.	INV	X	X	X
18.	INV	X	X	X
19.	INV	X	X	X
Estimated time to complete	76 min	60 min	44 min	48 min

FUND	=	Fundamentals of Financial Planning
INS	=	Insurance Planning
INV	=	Investment Planning
TAX	=	Income Tax Planning
RET	=	Retirement Planning
EB	=	Employee Benefits
EST	=	Estate Planning

*Questions marked with an asterisk (*) in CFP® Board Released Cases 13 through 16 are no longer accurate due to changes in the Federal Tax Code.

TOPIC LIST FOR THE CFP® CERTIFICATION EXAMINATION

The following topics, based on the 2004 Job Analysis Study, are the basis for the CFP® Certification Examinations. Each exam question will be linked to one of the following topics, in the approximate percentages indicated following the general headings. Questions will pertain to all levels in Bloom's taxonomy with an emphasis on the higher cognitive levels. Questions often will be asked in the context of the financial planning process and presented in an integrative format.

In addition to being used for the CFP® Certification Examination, this list indicates topic coverage requirements to fulfill the pre-certification educational requirement. Continuing education (CE) programs and materials that address these topics will be eligible for CFP Board CE credit.

(References to sections (§) in this list refer to sections of the Internal Revenue Code)

First Test Date: November 2006

GENERAL PRINCIPLES OF FINANCIAL PLANNING (11%)

1. Financial planning process
   A. Purpose, benefits, and components
   B. Steps
      1) Establishing client-planner relationships
      2) Gathering client data and determining goals and expectations
      3) Determining the client's financial status by analyzing and evaluating general financial status, special needs, insurance and risk management, investments, taxation, employee benefits, retirement, and/or estate planning
      4) Developing and presenting the financial plan
      5) Implementing the financial plan
      6) Monitoring the financial plan
   C. Responsibilities
      1) Financial planner
      2) Client
      3) Other advisors

2. CFP Board's *Code of Ethics and Professional Responsibility* and *Disciplinary Rules and Procedures*
   A. *Code of Ethics and Professional Responsibility*
      1) Preamble and applicability
      2) Composition and scope
      3) Compliance
      4) Terminology
      5) Principles
         a) Principle 1 – Integrity
         b) Principle 2 – Objectivity
         c) Principle 3 – Competence
         d) Principle 4 – Fairness
         e) Principle 5 – Confidentiality
         f) Principle 6 – Professionalism
         g) Principle 7 – Diligence
      6) Rules
   B) *Disciplinary Rules and Procedures*

3. CFP Board's *Financial Planning Practice Standards*
   A) Purpose and applicability
   B) Content of each series (use most current *Practice Standards*, as posted on CFP Board's Web site at www.CFP.net)
   C. Enforcement through *Disciplinary Rules and Procedures*

4. Financial statements
   A. Personal
      1) Statement of financial position
      2) Statement of cash flow
   B. Business
      1) Balance sheet
      2) Income statement
      3) Statement of cash flows
      4) *Pro forma* statements

5. Cash flow management
   A. Budgeting
   B. Emergency fund planning
   C. Debt management ratios
      1) Consumer debt
      2) Housing costs
      3) Total debt
   D. Savings strategies

6. Financing strategies
   A. Long-term vs. short-term debt
   B. Secured vs. unsecured debt
   C. Buy vs. lease/rent
   D. Mortgage financing
      1) Conventional vs. adjustable-rate mortgage (ARM)
      2) Home equity loan and line of credit
      3) Refinancing cost-benefit analysis
      4) Reverse mortgage

7. Function, purpose, and regulation of financial institutions
   A. Banks
   B. Credit unions
   C. Brokerage companies
   D. Insurance companies
   E. Mutual fund companies
   F. Trust companies

8. Education planning
   A. Funding
      1) Needs analysis
      2) Tax credits/adjustments/deductions
      3) Funding strategies
      4) Ownership of assets
      5) Vehicles
         a) Qualified tuition programs (§529 plans)
         b) Coverdell Education Savings Accounts
         c) Uniform Transfers to Minors Act (UTMA) and Uniform Gifts to Minors Act (UGMA) accounts
         d) Savings bonds
   B. Financial aid

9. Financial planning for special circumstances
   A. Divorce
   B. Disability
   C. Terminal illness
   D. Non-traditional families
   E. Job change and job loss
   F. Dependents with special needs
   G. Monetary windfalls

10. Economic concepts
    A. Supply and demand
    B. Fiscal policy
    C. Monetary policy
    D. Economic indicators
    E. Business cycles
    F. Inflation, deflation, and stagflation
    G. Yield curve

11. Time value of money concepts and calculations
    A. Present value
    B. Future value
    C. Ordinary annuity and annuity due
    D. Net present value (NPV)
    E. Internal rate of return (IRR)
    F. Uneven cash flows
    G. Serial payments

12. Financial services regulations and requirements
    A. Registration and licensing
    B. Reporting
    C. Compliance
    D. State securities and insurance laws

13. Business law
    A. Contracts
    B. Agency
    C. Fiduciary liability

14. Consumer protection laws
    A. Bankruptcy
    B. Fair credit reporting laws
    C. Privacy policies
    D. Identity theft protection

INSURANCE PLANNING AND RISK MANAGEMENT (14%)

15. Principles of risk and insurance
    A. Definitions
    B. Concepts
       1) Peril
       2) Hazard
       3) Law of large numbers
       4) Adverse selection
       5) Insurable risks
       6) Self-insurance
    C. Risk management process

   D. Response to risk
      1) Risk control
         a) Risk avoidance
         b) Risk diversification
         c) Risk reduction
      2) Risk financing
         a) Risk retention
         b) Risk transfer
   E. Legal aspects of insurance
      1) Principle of indemnity
      2) Insurable interest
      3) Contract requirements
      4) Contract characteristics
      5) Policy ownership
      6) Designation of beneficiary

16. Analysis and evaluation of risk exposures
    A. Personal
       1) Death
       2) Disability
       3) Poor health
       4) Unemployment
       5) Superannuation
    B. Property
       1) Real
       2) Personal
       3) Auto
    C. Liability
       1) Negligence
       2) Intentional torts
       3) Strict liability
    D. Business-related

17. Property, casualty and liability insurance
    A. Individual
       1) Homeowners insurance
       2) Auto insurance
       3) Umbrella liability insurance
    B. Business
       1) Commercial property insurance
       2) Commercial liability insurance
          a) Auto liability
          b) Umbrella liability
          c) Professional liability
          d) Directors and officers liability
          e) Workers' compensation and employers liability

18. Health insurance and health care cost management (individual)
    A. Hospital, surgical, and physicians' expense insurance
    B. Major medical insurance and calculation of benefits
    C. Continuance and portability
    D. Medicare
    E. Taxation of premiums and benefits

19. Disability income insurance (individual)
    A. Definitions of disability
    B. Benefit period

   C. Elimination period
   D. Benefit amount
   E. Provisions
   F. Taxation of premiums and benefits

20. Long-term care insurance (individual)
    A. Eligibility
    B. Services covered
    C. Medicare limitations
    D. Benefit period
    E. Elimination period
    F. Benefit amount
    G. Provisions
    H. Taxation of premiums and benefits

21. Life insurance (individual)
    A. Concepts and personal uses
    B. Policy types
    C. Contractual provisions
    D. Dividend options
    E. Nonforfeiture options
    F. Settlement options
    G. Illustrations
    H. Policy replacement
    I. Viatical and life settlements

22. Income taxation of life insurance
    A. Dividends
    B. Withdrawals and loans
    C. Death benefits
    D. Modified endowment contracts (MECs)
    E. Transfer-for-value
    F. §1035 exchanges

23. Business uses of insurance
    A. Buy-sell agreements
    B. Key employee life insurance
    C. Split-dollar life insurance
    D. Business overhead expense insurance

24. Insurance needs analysis
    A. Life insurance
    B. Disability income insurance
    C. Long-term care insurance
    D. Health insurance
    E. Property insurance
    F. Liability insurance

25. Insurance policy and company selection
    A. Purpose of coverage
    B. Duration of coverage
    C. Participating or non-participating
    D. Cost-benefit analysis
    E. Company selection
       1) Industry ratings
       2) Underwriting

2

26. Annuities
    A. Types
    B. Uses
    C. Taxation

EMPLOYEE BENEFITS PLANNING (8%)

27. Group life insurance
    A. Types and basic provisions
        1) Group term
        2) Group permanent
        3) Dependent coverage
    B. Income tax implications
    C. Employee benefit analysis and application
    D. Conversion analysis
    E. Carve-out plans

28. Group disability insurance
    A. Types and basic provisions
        1) Short-term coverage
        2) Long-term coverage
    B. Definitions of disability
    C. Income tax implications
    D. Employee benefit analysis and application
    E. Integration with other income

29. Group medical insurance
    A. Types and basic provisions
        1) Traditional indemnity
        2) Managed care plans
            a) Preferred provider organization (PPO)
            b) Health maintenance organization (HMO)
            c) Point-of-service (POS)
    B. Income tax implications
    C. Employee benefit analysis and application
    D. COBRA/HIPAA provisions
    E. Continuation
    F. Savings accounts
        1) Health savings account (HSA)
        2) Archer medical savings account (MSA)
        3) Health reimbursement arrangement (HRA)

30. Other employee benefits
    A. §125 cafeteria plans and flexible spending accounts (FSAs)
    B. Fringe benefits
    C. Voluntary employees' beneficiary association (VEBA)
    D. Prepaid legal services
    E. Group long-term care insurance
    F. Dental insurance
    G. Vision insurance

31) Employee stock options
    A. Basic provisions
        1) Company restrictions
        2) Transferability
        3) Exercise price
        4) Vesting
        5) Expiration
        6) Cashless exercise
    B. Incentive stock options (ISOs)
        1) Income tax implications (regular, AMT, basis)
            a) Upon grant
            b) Upon exercise
            c) Upon sale
        2) Holding period requirements
        3) Disqualifying dispositions
        4) Planning opportunities and strategies
    C. Non-qualified stock options (NSOs)
        1) Income tax implications (regular, AMT, basis)
            a) Upon grant
            b) Upon exercise
            c) Upon sale
        2) Gifting opportunities
            a) Unvested/vested
            b) Exercised/unexercised
            c) Gift tax valuation
            d) Payment of gift tax
        3) Planning opportunities and strategies
        4) Employee benefits analysis and application
    D. Planning strategies for employees with both incentive stock options and non-qualified stock options
    E. Election to include in gross income in the year of transfer (§83(b) election)

32. Stock plans
    A. Types and basic provisions
        1) Restricted stock
        2) Phantom stock
        3) Stock appreciation rights (SARs)
        4) Employee stock purchase plan (ESPP)
    B. Income tax implications
    C. Employee benefit analysis and application
    D. Election to include in gross income in the year of transfer (§83(b) election)

33. Non-qualified deferred compensation
    A. Basic provisions and differences from qualified plans
    B. Types of plans and applications
        1) Salary reduction plans
        2) Salary continuation plans
        3) Rabbi trusts
        4) Secular trusts
    C. Income tax implications
        1) Constructive receipt
        2) Substantial risk of forfeiture
        3) Economic benefit doctrine
    D. Funding methods
    E. Strategies

INVESTMENT PLANNING (19%)

34. Characteristics, uses and taxation of investment vehicles
    A. Cash and equivalents
        1) Certificates of deposit
        2) Money market funds
        3) Treasury bills
        4) Commercial paper
        5) Banker's acceptances
        6) Eurodollars
    B. Individual bonds
        1) U.S. Government bonds and agency securities
            a) Treasury notes and bonds
            b) Treasury STRIPS
            c) Treasury inflation-protection securities (TIPS)
            d) Series EE, HH, and I bonds
            e) Mortgage-backed securities
        2) Zero-coupon bonds
        3) Municipal bonds
            a) General obligation
            b) Revenue
        4) Corporate bonds
            a) Mortgage bond
            b) Debenture
            c) Investment grade
            d) High-yield
            e) Convertible
            f) Callable
        5) Foreign bonds
    C. Promissory notes
    D. Individual stocks
        1) Common
        2) Preferred
        3) American depositary receipts (ADRs)
    E. Pooled and managed investments
        1) Exchange-traded funds (ETFs)
        2) Unit investment trusts
        3) Mutual funds
        4) Closed-end investment companies

3

CFP | CERTIFIED FINANCIAL PLANNER | CFP®

Certified Financial Planner Board of Standards Inc. owns these certification marks in the U.S., which it awards to individuals who successfully complete CFP Board's initial and ongoing certification requirements.

5) Index securities
6) Hedge funds
7) Limited partnerships
8) Privately managed accounts
9) Separately managed accounts
F. Guaranteed investment contracts (GICs)
G. Real Estate
1) Investor-managed
2) Real estate investment trusts (REITs)
3) Real estate limited partnerships (RELPs)
4) Real estate mortgage investment conduits (REMICs)
H. Alternative investments
1) Derivatives
a) Puts
b) Calls
c) Long-term Equity AnticiPation Securities (LEAPS®)
d) Futures
e) Warrants and rights
2) Tangible assets
a) Collectibles
b) Natural resources
c) Precious metals

35. Types of investment risk
A. Systematic/market/nondiversifiable
B. Purchasing power
C. Interest rate
D. Unsystematic/nonmarket/diversifiable
E. Business
F. Financial
G. Liquidity and marketability
H. Reinvestment
I. Political (sovereign)
J. Exchange rate
K. Tax
L. Investment manager

36. Quantitative investment concepts
A. Distribution of returns
1) Normal distribution
2) Lognormal distribution
3) Skewness
4) Kurtosis
B. Correlation coefficient
C. Coefficient of determination (R²)
D. Coefficient of variation
E. Standard deviation
F. Beta
G. Covariance
H. Semivariance

37. Measures of investment returns
A. Simple vs. compound return

B. Geometric average vs. arithmetic average return
C. Time-weighted vs. dollar-weighted return
D. Real (inflation-adjusted) vs. nominal return
E. Total return
F. Risk-adjusted return
G. Holding period return
H. Internal rate of return (IRR)
I. Yield-to-maturity
J. Yield-to-call
K. Current yield
L. Taxable equivalent yield (TEY)

38. Bond and stock valuation concepts
A. Bond duration and convexity
B. Capitalized earnings
C. Dividend growth models
D. Ratio analysis
1) Price/earnings
2) Price/free cash flow
3) Price/sales
4) Price/earnings ÷ growth (PEG)
E. Book value

39. Investment theory
A. Modern portfolio theory (MPT)
1) Capital market line (CML)
a) Mean-variance optimization
b) Efficient frontier
2) Security market line (SML)
B. Efficient market hypothesis (EMH)
1) Strong form
2) Semi-strong form
3) Weak form
4) Anomalies
C. Behavioral finance

40. Portfolio development and analysis
A. Fundamental analysis
1) Top-down analysis
2) Bottom-up analysis
3) Ratio analysis
a) Liquidity ratios
b) Activity ratios
c) Profitability ratios
d) Debt ratios
B. Technical analysis
1) Charting
2) Sentiment indicators
3) Flow of funds indicators
4) Market structure indicators
C. Investment policy statements
D. Appropriate benchmarks
E. Probability analysis, including Monte Carlo
F. Tax efficiency
1) Turnover
2) Timing of capital gains and losses

3) Wash sale rule
4) Qualified dividends
5) Tax-free income
G. Performance measures
1) Sharpe ratio
2) Treynor ratio
3) Jensen ratio
4) Information ratio

41. Investment strategies
A. Market timing
B. Passive investing (indexing)
C. Buy and hold
D. Portfolio immunization
E. Swaps and collars
F. Formula investing
1) Dollar cost averaging
2) Dividend reinvestment plans (DRIPs)
3) Bond ladders, bullets, and barbells
G. Use of leverage (margin)
H. Short selling
I. Hedging and option strategies

42. Asset allocation and portfolio diversification
A. Strategic asset allocation
1) Application of client lifecycle analysis
2) Client risk tolerance measurement and application
3) Asset class definition and correlation
B. Rebalancing
C. Tactical asset allocation
D. Control of volatility
E. Strategies for dealing with concentrated portfolios

43. Asset pricing models
A. Capital asset pricing model (CAPM)
B. Arbitrage pricing theory (APT)
C. Black-Scholes option valuation model
D. Binomial option pricing

INCOME TAX PLANNING (14%)

44. Income tax law fundamentals
A. Types of authority
1) Primary
2) Secondary
B. Research sources

4

45. Tax compliance
   A. Filing requirements
   B. Audits
   C. Penalties

46. Income tax fundamentals and calculations
   A. Filing status
   B. Gross income
      1) Inclusions
      2) Exclusions
      3) Imputed income
   C. Adjustments
   D. Standard/Itemized deductions
      1) Types
      2) Limitations
   E. Personal and dependency exemptions
   F. Taxable income
   G. Tax liability
      1) Rate schedule
      2) Kiddie tax
      3) Self-employment tax
   H. Tax credits
   I. Payment of tax
      1) Withholding
      2) Estimated payments

47. Tax accounting
   A. Accounting periods
   B Accounting methods
      1) Cash receipts and disbursements
      2) Accrual method
      3) Hybrid method
      4) Change in accounting method
   C. Long-term contracts
   D. Installment sales
   E. Inventory valuation and flow methods
   F. Net operating losses

48. Characteristics and income taxation of business entities
   A. Entity types
      1) Sole proprietorship
      2) Partnerships
      3) Limited liability company (LLC)
      4) Corporations
      5) Trust
      6) Association
   B. Taxation at entity and owner level
      1) Formation
      2) Flow through of income and losses
      3) Special taxes
      4) Distributions
      5) Dissolution
      6) Disposition

49. Income taxation of trusts and estates
   A. General issues
      1) Filing requirements
      2) Deadlines
      3) Choice of taxable year
      4) Tax treatment of distributions to beneficiaries
      5) Rate structure
   B. Grantor/Nongrantor trusts
   C. Simple/Complex trusts
   D. Revocable/Irrevocable trusts
   E. Trust income
      1) Trust accounting income
      2) Trust taxable income
      3) Distributable net income (DNI)
   F. Estate income tax

50. Basis
   A. Original basis
   B. Adjusted basis
   C. Amortization and accretion
   D. Basis of property received by gift and in nontaxable transactions
   E. Basis of inherited property (community and non-community property)

51. Depreciation/cost-recovery concepts
   A. Modified Accelerated Cost Recovery System (MACRS)
   B. Expensing policy
   C. §179 deduction
   D. Amortization
   E. Depletion

52. Tax consequences of like-kind exchanges
   A. Reporting requirements
   B. Qualifying transactions
   C. Liabilities
   D. Boot
   E. Related party transactions

53. Tax consequences of the disposition of property
   A. Capital assets (§1221)
   B. Holding period
   C. Sale of residence
   D. Depreciation recapture
   E. Related parties
   F. Wash sales
   G. Bargain sales
   H. Section 1244 stock (small business stock election)
   I. Installment sales
   J. Involuntary conversions

54. Alternative minimum tax (AMT)
   A. Mechanics
   B. Preferences and adjustments
   C. Exclusion items vs. deferral items

   D. Credit: creation, usage, and limitations
   E. Application to businesses and trusts
   F. Planning strategies

55. Tax reduction/management techniques
   A. Tax credits
   B. Accelerated deductions
   C. Deferral of income
   D. Intra-family transfers

56. Passive activity and at-risk rules
   A. Definitions
   B. Computations
   C. Treatment of disallowed losses
   D. Disposition of passive activities
   E. Real estate exceptions

57. Tax implications of special circumstances
   A. Married/widowed
      1) Filing status
      2) Children
      3) Community and non-community property
   B. Divorce
      1) Alimony
      2) Child support
      3) Property division

58. Charitable contributions and deductions
   A. Qualified entities
      1) Public charities
      2) Private charities
   B. Deduction limitations
   C. Carryover periods
   D. Appreciated property
   E. Non-deductible contributions
   F. Appraisals
   G. Substantiation requirements
   H. Charitable contributions by business entities

RETIREMENT PLANNING
(19%)

59. Retirement needs analysis
   A. Assumptions for retirement planning
      1) Inflation
      2) Retirement period and life expectancy
      3) Lifestyle
      4) Total return
   B. Income sources
   C. Financial needs
      1) Living costs

5

  CERTIFIED FINANCIAL PLANNER™ | **CFP**®

2) Charitable and beneficiary gifting objectives
3) Medical costs, including long-term care needs analysis
4) Other (trust and foundation funding, education funding, etc.)
D. Straight-line returns vs. probability analysis
E. Pure annuity vs. capital preservation
F. Alternatives to compensate for projected cash-flow shortfalls

60. Social Security (Old Age, Survivor, and Disability Insurance, OASDI)
A. Paying into the system
B. Eligibility and benefit
1) Retirement
2) Disability
3) Survivor
4) Family limitations
C. How benefits are calculated
D. Working after retirement
E. Taxation of benefits

61. Types of retirement plans
A. Characteristics
1) Qualified plans
2) Non-qualified plans
B. Types and basic provisions of qualified plans
1) Defined contribution
a) Money purchase
b) Target benefit
c) Profit sharing
1) 401(k) plan
2) Safe harbor 401(k) plan
3) Age-based plan
4) Stock bonus plan
5) Employee stock ownership plan (ESOP)
6) New comparability plan
7) Thrift plan
2) Defined benefit
a) Traditional
b) Cash balance
c) 412(i) plan

62. Qualified plan rules and options
A. Nondiscrimination and eligibility requirements
1) Age and service requirements
2) Coverage requirements
3) Minimum participation
4) Highly compensated employee (HCE)
5) Permitted vesting schedules
6) ADP/ACP testing
7) Controlled group

B. Integration with Social Security/disparity limits
1) Defined benefit plans
2) Defined contribution plans
C. Factors affecting contributions or benefits
1) Deduction limit (§404(c))
2) Defined contribution limits
3) Defined benefit limit
4) Annual compensation limit
5) Definition of compensation
6) Multiple plans
7) Special rules for self-employed (non-corporations)
D. Top-heavy plans
1) Definition
2) Key employee
3) Vesting
4) Effects on contributions or benefits
E. Loans from qualified plans

63. Other tax-advantaged retirement plans
A. Types and basic provisions
1) Traditional IRA
2) Roth IRA, including conversion analysis
3) SEP
4) SIMPLE
5) §403(b) plans
6) §457 plans
7) Keogh (HR-10) plans

64. Regulatory considerations
A. Employee Retirement Income Security Act (ERISA)
B. Department of Labor (DOL) regulations
C. Fiduciary liability issues
D. Prohibited transactions
E. Reporting requirements

65. Key factors affecting plan selection for businesses
A. Owner's personal objectives
1) Tax considerations
2) Capital needs at retirement
3) Capital needs at death
B. Business' objectives
1) Tax considerations
2) Administrative cost
3) Cash flow situation and outlook
4) Employee demographics
5) Comparison of defined contribution and defined benefit plan alternatives

66. Investment considerations for retirement plans
A. Suitability

B. Time horizon
C. Diversification
D. Fiduciary considerations
E. Unrelated business taxable income (UBTI)
F. Life insurance
G. Appropriate assets for tax-advantaged vs. taxable accounts

67. Distribution rules, alternatives, and taxation
A. Premature distributions
1) Penalties
2) Exceptions to penalties
3) Substantially equal payments (§72(t))
B. Election of distribution options
1) Lump sum distributions
2) Annuity options
3) Rollover
4) Direct transfer
C. Required minimum distributions
1) Rules
2) Calculations
3) Penalties
D. Beneficiary considerations/ Stretch IRAs
E. Qualified domestic relations order (QDRO)
F. Taxation of distributions
1) Tax management techniques
2) Net unrealized appreciation (NUA)

ESTATE PLANNING (15%)

68. Characteristics and consequences of property titling
A. Community property vs. non-community property
B. Sole ownership
C. Joint tenancy with right of survivorship (JTWROS)
D. Tenancy by the entirety
E. Tenancy in common
F. Trust ownership

69. Methods of property transfer at death
A. Transfers through the probate process
1) Testamentary distribution
2) Intestate succession
3) Advantages and disadvantages of probate
4) Assets subject to probate estate
5) Probate avoidance strategies

6

 CERTIFIED FINANCIAL PLANNER™

6) Ancillary probate administration
B. Transfers by operation of law
C. Transfers through trusts
D. Transfers by contract

70. Estate planning documents
A. Wills
1) Legal requirements
2) Types of wills
3) Modifying or revoking a will
4) Avoiding will contests
B. Powers of Attorney
C. Trusts
D. Marital property agreements
E. Buy-sell agreements

71. Gifting strategies
A. Inter-vivos gifting

B. Gift-giving techniques and strategies
C. Appropriate gift property
D. Strategies for closely-held business owners
E. Gifts of present and future interests
F. Gifts to non-citizen spouses
G. Tax implications
1) Income
2) Gift
3) Estate
4) Generation-skipping transfer tax (GSTT)

72. Gift tax compliance and tax calculation
A. Gift tax filing requirements
B. Calculation
1) Annual exclusion
2) Applicable credit amount
3) Gift splitting
4) Prior taxable gifts
5) Education and medical exclusions
6) Marital and charitable deductions
7) Tax liability

73. Incapacity planning
A. Definition of incapacity
B. Powers of attorney
1) For health care decisions
2) For asset management
3) Durable feature
4) Springing power
5) General or limited powers
C. Advance medical directives (e.g. living wills)
D. Guardianship and conservatorship
E. Revocable living trust
F. Medicaid planning

G. Special needs trust
74. Estate tax compliance and tax calculation
A. Estate tax filing requirements
B. The gross estate
1) Inclusions
2) Exclusions
C. Deductions
D. Adjusted gross estate
E. Deductions from the adjusted gross estate
F. Taxable estate
G. Adjusted taxable gifts
H. Tentative tax base
I. Tentative tax calculation
J. Credits
1) Gift tax payable
2) Applicable credit amount
3) Prior transfer credit

75. Sources for estate liquidity
A. Sale of assets
B. Life insurance
C. Loan
76. Powers of appointment
A. Use and purpose
B. General and special (limited) powers
1) 5-and-5 power
2) Crummey powers
3) Distributions for an ascertainable standard
4) Lapse of power
C. Tax implications

77. Types, features, and taxation of trusts
A. Classification
1) Simple and complex
2) Revocable and irrevocable
3) Inter-vivos and testamentary
B. Types and basic provisions
1) Totten trust
2) Spendthrift trust
3) Bypass trust
4) Marital trust
5) Qualified terminable interest property (QTIP) trust
6) Pour-over trust
7) §2503(b) trust
8) §2503(c) trust
9) Sprinkling provision
C. Trust beneficiaries: Income and remainder
D. Rule against perpetuities
E. Estate and gift taxation

78. Qualified interest trusts
A. Grantor retained annuity trusts (GRATs)

B. Grantor retained unitrusts (GRUTs)
C. Qualified personal residence trusts (QPRTs or House-GRITs)
D. Valuation of qualified interests

79. Charitable transfers
A. Outright gifts
B. Charitable remainder trusts
1) Unitrusts (CRUTs)
2) Annuity trusts (CRATs)
C. Charitable lead trusts
1) Unitrusts (CLUTs)
2) Annuity trusts (CLATs)
D. Charitable gift annuities
E. Pooled income funds
F. Private foundations
G. Donor advised funds
H. Estate and gift taxation

80. Use of life insurance in estate planning
A. Incidents of ownership
B. Ownership and beneficiary considerations
C. Irrevocable life insurance trust (ILIT)
D. Estate and gift taxation

81. Valuation issues
A. Estate freezes
1) Corporate and partnership recapitalizations (§2701)
2) Transfers in trust
B. Valuation discounts for business interests
1) Minority discounts
2) Marketability discounts
3) Blockage discounts
4) Key person discounts
C. Valuation techniques and the federal gross estate

82. Marital deduction
A. Requirements
B. Qualifying transfers
C. Terminable interest rule and exceptions
D. Qualified domestic trust (QDOT)

83. Deferral and minimization of estate taxes
A. Exclusion of property from the gross estate
B. Lifetime gifting strategies
C. Marital deduction and bypass trust planning
D. Inter-vivos and testamentary charitable gifts

7

84. Intra-family and other business transfer techniques
   A. Characteristics
   B. Techniques
      1) Buy-sell agreement
      2) Installment note
      3) Self-canceling installment note (SCIN)
      4) Private annuity
      5) Transfers in trust
      6) Intra-family loan
      7) Bargain sale
      8) Gift or sale leaseback
      9) Intentionally defective grantor trust
      10) Family limited partnership (FLP) or limited liability company (LLC)
   C. Federal income, gift, estate, and generation-skipping transfer tax implications

85) Generation-skipping transfer tax (GSTT)
   A. Identify transfers subject to the GSTT
      1) Direct skips
      2) Taxable distributions
      3) Taxable terminations
   B. Exemptions and exclusions from the GSTT
      1) The GSTT exemption
      2) Qualifying annual exclusion gifts and direct transfers

86. Fiduciaries
   A. Types of fiduciaries
      1) Executor/Personal representative
      2) Trustee
      3) Guardian
   B. Duties of fiduciaries
   C. Breach of fiduciary duties

87. Income in respect of a decedent (IRD)
   A. Assets qualifying as IRD
   B. Calculation for IRD deduction
   C. Income tax treatment

88. Postmortem estate planning techniques
   A. Alternate valuation date
   B. Qualified disclaimer
   C. Deferral of estate tax (§6166)
   D. Corporate stock redemption (§303)
   E. Special use valuation (§2032A)

89. Estate planning for non-traditional relationships
   A. Children of another relationship
   B. Cohabitation
   C. Adoption
   D. Same-sex relationships

ADDENDUM

The following topics are an addendum to the *Topic List for CFP® Certification Examination*. Although individuals taking the CFP® Certification Examination will not be tested directly over these topics, CFP Board registered programs are strongly encouraged to teach them in their curricula) Continuing education (CE) programs and materials that address these topics will be eligible for CFP Board CE credit.

1. Client and planner attitudes, values, biases and behavioral characteristics and the impact on financial planning
   A. Cultural
   B. Family (e.g. biological; non-traditional)
   C. Emotional
   D. Life cycle and age
   E. Client's level of knowledge, experience, and expertise
   F. Risk tolerance
   G. Values-driven planning

2. Principles of communication and counseling
   A. Types of structured communication
      1) Interviewing
      2) Counseling
      3) Advising
   B. Essentials in financial counseling
      1) Establishing structure
      2) Creating rapport
      3) Recognizing resistance
   C. Characteristics of effective counselors
      1) Unconditional positive regard
      2) Accurate empathy
      3) Genuineness and self-awareness
   D. Nonverbal behaviors
      1) Body positions, movements, and gestures
      2) Facial expressions and eye contact
      3) Voice tone and pitch
      4) Interpreting the meaning of nonverbal behaviors
   E. Attending and listening skills
      1) Physical attending
      2) Active listening
      3) Responding during active listening; leading responses
   F. Effective use of questions
      1) Appropriate types of questions
      2) Ineffective and counterproductive questioning techniques

8

YOUR COMMENTS FOR VOLUME VII—CASE BOOK

Our goal is to provide a high-quality product to you and other CFP® candidates. With this goal in mind, we hope to significantly improve our texts with each new edition. We welcome your written suggestions, corrections, and other general comments. Please be as detailed as possible and send your written comments to:

Kaplan Financial
143 Mallard Street, Suite E
St. Rose, Louisiana 70087
(504) 461-9860 Fax

	Page	Question	Comments for Volume VII (please be as specific as possible)
1.			
2.			
3.			
4.			
5.			
6.			
7.			
8.			
9.			
10.			
11.			
12.			
13.			
14.			
15.			

Name

Address

Phone   (Work)   (Home)   (Fax)

E-mail _____ Do you require a response? _____YES _____NO

TABLE OF CONTENTS

I.   Nicholson Case
A. Case Scenario 3
B. Questions 13
C. Answer Summary... 21
D. Summary of Topics 21
E. Solutions 22

II.   Berger Case
A. Case Scenario 31
B. Questions 41
C. Answer Summary... 51
D. Summary of Topics 51
E. Solutions 53

III.   Savage Case
A. Case Scenario 65
B. Questions 75
C. Answer Summary... 85
D. Summary of Topics 85
E. Solutions 86

IV.   Topplemeir Case
A. Case Scenario 95
B. Questions 109
C. Answer Summary... 117
D. Summary of Topics 117
E. Solutions 118

V.   Farrell Case
A. Case Scenario 129
B. Questions 145
C. Answer Summary... 153
D. Summary of Topics 153
E. Solutions 154

VI.   Roth Case
A. Case Scenario 163
B. Questions 175
C. Answer Summary... 185
D. Summary of Topics 185
E. Solutions 186

VII.   **Ackerman Case**
    A. Case Scenario 195
    B. Questions 205
    C. Answer Summary.. 213
    D. Summary of Topics 213
    E. Solutions 214

VIII.   **Blocker Case**
    A. Case Scenario 225
    B. Questions 237
    C. Answer Summary.. 245
    D. Summary of Topics 245
    E. Solutions 246

IX.   **Klar Case**
    A. Case Scenario 253
    B. Questions 261
    C. Answer Summary.. 269
    D. Summary of Topics 269
    E. Solutions 270

X.   **Hobert Case**
    A. Case Scenario 277
    B. Questions 287
    C. Answer Summary.. 297
    D. Summary of Topics 297
    E. Solutions 299

XI.   **Martin Case**
    A. Case Scenario 309
    B. Questions 317
    C. Answer Summary.. 325
    D. Summary of Topics 325
    E. Solutions 326

XII.   **Wood Case**
    A. Case Scenario 335
    B. Questions 345
    C. Answer Summary.. 353
    D. Summary of Topics 353
    E. Solutions 354

XIII.   **Mathews Case**
    A. Case Scenario 361
    B. Questions 369
    C. Answer Summary.. 379
    D. Summary of Topics 379
    E. Solutions 380

XIV.   Kincaid Case
   A.   Case Scenario 387
   B.   Questions 393
   C.   Answer Summary 401
   D.   Summary of Topics 401
   E.   Solutions 402

XV.   Clarke Case
   A.   Case Scenario 407
   B.   Questions 413
   C.   Answer Summary 419
   D.   Summary of Topics 419
   E.   Solutions 420

XVI.   Davis Case
   A.   Case Scenario 425
   B.   Questions 435
   C.   Answer Summary 441
   D.   Summary of Topics 441
   E.   Solutions 442

XVII.   Item Sets
   A.   Questions 449
   B.   Answer Summary 505
   C.   Solutions 507

XVIII.   Cognitive Connections
   A.   Questions 557
   B.   Answer Summary 585
   C.   Solutions 586

XIX.   Appendix **611**

CHRIS AND FAITH NICHOLSON

Case Scenario

Chris and Faith Nicholson

Today is December 31, 2007. Chris and Faith Nicholson have come to you, a financial planner, for help in developing a plan to accomplish their financial goals. From your initial meeting together, you have gathered the following information:

PERSONAL BACKGROUND AND INFORMATION

Chris Nicholson (Age 27)

Chris is a correctional officer with a privately owned minimum security prison. He has a bachelor's degree in criminal justice and a master's degree in social work.

Faith Nicholson (Age 24)

Faith is an assistant manager for a clothing store.

The Children

Chris and Faith have no children from this marriage. Chris has two children, Jeremy (age 4) and Joshua (age 3) from a former marriage. Jeremy and Joshua live with their mother, Alice.

The Nicholsons

Chris and Faith have been married for 2 years.

Chris must pay $325 per month in child support until both Joshua and Jeremy reach age 18. In addition, the divorce decree requires Chris to create a life insurance trust for the benefit of the children and contribute $175 per month to the trustee. The trustee is Alice's father. There are no withdrawal powers on the part of the beneficiaries. The trust is to be used for the education and/or maintenance of the children in the event of Chris' death. The trustee has the power to invade any trust principal for the beneficiaries at the earlier of the death of Chris or Joshua reaching age 18.

During the current year, Chris paid his former spouse $3,000 in cash. The payment was not part of the original divorce agreement. Alice, the former spouse, used some of the money to fix the roof on her house and the remainder of the money was applied to her mortgage payment on her house. Both Chris and Alice occupied the house together when they were married, and the house was transferred solely into Alice's name upon their divorce.

PERSONAL AND FINANCIAL OBJECTIVES

- Save for an emergency fund.
- Eliminate debt.
- Save for a 20% down payment on their dream house. The current value of the house is $100,000. Property taxes and insurance would be $1,200 and $750, respectively. Both taxes and insurance are expected to increase at the rate of inflation.

- Contribute to tax-advantaged savings vehicles.

ECONOMIC INFORMATION

- Inflation is expected to be 4.0% annually.
- Salaries should increase 5.0% for the next five to ten years.
- No state income tax.
- Slow growth economy; stocks are expected to grow at 9.5% annually.

Bank lending rates are as follows:
- 15-year mortgages 7.5%.
- 30-year mortgages 8.0%.
- Secured personal loans 10.0%.
- Prime rate 6.0%.

INSURANCE INFORMATION

Life Insurance

	Policy A	Policy B	Policy C
Insured	Chris	Chris	Faith
Face amount	$250,000	$78,000[2]	$20,000
Type	Whole Life	Group Term	Group Term
Cash value	$2,000	$0	$0
Annual premium	$2,100	$156	$50
Who pays premium	Trustee	Employer	Employer
Beneficiary	Trustee[1]	Alice	Chris
Policyowner	Trust	Chris	Faith
Settlement options clause selected	None	None	None

[1] Joshua and Jeremy are beneficiaries of the trust.

[2] This was increased from $50,000 to $78,000 January 1, 2007.

Health Insurance

Chris and Faith are covered under Chris' employer plan which is an indemnity plan with a $200 deductible per person per year and an 80/20 major medical coinsurance clause with a family annual stop loss of $1,500.

Long-Term Disability Insurance

Chris is covered by an "own occupation" policy with premiums paid by his employer. The benefits equal 60% of gross pay after a 180-day elimination period. The policy covers both sickness and accidents.

Faith is not covered by disability insurance.

Renters Insurance

The Nicholsons have a HO4 renter's policy without endorsements.

Content Coverage $25,000; Liability $100,000.

Automobile Insurance

Both Car and Truck

Type	PAP
Bodily Injury	$25,000/$50,000
Property Damage	$10,000
Medical Payments	$5,000 per person
Physical Damage	Actual Cash Value
Uninsured Motorist	$25,000/$50,000
Comprehensive Deductible	$200
Collision Deductible	$500
Premium (annual)	$3,300

INVESTMENT INFORMATION

The Nicholsons think that they need 6 months of cash flow, net of all taxes, savings, vacation, and discretionary cash flow, in an emergency fund. They are willing to include in the emergency fund the savings account and Chris' 401(k) balance because it has borrowing provisions.

Chris has W-Mart stock, which was a gift to Chris from his Uncle Carter. At the date of the gift (July 1, 1999), the fair market value of the stock was $3,500. Uncle Carter's tax basis was $2,500, and Uncle Carter paid gift tax of $1,400 on the gift. Uncle Carter had already used up both his applicable credit and annual exclusion to Chris.

The 100 shares of Microsoft stock was a gift to Faith last Christmas from her Aunt Beatrice. At the date of the gift (December 25, 2007), the fair market value was $8,000, and Beatrice had paid $10,000 for the stock in 1998 (her tax basis).

Growth Mutual Fund
Current Value: $13,900
All earnings have been reinvested.

Year	Deposit	Earnings
2002	$1,000	$0
2003	$1,000	$200
2004	$2,000	$400
2005	$2,000	$400
2006	$2,500	$650
2007	$3,000	$750

INCOME TAX INFORMATION (FEDERAL)

The Nicholsons file married filing jointly. The children (Jeremy and Joshua) are claimed as dependents on the Nicholsons' tax return as part of the divorce agreement.

The Nicholsons live in a state that does not have state income tax.

Section 79 Uniform Premium Schedule	
Under 25	0.05 per month/per $1,000
25 to 29	0.06 per month/per $1,000

RETIREMENT INFORMATION

Chris' employer allows employees to contribute up to 25% of their compensation each year to their 401(k) plan, not to exceed Internal Revenue Code maximums. Chris' employer matches contributions dollar-for-dollar up to the first 6% of compensation contributed. Chris is currently contributing 3% of his compensation to the 401(k) plan.

The 401(k) plan allows employees to take loans from the plan at any time. The summary plan description imposes the following requirements on plan loans:

"If you had no loan balance within the immediate preceding 12 months, the maximum amount of the loan is the lesser of $50,000 or 50% of the vested account balance. All loans must be paid in full within 5 years from the date of the original loan. Loan payments can only be made through payroll deductions.

The interest rate will be established at the beginning of each month at one percent above the prime rate as published on the last business day of the previous month. Once an interest rate is established and assigned to a loan, it will remain unchanged for the term of that loan."

Chris has never borrowed from his 401(k) plan. He estimates that his average rate of return on the 401(k) investments is 8% per year.

GIFTS, ESTATES, TRUSTS, AND WILL INFORMATION

Chris has a will leaving all of his probate estate to his children. Faith does not have a will. The Nicholsons live in a common law state that has adopted the Uniform Probate Code.

STATEMENT OF CASH FLOWS
Chris and Faith Nicholson
Statement of Cash Flows (Expected to be similar next year)
Current Year

CASH INFLOWS

Salaries		
Chris—Salary	$26,000	
Faith—Salary	20,000	
Investment Income*	1,090	
Total Inflows		**$47,090**

CASH OUTFLOWS

Savings—House Down Payment	$1,200	
Reinvestment of Investment Income	1,090	
401(k) Contribution	780	
Total Savings	$3,070	

FIXED OUTFLOWS

Child Support	$3,900	
Payment to Former Spouse	3,000	
Life Insurance Payment (To Trustee)	2,100	
Rent	6,600	
Renters Insurance	480	
Utilities	720	
Telephone	360	
Auto Insurance	3,300	
Gas, Oil, Maintenance	2,400	
Student Loans	3,600	
Credit Card Debt	1,800	
Furniture Payments	1,302	
Total Fixed Outflows	$29,562	

VARIABLE OUTFLOWS

Taxes—Chris FICA	$1,989	
Taxes—Faith FICA	1,530	
Taxes—Federal	4,316	
Food	2,910	
Clothing	1,000	
Entertaining/Vacation	1,500	
Total Variable Outflows	$13,245	
Total Cash Outflows		$45,877
Discretionary Cash Flows		1,213
TOTAL CASH OUTFLOWS		$47,090

* $340 from dividends from W-Mart stock, and $750 from the Growth Mutual Fund.

STATEMENT OF FINANCIAL POSITION
Chris and Faith Nicholson
Balance Sheet
As of December 31, 2007

ASSETS[1]		LIABILITIES & NET WORTH	
Cash and Equivalents		**Liabilities[3]**	
Cash	$500	Credit Card Balance VISA	$9,000
Savings Account	1,000	Credit Card Balance M/C	0
Total Cash and Equivalents	$1,500	Student Loan—Chris[4]	45,061
		Auto Loan —Faith	14,796
Invested Assets		Furniture Loan	1,533
W-Mart Stock (100 Shares)[2]	$5,000	*Total Liabilities*	$70,390
Microsoft Stock (100 Shares)	7,200		
Growth Mutual Fund	13,900		
401(k) Account	1,500	**Net Worth**	$(46)
Total Invested Assets	$27,600		
Use Assets			
Auto—Faith	$18,494		
Truck—Chris	4,000		
Motorcycle—Faith	1,000		
Furniture & Personal Property	17,750		
Total Use Assets	$41,244		
Total Assets	$70,344	**Total Liabilities & Net Worth**	$70,344

Notes to Financial Statements:

[1] Assets are stated at fair market value.

[2] W-Mart's current dividend is $3.40.

[3] Liabilities are stated at principal only as of December 31 before January payments.

[4] Chris took out the loans to pay for qualified education costs. Chris paid $2,732 in interest in the current year.

INFORMATION REGARDING ASSETS AND LIABILITIES

Home Furnishings

The furniture was purchased with 20% down and 18% interest over 36 months. The regular monthly payment is $108.46.

Automobile

The automobile was purchased December 31 of this year, for $18,494 with 20% down and 8% financing over 60 months with payments of $300 per month.

Stereo System

The Nicholsons have a fabulous stereo system (fair market value $10,000). They asked and received permission to alter the apartment to install built-in speakers into every room. The agreement with the landlord requires them to leave the speakers if they move as they are permanently installed and affixed to the property. The replacement value of the installed speakers is $4,500, and the noninstalled components are valued at $5,500. The original cost of the system was $10,000, and it was purchased in late 2006.

CHRIS AND FAITH NICHOLSON

Questions

Chris and Faith Nicholson

QUESTIONS

1. Which of the following statements accurately describes the Nicholsons' current financial condition?

    1. The child support payment to Alice is fully deductible for income tax purposes.
    2. They are technically insolvent.
    3. They have inadequate life insurance.
    4. They have inadequate liability insurance.

        a. 1 and 3.
        b. 3 and 4.
        c. 1, 3, and 4.
        d. 2, 3, and 4.
        e. 1, 2, and 4.

2. If Chris and Faith sell the Microsoft stock at its current fair market value, what are the tax consequences?

    a. No gain or loss.
    b. $2,800 long-term capital loss.
    c. $2,800 short-term capital loss.
    d. $800 long-term capital loss.
    e. $800 short-term capital loss.

3. Assuming that Chris and Faith decide to sell the W-Mart stock next year, for a total price of $5,500, what are the tax consequences of such a sale?

    a. $2,600 long-term capital gain.
    b. $2,000 long-term capital gain.
    c. $3,000 long-term capital gain.
    d. $1,600 long-term capital gain.
    e. No gain or loss.

4. How many payments have been made on the purchased furniture as of today?

    a. 14.
    b. 16.
    c. 18.
    d. 20.
    e. 22.

5. Calculate the original purchase price of the furniture.

    a. $3,000.

    b. $3,250.

    c. $3,500.

    d. $3,750.

6. If the Nicholsons were burglarized and had their movable stereo system components stolen, would the burglary be covered under the HO4 policy, and if so, for what value?

    a. No, it would not be covered.

    b. Yes, covered but only up to $1,000, as it is a listed item.

    c. Yes, covered but only to the actual cash value (cost – depreciation) less the deductible.

    d. Yes, covered for full replacement value.

    e. Yes, covered for full replacement value less the deductible.

7. If there were a fire in the Nicholson's apartment building and their built-in speaker system was destroyed, would they be covered under the HO4 policy, and if so, to what extent?

    a. No, the system is part of the building, not personal property.

    b. No, the system is excluded.

    c. Yes, but the system is listed property $1,000 less deductible.

    d. Yes, but limited to $2,500 (10% of personal property) under building additions.

    e. Yes, at full replacement value less deductible.

8. If a fire forced them to move out of their apartment for a month, would the HO4 policy provide any coverage?

    a. No.

    b. Yes, up to $25,000.

    c. Yes, for loss of use up to $2,500.

    d. Yes, for loss of use up to $5,000.

9. Is Faith covered for liability on her motorcycle under the PAP?

    a. Yes, but only up to $10,000.

    b. No, motorcycles are excluded under the PAP.

    c. Yes, if the motorcycle is less than 80CC's.

    d. Yes, for liability but not for uninsured motorist.

10. Which of the following strategies may help Chris and Faith lower their tax liability?

    a. Contribute to a Traditional IRA.

    b. Purchase Series EE savings bonds.

    c. Create a SEP for Chris and contribute by the extended due date of the joint income tax return.

    d. Contribute to a Coverdell Education Savings Account for their children.

11. If the Nicholsons sell the Growth Mutual Fund for the current value, what will be the tax consequences?

    a. $2,400 long-term capital gain.

    b. $2,400 gain, part short-term and part long-term.

    c. $2,400 short-term capital gain.

    d. $2,400 ordinary income.

    e. No recognized gain or loss.

12. Which of the following may be appropriate planning strategies for the Nicholsons?

    1. Draft a will for Faith.

    2. Create Advanced Medical Directives for both Chris and Faith.

    3. Purchase a personal liability umbrella policy.

    4. Transfer their residence to a Qualified Personal Residence Trust (QPRT).

    a. 1 and 4.

    b. 1, 2, and 4.

    c. 1, 2, and 3.

    d. 1, 2, 3, and 4.

13. Do the payments of $175 a month to the trustee of the insurance trust for the children constitute a taxable gift from Chris?

    a. No, because the total payments are less than $12,000.

    b. Yes, because there is no Crummey provision in the trust.

    c. Yes, because the payments are a gift of a future interest.

    d. No, because the payments are a legal support obligation.

    e. No, because the payments are for the beneficial interest of his children.

14. Who will actually collect the proceeds of Chris' term life insurance if he were to die today, given that the Nicholsons live in a Uniform Probate Code state?

    a. Alice would get the entire insurance proceeds.

    b. Faith would get the entire insurance proceeds.

    c. Faith would get half and the children half.

    d. The children would get the entire proceeds of insurance.

    e. Alice would get half and Faith would get half.

15. Chris is considering borrowing from his 401(k) for a vacation. Which of the following statements is correct regarding this scenario?

    a. The maximum loan Chris can take from the 401(k) is $50,000.

    b. Interest paid on the loan will be deductible as a miscellaneous itemized deduction on Chris' federal income tax return.

    c. Chris would be better off taking a secured personal loan for the vacation.

    d. The loan will be repaid by Chris with after-tax dollars.

16. How much must Chris Nicholson's employer include in Chris' W-2 for 2007 for the group term life insurance? (Round to nearest dollar.)

    a. $0.
    b. $17.
    c. $20.
    d. $47.
    e. $56.

17. Chris and Faith are contemplating contributing to IRAs. Which of the following statements is/are correct regarding IRAs?

    1. Chris can rollover his employer's 401(k) into a Traditional IRA.
    2. If Faith establishes a Traditional IRA, she can take a lump-sum distribution and elect ten-year averaging when she retires.
    3. Chris is considered an active participant in a retirement plan.

    a. 3 only.
    b. 2 and 3.
    c. 1 or 2.
    d. 1, 2, and 3.
    e. 1 and 3.

18. What is the implied growth rate of W-Mart dividend based on the constant growth dividend model? (rounded to the nearest percent) Assume that the Nicholsons' required rate of return is 10%.

    a. 0%.
    b. 1%.
    c. 2%.
    d. 3%.
    e. 4%.

19. Assume Chris and Faith wanted to give the W-Mart stock on December 31, 2007 to State University, the school where Chris received his master's degree, but they only wanted to make the contribution if it would have positive tax consequences. Luckily, they came to you, their financial planner, prior to the donation and asked your advice. Which of the following would be the most appropriate advice?

    a. Chris and Faith should donate the W-Mart stock and take a charitable contribution using the 50% of the fair market value limit.
    b. Chris and Faith should donate the W-Mart stock and take a charitable contribution using the 30% of the basis limit.
    c. Chris and Faith should donate the W-Mart stock and take a charitable contribution for the full fair market value.
    d. Chris and Faith should donate the W-Mart stock and take a charitable contribution for the full adjusted basis.
    e. Chris and Faith should not donate the W-Mart stock because it would not yield the best tax consequences.

20. Assume Chris and Faith donated the W-Mart stock to State University this year and took a charitable contribution deduction. If the IRS audits Chris and Faith next year and disputes the charitable contribution deduction, which of the following can be cited as having the highest source of authority next to the Internal Revenue Code and as carrying the full force and effect of the law? (Assume each source is on point and is in the client's favor.)

    a. Treasury Regulation 1.170A-8.

    b. Revenue Ruling 67-178.

    c. Private Letter Ruling 9623035 (not issued to your client).

    d. Revenue Procedure 97-52.

21. The Nicholsons are interested in utilizing their discretionary cash flows in a manner that will make the most sense from a saving and net worth perspective. With respect to the discretionary cash flows, which of the following strategies would make the most sense for the Nicholsons based upon their current financial situation?

    a. Apply the discretionary income towards their outstanding student loan debt.

    b. Contribute an additional 3% of Chris' salary to his 401(k) plan.

    c. Set money aside in an S&P 500 index mutual fund to help fund a down payment on their dream home.

    d. Purchase a flexible premium deferred variable annuity to help provide an income stream for their retirement.

22. Which of the following statements is correct regarding the $3,000 cash payment made to Alice by Chris this year?

    a. The payment will be excluded from Alice's gross income for federal income tax purposes.

    b. The payment to Alice will be subject to alimony recapture, because it constitutes excess alimony.

    c. Only the portion of the $3,000 that was used to pay Alice's mortgage will be considered alimony for federal income tax purposes.

    d. The entire payment will be considered alimony because the payment was made in cash, and the home is solely in Alice's name.

CHRIS AND FAITH NICHOLSON

Solutions

Chris and Faith Nicholson

ANSWER SUMMARY

1. d	6. c	11. e	16. c	21. b
2. e	7. d	12. c	17. a	22. a
3. a	8. d	13. d	18. d	
4. d	9. b	14. a	19. e	
5. d	10. a	15. d	20. a	

SUMMARY OF TOPICS

1. Fundamentals—Financial Analysis
2. Tax—Basis of Gift
3. Tax—Basis of Gift
4. Fundamentals—Time Value of Money
5. Fundamentals—Time Value of Money
6. Insurance—Homeowners (HO4)
7. Insurance—Homeowners (HO4)
8. Insurance—Homeowners (Loss of Use)
9. Insurance—PAP Exclusions
10. Tax—Tax Liability
11. Tax—Basis of Investment
12. Fundamentals—Financial Recommendations
13. Estates—Gifts
14. Insurance—Contract
15. Retirement—401(k) Loan Provisions
16. Tax—Group Term Life Insurance
17. Retirement—IRAs
18. Investments—Constant Growth Dividend Model
19. Tax—Charitable Contributions
20. Tax—Sources of Law
21. Fundamentals—Budgeting
22. Tax—Alimony

SOLUTIONS

Fundamentals—Financial Analysis

1. **d**

The child support payment is for support of the children and is not deductible.

The Nicholsons are technically insolvent due to a small negative net worth. The debt ratios are especially revealing. The Nicholsons are in serious debt trouble when you include their monthly obligations to the child support and insurance payments. They are unlikely to qualify for a home loan until their financial situation changes. They have inadequate life insurance and inadequate liability insurance.

Tax—Basis of Gift

2. **e**

Sale price	$7,200
Faith's basis	(8,000)*
Gain or (loss)	($800)

This is a short-term capital loss due to the holding period beginning on the date of the gift and the holding period being less than one year and one day.

*The basis of a gift to a donee for an asset that has a fair market value less than the donor's basis is the fair market value for losses and the donor's basis for gains (double-basis rule). Since the stock was sold at a loss, the loss basis of $8,000 (fair market value on date of gift) is used.

Tax—Basis of Gift

3. **a**

Sale price	$5,500	Donor's basis	$2,500
Adjusted basis	(2,900)	Pro rata share of gift tax paid	400
Long-term capital gain	$2,600	Chris' adjusted basis	$2,900

FMV @ date of gift	$3,500
Donor's basis	(2,500)
Appreciation	$1,000

Gift tax paid	$1,400

Proportion attributed to appreciation ($1,000 ÷ $3,500) × $1,400 = $400

Since appreciated property was gifted, a portion of the gift tax paid by the donor is added to the donee's basis. Add $400 to the donor's basis. Therefore, Chris' adjusted basis is $2,900.

Fundamentals—Time Value of Money

4. **d**

The loan is 36 months.

The loan is 80% of the original value.

The interest rate is 18% annually.

The payment is $108.46 per month.

Therefore,

n	=	36
i	=	1.5 (18 ÷ 12)
PMT_{OA}	=	$108.46
PV	=	**($3,000.08)**

The current balance on the statement of financial position under liabilities is $1,533.

FV	=	($1,533)
PV	=	$3,000
PMT_{OA}	=	($108.46)
i	=	1.5 (18 ÷ 12)
n	=	20

Fundamentals—Time Value of Money

5. **d**

We use the result from the first half of the solution to number 4.

$3,000 = 0.80x

$\quad$ x = $3,750

Insurance—Homeowners (HO4)

6. **c**

Yes. It would be covered but only at the actual cash value (cost minus depreciation) less the deductible, because the policy is without endorsement.

Insurance—Homeowners (HO4)

7. **d**

Yes, but only to $2,500 (10% of personal property coverage under the building additions section).

Insurance—Homeowners (Loss of Use)

8. **d**

Yes. Loss of use up to 20% of the $25,000 based on their incremental loss.

Insurance—PAP Exclusions

9. b

No. Section B of the PAP specifically excludes liability for motorcycles even if not owned.

Tax—Tax Liability

10. a

Since they are below the AGI limits, they can each contribute to Traditional IRAs and take full deductions.

Option (b) is incorrect because there are no deductions for EE bonds.

Option (c) is incorrect because Chris is an employee and his employer already sponsors a plan; therefore, he cannot establish a SEP for himself.

Option (d) is incorrect because contributions to a Coverdell Education Savings Account are not deductible.

Tax—Basis of Investment

11. e

The question requires the determination of the adjusted basis of the growth fund.

<u>Basis Determination</u>:

Contributions (Deposits)	$11,500
Taxable Income (Earnings)	2,400 (2002 – 2007)
Adjusted Taxable Basis	$13,900

Sales Price	$13,900
Adjusted Taxable Basis	(13,900)
No Gain or Loss	$0

Fundamentals—Financial Recommendations

12. c

Statement 4 is incorrect because the Nicholsons don't own a home.

Estates—Gifts

13. d

No. This is legal support required by a divorce decree. Because there is no mention of a Crummey provision in the trust, this may appear to be a gift of a future interest but, in fact, it is legal support.

Insurance—Contract

14. a

The fact that they are in a Uniform Probate Code state is irrelevant in this situation because we are not concerned with probate property. In this instance, we are inquiring about the named beneficiary of an insurance contract. Alice would collect because she is the named beneficiary even though she and Chris are divorced.

Retirement—401(k) Loan Provisions

15. d

Since Chris will repay the loan through payroll deductions, he will essentially be paying back the loan with after-tax dollars.

A is incorrect. Chris' vested account balance is only $1,500. Therefore, his maximum loan would only be $750, because the maximum amount of the loan allowed is the lesser of $50,000 or 50% of the vested account balance.

B is incorrect. Interest paid on 401(k) loans is non-deductible personal interest for federal income tax purposes.

C is incorrect. The 401(k) interest rate is prime plus one, or 7% (6% prime rate plus 1%). The personal loan rate is 10%, and neither type of interest expense is deductible. Therefore, a 401(k) loan would be more appropriate than a personal loan.

Tax—Group Term Life Insurance

16. c

$(0.06 \times 28 \times 12) = \$20.16$

The amount of thousands over $50,000 times the Section 79 schedule per month times twelve months. ($78,000 − $50,000 = $28,000)

Retirement—IRAs

17. a

Chris could not roll his 401(k) balance over to an IRA while still employed. Rollovers are not the same as contributions; contributions are new (fresh) funds. The opportunity for ten-year forward averaging does not exist for a distribution from an IRA. Chris is considered an active participant in a retirement plan.

Investments—Constant Growth Dividend Model

18. d

$$V = \frac{D_1}{k - g}$$

$$\frac{\$3.40\,(1 + g)}{0.10 - g} = \$50$$

$$
\begin{aligned}
3.40\,(1 + g) &= 50\,(0.10 - g) \\
3.40 + 3.40g &= 5.00 - 50g \\
50g + 3.4g &= 5.00 - 3.40 \\
53.4g &= 1.60 \\
g &= 1.60 \div 53.4 \\
g &= 0.02996 = 3\%
\end{aligned}
$$

Tax—Charitable Contributions

19. e

Chris and Faith should not donate the W-Mart stock because it would not yield the best tax consequences. In order to take a charitable contribution, the recipient must itemize deductions. In this case, the charitable contribution would be less than the standard deduction. Since the problem specifically says that they only want to donate the property if it yields positive tax consequences, Option (e) is the most appropriate advice. Options (a) and (b) are incorrect because the limits apply to the contribution base, not the basis or fair market value. While Options (c) and (d) are both feasible options, they are not the best choice, as discussed above.

Tax—Sources of Law

20. a

Treasury regulations have the highest source of authority next to the code and have the full force and effect of the law. Revenue Rulings and Procedures can be relied on, but they do not have the same authority of the IRC or Treasury Regulations. Private Letter Rulings (PLRs) cannot be relied on by taxpayers. However, PLRs may give insight into the IRS's approach on certain transactions.

Fundamentals—Budgeting

21. b

Chris' employer offers a dollar-for-dollar match of employee contributions, up to 3% of salary. Since Chris is only contributing 3% of his salary to the 401(k), he is missing out on some matching contributions. By contributing an additional 3% to the 401(k), he is essentially doubling his money immediately.

A is incorrect. Although paying off debt is generally a good idea, the Nicholson's would be better served paying off their credit card debt first. In addition, the additional 3% contribution to the 401(k) would be more appropriate.

C is incorrect. Although this is not a bad planning idea, the Nicholsons should be more concerned with taking advantage of the employer match in the 401(k) and paying off debt.

D is incorrect. An annuity is probably not appropriate at this point, due to the charges imposed by the annuity company and the difficulty of accessing the money before retirement.

Tax—Alimony

22. a

Because the payment was not made pursuant to a written divorce agreement, the payment will not be considered alimony. Therefore, Chris will not receive an income tax deduction for the payment, and the payment will be excluded from Alice's gross income.

B, C, and D are incorrect. This payment is not considered alimony and, therefore, is not subject to recapture.

DEREK AND OLGA BERGER

■

Case Scenario

Derek and Olga Berger

CASE SCENARIO

Derek and Olga Berger have come to you, a financial planner, for help in developing a plan to accomplish their financial goals. From your initial meeting together, you have gathered the following information. Today is December 31, 2007.

PERSONAL BACKGROUND AND INFORMATION

Derek Berger (Age 26)

Derek Berger is employed at a computer store as a salesperson and trainer. He has been employed with this company for 5 years.

Olga Berger (Age 26)

Olga Berger is a German citizen and is employed as a floral designer for a local florist.

The Bergers

Derek and Olga have been married for 2 years.

Children

The Bergers have one child, Ursula (age 1).

Derek's Parents

Derek's parents, Adriana and Leonard, are fairly well off and live in Idaho. They own all of their property as community property. They have known Olga for a long time and any gift that they make will be to both Derek and Olga. Adriana and Leonard have made no previous taxable gifts.

The Bergers expect Derek's parents either to lend interest free or to give them a $30,000 down payment (27% of the purchase price) to purchase a house.

PERSONAL AND FINANCIAL INFORMATION AND OBJECTIVES

- Derek wants to start his own business in 10 years. In the meantime, he plans to advance in his current job. He wants to open a business similar to his current employer's and expects he'll need $100,000 in today's dollars to start the company.

- They want to buy a house in the price range of $110,000. They expect taxes and homeowners insurance to average $200 per month in total.

- They like to take vacations (twice a year) with an average cost of $2,250 per vacation. Derek and Olga also love to go out with friends or entertain weekly.

- They plan to retire in 30 years and expect that $50,000 per year (in today's dollars) would be sufficient during retirement.

- They expect raises to average 3.5% over their remaining work life expectancy.

- They both expect to live until age 90.

ECONOMIC INFORMATION

- Expected inflation will average 3.5% (CPI) annually.

- Expected return for the S&P 500 Index is 11%.

- T-Bills are currently yielding 5%. Treasury Bonds are currently yielding 7%.

- Current mortgage rates are:

  Fixed, 15-year mortgage: 7.5%

  Fixed, 30-year mortgage: 8.0%

- Home closing costs are expected to be 3% of any mortgage.

- Savings accounts currently yield 1.5% annually, compounded monthly.

- Certificates of Deposit are currently yielding 5% for 1 year.

- Unemployment is currently 6%.

INSURANCE INFORMATION

LIFE INSURANCE	
Insured	Derek
Owner	Derek
Beneficiary	Olga
Face Amount	$50,000
Cash Value	0
Type of Policy	Term
Settlement Options	Lump Sum
Premium	Paid by Employer

HEALTH INSURANCE	
Premium	Derek's premium paid by employer; Olga and Ursula are dependents under Derek's policy
Coverage	Major medical with a $500,000 lifetime limit on a 80/20 basis; maternity coverage also has 80/20; dental coverage is not provided
Deductible	$250 per person (3 person maximum)
Family Out-of-Pocket Limit	$2,500

DISABILITY INSURANCE
Neither Derek nor Olga has disability insurance.

AUTOMOBILE INSURANCE	
Premium	$1,000 total annual premium for both vehicles
Bodily Damage and Property Damage	$10,000/$25,000/$5,000 for each vehicle
Comprehensive	$250 deductible
Collision	$500 deductible

RENTER'S INSURANCE	
Type	HO-4
Contents Coverage	$35,000
Premium	$600 annually
Deductible	$250
Liability	$100,000
Medical Payments	$1,000 per person
Endorsements	None

INVESTMENT INFORMATION

Both Derek and Olga have a high tolerance for risk. They have a balance of $3,840 in Derek's 401(k) plan provided by his employer. He is currently deferring 4% of his salary, and the plan allows him to defer up to 10%. The 401(k) plan offers a variety of mutual funds ranging from aggressive growth stock funds to Treasury money market funds. Derek currently has 100% invested in the Growth Fund.

Several years ago, Derek's grandfather gave him URS stock. The fair market value at the date of the gift was $6,000. Derek's grandfather originally paid $2,000 for the stock and paid gift tax of $600 on the gift.

The Bergers' required rate of return for investments is 1% below the S&P 500 Index return.

INCOME TAX INFORMATION

Derek and Olga file a joint tax return. Their total tax rate including payroll is 24.65% (federal income tax average rate is 15%; state income tax amounts to 2% each year; FICA taxes amount to 7.65%).

RETIREMENT INFORMATION

Derek is a participant in his employer's 401(k) plan. The 401(k) plan has a 2–6 year graduated vesting schedule. The company has made matching contributions of $1,500, which is included in Derek's 401(k) balance above. The balance also includes $1,500 of contributions by Derek and prorated earnings of $840. The plan is not top heavy.

Olga and Derek each contributed $2,000 to an IRA for this year.

GIFTS, ESTATES, TRUSTS, AND WILL INFORMATION

Derek and Olga have simple handwritten wills leaving all probate assets to each other.

STATEMENT OF CASH FLOWS
Derek and Olga Berger
Statement of Cash Flows for Current Year
Monthly

CASH INFLOWS:

Salary—Derek[1]	$2,000	
Salary—Olga[2]	2,000	
Interest Income	1	
Total Inflows[3]		**$4,001**

CASH OUTFLOWS:

IRA Contributions	$333	
401(k) Deferral Savings	80	
Rent	650	
Groceries	323	
Utilities	70	
Water	25	
Telephone	40	
Auto Fuel	100	
Auto Repair	50	
Cable TV	35	
Child Care	200	
Entertainment	100	
Vacations[4]	375	
Auto Insurance	84	
Life Insurance	0	
Medical Insurance	0	
Renters (HO4) Insurance	50	
State Withholding	80	
Federal Withholding	500	
FICA	306	
Student Loan Derek 1	144	
Student Loan Derek 2	111	
Student Loans Olga	45	
Credit Card 1 Derek	51	
Gas Card Derek	9	
Credit Card 2 Olga	42	
Credit Card 3 Olga	165	
Credit Card 4 Olga	33	
Total Outflows		**$4,001**
Discretionary Cash Flow		**$0**

Notes to Financial Statements:

[1] $2,000/month salary = $24,000 per year.

[2] $2,000/month salary = $24,000 per year.

[3] Dividend income is reinvested and, therefore, not listed.

[4] Vacations = Two vacations costing $4,500 per year; $4,500 ÷ 12 months = $375.

STATEMENT OF FINANCIAL POSITION
Derek and Olga Berger
Statement of Financial Position
As of December 31, 2007

ASSETS[1]			LIABILITIES[7] AND NET WORTH		
Cash/Cash Equivalents			**Current Liabilities[8]**		
Checking[2]		$750	Credit Card 1 (Derek)[9]		$1,500
Savings[3]		1,000	Credit Card 2 (Olga)		1,200
Certificate of Deposit[4]		3,000	Credit Card 3 (Olga)		4,800
EE Savings Bonds[5]		500	Credit Card 4 (Olga)		950
Total Cash/Cash Equivalents		$5,250	Gas Card 1 (Derek)		200
			Total Current Liabilities		$8,650
Invested Assets					
URS Stock		$10,000	**Long-Term Liabilities[8]**		
Stock Portfolio[6]		22,000	Student Loans[9]		
Derek's 401(k) plan		3,840	Derek 1		20,000
Total Invested Assets		$35,840	Derek 2		15,000
			Olga 1		6,000
Personal-Use Assets			*Total Long-Term Liabilities*		$41,000
Auto 1		$7,500			
Auto 2		4,500	**Total Liabilities**		**$49,650**
Furniture		6,000			
Personal Property		7,000	**Net Worth**		**$16,440**
Total Personal-Use Assets		$25,000			
Total Assets		**$66,090**	**Total Liabilities & Net Worth**		**$66,090**

Notes to Financial Statements:

[1] All assets are stated at fair market value.

[2] Checking is a noninterest bearing account.

[3] Savings interest of 1.5% annually.

[4] Certificate of Deposit maturing December 1, 2008.

[5] EE savings bonds, 5 bonds with present value of $100 each; interest of 6% annually; maturity date of 2032.

[6] Stock Portfolio in stock account managed by Derek.

[7] Liabilities are stated at principal only.

[8] All liability payments are as indicated on monthly cash flow statement.

[9] The average interest rate for all credit cards is 15% and for student loans is 10%.

INFORMATION REGARDING ASSETS AND LIABILITIES

Detailed Investment Portfolio

Derek's 401(k) Plan

Description	Shares	Price/Share	Total Value	2006 Returns	2007 Returns
Growth Fund	93.00	$41.29	$3,840	13%	7%

Stock Portfolio

Stock	Date Acquired	Cost Basis	Fair Market Value as of 12/31/07	Beta	Current Dividend	Growth of Dividend
A	1/00	$300	$2,800	1.3	$200	3.50%
B	3/01	3,000	700	1.6	33	5.00%
C	5/06	5,000	7,000	1.0	400	4.00%
D	6/06	12,000	2,500	1.1	197	2.00%
E	7/06	9,000	9,000	1.2	500	4.25%
Total		$29,300	$22,000	N/A	$1,330	N/A

DEREK AND OLGA BERGER

Questions

Derek and Olga Berger

QUESTIONS

1. Assuming the Bergers have no savings set aside for the acquisition of Derek's future business, how much should be saved at the end of each month, beginning this month, to be able to acquire Derek's business? Assume they will invest in a no-load S&P 500 index fund and will pay any taxes on current earnings out of their regular budget. They will reinvest all earnings in this account.

    a. $456.65.

    b. $460.83.

    c. $566.55.

    d. $569.97.

    e. $650.05.

2. Which of the following insurance products would be most appropriate for Derek to purchase?

    a. Tax qualified long-term care policy with an inflation-adjusted benefit.

    b. Fixed annuity with a life and 20-year term certain options.

    c. Personal liability umbrella policy.

    d. Long-term disability insurance policy.

3. Regarding the planned contribution to Derek and Olga's IRA for 2007, which of the following statements is/are correct?

    1. Derek is an active participant in a qualified plan.

    2. Olga's contribution is fully deductible.

    3. Derek's contribution is nondeductible for income tax because he is covered by a qualified plan.

    4. Olga's contribution is partially deductible for income tax.

    a. 1 and 2.

    b. 2 only.

    c. 1 and 3.

    d. 1 and 4.

    e. 1, 2, and 3.

4. If Derek were to sell the URS stock today, what would be the current tax consequences to the Bergers?

    a. Long-term capital gain of $3,600.

    b. Long-term capital gain of $4,000.

    c. Short-term capital gain of $8,000.

    d. Long-term capital gain of $8,000.

    e. Long-term capital gain of $7,600.

5. Assume Derek had the following sale transactions in his stock trading account for 2007:

Sold Stock	Date	Sales Price/Net of Commissions
A	August 15, 2007	$2,750
B	August 15, 2007	$600
C	April 1, 2007	$8,000
D	April 1, 2007	$3,000
		$14,350 total proceeds

What are the net gains or losses from the above stock transactions during 2007?

    a. Long-term capital loss $2,400.

    b. Short-term capital gain $3,000.

    c. Long-term capital gain $2,450.

    d. Short-term capital loss $5,950.

    e. Short-term capital loss $9,000.

6. If the stock market yields 17%, what is the expected return for the Bergers' stock portfolio under the Capital Asset Pricing Model (CAPM), based on the value as of today?

    a. 19.4%.

    b. 19.0%.

    c. 18.8%.

    d. 18.5%.

    e. 18.2%.

7. Based on the constant dividend growth model, which of the stocks (A-E) in the Bergers' stock portfolio is overvalued as of today?

    a. A and E.

    b. B and C.

    c. A, D, and E.

    d. B, C, D, and E.

    e. A, B, C, D, and E.

8. If Derek's parents donate the down payment on the house ($30,000), which of the following statements is/are correct?

    1. The gift qualifies for the annual exclusion.

    2. The parents, Leonard and Adriana, must file a gift tax return.

    3. The parents are liable for a small amount of gift tax.

    4. This donation is a taxable gift.

    a. 1 only.

    b. 1 and 2.

    c. 1 and 3.

    d. 3 and 4.

    e. 1, 2, 3, and 4.

9. Assume Adriana and Leonard decide to loan the down payment to Olga and Derek instead of giving it to them. Which of the following statements regarding tax consequences is/are correct? The federal rate for imputed interest is 9%.

    a. The loan is less than $10,000. Therefore, there are no tax consequences.

    b. Adriana and Leonard have made a taxable gift of $2,700 to Derek and Olga.

    c. Olga and Derek must impute the $2,700 of taxable income.

    d. Adriana and Leonard must impute $2,700 of taxable income.

    e. This loan has no adverse tax consequences to Olga and Derek.

10. Which of the following statements is true regarding Derek's options for his 401(k) plan assuming he left his current job?

    a. Derek could have the distribution transferred directly from the 401(k) plan to an IRA account, but only 80% of the balance would transfer since the 20% withholding would apply.

    b. Derek could transfer the distribution to an IRA account, but would only receive 60% of the employer contributions and earnings in his account since he is only partially vested.

    c. Derek could have the distribution rolled over (converted) directly into a Roth IRA account.

    d. Derek could receive a distribution payable directly to himself from the 401(k) plan (subject to a 20% withholding), wait 60 days, and contribute the full amount of the distribution to a Roth IRA.

    e. Derek could transfer the distribution directly to a trustee for a traditional IRA and then have the trustee convert the traditional IRA to a Roth IRA.

11. Reviewing Derek's retirement accounts and assuming Derek terminated employment when the account balances are as stated after five years of employment, how much could Derek take with him, plan permitting?

    a. $2,304.

    b. $3,372.

    c. $3,456.

    d. $3,540.

    e. $3,840.

12. Olga's employer just instituted a cafeteria plan with a flexible spending account (FSA). She wants to know her best option regarding her child care cost.

    a. Olga should use the FSA for her child care expenditures.

    b. Olga should not use the FSA so that she can take a credit for the full cost of the child care expenditures.

    c. Olga should not use the FSA so that she may take the dependent care credit equal to 20% of her actual cost.

    d. Olga may use the FSA and take a reduced dependent care credit of 20% of actual cost.

13. Which of the following would be an appropriate estate planning strategy for Derek and Olga?

   1. Have an attorney draft a durable power of attorney for both Derek and Olga.
   2. Create a QTIP trust to hold assets at the death of the first decedent.
   3. Begin an annual gifting program to take advantage of the annual exclusion afforded to Derek and Olga.
   4. Gift the EE savings bonds to Ursula to take advantage of these bonds when Ursula is ready for college.

      a. 1 only.
      b. 1 and 4.
      c. 2 and 3.
      d. 1, 3, and 4.
      e. 1, 2, 3, and 4.

14. What is the best course of action for the Bergers regarding their debt situation?

   a. There is no reason to adjust their debt situation in any way at this time since it would reduce their emergency fund (liquid assets).
   b. They should sell their stock portfolio and pay off Derek's $20,000 student loan.
   c. They should not liquidate their stock portfolio but should sell the URS stock and use the proceeds to pay off their credit card debt.
   d. They should liquidate all or a portion of their stock portfolio and use the proceeds to pay off the credit card debt.

15. Which of the following is/are correct regarding deficiencies in the Bergers' current estate planning?

   1. They are subject to probate.
   2. They have each currently overqualified their estate.
   3. They have made no provision for guardianship of their children.
   4. They have made no provision for an advanced medical directive.

      a. 1 and 2.
      b. 1, 3, and 4.
      c. 1, 2, and 3.
      d. 2, 3, and 4.
      e. 1, 2, 3, and 4.

USE THE FOLLOWING INFORMATION FOR QUESTIONS 16 THROUGH 21

While on a vacation in Montana, the Bergers experienced several unfortunate incidents.

- A deer collided with their car causing $800 worth of damage to the front of the car.

- Derek rented a motorcycle. While riding the motorcycle, his wallet was stolen. He thought he had lost the wallet on the mountain during a fall, so he did not report the loss to the credit card company until he returned home.

- Derek, not experienced driving in the mountains, drove the motorcycle into another motorcycle on the road causing damage to both motorcycles and to Derek. The driver of the other motorcycle, Oscar Applebaum, had minor medical injuries.

- Upon returning home, they discovered that their apartment building had been destroyed by fire.

16. How much will the insurance company pay to have the front of the car repaired from the collision with the deer?

    a. $0.
    b. $250.
    c. $300.
    d. $550.
    e. $800.

17. When Derek and Olga received their credit card statements, they discovered that the following amounts had been charged to their credit cards by the thief:

Credit Card 1	$200
Credit Card 2	$450
Credit Card 3	$35
Credit Card 4	$60

    How much of the above charges will the Bergers be responsible for?

    a. $0.
    b. $50.
    c. $185.
    d. $200.
    e. $745.

18. The fire that destroyed the apartment building also destroyed all of their personal property. While the depreciated or actual cash value of all their property is $5,000, it would cost the Bergers about $37,000 to replace all of their lost items. How much will the insurance company pay for this loss?

    a. $4,750.
    b. $5,000.
    c. $12,750.
    d. $35,750.
    e. $36,750.

19. Derek's collision with the motorcycle caused $1,200 of damage to the motorcycle owned by Mr. Applebaum. Which of the following is correct?

    a. The HO-4 will cover the entire loss if Derek is found to be responsible.

    b. The HO-4 will cover the $1,200 loss less the $250 deductible.

    c. The HO-4 will not pay anything because this situation is excluded under all homeowners policies.

    d. The HO-4 will not pay anything because this is property damage and the liability coverage extends only to bodily injury.

20. Mr. Applebaum, the motorcycle owner, suffered $200 in emergency medical expense to reset his broken arm caused by the incident. Which of the following is correct?

    a. The liability section of the HO-4 will pay for the full $200.

    b. The medical payments section of the HO-4 will pay for the full $200.

    c. The automobile policy will pay these medical expenses.

    d. Neither the HO-4 nor the automobile policy will pay these medical expenses.

21. In the motorcycle accident, Derek suffered medical expenses of $1,450. Which of the following is correct?

    1. The HO-4 will cover the expenses, but only up to $1,000.

    2. The HO-4 will not cover these expenses at all.

    3. The major medical policy will cover 80/20 after the $250 deductible.

    4. The major medical will not cover this situation because the motorcycle is rented.

        a. 1 only.

        b. 1 and 3.

        c. 1 and 4.

        d. 2 only.

        e. 2 and 3.

22. Which of the following is the best reason for the Bergers to <u>avoid</u> purchasing a house?

    a. Do not want to pay property tax.

    b. Expect to relocate within 1-3 years.

    c. Do not want to tie themselves to doing yard work.

    d. Do not want to purchase any homeowners insurance.

23. Derek's company sponsors a Death-Benefit-Only (DBO) plan. Under the plan, the company will pay a $30,000 death benefit to Derek's wife in the event of his death. How much of the death benefit will be taxable to his wife if Derek dies?

    a. $0.

    b. $5,000.

    c. $15,000.

    d. $25,000.

    e. $30,000.

24. Olga is interested in purchasing a bond for the Berger's investment portfolio. Which of the following bonds would have the least volatility from changing interest rates, assuming all of the bonds listed below have a 20-year maturity?

    a. Zero-coupon bond with a 6% yield.

    b. Zero-coupon bond with a 4% yield.

    c. Corporate bond priced at par with a 6% yield.

    d. Corporate bond priced at par with a 4% yield.

25. Derek will undergo gall bladder surgery in March. If the hospital costs for the surgery are $8,000, how much will the insurance company pay?

    a. $8,000.

    b. $6,450.

    c. $6,400.

    d. $6,200.

    e. $6,150.

26. You recommend that the Bergers develop an investment policy statement. Which one of the following is not included in an investment policy statement?

    a. Current income needs.

    b. Investment selection.

    c. Time horizon.

    d. Risk tolerance.

    e. Portfolio objectives.

27. The Bergers are trying to decide what education funding investment vehicle they should use to reach their goal to pay for college education. Which of the following would best suit their needs for the monthly investment, assuming the Bergers will try to increase the amount of each deposit in the future?

    a. 529 plan.

    b. Coverdell Education Savings Account.

    c. Series EE bonds.

    d. Roth IRA.

28. The Bergers are concerned about funding their children's education. They are planning to develop an asset allocation for the funds for this goal and need some assistance. Based on the Bergers' risk tolerance and objectives, what is the most appropriate asset allocation?

    a. 10% Growth Fund, 15% Value Fund, 25% Balanced Fund, 30% Bond Fund, 10% Small Cap Fund, 10% Cash.

    b. 20% Growth Fund, 20% Value Fund, 35% Balanced Fund, 10% Small Cap Fund, 15% Cash.

    c. 25% Growth Fund, 30% Value Fund, 20% Bond Fund, 15% Small Cap Fund, 10% International Fund.

    d. 45% Growth Fund, 10% Value Fund, 20% Balanced Fund, 15% Small Cap Fund, 10% International Fund.

    e. 20% Growth Fund, 25% Value Fund, 10% Balanced Fund, 25% Small Cap Fund, 20% International Fund.

29. Although the Bergers have Series EE bonds, they do not really understand all of the rules and features that are available. They have come to you for assistance. You tell them all of the following are incorrect regarding Series EE bonds, except:

    a. The taxation of interest on a Series EE bond is always deferred until redeemed or until the bond reaches maturity.

    b. The interest accrued on Series EE bonds can continue to be deferred by exchanging the bonds for I bonds. The interest deferral continues until the I bonds are sold or mature.

    c. The proceeds from Series EE bonds can always be rolled over into a Coverdell Education Savings Account or a Qualified Tuition Program.

    d. Both Series I bonds and Series EE bonds have the same advantages regarding the exclusion from income for qualifying higher educational costs.

    e. Like I bonds, Series EE bonds are issued at 50% of their face value.

30. Assume Derek's long lost uncle died in 2007 and left Derek $100,000. Derek gave a gift of $20,000 cash to Olga. What are the gift tax ramifications of this gift assuming Derek did not make any other gifts to Olga?

    a. $12,000 of the gift is subject to the annual exclusion (for 2007) and gift tax is owed on the remaining $8,000.

    b. No gift tax is owed because of the unlimited marital deduction.

    c. Olga does not qualify for the unlimited marital deduction, so the entire gift is subject to gift tax.

    d. $125,000 (for 2007) of present interest gifts from Derek to Olga per year are not subject to gift tax.

31. Assume Derek dies while Olga has a dependent at home. Will Olga qualify for Social Security benefits if she and the children move to Germany?

    a. No—she must reside in the US to receive Social Security.

    b. No—only citizen spouses qualify for Social Security.

    c. Yes—a survivor's benefit can be paid to noncitizen spouses outside the US

    d. Yes—she can receive a benefit if the child remains a US citizen.

DEREK AND OLGA BERGER

Solutions

Derek and Olga Berger

ANSWER SUMMARY

1. e	6. c	11. c	16. d	21. e	26. b	31. c
2. d	7. b	12. a	17. c	22. b	27. a	
3. a	8. a	13. a	18. a	23. e	28. c	
4. e	9. e	14. d	19. c	24. c	29. d	
5. d	10. e	15. b	20. d	25. d	30. d	

SUMMARY OF TOPICS

1. Fundamentals—Time Value of Money
2. Insurance—Needs Analysis
3. Tax—Traditional IRA
4. Tax—Sale Capital Assets
5. Tax—Sale Capital Assets
6. Investments—Capital Asset Pricing Model
7. Investments—Constant Dividend Growth Model
8. Estates—Gift Tax
9. Estates—Gift Tax
10. Retirement—401(k) Plan Distributions
11. Retirement—Vesting
12. Tax—Dependent Care Credit
13. Estates—Estate Planning
14. Fundamentals—Debt Management
15. Estates—Estate Tax
16. Insurance—Auto Insurance
17. Fundamentals—Consumer Protection Laws
18. Insurance—Homeowners Insurance
19. Insurance—Liability Insurance
20. Insurance—Medical Expenses
21. Insurance—Medical Expenses
22. Fundamentals—Financing Strategies
23. Insurance—Life Insurance Taxation
24. Investments—Volatility of Bonds
25. Insurance—Medical Insurance
26. Investments—Investment Policy Statement

27. Fundamentals—Educational Funding
28. Investments—Asset Allocation
29. Investments—Series EE Bonds
30. Estates—Alien Spouse
31. Estates—Alien Spouse

SOLUTIONS

Fundamentals—Time Value of Money

1. e

    In order for Derek to start his own business in ten years with an estimated cost of $100,000 in today's dollars, the Bergers would have to save $650.05 by the end of each month since they have no savings set aside.

    First calculate the future value of $100,000 over a ten-year period with an interest rate (inflation) of 3.5% per year.

    The next step is to calculate the monthly payment of the future value calculated in Step 1 of $141,060.

Step 1:			Step 2:		
PV	=	$100,000	FV	=	$141,060
n	=	10	n	=	120 (10 × 12)
i	=	3.5000	i	=	0.9167 (11 ÷ 12)
FV	=	$141,060	PMT_{OA}	=	$650.05

Insurance—Needs Analysis

2. d

    Option (a) is incorrect. Since Derek is young, and the fact pattern does not indicate a family history of long-term care needs, a long-term care policy is not a priority.

    Option (b) is incorrect. Derek should take advantage of a traditional IRA or a Roth IRA before considering an annuity.

    Option (c) is incorrect. Although Derek may need an umbrella policy, the question asks for the _most_ appropriate product, which would be a disability policy.

Tax—Traditional IRA

3. a

    Statement 1 is correct. Derek is an active participant in a qualified plan. Statement 2 is also correct.

    Any contribution by Olga will be fully deductible. The beginning of the traditional IRA deduction phaseout is $83,000 for 2007, for married couples filing jointly, and a spouse who is an "active" participant will not preclude deduction of the entire amount of the other spouse until the AGI reaches the phaseout limits for 2007 of $156,000–$166,000, when the deduction is phased out completely.

Tax—Sale Capital Assets

4. e

The Bergers would have a long-term capital gain of $7,600. It is necessary to first calculate Derek's basis in the stock and then the gain or loss.

Step 1: Establish Derek's Basis		Step 2: Determine Gain	
Carryover basis of donor	$2,000	Proceeds	$10,000
Pro rata share of gift tax paid by donor*	400	Basis	(2,400)
Derek's basis	$2,400	Gain	$7,600

$$* \ \frac{\text{Appreciation}}{\text{FMV}} \ \times \ \text{gift tax paid} \ = \ \frac{\$4,000}{\$6,000} \ \times \ 600 \ = \ \$400$$

Tax—Sale Capital Assets

5. d

The net result of the sale transactions is a short-term capital loss of $5,950.

Property held longer than 12 months qualifies for long-term capital gain/loss treatment. Property that is held for a period of one year or less is treated as a short-term gain/loss. The day of disposition is included in the holding period. Consequently, the sale of Stock A results in a long-term capital gain of $2,450, and the sale of Stock B results in a long-term capital loss of $2,400. The net long-term capital gain is $50. The sale of Stock C results in a short-term capital gain of $3,000. The sale of Stock D results in a short-term capital loss of $9,000. The net short-term capital loss is $6,000. The net of all gains and losses is a $5,950 net short-term capital loss.

STCG	$3,000	C	LTCG	$2,450	A
STCL	(9,000)	D	LTCL	(2,400)	B
Net STCL	($6,000)		Net LTCG	$50	

Net STCL	$6,000
Net LTCG	(50)
Net STCL	$5,950

Investments—Capital Asset Pricing Model

6. c

The expected return for the Bergers' stock portfolio under the Capital Asset Pricing Model (CAPM) based on a stock market yield of 17% is 18.8%.

The first step in calculating the expected return is to find the beta for the portfolio. Using this calculated beta of 1.15, the second step is to determine expected return of 18.8%.

<table>
<tr><td colspan="5" style="text-decoration: underline;">Step 1: Find the Beta for the Portfolio</td><td colspan="2" style="text-decoration: underline;">Step 2: Determine Expected Return</td></tr>
<tr><td>$2,800</td><td>×</td><td>1.3</td><td>=</td><td>$3,640</td><td colspan="2">$E(R) = Rf + B(R_M - Rf)$</td></tr>
<tr><td>700</td><td>×</td><td>1.6</td><td>=</td><td>1,120</td><td colspan="2">$E(R) = 0.05 + 1.15 (0.17 - 0.05)$</td></tr>
<tr><td>7,000</td><td>×</td><td>1.0</td><td>=</td><td>7,000</td><td colspan="2">$E(R) = 18.8\%$</td></tr>
<tr><td>2,500</td><td>×</td><td>1.1</td><td>=</td><td>2,750</td><td colspan="2"></td></tr>
<tr><td>9,000</td><td>×</td><td>1.2</td><td>=</td><td>10,800</td><td colspan="2">Note: The T-Bill rate of 5% is used to</td></tr>
<tr><td>$22,000</td><td></td><td></td><td></td><td>$25,310</td><td colspan="2">estimate R_f.</td></tr>
</table>

$25,310 ÷ $22,000 = 1.15045$

Investments—Constant Dividend Growth Model

7. b

Stocks B and C are overvalued.

The constant dividend growth model is used to determine the price for a security that pays dividends that are growing at a constant rate. The formula for this model is:

$P_0 = D_1 ÷ (k-g)$ where:

P_0 = Price for the security.

D_1 = The dividend paid at period 1.

k = The investors required rate of return.

g = The growth rate of the dividends.

Note: Problems will often provide the dividend today, which is D_0. D_1 can be determined by multiplying D_0 by $(1 + g)$.

Stock	Current Dividend	D_1	Required Return	Growth Rate	Diff.	D_1/diff.	FMV	Valued
A	$200	$207.00	10%	3.50%	6.50%	$3,185	$2,800	Undervalued
B	33	34.65	10%	5.00%	5.00%	693	700	Overvalued
C	400	416.00	10%	4.00%	6.00%	6,933	7,000	Overvalued
D	197	200.94	10%	2.00%	8.00%	2,512	2,500	Undervalued
E	500	521.25	10%	4.25%	5.75%	9,065	9,000	Undervalued

Estates—Gift Tax

8. a

The gift qualifies for the annual exclusion. The gift is from community property. Therefore, it is a joint gift and not a split gift. It qualifies for the annual exclusion, as Adriana and Leonard are each making a gift of $7,500 to Derek and $7,500 to Olga. No gift tax return is required to be filed. This is not a taxable gift because the gift from each spouse is less than the annual exclusion.

Estates—Gift Tax

9. e

Derek and Olga will have no adverse tax consequences because of the loan. Adriana and Leonard do not have to impute the $2,700 ($30,000 × 0.09$) of interest because the loan is under $100,000 and Derek and Olga's portfolio income is less than $2,700. Thus, Adriana and Leonard would impute Derek and Olga's net investment income, which is approximately $1,345.

Savings	15	$(0.015 × \$1,000)$
Stocks	1,330	
	$1,345	

Option (a) is incorrect. The loan is $30,000.

Option (b) is incorrect because the loan interest is not a taxable gift.

Option (c) is incorrect because the borrower does not impute the interest, the lender does.

Option (d) is incorrect because the loan is under $100,000, and Derek and Olga's portfolio income is only $1,345. Therefore, $1,345 is what Adriana and Leonard would have to impute.

Retirement—401(k) Plan Distributions

10. e

Option (a) is false because direct transfers are not subject to 20% withholding.

Option (b) is false because Derek is 100% vested in his own contributions and 80% vested in the contributions and earnings of his employer.

Option (c) is false because a transfer cannot be made directly from a qualified plan into a Roth IRA until 2008. The distribution could be to a traditional IRA, and the traditional IRA could be converted to a Roth IRA.

Option (d) is false because "only amounts in another IRA can be converted to a Roth IRA."

Option (e) is true.

Retirement—Vesting

11. c

The 401(k) matching contribution must vest over 2–6 years. Therefore, Derek has a vested interest of 80% in the employer's contribution and the earnings on those contributions of the 401(k) plan. Derek's own contributions and the earnings on those contributions to the plan are immediately 100% vested.

401(k) plan (employer match): ($1,500 + $420) × 0.80 = $1,536.
Total Vested: $1,500 + $420 + $1,536 = $3,456.

Tax—Dependent Care Credit

12. a

Olga has the choice to use the FSA or take a dependent care credit. The FSA will shelter 100% of the cost of providing the child care, and the amounts contributed to the FSA are not subject to payroll tax. The other option is for Olga to take a credit equal to 20% of any qualified child care expenses. The FSA is preferred because the Bergers would save 15% of federal tax plus 7.65% for FICA for a total of 22.65% versus a 20% credit.

Estates—Estate Planning

13. a

Statement 1 is correct. A durable power of attorney would be an appropriate document in any estate plan.

Statement 2 is incorrect. A QTIP trust would only be appropriate in certain situations, such as a second marriage.

Statement 3 is incorrect. Derek and Olga's estate is not large enough for an annual gifting program.

Statement 4 is incorrect. To take advantage of the income exclusion for EE bonds, the bonds must be redeemed by the original purchaser.

Fundamentals—Debt Management

14. d

The credit card debt has an interest rate of 15% while the student loans carry a rate of 10%, and the interest on them is deductible up to $2,500. Since the Bergers' required return of 10% (1% less than the S&P 500) and their after-tax return is certainly lower, it would be prudent to eliminate the higher interest rate debt. In addition, the stock portfolio has several loss positions that could generate a capital loss to reduce their current income tax.

Estates—Estate Tax

15. b

Statement 2 is incorrect. The value of their estate is considerably less than the applicable credit. Statements 1, 3, and 4 are deficiencies that the Bergers should correct.

Insurance—Auto Insurance

16. d

Derek's insurance company will have to pay $800 for the damage to the car less the comprehensive deductible for a total payment of $550.

Damage	$800
Less: Comprehensive deductible	(250)
Insurance company payment	$550

Fundamentals—Consumer Protection Laws

17. c

According to the Fair Credit Billing Act, Derek will not be liable for more than $50 per card because the use of the cards was unauthorized, and notices were given to each card issuer. Derek will only be responsible for $185.

Credit Card 1	$50
Credit Card 2	50
Credit Card 3	35
Credit Card 4	50
Derek's Liability	$185

Insurance—Homeowners Insurance

18. a

Under the HO-4 policy (renter's insurance), the insurance company will pay $4,750 (depreciated or actual cash value less deductible) for the loss of the Bergers' personal property that resulted from the fire in the apartment building. Even though the contents coverage under this policy is $35,000 and the replacement cost of the lost items is $37,000, the insurance company is obligated to pay the lesser of the depreciated or actual cash value and the replacement cost because the policy was issued without an endorsement for replacement cost on personal property.

$5,000	Actual cash value
250	Deductible
$4,750	Insurance company payment

Insurance—Liability Insurance

19. c

The HO-4 policy will pay nothing because the situation, rental of a motorcycle, is excluded under all homeowners and renters policies.

Insurance—Medical Expenses

20. d

The HO-4 policy will not pay for these medical expenses because the motorcycle rental is excluded under all homeowners and renters policies. The automobile policy also excludes two-wheeled vehicles. Derek may have to personally pay for any liability.

Insurance—Medical Expenses

21. e

The major medical policy will pay 80% of the medical expenses after the $250 deductible. The HO-4 will not cover the medical expenses because it was the result of an excluded activity.

Fundamentals—Financing Strategies

22. b

Option (b) is correct. If the Bergers expect to relocate within 1-3 years, they should not buy the house.

Option (a) is incorrect. Although it is true that renters do not pay property taxes, this answer is not the BEST reason to rent as opposed to purchasing a home. Note: Property taxes are tax deductible.

Option (c) is incorrect because this is not the BEST reason to rent. Landscaping services are available at reasonable costs.

Option (d) is incorrect. Renters should purchase an HO-4 (renters) policy to protect their contents and provide liability protection.

Insurance—Life Insurance Taxation

23. e

$30,000 will be taxable to Olga if Derek dies. The death benefit is paid by the company; it is not part of a group-term life insurance policy. Death benefits paid by an employer under a DBO plan are 100% taxable to the beneficiary.

Investments—Volatility of Bonds

24. c

The corporate bond priced at par with a 6% yield would have the least volatility.

Options (a), (b), and (d) are incorrect because there is an inverse relationship between coupon rate and volatility.

Insurance—Medical Insurance

25. d

Total hospital cost	$8,000
Less deductible	(250)
Net cost	$7,750
Insurance percentage	× 80%
Amount insurance company pays	$6,200

Investments—Investment Policy Statement

26. b

Investment selection is not included in an investment policy statement.

Fundamentals—Educational Funding

27. a

Option (b) is not the best answer because a Coverdell ESA has annual contribution limits that do not adjust with inflation. Option (c) is not the best answer because the Series EE bonds would not provide the return close to the S&P 500 Index that the Bergers desire. Option (d) is not the best choice because of low annual contribution limits and because a portion of the distribution may be subject to income taxation. A 529 plan would allow for the largest contributions and tax-free distributions.

Investments—Asset Allocation

28. c

Important issues:

1. The Bergers' risk tolerance is high, and they expect to earn a return equal to one percent less than the S&P 500.

2. Their child is age one. They have a 17-year time horizon.

3. Conclusion: They should have a large allocation to equities.

Option (a) is not correct because it is too conservative. Option (b) is not correct because it is too conservative with the cash allocation and the balanced fund allocation. Option (d) is not correct because it is too heavy in equities; greater bond allocation would be preferred. Growth and value should be relatively balanced. Option (e) is not correct because it is too heavily weighed toward small cap and international.

Investments—Series EE Bonds

29. d

Option (a) is incorrect because the Series EE purchaser has the option to recognize interest for tax purposes as it is earned. Option (c) is incorrect because the proceeds from EE bonds cannot be rolled over into a Coverdell Education Savings Account or a Qualified Tuition Program if the owner's income exceeds certain limits. Option (b) is incorrect because EE bonds cannot be exchanged for I bonds. Option (d) is correct. Option (e) is incorrect because I bonds are issued at face value.

Estates—Alien Spouse

30. d

Olga is a German citizen and does not qualify for the unlimited marital deduction. However, a noncitizen spouse can receive up to $125,000 (in 2007) per year free of gift tax. This noncitizen spouse annual exclusion is subject to the same rules as the $12,000 (for 2007) annual exclusion applicable to gifts to noncitizen spouses (i.e., must be of present interest, etc.).

Estates—Alien Spouse

31. c

A survivor's benefit can be paid to noncitizen spouses residing outside the United States. The rules on this are complex and can vary depending on the country of citizenship and residence. Note: Survivor benefits are subject to the earnings limit until full retirement age.

WILLIAM AND PAULA SAVAGE

■

Case Scenario

William and Paula Savage

William and Paula Savage have come to you, a financial planner, for help in developing a plan to accomplish their financial goals. From your initial meeting, you have gathered the following information. Today is December 31, 2007.

PERSONAL BACKGROUND AND INFORMATION

William Savage (Age 37)

William is the owner/manager of a bar named The Tack Room. The Tack Room is a small, neighborhood bar open only at nights and has five part-time employees (< 1,000 hours each). He inherited the bar six years ago from his Uncle Wesley. In January of 2002, he left General Construction Services, Inc. and now dedicates all of his efforts to The Tack Room.

Paula Savage (Age 37)

Paula is a loan officer at Bank of Texas. She has been employed by the bank for eight years. She has a BBA in finance and also attended State University where she earned her MBA.

The Savages

William and Paula have been married for 11 years. They both plan to retire in 25 years. They own a three-bedroom house with a pool, two cars, and a bar (The Tack Room) in Dallas, Texas. They have three children and do not plan to have any more.

Shane Savage (Age 10)

Shane attends Sunshine Grammar School (the local public school) and is in the fourth grade.

Lorraine Savage (Age 5)

Lorraine also attends Sunshine Grammar School and is in kindergarten. Lorraine spends the afternoon at Discovery Day Care.

Gretchen Savage (Age 2)

Gretchen attends Discovery Day Care Center for nine hours a day, Monday through Friday.

Dionne Savage (Age 62)

William's mother, Dionne, was widowed four years ago when her husband was age 60. Her income is $600 a month from Social Security and $500 a month from William and Paula. She does not spend the $600 from Social Security; she simply saves it in her money market account. She lives 100 miles from William and Paula.

Benita St. Martin (Age 70)

Paula's mother, Benita, is a lifelong resident and citizen of Peru and is fully supported by William and Paula. It costs them $300 per month to support Benita.

PERSONAL AND FINANCIAL GOALS

The Savages have the following financial objectives in order of priority:

1. Provide a standard of living after retirement of 80% of their preretirement income.

2. Accumulate sufficient assets to send the children to a state university away from home, but in the state of Texas.

3. Minimize their current tax liabilities.

4. Expand The Tack Room to include a daytime grill within the next 5 years.

5. Be mortgage free at retirement.

6. Develop an estate plan to minimize estate tax liabilities.

ECONOMIC INFORMATION

- The Savages expect inflation to average 3% annually, both currently and for the long term.

- The Savages expect Paula's salary to increase 5% annually, both currently and long term.

- Current mortgage rates are 7.5% for 15 years and 8.0% for 30 years. Closing costs of 3% will be added to any refinanced loan.

INSURANCE INFORMATION

Life Insurance

	Policy 1	Policy 2
Insured	Paula	William
Policy Through	Employer	All Farm
Face Amount	$50,000	$150,000
Type	Term (Group)	Whole
Cash Value	$0	$21,250*
Annual Premium	$102 (Employer paid)	$2,361
Beneficiary	William	Paula
Contingent Beneficiary	3 children	None
Policyowner	Paula**	William**
Settlement Options	None	Life Annuity

*William's after-tax savings rate is 6%. Cash value at December 31, 2007 was $20,900 and the 2007 dividend was $100.

**Community property.

Paula also has an accidental death and dismemberment policy through her employer. She is covered for $100,000 under this policy. She pays a premium of $68 per year for this coverage.

Health Insurance

All family members are covered by Paula's employer under a group health plan with an annual family deductible of $400. After the deductible is met, the plan pays 100% of the first $2,000 of covered hospital charges for each hospital stay, and 80% thereafter. There is a stop-loss maximum of $2,000 including the deductible. The plan will then pay 100% of any other covered expenses, as long as they are reasonable and customary, incurred that year—no matter how high the amount.

Dental Insurance

The Savages have dental insurance. Premiums are $216 annually.

Disability Insurance

William has a personal disability policy with an *own occupation* definition that provides a benefit of $2,000 per month disability income and has a 14-day elimination period. The policy was purchased from a local insurance company. This policy covers both accidents and sickness and has a benefit period of five years. His annual premium is $608. Paula has an *own occupation* definition policy that provides a benefit of 65% of gross pay and has a 90-day elimination period. The policy covers both accidents and sickness to age 65. The annual premium is $460 and the employer pays half of the premiums and Paula pays half of the premiums.

Homeowners Insurance

The Savages have a HO-3 Policy (replacement value) with a $250 deductible and a dwelling value of $97,000 purchased through All State Insurance Company (premium is $739 per year). It offers $100,000 liability per person.

Automobile Insurance

Both Cars	
Type	Personal Auto Policy (PAP)
Liability	$100,000/300,000
Medical Payments	$5,000 per person/accident
Physical Damage, Own Car	Actual cash value
Uninsured Motorist	$50,000/accident
Collision Deductible	$100
Comprehensive Deductible	$250
Premium (Per Year)	$1,080

INVESTMENT DATA

The Savages' tolerance of risk on a scale of "1 to 10" ("1" being most risk averse) is considered to be a "7". They expect to be more conservative as they get closer to retirement.

INCOME TAX INFORMATION

Their marginal income tax rate is currently 25% for federal income taxes. There is no state income tax in Texas.

RETIREMENT INFORMATION

The Savages plan to retire in 25 years when they are 62 years old. They would like to have a standard of living equal to 80% of their preretirement income. At or before retirement, the Savages plan to sell the bar and travel. They expect to be in retirement for 28 years.

Paula has a 401(k) plan through Bank of Texas. The Bank of Texas matches $1 for every $4 contributed by Paula up to an employer maximum contribution of 2% of her salary. The maximum employee contribution without regard to the match is 70% of her salary. She has been contributing 5% of her salary since she began working there in 1998. Her 401(k) has averaged an annual return of 7% over the past eight years. Her estate is currently designated as the beneficiary.

William has an IRA account through his banker. He opened the account ten years ago and has been contributing $2,000 each year. He is hoping to contribute $3,000 in 2007. He has averaged a 6% annual return over the past ten years. His estate is the designated beneficiary.

William expects to collect $13,500 in Social Security benefits at full retirement or 70% of that amount at age 62 (in today's dollars). Paula expects to collect $9,000 in Social Security benefits at full retirement age or 70% at age 62 (in today's dollars). They expect to receive Social Security benefits as soon as they retire.

GIFTS, ESTATES, TRUSTS, AND WILL INFORMATION

The Savages have simple wills leaving all assets to one another.

STATEMENT OF CASH FLOWS
William and Paula Savage
For the Year Ended December 31, 2007 (Annual Basis)

INFLOWS

William's Net Income from the Bar (Schedule C)	$64,000	
Paula's Salary	57,200	
Dividend Income	777	
Checking Interest Income	130	
Savings Interest Income	400	
Certificate of Deposit Interest Income	275	
Total Inflows		$122,782

OUTFLOWS

Planned Savings

401(k) Plan 5% for Paula	$2,860	
IRA for William	2,000	
Total Planned Savings	$4,860	

Ordinary Living Expenses

Mortgage (P&I)	$10,267	
Homeowners Insurance Premium	739	
Church Donations—Cash	5,200	
Lease on Honda	3,588	
P&I on Cherokee	7,800	
Gas/Oil/Maintenance	2,000	
Auto Insurance Payments (Both Cars)	1,080	
Credit Card Payments	6,200	
Taxes on Income	41,767	
Property Taxes on Residence	2,657	
Utilities	1,200	
Telephone	600	
Life Insurance Premiums (William)	2,361	
Accidental Death & Dismemberment (Paula)	68	
Support for Dionne and Benita	9,600	
Health	2,592	
Dental Insurance	216	
Child Care (Paid to Discovery)	4,500	
Disability Premium (Both)	838	
Vacation Expense	4,000	
Entertainment Expense	3,250	
Food	3,250	
Clothing	3,000	
Total Ordinary Living Expenses	116,773	
Total Outflows		$121,633
Discretionary Funds Available		$1,149

Notes on Taxes:

Self-employment Tax—William (15.3% on $64,000)	$9,792	
FICA - Paula (7.65% on $57,200)	4,375	
Estimated Payments—William	12,600	
Federal Withholding—Paula	15,000	
Total Income Taxes	$41,767	

STATEMENT OF FINANCIAL POSITION
William and Paula Savage
December 31, 2007

ASSETS[1]			LIABILITIES[3] & NET WORTH	
Cash/Cash Equivalents			**Current Liabilities**	
Checking Account (2.5%)	CP	$5,200	Credit Card Balances (14.7%)	$8,200
Savings Account (3.25%)[2]	CP	12,300	Car Loan (Jeep Cherokee)	11,000
Total Cash/Cash Equivalents		$17,500	*Total Current Liabilities*	$19,200
Invested Assets			**Long-Term Liabilities**	
Certificate of Deposit	CP	$5,000	Home Mortgage (9.25% for 30 yrs.)	$98,836
(5.5%, 2 yrs., mat. January 1, 2007)			*Total Long-Term Liabilities*	$98,836
Savings Bonds (zero-coupon EE bonds)	CP	4,000		
Mutual Funds (see detail)	CP	18,800		
Stocks	CP	13,600		
401(k) Plan (Paula)	CP	31,331	**TOTAL LIABILITIES**	$118,036
IRA (William)	CP	27,942		
The Tack Room	CP	138,000		
Rental Property	W	84,000		
Cash Value Life Insurance	CP	21,250		
Total Investments		$343,923		
			NET WORTH	$402,787
Personal-Use Assets				
House (Land value is $20,000)	CP	$125,000		
Jewelry (1 Diamond)	CP	8,000		
Jeep Grand Cherokee	CP	24,000		
Baseball Card Collection	H	2,400		
Total Personal Use		$159,400		
Total Assets		$520,823	**Total Liabilities and Net Worth**	$520,823

CP = Community property
H = Husband's separate property
W = Wife's separate property

Notes to Financial Statements:

[1] Assets are stated at fair market value.

[2] The savings account is currently serving as their emergency fund.

[3] Liabilities are stated at principal only and are all community obligations.

General Note: The bracketed percentages indicate the interest rate.

INFORMATION REGARDING ASSETS AND LIABILITIES

The Tack Room

Wesley had a tax basis in the bar of $10,000 at his death. The fair market value at the time of Wesley's death was $40,000. In 2005, William executed a legal document making The Tack Room community property with Paula.

William completely refurbished the bar in 2001 at a cost of $30,000. The building and property are currently valued at $78,000. Property taxes are high in this district; they are currently $2,278. The bar could be sold at its fair market value of $138,000 and is increasing in value at 3.5% per year. The bar's net income for the last three years was $64,000 (2007), $59,600 (2006), and $57,500 (2005).

They also expect William's net income and cash flows from The Tack Room to increase at 3.5% annually, both currently and over the long run.

William is considering the implementation of some or all of the following benefit plans for The Tack Room:

- A group term life insurance arrangement in which William and all of the employees of The Tack Room would receive $25,000 of insurance coverage. Premiums would be paid exclusively by The Tack Room.
- A cafeteria plan that includes benefits for long-term care, disability income insurance, dental insurance, and up to two weeks of additional vacation time.
- $50 of free parking at the local garage provided each month only to William and two selected employees of The Tack Room.
- Membership for all employees at the local health club.

All costs of these benefits would be paid solely by The Tack Room, and not the employees.

Personal Residence

The Savages purchased their house and financed the mortgage over 30 years at 9.25%. The house is a two-story, three-bedroom, brick house. It has a pool in the backyard and a monitored burglar alarm.

Rental Property

The rental property, which is valued at $84,000, is located in Tallahassee, Florida, and consists of a small strip shopping center. It is in a poor location and is currently a break-even proposition with income equaling expenses. The property was acquired from Paula's Aunt Olivia in 2002 as a gift. Olivia had a basis in the property of $20,000 and paid gift tax on the transfer of $24,000. At the time of the gift, the property had a fair market value of $60,000. Olivia died recently, and at the time of her death the property was valued at $84,000.

Prior to Olivia's death, Paula and William would never dispose of the rental property for fear of offending Olivia. Now, however, they want to buy a strip shopping center in Dallas at a cost of $100,000, assuming a small mortgage of $16,000. There is a tenant in the Tallahassee property that would buy the rental property for the fair market value of $84,000.

Mutual Funds

	FMV	Beta	Expected Return	R^2	Sharpe Ratio
Balanced Fund	$5,600	0.65	8.5%	0.56	0.70
Growth Fund	2,400	1.24	12.4%	0.85	0.49
Bond Fund	10,800	0.55	6.5%	0.92	0.51
Total	$18,800				

WILLIAM AND PAULA SAVAGE

Questions

William and Paula Savage

1. How much dividend income could Gretchen receive in 2007 without being subject to income tax (assuming she has no other sources of income)?

    a. $0.

    b. $850.

    c. $1,700.

    d. $5,350.

2. Which of the following statements accurately reflect(s) the dependency status of Dionne and Benita relative to the Savages for income tax purposes?

    1. Dionne is a dependent.

    2. Dionne is not a dependent.

    3. Benita is a dependent.

    4. Benita is not a dependent.

        a. 1 only.

        b. 2 and 4.

        c. 1 and 3.

        d. 2 and 3.

        e. 1 and 4.

3. How much of a dependent care credit can the Savages take for the year 2007?

    a. $0.

    b. $480.

    c. $900.

    d. $960.

    e. $1,200.

4. Which of the following retirement plans would William be permitted to adopt for The Tack Room?

    1. SEP.

    2. Profit-sharing plan.

    3. SIMPLE plan.

    4. Defined-benefit plan.

        a. 1 only.

        b. 1 and 2.

        c. 1, 2, and 3.

        d. 2, 3, and 4.

        e. 1, 2, 3, and 4.

5. Which type of retirement plan should William adopt if he wishes to both maximize his contribution potential and minimize his cash flow commitment?

        a. SEP.

        b. Money-purchase plan.

        c. Profit-sharing plan.

        d. SIMPLE plan.

        e. Defined-benefit plan.

6. What is the maximum contribution William can make to a profit-sharing plan in the current year without a cash or deferred arrangement?

        a. $10,841.

        b. $11,821.

        c. $12,800.

        d. $14,000.

        e. $42,000.

7. If Paula were to become disabled on March 1, 2008, and receive benefits beginning June 1, 2008, for the remainder of 2008, how much of her disability benefits would be included in the Savages' gross income for federal income tax purposes? (For purposes of this problem, use Paula's 2007 salary).

        a. $0.

        b. $9,295.

        c. $10,844.

        d. $18,590.

        e. $21,688.

8. Which of the following qualifying events that could happen to Paula would allow extended coverage to her dependents (the children) under COBRA for a maximum of 18 months?

    1. Paula reduces her hours from full-time to part-time.

    2. Paula's employer terminates the master plan.

    3. Paula is fired because the company is downsizing (considered a normal termination).

    4. Paula suffers an untimely death in the current year.

        a. 1 and 2.

        b. 1 and 3.

        c. 1, 2, and 3.

        d. 2, 3, and 4.

        e. All of the above.

9. Which chart best describes the strengths and weaknesses of disability insurance coverage for William and Paula?

1	2
Strengths • Own occupation—both • Benefit period—both • Paula's benefit **Weaknesses** • Taxable benefits—both • William's benefit	**Strengths** • Own occupation—both • Benefit period—both **Weaknesses** • Elimination period—both • Benefit amount—both

3	4
Strengths • Own occupation—both • Benefit period—Paula • Nontaxable benefits —William **Weaknesses** • Benefit period—William • Benefit amount—William • Taxable benefits—Paula	**Strengths** • Own occupation—both • Benefits— both • Elimination period—both **Weaknesses** • Payor of premiums—Paula • Benefit period—William

        a. 1.

        b. 2.

        c. 3.

        d. 4.

10. Which of the following assets would be included in William's probate estate if he died today?

    a. Individual Retirement Account.

    b. Proceeds from the life insurance policy on William's life.

    c. Rental property.

    d. Proceeds from the life insurance policy on Paula's life.

11. Calculate the value of William's gross estate assuming he died today.

    a. $206,587.

    b. $208,987.

    c. $224,969.

    d. $283,987.

    e. $358,987.

12. What are the tax consequences of a sale of the Tallahassee rental property?

    a. No gain or loss.

    b. $48,000 long-term capital gain.

    c. $40,000 long-term capital gain.

    d. $64,000 long-term capital gain.

    e. $84,000 long-term capital gain.

13. If instead of a sale of the Tallahassee property, Paula uses a tax-free exchange (1031) to acquire the Dallas property, what is her recognized gain or loss from the Tallahassee property and her basis in the new property?

	Tallahassee Gain or Loss	Dallas Basis in New Property
a.	$0	$36,000
b.	$0	$52,000
c.	$24,000 LTCG	$76,000
d.	$48,000 LTCG	$48,000
e.	$16,000 STCG	$36,000

14. If William were to die today and Paula inherited and sold The Tack Room for the current balance sheet value, what would be her adjusted taxable basis at the time of the sale?

    a. $35,000.

    b. $70,000.

    c. $104,000.

    d. $138,000.

15. William and Paula are concerned that they do not have enough money saved for Shane, Lorraine, and Gretchen for college. Assuming each child begins college at age 18 and is in college for 4 years, what steps can they take to put funds away? (assume contribution limits for 2007)

   1. Set up a Coverdell Education Savings Account for the children and deposit $6,000 per year in the account.

   2. Set up three separate Coverdell Education Savings Accounts, one for each child, and deposit $2,000 in each.

   3. Fund their own traditional IRAs each year since penalty-free withdrawals can be taken to pay qualified education expenses at an eligible educational institution.

   4. Fund a Roth IRA since they can withdraw funds tax free after age 59½ to pay college costs.

   5. Each year fund Roth IRAs for $8,000, traditional IRAs for $8,000, and Coverdell Education Savings Accounts for $6,000.

      a. 2 only.
      b. 1 and 5.
      c. 2 and 3.
      d. 1, 3, and 5.
      e. 2, 3, and 4.

16. William has decided to adopt a SIMPLE IRA plan for The Tack Room. Which of the following apply?

   1. William must meet ADP testing to fund his own plan.

   2. William can contribute 2% to all eligible participants to comply with IRS rules.

   3. William can choose to make matching contributions to only those participants who make elective contributions.

   4. William could rollover his existing Traditional IRA balance into his SIMPLE IRA.

      a. 1, 2, and 4.
      b. 3 and 4.
      c. 2 and 3.
      d. 1, 2, and 3.
      e. 1 and 4.

17. William is considering his current life insurance policy. He understands that there is an economic model to determine whether he should keep his existing policy or replace it with a new policy. Which of the following models would you use to determine whether he should replace his policy?

      a. Jensen model.
      b. Gordon growth model.
      c. Virgie model.
      d. Belth model.
      e. Phelps model.

18. William had an accident at the bar and was hospitalized. The cost of the surgery was $10,245. The hospital stay cost was $16,000. Due to an infection, William needed continued physician care after going home. The additional cost for the doctor was $585. How much did William have to pay? All costs were considered reasonable and customary.

    a. $3,200.

    b. $2,000.

    c. $2,585.

    d. $2,400.

19. The Savages have identified their nonretirement mutual funds as funds available for college costs for the children. Which of the following recommendations would be most appropriate?

    a. With the time frame for college funding and the risk tolerance level, the current portfolio is appropriate.

    b. With the time frame for college funding and the risk tolerance level, the current portfolio should be reallocated placing more in the Balanced Fund.

    c. With the time frame for college funding and the risk tolerance level, the current portfolio should be balanced to shift more to the Growth fund.

    d. With the time frame for college funding and the risk tolerance level, the current portfolio should be rebalanced to increase the Bond Fund weighting.

20. What is the weighted beta and weighted expected return for the mutual fund portfolio?

	Beta	Weighted Expected Return
a.	0.70	9.13%
b.	0.67	7.85%
c.	0.81	9.11%
d.	0.60	7.87%

21. In the current year, William's uncle died. He bequeathed the Balanced Mutual Fund to William. The Balanced Mutual Fund happens to have the exact same standard deviation and expected return as the Savages' current mutual fund portfolio. What can the Savages expect to happen to the standard deviation (SD) and expected return (ER) of their current mutual fund portfolio once Balanced Mutual Fund is added to the portfolio?

    a. SD goes down; ER goes down.

    b. SD remains the same; ER remains the same.

    c. SD goes down; ER remains the same.

    d. SD remains the same; ER goes down.

    e. Not enough information given to solve the problem.

22. William and Paula have three mutual funds in their portfolio. They have been trying to learn more about investments and now understand some basics about risk and return. Of the funds in the portfolio, which one has historically had the highest risk-adjusted return?

    a. Balanced Fund.

    b. Growth Fund.

    c. Bonds Fund.

    d. Two of the funds have the same risk-adjusted return.

    e. Not enough information to answer the question.

23. Which of the following statements is correct with respect to William's goal to implement additional employee benefit plans for The Tack Room?

    a. William can establish the cafeteria plan based upon his desired objectives.

    b. The entire cost of his own group term life insurance coverage will be taxed to William each year.

    c. The health club dues will not be taxable to the employees because the plan is nondiscriminatory.

    d. The parking benefit provided to William will be taxable because the plan is discriminatory.

WILLIAM AND PAULA SAVAGE

Solutions

William and Paula Savage

1. b	6. b	11. d	16. c	21. e
2. e	7. c	12. b	17. d	22. a
3. c	8. b	13. b	18. b	23. b
4. e	9. c	14. d	19. c	
5. c	10. a	15. c	20. b	

SUMMARY OF TOPICS

1. Tax—Standard Deduction
2. Tax— Dependency Exemption
3. Tax—Dependent Care Credit
4. Retirement—Plan Options
5. Retirement—Plan Selection
6. Retirement—Keogh
7. Insurance—Taxability of Disability Benefits
8. Insurance—COBRA
9. Insurance—Adequacy of Disability Benefits
10. Estates—Probate Estate
11. Estates —Gross Estate
12. Estates—Basis of Gift
13. Tax—Tax-Free Exchanges
14. Estates—Basis of Inherited Community Property
15. Retirement—Education Funding with Various Savings Vehicles
16. Retirement—SIMPLE Plan
17. Insurance—Life Insurance Replacement
18. Insurance—Health Insurance Coverage
19. Investments—Recommendation
20. Investments—Weighted Beta/Weighted Expected Return
21. Investments—Portfolio Diversification
22. Investments—Sharpe Ratio
23. Tax—Fringe Benefits/Cafeteria Plans

SOLUTIONS

Tax—Standard Deduction

1. b

$850. Gretchen is age 2 and claimed as a dependent by her parents. Therefore, she will not receive a personal exemption, and her standard deduction will be limited to the greater of:

1. $850, or
2. Earned income + $300.

Since she has no earned income, her standard deduction will be $850, allowing her to receive up to $850 of unearned income (interest, dividends, etc.) tax free.

Tax— Dependency Exemption

2. e

Statements 1 and 4 are correct. The Savages contribute more than half of Dionne's support. Unspent Social Security is not counted as support. Benita is a citizen and lifelong resident of Peru. The exception for the citizenship and residency test extends only to those in contiguous countries (Mexico and Canada).

Tax—Dependent Care Credit

3. c

They can take a credit of $900 ($4,500 × 20%).

The employment-related expenses eligible for the credit are limited to $3,000 if there is one qualifying individual or $6,000 if there are two or more qualifying individuals. The $4,500 is the actual child care expense per the Statement of Cash Flows.

Retirement—Plan Options

4. e

All of the following retirement plans are permissible for the Tack Room:

- SEP.
- Money-purchase plan.
- Profit-sharing plan.
- SIMPLE plan.
- Defined-benefit plan.

Retirement—Plan Selection

5. c

He should adopt a profit-sharing plan (the maximum deductible employer contribution to a profit-sharing plan is 25% of compensation). Because he is self employed, he will be limited to 20% of his net income after a reduction for one-half of his Social Security taxes paid. Since a profit-sharing plan is a qualified plan, he could exclude part-time employees working less than 1,000 hours.

Retirement—Keogh

6. b

Schedule C Income	$64,000
Less ½ SE Tax	(4,896) ($9,792 × ½)
Net	$59,104
Contribution %	× 20% (Self employed)
Maximum Contribution	$11,821

Since this is a Keogh plan, the contribution percentage is calculated by using the formula $[(\%) \div (1 + \%)]$, or $[(0.25) \div (1.25)] = 20\%$.

Insurance—Taxability of Disability Benefits

7. c

Any disability benefits received by Paula will be 50% taxable as income "in lieu of wages" because her employer pays one-half of the premiums. She will receive 7 months of benefits at 65% of $57,200. One-half will be taxable = $10,844. $[(($57,200 \times 0.65) \times {}^{7}/_{12}) \times 0.5] = \$10,844$.

Insurance—COBRA

8. b

The term of coverage is 18 months for both a reduction in hours and a normal termination from the job. If the master plan is terminated or the employee dies, the term of coverage is 36 months.

Insurance—Adequacy of Disability Benefits

9. c

STRENGTHS	WEAKNESSES
William • Own occupation • Nontaxable benefit • 14-day elimination • Accident and sickness	**William** • Amount is only $2,000/month (37.5% of compensation) • High premiums • 5-year benefit period
Paula • Premiums partially paid by employer • Own occupation • 65% gross pay • 90-day elimination period • Coverage for sickness and accidents • Coverage to age 65	**Paula** • ½ premium paid by Paula • ½ is taxable

Estates—Probate Estate

10. a

IRA will be included because William's estate is the named beneficiary. Since the beneficiary of William's life insurance is not deceased for his estate, it will not pass through probate. The rental property is owned by Paula. The life insurance on Paula's life will not pay out at William's death.

Estates —Gross Estate

11. d

Community property ($520,823 − $21,250* − $84,000** − $2,400)	$413,173
	× ½
One-half of community property	$206,587
Plus baseball card collection	2,400
Plus insurance policy #2 ***	75,000
Gross Estate	**$283,987**

The term policy #1 (Paula) has no value.

* Life insurance.

** Rental property.

*** 50% of face value is included because William has incidence of ownership and it is community property.

Estates—Basis of Gift

12. b

The adjusted taxable basis of the gift to a donee is generally the carryover basis of the donor; however, an adjustment is made for the gift tax paid on the portion of the asset that has appreciated.

Donor's adjusted taxable basis	$20,000
Adjustment [($40,000 ÷ $60,000) × $24,000]	16,000
Donee's basis	$36,000
Sales price	$84,000
Basis	(36,000)
Long-term capital gain	$48,000

Tax—Tax-Free Exchanges

13. b

Old Property		New Property	
FMV	$84,000	FMV	$100,000
Basis	(36,000)		
Realized gain	$48,000		

No gain recognized

Boot Given
Assumed mortgage adds $16,000 to basis.

FMV of new property		$100,000
Boot given	$16,000	
Old property basis	36,000	
New basis		(52,000)
Remaining potential gain		$48,000

There is no gain or loss recognized, and the basis of the new property is $52,000 ($36,000 + $16,000).

Estates—Basis of Inherited Community Property

14. d

She owns half.

	His	Hers	Total
Basis before date of death	$35,000	$35,000	$70,000
Step-up to FMV at date of death	$69,000	$69,000	$138,000

Community property receives an adjustment to fair market value on both halves of the property, not just the portion belonging to the decedent.

Sale Price	$138,000
Basis	(138,000)
No gain or loss	$0

Retirement—Education Funding with Various Savings Vehicles

15. c

Statement 1 is incorrect since a Coverdell Education Savings Account has a maximum contribution per account of $2,000 per year.

Statements 2 and 3 are correct.

Statement 4 is not correct because Shane and Lorraine will be out of college and Gretchen will be finishing college when William and Paula turn 59½.

Statement 5 is incorrect since total IRA contributions cannot exceed $8,000 for 2007 ($4,000 each for William and Paula).

Retirement—SIMPLE Plan

16. c

Statement 1 is incorrect. ADP testing does not apply to SIMPLE plans since the employer is required to make mandatory matching contributions. ADP testing does apply to 401(k) plans and existing SARSEP plans.

Statement 2 is correct. The employer can choose to make a 2% nonelective contribution for each eligible employee.

Statement 3 is correct. The employer can match employee elective contributions dollar-for-dollar up to 3% of compensation; however, the employer can match as little as 1% in no more than 2 out of 5 years.

4 is incorrect. Individuals cannot transfer or rollover traditional IRA assets or qualified plan assets into a SIMPLE IRA.

Insurance—Life Insurance Replacement

17. d

The Belth model is used to determine whether or not someone should keep their existing life insurance policy.

Insurance—Health Insurance Coverage

18. b

There is a stop-loss provision that limits William to a maximum out-of-pocket cost of $2,000, including the deductible. The plan will then pay 100% of any other covered expenses as long as they are reasonable and customary.

Investments—Recommendation

19. c

Given the ages of the children and the risk tolerance level of the Savages (7 on a scale of 1-10), they can accept the additional risk of the growth fund to have an opportunity to increase the return of their mutual fund portfolio.

Investments—Weighted Beta/Weighted Expected Return

20. b

	FMV	Beta	FMV × Beta
Balanced Fund	$5,600.00	0.65	$3,640
Growth Fund	$2,400.00	1.24	$2,976
Bond Fund	$10,800.00	0.55	$5,940
Total	$18,800.00		$12,556

Weighted Beta = ($12,556 ÷ $18,800) = 0.6679

	FMV	Average Exp. Return	Expected Earnings
Balanced Fund	$5,600.00	8.50%	$476.00
Growth Fund	$2,400.00	12.40%	$297.60
Bond Fund	$10,800.00	6.50%	$702.00
Total	$18,800.00		$1,475.60

Weighted Expected Return = ($1,475.60 ÷ $18,800.00) = 7.85%

Investments—Portfolio Diversification

21. e

Since the correlation coefficient between the Balanced Mutual Fund and the existing portfolio was not given, there is not enough information to solve the problem.

Investments—Sharpe Ratio

22. a

The Balanced Mutual Fund has the highest Sharpe ratio. The Sharpe ratio is a measure of incremental return divided by standard deviation and, thus, provides us with a measure of the risk-adjusted return.

Tax—Fringe Benefits/Cafeteria Plans

23. b

Although he only has $25,000 of coverage for himself, William will be taxed on the full cost of this coverage each year. Self-employed individuals do not receive the $50,000 exclusion for group term life insurance.

A is incorrect. Cafeteria plans do not permit the inclusion of long-term care insurance.

C is incorrect. Dues to the local health club paid by the employer are taxable to the employee, regardless of whether or not the plan is discriminatory.

D is incorrect. Nondiscrimination requirement do not apply to the transportation fringe benefits.

EDDIE AND TINA TOPPLEMEIR

Case Scenario

Eddie and Tina Topplemeir

Today is December 31, 2007. Eddie and Tina Topplemeir have come to you, a financial planner, for help in developing a plan to accomplish their financial goals. From your initial meeting together, you have gathered the following information:

PERSONAL BACKGROUND AND INFORMATION

Eddie Topplemeir (Age 47)

Eddie Topplemeir is an executive in the Amadeus Company, a closely held corporation. His salary is $100,000 and he expects increases of approximately 5% per year.

Tina Topplemeir (Age 50)

Tina Topplemeir is Eddie's secretary. Her present salary is $24,000. She expects raises of 5% each year.

This is a second marriage for Tina. Her first husband, Reggie, was killed several years ago. Tina was the beneficiary of his $250,000 life insurance policy with which she created her investment portfolio.

Tina is very vigorous, and women on her family's side have continued to have children into their fifties.

The Topplemeirs

Eddie and Tina have been married for 3 years. They do not currently reside in a community property state.

The Children

Tina has two children from her first marriage, Brooks, age 16 and Hunter, age 12. Eddie and Tina have a daughter, Emily, who is now 2 years old. All children live with them. They are considering having additional children. The children are cared for during the day by their grandmother who lives next door.

When they were first married, Eddie wanted to adopt Brooks and Hunter, but the children did not agree. Since then, Eddie and the two boys have been in continual conflict. As a result, Tina expects to use her investment portfolio to pay for the boys' education without any assistance from Eddie.

PERSONAL AND FINANCIAL GOALS

1. The Topplemeirs want to aggressively start planning for their children's college education. They plan for each child to attend a private institution for five years at age 18 at a cost of $25,000 a year per child (today's cost). The expected educational inflation rate is 6%.

2. Eddie and Tina want to retire at 80% of their preretirement income. Both Tina and Eddie would like to retire at age 65. They expect the retirement period to be 30 years.

3. Eddie wants to review both his and Tina's life insurance needs and have wills drafted for both of them.

4. They would like to minimize any estate tax liability.

5. During retirement, Eddie and Tina plan to travel extensively.

6. They want to be free of all debt by the time they retire.

ECONOMIC INFORMATION

*   Inflation has averaged 4% over the last 20 years.

*   Inflation is expected to be 3.5% in the future.

Current Yields for Treasury Securities

3 months	6 months	9 months	1 year	3 years	5 years	10 years	20 years	25 years	30 years
4.0%	4.5%	4.7%	5.0%	6.0%	7.5%	8.5%	9.0%	9.0%	8.8%

Current Mortgage Rates

*   8.75% for 30-year loans.

*   8.25% for 15-year loans.

Refinancing will cost 3% of any mortgage as closing costs and will be included in any new mortgage.

Economic Outlook—Investments

	Expected Returns (Pretax)	Expected Standard Deviation
Aggressive Stocks	18%	15%
Growth Stocks	14%	10%
S&P 500	11%	8%
Bonds	8%	3%
Insurance Contracts	6%	2%
Money Markets	5%	1%
T-bills	4%	1%

INSURANCE INFORMATION

Life Insurance

	Policy A	Policy B	Policy C	Policy D
Insured	Eddie	Eddie	Tina	Tina
Owner	Eddie	Eddie	Tina	Eddie
Beneficiary	Eddie's mother	Estate of Eddie	Brooks & Hunter	Brooks & Hunter
Original Amount	$200,000	$100,000	$72,000	$50,000
Type	Group Term	Term 30-year declining balance	Group Term	Whole Life
Cash Value*	$0	$0	$0	$5,000
Settlement Options	N/A	N/A	N/A	N/A
Annual Premium	$250	$100	$60	$420
Who Pays Premium	Employer	Eddie	Employer	Eddie
Date Purchased	Annually	1978	Annually	1997
Current Coverage	$200,000	$75,000	$72,000	$50,000
*Equal to interpolated terminal reserve.				

Health Insurance

The entire family is covered under the Amadeus health plan. The Topplemeirs currently pay $200 per month for the employer-provided indemnity plan. The deductible is $200 per person up to three persons. There is a stop loss of $2,000 per year and an 80/20 major medical coinsurance provision.

Disability Insurance

Eddie has a personally owned disability insurance policy that covers accident and sickness and has an *own occupation* definition with a 180-day elimination period. The policy pays benefits of 60% of current pay (payable to age 65).

Homeowners Insurance

HO-2 Policy	
Dwelling	$150,000
Other Structure	$15,000
Personal Property	$75,000
Loss of Use*	$30,000 (20% of dwelling)

*There is no rider for replacement value on personal property.
There is an endorsement for furs and jewelry (annual premium of $30).

SPECIAL LIMITS ON PERSONAL PROPERTY

Property Description	Special Limits
Money, bank notes, bullion, gold other than goldware, silver other than silverware, platinum, coins, and medals.	$200
Securities, accounts, deeds, evidences of debt, letters of credit, notes other than bank notes, manuscripts, personal records, passports, tickets, and stamps.	$1,000 regardless of whether printed on paper or stored on computer disks
Watercraft – including outboard motors, furnishings, equipment, and trailers.	$1,000
Any trailer not used with watercraft, such as a utility or camping trailer.	$1,000
Jewelry, watches, furs, and precious and semiprecious stones.	$1,000 for loss by theft
Firearms of any type.	$2,000 for loss by theft
Silver and silver-plated ware, gold and gold-plated ware, and pewterware.	$2,500 for loss by theft
Property used at any time, in any manner, for any business purpose.	$2,500 on premises $250 off premises
Electronic apparatus, such as a citizens band radio or tape deck, that can be plugged into a cigarette lighter while in or upon a motor vehicle or other motorized land conveyance, if it can be powered by the electronic system of, or another source of power within, the vehicle or conveyance.	$1,000 including accessories, antennas, tapes, wires, records, discs, or other medical for use with this electronic apparatus

INVESTMENT INFORMATION

During Tina's marriage to Reggie, an education fund was established for Brooks and Hunter. These funds were intended for the children's education. When Reggie died, Tina no longer contributed to this fund. At the present time, the balance is $22,747. The money was invested short term at 6%, and the Topplemeirs have the option of renewing the short-term CDs in April at an interest rate of 4%.

When Tina received the life insurance proceeds of $250,000 from Reggie's death, she asked a broker to help her manage the money. Her broker, Randall, has her in a wrap account with a 3% annual fee. Randall has full discretion over the account and determines which securities to buy and sell and when to buy and sell. Randall's record regarding Tina's investment portfolio over the last 5 years has been as follows:

	2003	2004	2005	2006	2007
Load Adjusted Return	(10.0)	?	(8.5)	12.0	3.0

Tina did not have the information for 2004 and has been unable to acquire it from Randall.

Tina considers herself to be a conservative to moderate investor and has had little experience and little education in the area of investments. Eddie believes that he is a more moderate investor. He has more experience with investments than Tina.

INCOME TAX INFORMATION

The Topplemeirs are in the 25% marginal tax bracket for federal income tax and 8% for state income tax.

GIFTS, ESTATES, TRUSTS, AND WILL INFORMATION

The Topplemeirs have not done any estate planning, nor do they have wills.

RETIREMENT INFORMATION

They both plan to retire when Tina reaches age 65. They expect the retirement period to be 30 years. They expect their retirement portfolio to average 10% pretax. Social Security benefits for Eddie today would be $14,000 at age 67. The benefits for Tina at age 67 on her own earnings would be $9,600.

Amadeus provides a profit-sharing plan and a 401(k) plan. The 401(k) plan allows them to save up to 16% of their salary with a 3% employer match when they save 6%; maximum savings is $10,000. Neither Eddie nor Tina has ever participated in the 401(k) plan, but both have fully vested balances in the profit-sharing plan as follows:

	Vested Balance
Eddie	$80,000
Tina	$12,000

The Amadeus profit-sharing plan allows the participant to choose between self-directing the retirement assets through the available mutual funds or having the company's fund manager manage the assets. The Topplemeirs, not being confident in their ability to manage assets, have chosen to let the fund manager direct their assets. The 401(k) plan assets can only be self-directed.

Total Return and Annualized Rates of Return

The company has made the following contributions to the profit-sharing plan for Eddie and Tina for each of the related years:

	Eddie	Tina
2008	none yet	none yet
2007	$15,000	$3,600
2006	$0	$0
2005	$13,605	$3,265
2004	$10,366	$2,488
2003	$8,954	$2,369
Balance January 1, 2003	$25,000	$0

All contributions are made December 31 of the indicated year.

STATEMENT OF CASH FLOWS
Eddie and Tina Topplemeir
Statement of Cash Flows
For the year ended December 31, 2007

CASH INFLOWS

Salaries

Eddie's	$100,000	
Tina's	24,000	
Total Salaries	$124,000	

Investment Income

Brokerage account	$3,050	
Tina's investment portfolio	4,771	
Savings account	618	
Tina's education fund	1,062	
Investment Income	$9,501	

Total Cash Inflows	$133,501

CASH OUTFLOWS

Living Expenses

Food	$4,300	
Clothing	4,000	
Entertainment	6,500	
Utilities, cable, and phone	5,000	
Auto maintenance	1,200	
Church	2,000	
Home mortgage	14,934	
Auto loan	18,818	
Credit card	4,300	
Total Living Expenses	$61,052	

Insurance

Health premiums	$2,400	
Auto premiums	1,660	
Life premiums	520	
Homeowners premiums	920	
Fur and jewelry endorsement	30	
Disability	1,677	
Total Insurance	$7,207	

Taxes

Property (residence)	$5,550	
Federal Income (withholdings)	37,200	
State Income	4,122	
Payroll (FICA)	7,665	
Total Taxes	$54,537	

Total Cash Outflows	$122,796
Discretionary Cash Flow	$10,705

STATEMENT OF FINANCIAL POSITION
Eddie and Tina Topplemeir
Balance Sheet
As of December 31, 2007

ASSETS[1]

Liquid Assets

JT	Checking[3]	$2,500
JT	Savings[4]	15,450
W	Cash Value Life Insurance	5,000
	Total Liquid Assets	22,950

Invested Assets

H	First Mutual Growth Fund[5]	7,950
H	Brokerage Account[6]	100,000
W	Tina's Investment Portfolio	210,000
W	Tina's Education Fund	22,747
H	Eddie's Profit-Sharing Plan	80,000
W	Tina's Profit-Sharing Plan	12,000
H	Eddie's IRA[8]	9,000
	Total Invested Assets	441,697

Use Assets

JT	Home	185,000
H	Lexus	32,000
W	BMW	21,000
H	Boat	10,000
W	Furs and Jewelry	7,000
JT	Furniture and Household	30,000
	Total Use Assets	285,000
	Total Assets	**$749,647**

LIABILITIES[2] AND NET WORTH

Short-Term Liabilities

W	Credit Cards	$4,300

Long-Term Liabilities

JT	Home Mortgage	144,981
H/W	Auto Loans	40,069
H	Margin Loan[7]	7,500
	Total Long-Term Liabilities	192,550

Total Liabilities	196,850
Net Worth	552,797
Total Liabilities and Net Worth	**$749,647**

Notes to Financial Statements:

[1] All assets are stated at fair market value.

[2] Liabilities are stated at principal only.

[3] The checking account is a noninterest bearing account.

[4] The savings account earns 4% per year.

[5] See detail of mutual fund.

[6] Brokerage Account is stated at gross value that does not include margin loan of $7,500.

[7] Margin loan is for Brokerage Account. Interest rate is currently 8%.

[8] Eddie's IRA is currently invested in CDs at a local bank.

H	=	Husband
W	=	Wife
JT	=	Joint tenancy

INFORMATION REGARDING ASSETS AND LIABILITIES

Investment Income

Brokerage Account	
MM	$300
Bonds	3,350
Margin Interest	(600)
Total	$3,050
Tina's Investment Portfolio	
Bonds	$1,300
Stocks	3,471
Total	$4,771
Savings Account	$618
Tina's Education Fund	$1,062
TOTAL	**$9,501**

House

Principal Residence	January 1, 2005 (Purchase)
FMV (Current)	$185,000
Original Loan	$148,000
Term	30 years
Interest Rate	9.5%
Payment	$1,244.46
Remaining Mortgage	$144,981
Remaining Term	27 years

Boat

The original purchase price of the boat was $10,000. It is completely paid for. The boat is a 90-horsepower fishing boat.

Automobiles

	Eddie's Lexus	Tina's BMW
Purchase Price	$40,000	$35,000
Down Payment	$0	$10,000
Term	48 months	48 months
Interest Rate	7%	8%
Monthly Payment	$957.85	$610.32
Payments Remaining	33	20
Balance	$28,677.07	$11,392.23

Brokerage Account

ACCOUNT NAME: EDDIE TOPPLEMEIR				
ACCOUNT NUMBER: AB100402				
BALANCES				
Money Market	Price/Share	Shares	Current Yield	FMV
Money Market	$1.00	7,324.71	4.5%	$7,324.71
Bonds	Maturity	Coupon	Cost Basis	FMV
10,000 US Treasury Note	5	7.5%	$10,351.18	$10,000.00
15,000 US Treasury Bond	25	6.0%	$13,138.64	$10,579.83
50,000 US Treasury Bond	30	0%	$4,093.40	$3,982.02
20,000 Davidson Debenture	20	8.5%	$17,455.93	$16,288.44
			$45,039.15	$40,850.29
Stocks	Price/Share	Shares	Cost Basis	FMV
Stock 1 *	$5.20	2,000	$10,000	$10,400
Stock 2 *	$4.85	1,500	$6,750	$7,275
Stock 3 *	$26.00	500	$11,250	$13,000
			$28,000	$30,675
* These stocks do not currently pay dividends				
Mutual Funds	Price/Share	Shares	Cost Basis	FMV
Emerging Growth Fund	$21.00	500	$12,250	$10,500
Balanced Fund	$18.00	425	$8,925	$7,650
Municipal Bond Fund	$12.00	250	$3,500	$3,000
			$24,675	$21,150
Note: All distributions from these funds are reinvested				
Options	# of Option Contracts	Option Premium	Exercise Price	Option Expiration
Stock 2 Call Options	5	$3.00	$5.50	July 08
Stock 3 Put Options	5	$5.00	$24.00	March 08
Margin Balance				
Outstanding Balance				$7,500
Net Account Value				$92,500
Total Account Value				$100,000

First Mutual Growth Fund

ACCOUNT NAME: EDDIE TOPPLEMEIR						
ACCOUNT NUMBER: SN15135						
Transaction	Date	Cost Basis	Price/Share	Shares	Total Shares	Total Value
Buy	04/01/06	$2,500.00	$25.00	100	100	$2,500.00
Buy	08/01/06	$4,000.00	$20.00	200	300	$6,000.00
Reinvest Div	12/01/06	$500.00	$12.50	40	340	$4,250.00
Buy	02/01/07	$3,000.00	$15.00	200	540	$8,100.00
Buy	04/01/07	$2,000.00	$20.00	100	640	$12,800.00
Buy	06/01/07	$1,500.00	$25.00	60	700	$17,500.00
Sell	12/01/07	$11,880.00	$27.00	(440)	260	$7,020.00
Reinvest Div	12/01/07	$1,080.00	$27.00	40	300	$8,100.00
Balance	12/31/07	—	$26.50	—	300	$7,950.00

Note: All income from this fund is reinvested.

Tina's Investment Portfolio

Bonds

Bonds	Term	Duration	Current FMV
10,000 US Treasury Bonds	10	7.12 years	$10,000
5,000 US Treasury Bonds	20	9.95 years	$5,000
		Total Value of Bonds	$15,000

Stocks

Shares	Stock	$\bar{x}$	Beta	σ	R^2	P/E Ratio	Dividend Yield	Basis	FMV
1,000	Stock A	6%	0.65	11%	75	13.0	3.0%	$30,000	$38,000
575	Stock B	11%	0.75	9%	65	14.0	3.7%	$45,000	$46,000
200	Stock C	7%	0.65	10%	30	15.1	3.7%	$20,000	$17,000
500	Stock D	3%	0.70	8%	45	25.2	0.0%	$11,000	$8,500
1,000	Stock E	25%	0.95	15%	70	14.4	0.0%	$20,000	$18,000
1,250	Stock F	22%	1.10	18%	20	11.1	0.0%	$23,000	$25,000
							Total Value of Stocks		$152,500

Mutual Funds

Shares	Mutual Fund	Style	$\bar{x}$	Alpha	Beta	σ	R^2	Front End Load	Expense Ratio	Basis	FMV
210	Fund A	MG	14%	3%	1.10	12%	57	8.5%	0.71%	$2,500	$2,625
300	Fund B	LG	11.5%	0.5%	0.94	8%	81	8.5%	1.0%	$5,000	$5,100
443	Fund C	MV	6%	(4%)	0.65	8%	42	8.5%	3.5%	$10,000	$11,075
1,000	Fund D	MG	-6%	(10%)	0.70	20%	4	8%	7.0%	$8,000	$7,500
320	Fund E	LG	4%	(3%)	1.10	5%	60	5%	2.5%	$9,500	$8,000
410	Fund F	LG	7%	(2.5%)	0.90	3%	78	3%	1.5%	$10,000	$8,200
								Total Value of Mutual Funds			$42,500

Note: All income distributions from the mutual funds are reinvested.

TOTAL PORTFOLIO VALUE — $210,000

$\bar{x}$	=	Five-Year Average Return	L	=	Large
σ	=	Standard Deviation	M	=	Medium
R^2	=	Coefficient of Determination	G	=	Growth
			V	=	Value

EDDIE AND TINA TOPPLEMEIR

Questions

Eddie and Tina Topplemeir

1. What is the character and amount of the taxable gain on the sale of the 440 shares of First Mutual Growth Fund (December 1, 2007), and how will it be classified for income tax purposes? Assume that the basis in the shares is determined using a FIFO method. (Round to the nearest dollar.)

	Short Term	Long Term
	Capital Gain	
a.	$0	$3,380
b.	$1,780	$1,600
c.	$1,600	$1,780
d.	$1,200	$2,180
e.	$2,180	$1,200

2. Which of the following methods are permitted for determining the basis of the 440 shares of First Mutual Growth Fund sold on December 1?

    1. FIFO method.
    2. Specific identification method.
    3. LIFO method.
    4. Average cost method.

        a. 4 only.
        b. 1 and 4.
        c. 1, 2, and 3.
        d. 1, 2, and 4.
        e. 1, 2, 3, and 4.

3. Eddie and Tina are interested in maintaining an emergency fund to pay expenses in the event that Eddie loses his job. Which of the following would be the best option for their emergency fund?

    a. GNMA fund.
    b. Money market fund.
    c. Exchange traded fund.
    d. Hedge fund.
    e. Cash value of life insurance policy.

4. Tina is considering the purchase of a $1,500 van with 120,000 miles on it for her 16-year-old son, Brooks. With respect to collision coverage for this vehicle, what is the most appropriate risk management technique?

    a. Insure.

    b. Subrogate.

    c. Share.

    d. Retain.

    e. Aleate.

5. The Topplemeirs should purchase separate insurance coverage in addition to their HO-2 policy for which of the following?

    1. Jewelry.

    2. Boat.

    3. Fur.

    4. Fine Art.

        a. 1 and 3.

        b. 2 only.

        c. 1, 2, and 3.

        d. 2, 3, and 4.

        e. 1, 2, 3, and 4.

6. Which of the following is the most appropriate strategy for the allocation of Tina's mutual funds among the different styles of mutual funds?

    a. Because Tina has a relatively even balance between the growth and value styles, she should maintain this balance.

    b. Although she has an even split between growth and value, she should sell an even amount of each of these groups to purchase an even amount of blend funds.

    c. She should maintain the balance that she has because she has a good split between large-sized and medium-sized companies.

    d. She should sell some of the growth funds and buy more value and blend funds.

    e. She should sell all of her value funds and buy small company funds.

7. If one was to plot the current yields for Treasury securities given in the case, the derived yield curve is consistent with which of the following investment theories?

    1. Liquidity premium theory.

    2. Market segmentation theory.

    3. Expectation theory.

        a. 1 only.

        b. 2 only.

        c. 1 and 2.

        d. 2 and 3.

        e. The yield curve is consistent with all three of the above theories.

8. If interest rates for all maturities increase by 1.0%, what will be the approximate value of the bonds in Tina's investment portfolio?

    a. $13,759.
    b. $13,887.
    c. $14,324.
    d. $15,000.
    e. $16,112.

9. What is the holding period return that Eddie would receive if the price of Stock 2 increases to $7.50 (in brokerage account)?

    a. 75%.
    b. 67%.
    c. 55%.
    d. 44%.
    e. 33%.

10. Tina has decided that the CDs and her investment account will be used to fund the cost of college for the boys. Tina wants to set aside enough of these assets to fund their education with the remainder being used to fund Emily's college education. Ignoring the transaction costs of selling the current assets, how much does she need to set aside for the boys' college education if she wants to invest in an even mix of 5-year and 10-year Treasury bonds? Assume all taxes will be paid out of current expenditures.

    a. $223,711.15.
    b. $219,568.33.
    c. $211,463.02.
    d. $194,714.06.
    e. $186,600.98.

11. How much of their current gross income in dollars are the Topplemeirs currently saving toward their retirement goal?

	Eddie	Tina
a.	$18,000	$3,840
b.	$19,000	$4,560
c.	$6,000	$1,440
d.	$9,000	$2,160
e.	$0	$0

12. When Tina dies, which one of the following assets will be considered an income in respect of a decedent (IRD) asset?

    a. Life insurance Policy D owned by Tina.

    b. Personal residence owned joint tenancy between Eddie and Tina.

    c. Tina's investment portfolio.

    d. Tina's profit-sharing plan.

    e. BMW owned by Tina.

13. Which of the following correctly describes the insurance situation of the Topplemeirs?

    1. The Topplemeirs are underinsured for life insurance.

    2. The life insurance beneficiary designations need to be revised.

    3. None of the life insurance would be included in the probate estate due to the contractual nature of life insurance.

    a. 1 only.

    b. 3 only.

    c. 2 and 3.

    d. 1 and 2.

    e. 1, 2, and 3.

14. Which of the following are the Topplemeirs' estate planning deficiencies?

    1. Failure to plan for incapacity.

    2. Underqualified estates.

    3. Lack of wills.

    a. 1 only.

    b. 1 and 2.

    c. 2 and 3.

    d. 1 and 3.

    e. 1, 2, and 3.

15. The Topplemeirs qualify for which of the following tax benefits for 2007?

    1. Tax credit of $1,000 per child for Brooks, Hunter, and Emily.

    2. Tax credit of $1,000 per child for Hunter and Emily.

    3. Deductible Coverdell Education Savings Account contributions of $2,000 each for Brooks, Hunter, and Emily.

    4. Nondeductible Coverdell Education Savings Account contributions of $2,000 for Brooks, Hunter, and Emily.

    5. Hope Scholarship Credit for Brooks.

    a. 2 and 4.

    b. 1 and 3.

    c. 2, 4, and 5.

    d. 4 only.

    e. 1, 3, and 5.

16. Assuming that the Topplemeirs invest $10,000 in an S&P 500 index fund, what is the probability that they will have return over 3%?

    a.   0%.

    b.   16%.

    c.   34%.

    d.   84%.

    e.   95%.

17. What is the annualized rate of return that Eddie has earned on the assets held in the profit-sharing plan from January 1, 2003 to December 31, 2007?

    a.   2.0%.

    b.   2.3%.

    c.   2.6%.

    d.   2.9%.

    e.   3.1%.

18. Which of the following strategies would help the Topplemeirs reduce their federal income tax liability for 2008?

    1.   Have Eddie contribute to the Amadeus 401(k) plan.

    2.   Have Tina contribute to a deductible traditional IRA.

    3.   Have both Eddie and Tina contribute to a deductible single-premium deferred annuity.

    4.   Purchase a $1,000 computer for Eddie's business use, and elect Section 179 expensing.

        a.   1 only.

        b.   1 and 4.

        c.   2 and 3.

        d.   1, 2, and 4.

        e.   2, 3, and 4.

19. Tina has decided to go back to night school to earn her undergraduate degree in Business Management. She also wants to take advantage of an educational assistance program that was recently adopted by Amadeus Company. All of the following statements are correct regarding Employer Educational Assistance Programs, except:

    a.   Up to $5,250 of qualified educational expenses can be paid by the employer for an employee's undergraduate or graduate education expenses and is not taxable to the employee.

    b.   Qualified educational expenses under the Employer Educational Assistance Program include tuition, enrollment fees, books, supplies, and equipment.

    c.   The $5,250 benefit is taxed to the employee as ordinary income and deductible by the employer.

    d.   A Hope Scholarship or Lifetime Learning Credit can be taken for qualified educational expenses over $5,250 (if an employee meets the requirements for educational credits).

20. If Eddie died today, what amount of life insurance would be included in his gross estate for federal estate tax purposes?

    a. $125,000

    b. $200,000

    c. $280,000

    d. $325,000

21. Assuming Tina died today, which of the following statements is correct?

    a. The death benefit of the whole life policy will be included in Tina's gross estate.

    b. The death benefit of the whole life policy will be considered a gift from Eddie to Brooks and Hunter.

    c. The group term policy will be included in Tina's probate estate.

    d. $22,000 of the group term policy death benefit will be subject to income tax to the beneficiaries.

EDDIE AND TINA TOPPLEMEIR

Solutions

Eddie and Tina Topplemeir

ANSWER SUMMARY

1.	b	6.	d	11.	e	16.	d	21.	b
2.	d	7.	e	12.	d	17.	e		
3.	b	8.	b	13.	d	18.	a		
4.	d	9.	b	14.	d	19.	c		
5.	b	10.	a	15.	d	20.	c		

SUMMARY OF TOPICS

1. Tax—Sale of Mutual Fund Shares
2. Tax—Sale of Mutual Fund Shares
3. Fundamentals—Emergency Fund
4. Insurance—Collision
5. Insurance—Personal Property/HO-2 Loss of Use Coverage
6. Investments—Allocation of Funds (Asset Allocation)
7. Investments—Yield Curve and the Liquidity Premium Theory
8. Investments—Bond Analysis with Increasing Interest Rate
9. Investments—Calculation of Gains and Losses
10. Fundamentals—Education Funding
11. Retirement—Savings Rate
12. Tax—IRD
13. Insurance—Life Insurance Coverage
14. Estates—Planning Deficiencies
15. Tax—Educational Tax Benefits
16. Investments—Probability of a Return
17. Investments—Internal Rate of Return
18. Tax—Reduction of Tax Liability
19. Fundamentals—Employer Educational Assistance
20. Estates—Gross Estate
21. Estates—Life Insurance Benefits

SOLUTIONS

Tax—Sale of Mutual Fund Shares

1. b

Purchase Date	Sales Date	Shares	Sales Price	Purchase Price	Short-Term Gain/Loss	Long-Term Gain/Loss
04/01/06	12/01/07	100	$2,700	$2,500		$200
08/01/06	12/01/07	200	5,400	4,000		1,400
12/01/06	12/01/07	40	1,080	500	$580	
02/01/07	12/01/07	100	2,700	1,500	1,200	
Total			$11,880	$8,500	$1,780	$1,600

Long-term holding period rule: Must be held for *more* than 12 months (sales price is $27.00 per share).

Tax—Sale of Mutual Fund Shares

2. d

The methods of determining the basis include FIFO, specific identification, and the average cost method. Under the specific identification method, the taxpayer identifies specific shares to be sold and uses compounding basis for those shares. Generally, the shares with the highest basis would be selected. The average cost method calculates basis by determining the total basis for all shares owned and dividing the sum by the total number of shares.

Fundamentals—Emergency Fund

3. b

The money market fund would be the most appropriate investment for their emergency fund because it is the least risky of the choices given.

The cash value of their existing policy is insufficient for their emergency fund.

Insurance—Collision

4. d

Tina should not purchase collision insurance due to the low amount at risk and the high cost of the insurance.

Insurance—Personal Property/HO-2 Loss of Use Coverage

5. b

The boat is not covered for liability under the homeowners policy because of its engine size. A separate watercraft policy should be purchased. Their HO-2 policy includes an endorsement for furs and jewelry. There is no indication that the Topplemeirs own fine art.

Investments—Allocation of Funds (Asset Allocation)

6. d

	Value	Blend	Growth
Large			**Fund** B $5,100 E 8,000 F 8,200 Total $21,300
Medium	**Fund** C $11,075 Total $11,075		**Fund** A $2,625 D 7,500 Total $10,125
Small			

	Value	Blend	Growth
Large			50.12%
Medium	26.06%		23.82%
Small			

Tina's portfolio is heavily concentrated in the growth style and is evenly split between large-sized and medium-sized companies. She should shift some of her investments to the value or blend style based on her risk tolerance.

Investments—Yield Curve and the Liquidity Premium Theory

7. e

The Liquidity Premium Theory is based on the concept that longer-term bonds are more price sensitive to interest rate changes than shorter-term bonds. The Liquidity Premium Theory also implies that investors pay a premium (i.e., lower yields) for shorter-maturity bonds to avoid the high interest rate risk associated with long-term bonds. Under this theory, long-term rates will generally be higher than short-term rates. Although the 25-year and 30-year rates are lower than the 20-year rate, the yield curve is generally upward sloping.

The Market Segmentation Theory relies on the concepts of supply and demand for various maturities of borrowing and lending. Bonds with different maturities make up distinct markets. The markets for borrowing and lending can be broken into three categories.

Lenders in each market will match their assets, or lending, with their liabilities, or debts. Borrowers attempt to match the term of indebtedness with the period of time they need to borrow the funds.

Supply and demand in the various markets are believed to be independent, which allows for the shape of the yield curve to change over time. Based on this theory, the yield curve can take on almost any shape. The derived yield curve is consistent with this theory.

The Expectations Theory is based on the concept that long-term rates consist of a series of short-term rates. The long-term rates will be the average (or geometric mean) of the short-term rates.

Investments—Bond Analysis with Increasing Interest Rate

8.   b

Formula: $\dfrac{\Delta P}{P} = \dfrac{-D}{1 + YTM} \times \Delta YTM$

$-6.56\% = \dfrac{-7.12}{1.085} \times 0.01$ 10,000 T-bonds

$-9.13\% = \dfrac{-9.95}{1.09} \times 0.01$ 5,000 T-bonds

Note: The yield to maturity for each bond is determined by analyzing the current yield curve.

	New FMV
10,000 US Treasury bonds	$9,343.78
5,000 US Treasury bonds	4,543.58
	$13,887.36

10,000 US Treasury Bonds	
Duration	7.12
YTM	8.50%
Change in interest rates	1.00%
Old price of bond	$10,000.00
Percent change	−6.5622%
New price of bond	$9,343.78

5,000 US Treasury Bonds	
Duration	9.95
YTM	9.00%
Change in interest rates	1.00%
Old price of bond	$5,000.00
Percent change	−9.1284%
New price of bond	$4,543.58

Adjusted value of the bonds in Tina's investment portfolio: $9,343.78 + 4,543.58 = $13,887.

Investments—Calculation of Gains and Losses

9.   b

	# Shares	Price	Total	%
Sales Price	1,500	$7.50	$11,250	166.66%
Cost Basis	1,500	(4.50)	(6,750)	(100.00%)
Gain	N/A	$3.00	$4,500	66.66%

The holding period return is 67%.

The gain would be a capital gain (short or long term depending on the holding period).

The options are not considered here, as the options can be assumed to be exercised only when in-the-money on the date of expiration. In this case, we do not know the date.

Fundamentals—Education Funding

10. a

PMT	=	($25,000)
n	=	5
i	=	1.8868% [[(1.08 ÷ 1.06) − 1] × 100]
FV	=	$0
$PV_{AD@18}$	=	$120,455.30

Note: Ten-year bonds are yielding 8.5%. Therefore, five-year bonds are yielding 7.5%, and the average yield is 8.0%.

		Brooks	Hunter
FV_{18}	=	$120,455.30	$120,455.30
n	=	2	6
i	=	1.8868	1.8868
PMT	=	$0	$0
PV	=	$116,035.28	$107,675.87

Therefore, Tina should set aside $223,711.15 to fund her boys' college education.

Retirement—Savings Rate

11. e

They are currently saving nothing (Statement of Cash Flows).

Tax—IRD

12. d

Retirement plans are considered IRD assets, and therefore, will receive no step-up in basis at death.

Insurance—Life Insurance Coverage

13. d

Statement 3 is incorrect because the beneficiary designation on Policy B (Eddie's estate) subjects the proceeds to probate. Statement 2 is true since none of the policies provide for Tina or Emily, and Eddie's estate is generally an inappropriate beneficiary. Statement 1 must be true by the process of elimination.

Estates—Planning Deficiencies

14. d

- The life insurance is improperly held.
- There are no wills.
- The estates may be overqualified depending on intestate law.
- There are no provisions for the care of children.
- There are no durable powers of attorney for health care.

Tax—Educational Tax Benefits

15. d

Statements 1 and 2 are false. Even though all three children are under 17, the Topplemeirs' AGI is over $114,000 (The beginning phaseout threshold). Thus, the $1,000 credit will be reduced.

Statement 3 is false because the contributions to a Coverdell Education Savings Account are always nondeductible.

Statement 4 is true. The contributions are nondeductible and may be made until the child reaches age 18. Therefore, all children qualify in 2007. AGI for a joint return cannot exceed $190,000 before phaseout begins.

Statement 5 is false. Hope Scholarship Credit applies to the first two years of postsecondary education at an eligible educational institution.

Investments—Probability of a Return

16. d

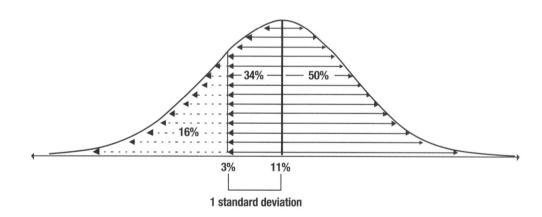

Since 3% is one standard deviation from the mean (11%), the probability of getting a return between 3% and 11% is 34% (one half of 68%). The probability of getting a return above 11% is 50%. Therefore, the probability of a return above 3% is 84% (50% + 34%).

Investments—Internal Rate of Return

17. e

Period	Cash Flow	
0	($25,000)	
1	($8,954)	
2	($10,366)	
3	($13,605)	
4	$0	
5	$65,000	($80,000 – $15,000)
IRR	3.0745%	

Tax—Reduction of Tax Liability

18. a

Statement 1 is correct. Contributions to the 401(k) would be pretax, thereby reducing the amount of salary that would be taxed to Eddie.

Statement 2 is incorrect. Tina is an active participant in the profit-sharing plan. Their AGI is too high for Tina to deduct her contribution to a traditional IRA.

Statement 3 is incorrect. Contributions to annuities would be nondeductible.

Statement 4 is incorrect. Eddie is an employee of Amadeus. Therefore, his unreimbursed business expenses would be considered miscellaneous itemized deductions subject to the 2% of AGI floor.

Fundamentals—Employer Educational Assistance

19. c

Option (c) is incorrect because the benefit is excluded from the employee's income up to $5,250 per year for 2007.

Estates—Gross Estate

20. c

$280,000 will be included in Eddie's gross estate, based on the following:

Policy	Amount	Rationale
Policy A	$200,000	Current coverage is included in the gross estate because Eddie is the owner and the insured.
Policy B	$75,000	Current coverage is included in the gross estate because Eddie is the owner and the insured.
Policy C	$0	Coverage is excluded from the estate because Tina is the owner.
Policy D	$5,000	Interpolated terminal reserve is included in the gross estate, because Eddie is the owner and Tina is the insured.
Total	$280,000	

Estates—Life Insurance Benefits

21. b

Since Eddie is the owner and the children are the beneficiaries, Eddie will have given the children a gift for federal gift tax purposes equal to the death benefit. The gift will be eligible for the gift tax annual exclusion.

A is incorrect. The whole life policy will be excluded from Tina's gross estate because Eddie is the owner.

C is incorrect. The group term policy will be included in Tina's gross estate, but will be excluded from her probate estate because the death benefit will pass by contract to the beneficiaries.

D is incorrect. The group term policy will be received by the beneficiaries completely income tax free.

ROBERT AND ROBIN FARRELL

Case Scenario

Robert and Robin Farrell

CASE SCENARIO

Robert and Robin Farrell have come to you, a financial planner, for help in developing a plan to accomplish their financial goals. From your initial meeting together, you have gathered the following information. Today is December 31, 2007.

PERSONAL INFORMATION

Robert Farrell (Age 65)

Robert is in excellent health. He owns Farrell's Animal Care Center, a local animal hospital with 25 employees. Robert has a salary of $250,000.

Robin Farrell (Age 50)

Robin is in excellent health. She works as a CPA for an international accounting firm, where she is currently a manager in the area of litigation support. She has a daughter, Payton, from a previous marriage who is 30 and living on her own. Robin has a salary of $50,000.

The Farrells

They have been married for 25 years.

Children

Robert and Robin have three children from their marriage.

Nicole—Age 23
Ryan—Age 21
Danielle—Age 5

Marleen Burke

Robin's mother, Marleen, turned age 71 on December 1, 2007, and is a widow with substantial net worth. In addition to sizable holdings of real estate, stocks, and bonds, Marleen has $450,000 in her IRA rollover account, as of December 31, 2007 (her account grew by $25,000 during 2007). Because she is in extremely poor health, she had an attorney draft a will leaving her entire estate to Robin. The will provides that in the event that Robin should disclaim any or all of the inheritance, the disclaimed amount will be left in trust for Robin's four children.

PERSONAL AND FINANCIAL OBJECTIVES

1. Robert wants to sell his business during 2008 and retire. He expects to live 30 years.

2. Robert wants to continue to transfer some of his wealth to his children to avoid estate taxes. He will consider using the Family Limited Partnership that is currently in place.

ECONOMIC INFORMATION

General

They expect inflation to average 4.0% annually both currently and for the long term.

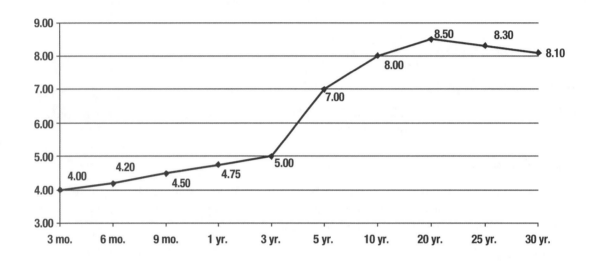

US Treasury
Current Yield Curve

Economic Outlook—Investments

	Expected Returns (pretax)		Expected Deviation
Aggressive stocks	18%	±	15%
Growth stocks	14%	±	10%
S&P 500	11%	±	8%
Bonds	8%	±	3%
Insurance contracts	6%	±	2%
Money markets	5%	±	1%
T-bills	4%	±	1%

Banking

The Farrells have favorable banking relationships and could borrow money for any purpose at the following rates:

Type of Loan	Rates
Installment Loans—Secured	6.5%
Personal Signature Bank Loans	9.0%
Mortgage Loan—30-year fixed	8.5%
Mortgage Loan—15-year fixed	8.0%

INVESTMENT INFORMATION

They consider $100,000 adequate for an emergency fund. They indicate a moderate level of risk tolerance in investments.

INCOME TAX INFORMATION

The Farrells are in a marginal income tax bracket of 35% for federal and 6% for state. They pay on average 31% and 5% for federal and state tax, respectively. Capital gains are taxed at 15% for federal (no special rate at the state level).

In an effort to reduce their income tax liability, the Farrells would like to donate some cash and other assets to charity, but they are not certain which specific charity they would like to donate to. They do not need cash flow from the assets donated, and do not want to deal with administrative headaches. Although today is December 31, they would like to receive an income tax deduction for the current year if possible.

INSURANCE INFORMATION

Life Insurance	Policy 1	Policy 2
Insured	Robert Farrell	Robert Farrell
Face amount	$1,500,000	$250,000
Cash value	$25,000	0
Type of policy	Whole Life	Variable Universal Life
Annual premium	$4,500	$40,706 (single premium)*
Beneficiary	Payton, Nicole, Ryan, Danielle	Robin Farrell
Contingent beneficiary	Robert's Estate	Farrell Children's Trust
Policyowner	Farrell Children's Trust**	Robert
Settlement options	N/A	Single Life Annuity (guaranteed for 10 years)

* Robert is considering purchasing the variable universal life insurance policy.

** The original owner of the policy was Robert; however, he transferred the policy to the trust on June 30, 2007. William Bradley, who has been a friend of Robert since college, is the trustee for the Farrell Children's Trust. Interpolated terminal reserve at date of transfer was $25,000. The policy was purchased January 1, 1996.

Robin also has term insurance provided through her employer. She has $100,000 of term coverage. The primary beneficiary is Robert.

HEALTH INSURANCE

Robert

Currently he has a good health insurance plan through Farrell's Animal Care Center, but will not be covered once the sale of the business has been finalized. Robert's health plan has the following features:

- $1,000 individual deductible.
- $2,500 family deductible.
- $3,500 stop loss provision.
- 80% coinsurance clause.
- $5 million major medical limit.

Robin

Coverage is available through Robin's employer, but she is currently covered under Robert's policy.

Disability Insurance

Robert does not have disability insurance.

Robin has disability insurance provided by her employer. The policy provides for a benefit of 60% of gross pay with an "own occupation" definition and a 180-day elimination period. The policy covers both accidents and sickness.

Property and Liability Auto Insurance (both cars)

Type	PAP
Liability (Bodily injury)	$100,000/$300,000
Property Damage	$50,000
Medical Payments	$1,000
Physical Damage, own car	Actual Cash Value
Uninsured Motorist	$100,000/$300,000
Collision Deductible	$1,000
Comprehensive Deductible	$500
Annual Premium (2 cars)	$1,800

Homeowners Insurance

Type	HO-3
Dwelling	$700,000
Other Structures	$70,000
Personal Property	$350,000
Personal Liability	$100,000
Medical Payments	$1,000
Deductible	$100
Coinsurance Clause	80/20
Annual Premium	$2,200

Umbrella Insurance

The policy is for $3 million, and their premium is $500 per year.

RETIREMENT INFORMATION

Robert

- Robert has a profit-sharing plan and a money-purchase pension plan at Farrell's Animal Care Center, with a combined balance of $1,350,000.

- Robert also has an IRA account with a balance of $30,000 (see details). This account was established in 1990.

- Robin is the beneficiary of all of Robert's retirement accounts.

Robin

- Robin has a 401(k) plan where she is able to defer up to 20% of her salary. The accounting firm matches $0.25 for each $1.00 she defers, up to 6% of her salary.

- Robert is the beneficiary of all of Robin's retirement accounts.

Robert and Robin

- They anticipate retiring today and both expect to live until age 95.

- They have estimated that they need $250,000 per year, in today's dollars, for retirement. This amount would drop by 25% if only one was alive.

Asset Allocation

The Farrells plan to have a separate fund to provide for their retirement income. They expect to maintain a portfolio with the following asset allocation.

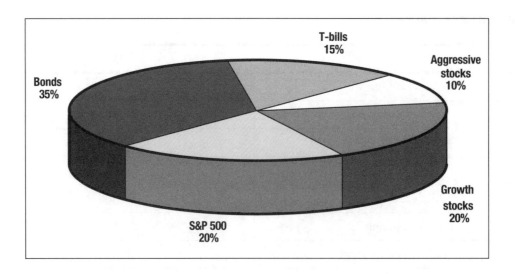

EDUCATION INFORMATION

Nicole and Ryan are both enrolled at Davidson University. The annual tuition is currently $30,000 per year for each child and is expected to increase by approximately 7% per year. This cost is being funded from current earnings and savings. They are concerned about funding Danielle's education, because Robert and Robin are retiring and will not be working while Danielle is in school. They expect tuition to be $30,000 (today's cost) and to increase by 7% each year. They expect Danielle, beginning at age 18, will attend four years of undergraduate and two years of graduate school. They would like to set aside money today, which would be invested in bonds, to fund the cost of Danielle's college education.

INFORMATION REGARDING WILLS, TRUSTS, AND ESTATES

Wills

Both Robert and Robin have wills. Each of the wills provides for all assets to be left in a QTIP trust with the surviving spouse as the income beneficiary and the children as the remaindermen. They think they need to have their wills updated.

The Farrell Family Trust

This trust was established in 1993 for the purpose of reducing the Farrells' estate tax. The primary beneficiaries of the trust are the four children with the contingent beneficiary being the Heart Association. If a child should die, his interest would pass to that child's heirs. If no heir exists, then the interest would pass to the remaining children of the trust. If all children should die without heirs, then the Heart Association would receive the corpus of the trust. The trust is currently valued at $3,000,000.

The Farrell Children's Insurance Trust (All 4 children)

This trust was set up in early 2007 for the purpose of reducing the Farrells' estate tax liability. On June 30, 2007, Robert Farrell transferred life insurance Policy 1 to the trust. There is a Crummey provision in the trust.

RARF Family Limited Partnership

P.K. Keller, one of the area's best estate planning attorneys, discussed the benefits of setting up a Family Limited Partnership with the Farrells. With his help, the Farrells established RARF Family Limited Partnership (RARF FLP) in 2003. All of the assets transferred to the trust were Robert's separate property. Robert currently owns 100% of the RARF FLP but intends to begin transferring some ownership to his children and possibly to Robin.

STATEMENT OF FINANCIAL POSITION
Robert and Robin Farrell
Statement of Financial Position
As of December 31, 2007

	ASSETS[1]			LIABILITIES & NET WORTH	
	Cash/Cash Equivalents			**Liabilities[7]**	
H	Cash and Checking[2]	$250,000	W	Credit Card Balances[8]	$15,000
H	Money Market Fund[3]	875,000	H	Short-Term Note	230,000
	Total Cash/Equivalents	$1,125,000		Auto Note Balances	0
				Mortgage Note	0
	Invested Assets			*Total Liabilities*	$245,000
H	Profit-Sharing Keogh	$1,350,000			
H	IRA—Robert	30,000			
W	IRA—Robin 401(k)	150,000			
H	Growth Mutual Fund	53,100			
H	Due from RARF	70,500			
H	RARF Family Limited Partnership (see detail)	1,193,600			
H	Common Stock Portfolio[4]	100,000			
H	Farrell's Animal Care Center Common Stock[5]	2,250,000			
	Total Invested Assets	$5,197,200		**Net Worth**	$7,519,200
	Use Assets				
JT	Residence[6]	$1,000,000			
JT	Personal Property	400,000			
JT	Autos	42,000			
	Total Use Assets	$1,442,000			
	Total Assets	$7,764,200		**Total Liabilities & Net Worth**	$7,764,200

Notes to Financial Statement:

[1] Presented at fair market value.

[2] Cash and checking earn 3% annually.

[3] Money market earns 5% annually.

[4] Publicly traded stock.

[5] The value is an approximation of the value of the business made by Dr. Farrell. The company is a C corporation with a basis of $25,000.

[6] Basis of home $200,000 (Robert contributed 75%, Robin contributed 25% to the purchase of house).

[7] All liabilities are stated at principal only. All liabilities are owned jointly.

[8] Credit card interest rate is 18%.

H = Husband only

W = Wife only

JT = Joint tenancy with survivorship rights

STATEMENT OF CASH FLOWS
Robert and Robin Farrell
2007 Statement of Cash Flows
January 1, 2007 to December 31, 2007

INFLOWS—ANNUAL

Robert's Salary	$250,000	
Robin's Salary	50,000	
Dividend Income	7,373	
Interest Income	49,227	
Total Inflows		**$356,600**

OUTFLOWS—ANNUAL

Savings and Investments	$56,600	**$56,600**

Fixed Outflows—Annual

Mortgage (P&I)	$0	
Property Taxes	20,000	
Homeowners Insurance	2,200	
Utilities	7,800	
Telephone	600	
Auto (P&I) Payment	0	
Auto Insurance	1,800	
Gas/Oil/Maintenance	1,800	
Credit Card Payments	12,000	
Umbrella Insurance	500	**$46,700**

Variable Outflows

Taxes	$119,691	
Food	7,800	
Medical/Dental	2,000	
Clothing/Personal Care	6,000	
Child Care	5,200	
Entertainment/Vacation	10,000	
College	60,000	
Kindergarten	6,000	**$216,691**
Total Outflows		**$319,991**
Discretionary Cash Flow		**$36,609**

INFORMATION REGARDING ASSETS AND LIABILITIES

FARRELL'S ANIMAL CARE CENTER	
	Cash Flows (NOI)
Year 1	$400,000
Year 2	$420,000
Year 3	$435,000
Year 4	$440,000
Terminal Value	$3,000,000*

* The terminal value was calculated by dividing the forecasted NOI for Year 5 of $450,000 by an assumed discount rate of 15%.

GROWTH MUTUAL FUND

Account Name: Robert Farrell   **Account No.:** SIN852741

Date	Amount	Price/Share	Shares	Share Balance
2/1/06				0
3/1/06	$7,500	$15.00	500	500
4/1/06	7,500	18.75	400	900
5/1/06	1,000	20.00	50	950
6/1/06	1,000	20.00	50	1,000
7/1/06	1,000	25.00	40	1,040
8/1/06	1,000	25.00	40	1,080
9/1/06	1,000	25.00	40	1,120
10/1/06	1,000	20.00	50	1,170
11/1/06	1,000	25.00	40	1,210
12/1/06	1,000	25.00	40	1,250
3/1/07	2,300	23.00	100	1,350
6/1/07	4,800	24.00	200	1,550
9/1/07	3,000	30.00	100	1,650
12/1/07	4,200	28.00	150	1,800
12/1/07	2,700*	27.00	100	1,900

*Reinvest Dividend

Account Value as of 12/31/07: $53,100

Notes:

1. The NAV of the fund on December 31, 2006 was $26.00.

2. No dividends were paid in 2006.

3. Dividend of $1.50 per share was paid December 1, 2007.

4. The NAV of the fund on December 31, 2007 was $27.9474.

COMMON STOCK PORTFOLIO						
Account Name: Robert Farrell						
Stock	Average Expected Return	Price/Share	Total Shares	Cost Basis	FMV	Current Dividend
A	25%	$25.55	1,250.00	$7,500.00	$31,937.50	3.0%
B	23%	$37.50	850.00	$10,000.00	$31,875.00	4.0%
C	15%	$87.00	175.00	$18,000.00	$15,225.00	0.0%
D	20%	$43.00	487.50	$16,000.00	$20,962.50	2.5%
Total			2,762.50	$51,500.00	$100,000.00	

1. The standard deviation of the portfolio has been 10.9% in the past and is expected to be the same in the future.

2. Stocks were purchased as follows:

Stock A	3/5/90
Stock B	4/7/95
Stock C	6/30/07
Stock D	6/30/07

RARF FAMILY LIMITED PARTNERSHIP				
Investment	FMV	Average Expected Return	Standard Deviation	Beta
Growth & Income Mutual Fund	$178,000	10.0%	9%	0.92
Balanced Mutual Fund	246,500	8.5%	7%	0.72
Foreign Mutual Fund	138,500	9.7%	15%	0.30
Brokerage Account A	216,000	11.2%	13%	1.22
Brokerage Account B	350,000	10.4%	10%	1.12
Total	$1,129,000			

STATEMENT OF FINANCIAL POSITIONS (RARF)
RARF Family Limited Partnership
Balance Sheet as of December 31, 2007

ASSETS[1]

Cash/Cash Equivalent

Cash	$45,000	
Money Market	55,000	
Total Cash/Cash Equivalent		$100,000

Invested Assets (see detail)

Growth and Income Mutual Fund	$178,000	
Balanced Mutual Fund	246,500	
Foreign Mutual Fund	138,500	
Brokerage Account A	216,000	
Brokerage Account B	350,000	
Total Invested Assets		$1,129,000

Use Assets[2]

Computer Equipment	$4,000	
Luxury Auto	37,500	
Depreciation[3]	(6,400)	
Total Use Assets		$35,100
Total Assets		**$1,264,100**

LIABILITIES

Due to Robert Farrell	$70,500	
Total Liabilities		$70,500

Partner's Capital		$1,193,600
Total Liabilities & Partner's Capital		**$1,264,100**

Notes:

[1] All assets, other than use assets, are stated at fair market value.

[2] Use assets are listed at historical cost.

[3] Depreciation (computer = $4,000 and automobile = $2,400).

ROBERT AND ROBIN FARRELL

Questions

Robert and Robin Farrell

QUESTIONS

---

1. Farrell's Animal Care Center has been profitable for the past several years. Last year net income was $400,000. If you used a discount rate of 3% above the expected return for aggressive stocks, what would be the value of the business under the capitalization of earnings approach?

   a. $1,388,889.

   b. $1,904,762.

   c. $1,990,476.

   d. $2,222,222.

   e. $2,250,000.

2. Because of her financial stability and sizable net worth, Marleen Burke is intending to simply leave the funds in her IRA untouched. When she dies, she believes that this asset will get a step-up in basis for her heirs. Which of the following statements regarding her IRA is correct?

   a. She must receive minimum distributions after attaining the age of 70½, but any remaining assets at her death will get a step-up in basis.

   b. She is correct in her belief, and this is a great strategy.

   c. She is incorrect in her belief and will be subject to minimum distribution penalties and the assets will not be stepped up.

   d. The heirs will not receive a step-up in basis, and she will be penalized if she does not receive distributions beginning in 2008.

3. What is the time-weighted return from March 1, 2006, to December 31, 2006, for the Growth Mutual Fund (listed on the Statement of Financial Position)?

   a. 12.68%.

   b. 21.82%.

   c. 26.19%.

   d. 53.55%.

   e. 67.85%.

4. What is the dollar-weighted return from March 1, 2006, to December 31, 2006, for the Growth Mutual Fund (listed in the Statement of Financial Position)?

   a. 12.68%.

   b. 21.82%.

   c. 26.19%.

   d. 53.55%.

   e. 67.85%.

5. Explain the difference between time-weighted return and dollar-weighted return.

    1. Time-weighted return is primarily focused on how an investment has performed over a specific period of time without regard to the cash flows of specific investors.

    2. Time-weighted return is the same as dollar-weighted return.

    3. Dollar-weighted return is used primarily by mutual funds.

    4. Dollar-weighted return considers the return an investor receives from an investment based on his cash flows.

    5. Time-weighted return is the same as average return.

        a. 4 only.

        b. 1 and 4.

        c. 1 and 5.

        d. 2, 3, and 4.

        e. 1, 2, 4, and 5.

6. What was the gift tax valuation of the life insurance policy transferred to the Farrell Children's Trust?

    a. $0—due to the annual exclusion.

    b. $15,000—due to the annual exclusion.

    c. $25,000—interpolated terminal reserve.

    d. $27,250—interpolated terminal reserve and one-half of the annual premium.

    e. $29,500—interpolated terminal reserve plus the annual premium.

7. What are the implications of Robert's estate being the contingent beneficiary of the life insurance policy 1?

    a. There are no implications as long as the estate is simply the contingent beneficiary.

    b. This could cause inclusion of the proceeds in Robert's estate.

    c. There are no implications if Robert lives 3 years.

    d. Because there are four beneficiaries, there is no problem.

8. What are the ramifications if Robin assigns her $100,000 of term insurance to the Farrell Children's Trust?

    a. She cannot assign group term because vendors change yearly.

    b. She has made a taxable gift of $100,000.

    c. She has made a gift equal to the cash value of the policy.

    d. She has made a gift equal to the remaining prorated premiums.

9. The Farrells are currently designing an education investment program to fund the education for Danielle. Robert wants a portion of the investment portfolio to be invested in tax-exempt securities. Which one of the following investments would produce interest or dividends that are free from federal income tax?

    a. Zero-coupon Treasury bonds.

    b. State of Louisiana bonds with a 5% coupon rate.

    c. Zero-coupon corporate bond with a duration of 7.3 years.

    d. Series EE savings bonds.

10. If Robert were to die today, which one of the following assets would be included in his probate estate?

    a.   Personal residence.

    b.   Profit-sharing plan.

    c.   RARF FLP.

    d.   Autos.

    e.   Life Insurance Policy 1.

11. Assume the Farrells decide to update their wills. Which of the following should be included in their new wills?

    1.   Provision for guardians of minors.

    2.   Funeral instructions.

    3.   Transfer of IRA assets.

    4.   Attestation clause.

        a.   1 and 2.

        b.   1 and 4.

        c.   3 and 4.

        d.   2, 3, and 4.

        e.   1, 2, 3, and 4.

12. Which of the following results from Robert creating a Charitable Remainder Annuity Trust (CRAT) or Charitable Remainder Unitrust (CRUT) and donating his ownership of Farrell's Animal Care Center to such a trust, as opposed to a direct sale of the business?

    1.   He avoids capital gains tax upon the transfer of the business to the trust.

    2.   He gets an immediate charitable income tax deduction.

    3.   He may select a joint life annuity.

    4.   He can receive annuity income.

        a.   2 only.

        b.   2 and 4.

        c.   1, 2, and 4.

        d.   1, 3, and 4.

        e.   1, 2, 3, and 4.

13. If Marleen died and Robin decided to disclaim part or all of her inheritance, which of the following are steps Robin should take to make sure that any such disclaimer is effective?

    1. The disclaimer should be made to the executor.

    2. The disclaimer must be in writing.

    3. The disclaimer must be filed within 6 months of Marleen's death.

    4. Robin cannot have benefited from any disclaimed assets prior to the disclaimer.

      a. 1 and 2.

      b. 2 and 4.

      c. 2, 3, and 4.

      d. 1, 2, and 4.

      e. 1, 2, 3, and 4.

14. What is the weighted rate of return of the common stock portfolio?

      a. 20.69%.

      b. 20.75%.

      c. 21.78%.

      d. 22.50%.

      e. 24.55%.

15. What is the probability that Robert's common stock portfolio (listed on the Statement of Financial Position) will have a return above 10.88%?

      a. 34%.

      b. 50%.

      c. 68%.

      d. 84%.

      e. 95%.

16. Which of the following options are available to the Farrells to provide health insurance once Robert sells his business?

    1. Robert qualifies for Medicare Part A and Part B.

    2. Robin qualifies under Medicare as Robert's spouse.

    3. Danielle qualifies under COBRA to continue health insurance for 36 months.

    4. Robin qualifies under COBRA to continue health insurance for 36 months.

      a. 1, 2, and 3.

      b. 1 and 2.

      c. 1 and 3.

      d. 2 and 4.

17. Using the discounted cash flow analysis and a discount rate of 3% above the expected return for aggressive stock, what would be the value of Farrell's Animal Care Center?

    a. $1,388,889.

    b. $1,904,762.

    c. $2,145,000.

    d. $2,224,883.

    e. $2,467,776.

18. Using the Sharpe Index, which of the RARF Family Limited Partnership accounts (mutual funds) has the highest risk-adjusted return?

    a. Growth and Income Mutual Fund.

    b. Balanced Mutual Fund.

    c. Foreign Mutual Fund.

    d. Account A.

    e. Account B.

19. Robert's nephew, Tom, has always been Robert's favorite. Robert has always thought of him as a son. Tom has worked closely with Robert at Farrell's Animal Care Center and is considered by Robert to be a top-notch veterinarian. Assume Robert is considering retirement and has decided to transfer Farrell's Animal Care Center to Tom using a self-canceling installment note (SCIN). All of the following statements are correct regarding SCINs, except:

    a. Installment payments cease upon Robert's death.

    b. Robert is able to bargain for a higher price or higher interest rate.

    c. The value of the note cancelled at Robert's death is not included in his estate.

    d. Any remaining gain on the transaction is not included in Robert's estate income tax return.

20. Assume Robert decides to purchase the $250,000 variable universal life policy and the policy is classified as a modified endowment contract (MEC). All of the following statements regarding the policy are correct, except:

    a. The policy is classified as an MEC because too much premium has been paid into the policy.

    b. This policy has taken in more premium than the sum of the net level premiums that are needed to result in a paid-up policy after seven years.

    c. Should Robert make a loan or withdrawal from the cash value of the policy, he will be subject to a 10% penalty.

    d. This policy is subject to LIFO income tax treatment for loans from the policy.

21. Based on the Farrell's charitable income tax planning goal, what would be the best strategy to implement today?

    a. Charitable Remainder Annuity Trust.

    b. Outright gift to charity.

    c. Private foundation.

    d. Donor advised fund.

22. Which of the following strategies will assist the Farrells in lowering their personal income tax liability for next year?

    a. Donate their personal residence to charity, retaining a life estate.

    b. Contribute to a Section 529 plan to help fund Danielle's college education.

    c. Have the Animal Care Center purchase equipment and elect section 179 expense.

    d. Have Robert purchase a personal disability income replacement policy.

ROBERT AND ROBIN FARRELL

Solutions

Robert and Robin Farrell

1.	b	6.	d	11.	b	16.	c	21.	d
2.	d	7.	b	12.	e	17.	e	22.	a
3.	e	8.	d	13.	d	18.	a		
4.	d	9.	b	14.	c	19.	d		
5.	b	10.	c	15.	d	20.	c		

SUMMARY OF TOPICS

1. Investments—Capitalized Earnings
2. Retirement—Traditional IRA
3. Investments—Time-Weighted Return
4. Investments—Dollar-Weighted Return
5. Investments —Time-Weighted and Dollar-Weighted Returns
6. Estates—Gift Tax
7. Estates—Gifting Strategies
8. Estates—Gift Tax
9. Fundamentals—Educational Funding Strategies
10. Estates—Probate Estate
11. Estates—Wills
12. Estates—CRAT
13. Estates—Wills
14. Investments—Investments Returns
15. Investments—Normal Distribution
16. Insurance—Health Insurance
17. Fundamentals—TVM
18. Investments—Sharpe Ratio
19. Estates—SCINs
20. Insurance—Modified Endowment Contracts
21. Income Tax—Charitable Contributions
22. Income Tax—Tax Planning

SOLUTIONS

Investments—Capitalized Earnings

1. b

Discount Rate = 18% + 3% = 21%

$$\text{Value} = \frac{\text{Earnings}}{\text{Discount Rate}} = \frac{\$400,000}{0.21} = \$1,904,762$$

Retirement—Traditional IRA

2. d

There are a couple of problems with Marleen's plan. First, she is required to take a minimum distribution for 2007 by April 1, 2008, and another distribution in 2008 by December 31, 2008. She will continue to be required to take minimum distributions annually for years after 2008. Second, retirement accounts are considered income in respect of a decedent (IRD) assets and do not receive a step-up in basis at the owner's death.

Investments—Time-Weighted Return

3. e

FMV @ 12/31/06 = $26

FMV @ 3/1/06 = $15

PV	=	($15)
FV	=	$26
n	=	10
i	=	5.655 per month

5.655% × 12 = 67.85%

Investments—Dollar-Weighted Return

4. d

IRR = 4.46% per month, which equates to 53.55% per year.

CF_0	($7,500)
CF_1	($7,500)
CF_2	($1,000)
CF_3	($1,000)
CF_4	($1,000)
CF_5	($1,000)
CF_6	($1,000)
CF_7	($1,000)
CF_8	($1,000)
CF_9	($1,000)
CF_{10}	$32,500 (1,250 shares @ $26.00)

Investments —Time-Weighted and Dollar-Weighted Returns

5. b

The time-weighted return is primarily focused on how the investment has performed over a specific period of time without regard to cash flows of specific investors. The dollar-weighted return considers the return an investor receives from an investment based on his cash flows.

Estates—Gift Tax

6. d

The amount of the gift is the fair market value at the date of the gift. Since the policy has been in force for several years and further premiums are to be paid, the gift tax valuation may be approximated by adding to the interpolated terminal reserve the proportionate part of the gross premium last paid before the gift (unearned premium), which covers the period extending beyond the gift (i.e., $2,250 - one half of the yearly premium). The interpolated terminal reserve is equal to $25,000 and the valuation for gift taxation is $27,250.

Estates—Gifting Strategies

7. b

Robert has potentially undone some of the planning that he had previously put into place. The contingent beneficiary status, which is very unlikely to occur, causes the inclusion of the proceeds in Robert's estate at his death. He should seek to amend the beneficiary status by permanently and irrevocably disclaiming any rights and do so in writing to the trustee.

Estates—Gift Tax

8. d

The assignment itself will be a gift to the trust beneficiaries. The gift is equal to the prorated premium for the remainder of the premium period. Also, the continuing payment of premiums by the employer will result in continuing gifts from Robin to the trust beneficiaries.

Fundamentals—Educational Funding Strategies

9. b

Option (a) is incorrect. Although the bonds are zero-coupon bonds, the taxpayer will still be responsible for paying federal income tax on the accrued interest each year.

Option (b) is correct. Interest on municipal bonds is not taxed at the federal level.

Option (c) is incorrect. Although the bonds are zero-coupon bonds, the taxpayer will still be responsible for paying federal income tax on the accrued interest each year.

Option (d) is incorrect. Series EE bonds are not taxed if the proceeds are used for education purposes. However, the tax benefit of Series EE bonds is phased out at certain AGI levels, and the Farrells are well above those levels.

Estates—Probate Estate

10. c

The FLP interest will be included in the probate estate.

Estates—Wills

11. **b**

Statements 1 and 4 are correct.

Statement 2 is incorrect. The will is often read after the funeral.

Statement 3 is incorrect. IRA assets will automatically pass to the IRA beneficiaries, regardless of the will.

Estates—CRAT

12. **e**
   1. He avoids capital gains tax upon the transfer of the business to the trust. However, the character of income for the annuity or unitrust payment will be determined based on the income earned in the CRT. The ordinary rules require ordinary income to be used first, followed by capital gain income, then followed by tax-exempt income. If there is a subsequent sale of the business from the CRT, it will create capital gain income. Therefore, all or a portion of the CRT payment may be capital gain income.
   2. He gets an immediate tax deduction.
   3. He is able to get a retirement annuity from the CRAT or CRUT, and the assets will not be in his estate at death.
   4. He can choose a joint life expectancy for either the CRAT or CRUT. The problem is the loss of asset to the surviving heirs, but that can be mitigated with a second-to-die life insurance policy purchased by an irrevocable life insurance trust.

Estates—Wills

13. **d**
   1. Make the disclaimer in writing to the executor.
   2. Make sure that it is filed with the executor within 9 months, not 6 months.
   3. Make sure Robin has not or does not benefit from disclaimed assets.
   4. Make sure Robin does not try to direct Marleen's disclaimed assets to particular heirs.

Investments—Investments

14. **c**

	Fair Market Value	% of Portfolio	Avg/Exp Return	Weighted Return
Stock A	$31,937.50	31.94%	25%	7.98%
Stock B	31,875.00	31.88%	23%	7.33%
Stock C	15,225.00	15.22%	15%	2.28%
Stock D	20,962.50	20.96%	20%	4.19%
Total	$100,000.00	100.00%		21.78%

Investments—Normal Distribution

15. d

68% of outcomes will fall within one standard deviation of the mean. Since 10.88% is one standard deviation from the mean of 21.78% (weighted average), the probability of having a return between 10.88 and 21.78% is 34% (1/2 of 68%), and the probability of a return above 10.88% is 84% (34% plus 50% (probability to the right of the mean)).

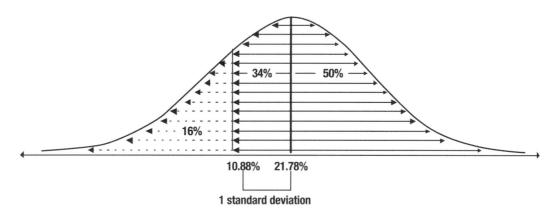

Insurance—Health Insurance

16. c

Robert is 65 and qualifies for Medicare. As a dependent (under 18 years of age) of someone qualifying for Medicare, Danielle can be covered for 36 months under COBRA.

Fundamentals—TVM

17. e

Period	Cash Flow
0	$0
1	$400,000
2	$420,000
3	$435,000
4	$3,440,000 ($3,000,000 + $440,000)
i =	21% (18% + 3%)
NPV =	$2,467,776

Investments—Sharpe Ratio

18. a

According to the Sharpe Index, Growth and Income Mutual Fund has the highest return.

$$\text{Sharpe Index} \quad \frac{R_P - R_F}{\sigma_P}$$

$$\text{Growth \& Income Mutual Fund} \quad \frac{10\% - 4\%}{9\%} \quad = 0.67$$

$$\text{Balanced Mutual Fund} \quad \frac{8.5\% - 4\%}{7\%} \quad = 0.64$$

$$\text{Foreign Mutual Fund} \quad \frac{9.7\% - 4\%}{15\%} \quad = 0.38$$

$$\text{Account A} \quad \frac{11.2\% - 4\%}{13\%} \quad = 0.55$$

$$\text{Account B} \quad \frac{10.4\% - 4\%}{10\%} \quad = 0.64$$

Estates—SCINs

19. d

Option (d) is incorrect because any remaining gain may be included in Robert's estate income tax return as income in respect of decedent.

Insurance—Modified Endowment Contracts

20. c

Option (c) is incorrect because Robert is over 59½ years old and, therefore, would not be subject to the 10% penalty for loans or withdrawals from the MEC.

Income Tax—Charitable Contributions

21. d

A donor advised fund is easy to setup and administer, and would allow an immediate income tax deduction, even though they are not certain of the charity at this time.

A is incorrect. A CRAT would provide them with an annuity payment, which is not needed. In addition, it would be difficult to establish a CRAT today, which is the goal.

B is incorrect. They do not know which specific charity they would like to donate to.

C is incorrect. Private foundations are expensive and have restrictions and regulatory requirements.

Income Tax—Tax Planning

22. a

If they donated their personal residence to charity, retaining a life estate, they will receive an immediate income tax deduction equal to the present value of the remainder interest in the residence.

B is incorrect. Contributions to a Section 529 plan are nondeductible.

C is incorrect. Since the Animal Care Center is a C corporation, the Farrells will not receive any personal income tax benefit from deductions received by the corporation.

D is incorrect. Premiums for disability insurance are not deductible if the policy is purchased by and paid for by an individual.

PAUL AND KRISTI ROTH

Case Scenario

Paul and Kristi Roth

Today is December 31, 2007. Paul and Kristi Roth have come to you, a financial planner, for help in developing a plan to accomplish their financial goals. From your initial meeting together, you have gathered the following information:

PERSONAL BACKGROUND AND INFORMATION

Paul Roth (Age 45)

Paul owns an 80% interest in a closely held company, Roth Printing. He has recently been diagnosed with diabetes and is considering selling or transferring some or all of the business to his son, Anthony, and retiring earlier than age 65.

Kristi Roth (Age 24)

Kristi is the office manager of Blue Moon, a paper supply store with 45 employees.

The Roths

Paul and Kristi met at Blue Moon when Paul purchased paper for Roth Printing. They have been married for 2 years. They live in a community property state but have a prenuptial agreement declaring that all property is separate.

The Children

Paul and Kristi have no children of their own, but Paul has 2 children from a former marriage (former spouse is deceased). Paul's children are Julia, who is an 18-year-old college student, and Anthony, who is age 27 and works in the printing business with Paul.

PERSONAL AND FINANCIAL OBJECTIVES

1. Retire at age 65.
2. Provide adequate retirement income.
3. Avoid or minimize death taxes at the death of the first spouse.
4. Minimize death taxes at the death of the second spouse.
5. Provide adequate estate liquidity.

ECONOMIC INFORMATION

- They expect inflation to average 4.0% annually, both currently and for the long term.
- They each expect salaries and net income to increase at 4.0% annually, both currently and long term.
- They believe the S&P 500 is a good measure of the market's performance. Its historical rate of return of 12% is expected to continue.

ASSUMED
TREASURY YIELD CURVE

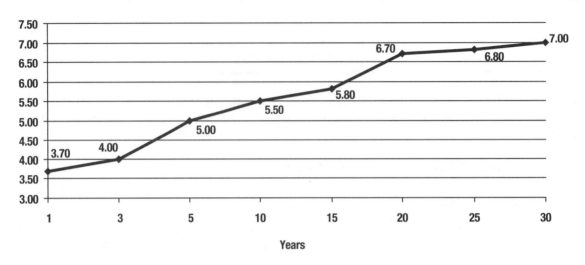

Economic Outlook—Investments

	Return	Standard Deviation
Small Company Stocks	13.0%	15.0%
Large Company Stocks	11.0%	12.0%
S&P 500	12.0%	12.0%
Corporate Bonds	8.5%	6.0%
Long-Term Treasury Bonds	7.0%	5.0%
T-Bills	3.7%	2.0%

INSURANCE INFORMATION

Life Insurance

	Policy 1	Policy 2	Policy 3[1]
Insured	Paul Roth	Paul Roth	Kristi Roth
Face Amount	$500,000	$150,000	$28,000
Type of Policy	Whole life	Term	Term
Cash Value	$5,000	$0	$0
Annual Premium	$1,500	$150	$28
Beneficiary	Kristi Roth	Kristi Roth	Paul Roth
Owner	Paul Roth	Paul Roth	Kristi Roth
Contingent Beneficiary	Estate of Paul Roth[2]	Estate of Paul Roth[2]	Anthony and Julia

[1] Kristi's term policy is employer provided. The 2008 premium has not yet been paid.

[2] Paul listed his estate as the contingent beneficiary because he was concerned about his wife's ability to pay off their debt obligations in the event that he should suffer an untimely death.

Health Insurance

Kristi currently has a health plan provided by her employer (Blue Moon). Kristi and Paul are both currently covered by her plan. Kristi's plan has the following characteristics:

- $1,500 individual deductible/ $3,000 family deductible
- Stop-loss provision individual: $4,000, family: $6,000
- 80% coinsurance clause
- $3 million major medical lifetime limit

Note: Julia is also covered under this plan and is eligible to continue coverage until age 25. Roth Printing does not have a health insurance plan. Anthony is currently covered under his wife's health policy.

Disability Insurance

Kristi has disability coverage provided by her employer (60% of gross pay coverage, own occupation, and a 90-day elimination period). Since Roth Printing is a small business, it does not provide disability insurance to its employees. Paul has purchased a disability policy on his own. The policy is an *own occupation* policy that provides 65% of gross pay coverage and a 180-day elimination period. The premium for this policy is $1,200 per year, and the policy provides benefits to age 65.

Property and Liability Auto Insurance

	PAUL AND KRISTI'S AUTOS	JULIA'S AUTO
Type of Policy	PAP	PAP
Liability (Bodily Injury)	$100,000/$300,000	$50,000/$100,000
Property Damage	$50,000	$25,000
Medical Payments	$1,000	$1,000
Physical Damage, Own Car	Actual Cash Value	Actual Cash Value
Uninsured Motorist	$100,000/$300,000	N/A
Collision Deductible	$1,000	N/A
Comprehensive Deductible	$500	N/A
Annual Premium	$1,800 (2 autos)	$1,350

Homeowners Insurance

	PERSONAL RESIDENCE	BEACH CONDO
Type of Policy	HO-3	HO-3
Dwelling	$150,000	$150,000
Other Structures	$15,000	$15,000
Personal Property	$75,000	$75,000
Personal Liability	$100,000	$100,000
Medical Payments	$1,000	$1,000
Deductible	$250	$500
Coinsurance Clause	80/20	80/20
Annual Premium	$1,500	$1,100

Umbrella Insurance

Policy is for $2 million and their premium is $300/year.

INVESTMENT INFORMATION

The Roths have a required and expected rate of return of 9%. They consider themselves to be moderate to moderate-aggressive investors, and they consider $50,000 adequate for an emergency fund.

INCOME TAX INFORMATION

The Roths are in the 25% marginal tax bracket for federal income tax purposes. Long-term capital gains are taxed at 15%. There is no state income tax.

RETIREMENT INFORMATION

Kristi is eligible to participate in her employer's 401(k) plan, but has chosen not to participate. Her employer provides a match of dollar-for-dollar up to 3% of her gross salary.

Paul does not have a retirement plan at Roth Printing, but usually makes IRA contributions for Kristi and himself.

Paul has several other retirement accounts from previous employers, all of which consist of qualified assets.

Paul and Kristi would both like to retire when Paul reaches age 65. They believe that together they would need about $75,000 (in today's dollars) pretax income during their retirement. This amount would decrease by 1/3 at the death of the first spouse.

Although Paul is battling diabetes, they believe his condition is not terminal and expect him to live to age 95. Kristi also expects to live to age 95.

GIFTS, ESTATES, TRUSTS, AND WILL INFORMATION

Gifts

Neither Paul nor Kristi have made any previous taxable gifts.

Estates

Paul and Kristi estimate that funeral expenses will be $25,000 each and administrative expenses will be $40,000 for each of them.

Wills

Paul and Kristi both have wills that leave $100,000 outright to each child with the remainder of the estate going to the surviving spouse. The wills also establish credit equivalency trusts with all expenses and taxes to be paid from the residue of the estate.

STATEMENT OF CASH FLOWS
Paul and Kristi Roth
Statement of Cash Flows
For the Year 2007

CASH INFLOWS

Salary—Paul	$60,000	
Salary—Kristi	28,000	
Investment Income[1]	9,508	
Rental Income	2,100	
Total Cash Inflows		**$99,608**

CASH OUTFLOWS

Savings—IRA Contributions	$6,000	
Ordinary Living Expenses		
Food	$4,800	
Clothing	2,500	
Travel	3,500	
Entertainment at Home	1,500	
Utilities	3,000	
Telephone	3,600	
Auto Maintenance	400	
Pool Service	700	
Lawn Service	840	
Church	1,200	
Total Ordinary Living Expenses & Savings	$28,040	
Other Payments		
Automobile Payment	$7,200	
Mortgage Payment (Principal Residence)	11,747	
Mortgage Payment (Beach Condo)	12,943	
Total Other Payments	$31,890	
Insurance Premiums		
Automobile	$3,150	
Disability	1,200	
Health	0	
Homeowners	2,600	
Life	1,650	
Umbrella	300	
Total Insurance Premiums	$8,900	
Taxes		
Federal Income Tax	$22,000	
FICA—Kristi ($28,000 @ 7.65%)	2,142	
FICA—Paul ($60,000 @ 7.65%)	4,590	
Property Tax (Principal Residence)	500	
Property Tax (Beach Condo)	300	
Total Taxes	$29,532	
Total Expenses and Planned Savings		**$98,362**
Balance Available for Discretionary Investment		**$1,246**

(Continued on next page)

Notes:

[1]Investment Income:

Checking	$0	
Savings	764	
Roth Printing Stock	0	
Brokerage Account	1,594	
Bond Mutual Fund	0*	
Bond Portfolio	6,250	
High Tech Stock	800	
Fox Stock	100	
TOTAL	$9,508	

* All income is automatically reinvested in the fund.

STATEMENT OF FINANCIAL POSITION
Paul and Kristi Roth
Balance Sheet as of December 31, 2007

ASSETS[1]			LIABILITIES[9] & NET WORTH		
Cash & Cash Equivalents			**Current Liabilities**		
JT	Checking[2]	$8,000	H	Automobile Notes Payable	$19,000
JT	Savings[3, 4]	25,475	W	Credit Cards	3,500
	Total Cash & Equivalents	$33,475		*Current Liabilities*	$22,500
Invested Assets					
H	Stock in Roth Printing[5]	$160,000	**Long-Term Liabilities**		
H	Brokerage Account	58,121	JT	Mortgage on Residence	$139,150
H	Bond Mutual Fund Portfolio	136,000	H	Mortgage on Beach Condo	107,627
H	Bond Portfolio	100,000		*Long-Term Liabilities*	$246,777
H	High Tech Stock[6]	20,000			
W	Fox Stock[7]	5,000		*Total Liabilities*	$269,277
H	Pension Plan #1[8]	34,594			
H	Pension Plan #2[8]	98,676			
H	IRA Rollover[8]	65,078			
H	IRA—Paul	14,650			
W	IRA—Kristi	17,350			
H	Cash Value Life Insurance	5,000			
	Total Invested Assets	$714,469	Net Worth		$965,667
Use Assets					
JT	Personal Residence[3]	$180,000			
H	Beach Condo	120,000			
JT	Personal Property[3]	100,000			
H	Automobiles	87,000			
	Total Use Assets	$487,000			
	Total Assets	**$1,234,944**	**Total Liabilities & Net Worth**		**$1,234,944**

Notes to Financial Statements:

[1] Assets are stated at fair market value with exception of Roth Printing stock.

[2] Joint tenancy with survivorship rights with son, Anthony. Checking account doesn't earn interest. Paul contributed 100%.

[3] Joint tenancy with survivorship rights with spouse.

[4] The current rate for savings is 3%.

[5] This is Paul's guess at what Roth Printing is worth. His basis is $25,000.

[6] 2,000 shares @ $10 per share. The current dividend is $0.40 per share and is expected to grow at 3% per year.

[7] 100 shares.

[8] All pension plans have the spouse of participant as named beneficiary.

[9] Liabilities are stated at principal only. All liabilities go with the associated asset for title purposes.

Title Designations:

H = Husband (sole owner).   W = Wife (sole owner).   JT = Joint tenancy with survivorship rights.

INFORMATION REGARDING ASSETS AND LIABILITIES

High Tech Stock

This stock was given to Paul as a Christmas present several years ago by Paul's brother, David. David's basis in the High Tech Stock was $13,500, and the value at the date of the gift was $25,000. See footnote on Statement of Financial Position.

Mutual Fund Portfolio of Bonds

The bond fund was inherited from Paul's uncle, Fred, who died December 10, 2007, at which time the bond fund was valued at $148,000. Uncle Fred had just bought the bond fund on November 1, 2007, and paid $145,000 for it. All earnings are automatically reinvested in the fund, and Paul has had no distributions since inheriting it. The fund earned $6,000 in 2007, but unfortunately is only valued at $136,000 today, due to fluctuations in interest rates.

Bond Portfolio

Description	Maturity	Coupon[3]	Cost Basis	FMV
10,000 US T-Bills	1	N/A	$9,640.00	$9,643.20
20,000 US T-Bonds	30	8%	20,000.00	22,494.47
10,000 US T- Bonds	20	0%	1,313.00	2,625.30
20,000 Big Co. Bonds[1]	20	9%	20,000.00	24,271.01
15,000 Weak Co. Bonds[2]	25	9%	15,000.00	3,000.47
25,000 Texas Municipal Bonds	15	6%	25,000.00	27,616.29
			$90,953.00	$89,650.74
Money Market Account				10,349.26
TOTAL				$100,000.00

Account Value as of 12/31/07:	$100,000.00

Notes:
[1] Bonds are investment quality.
[2] Bonds are noninvestment quality.
[3] Assume all coupon payments are made once a year at the end of the year.

Brokerage Account

Stock	Shares	Beta	Std. Dev.	Div. Yield[2]	Average Return	Cost	FMV
Big Co.	1,000	0.88	12.5%	4.0%[3]	12.5%	$8,046.47	$14,500.00
Small Co.	1,000	1.24	18.0%	0.0%	15.0%	10,724.35	12,333.00
Oil Co.	1,000	1.00	10.0%	3.5%[3]	8.0%	11,135.70	15,150.00
Auto Co.	1,000	1.12	10.0%	3.0%[4]	10.0%	12,124.72	16,138.00
					Total	$42,031.24	$58,121.00

Notes:

[1]The stock portfolio has a correlation coefficient with the market of 0.80.

[2]The dividend yield is the current yield.

[3]Growth of dividend is expected to remain at 3%.

[4]The expected growth of the dividend is zero.

Fox Stock

Kristi inherited the Fox stock from her great aunt, Joyce, who had bought the stock when the price was $42.00 per share. When Joyce died, she left Kristi 50 shares of Fox stock. Kristi knows that when Joyce died, Fox stock closed at $35.00 per share with a high price of $38.00 and low price of $34.00. The stock has since split 2 for 1 and has a current dividend yield of 2%.

Personal Residence

The Roths purchased their personal residence for $175,000 eight months ago. They made a down payment of 20% from the sale of their previous home. They were able to obtain a mortgage rate of 7.5% financed over 30 years. Their monthly payment is $978.90 with a balance of $139,150.39 remaining.

Beach Condo

Paul purchased the beach condo 3 years ago for $150,000 and put 20% down. The balance was financed over 15 years at 7%. The monthly payment is $1,078.59, and they have made 30 payments. The balance on the loan is $107,627.07. Since the purchase, Paul has paid $9,200 in restoration costs. The Roths personally use the condo often in both the winter and summer. Paul and Kristi generally let some of their friends rent the condo during the year. This year, they rented the condo to Paul's best friend for one week and to Kristi's sister for a long weekend (five days).

PAUL AND KRISTI ROTH

Questions

Paul and Kristi Roth

QUESTIONS

1. Which of the following accurately describes Paul's current estate plan?

    1. Inappropriate ownership of life insurance.
    2. The will arrangement adequately protects both children regarding inheritance.
    3. A QTIP would be useful in this case.
    4. Inadequate health and medical directives.

        a. 1 only.
        b. 2 and 4.
        c. 3 and 4.
        d. 1, 3, and 4.
        e. 1, 2, 3, and 4.

2. If Kristi were to die today, what would be the value of her gross estate?

    a. $157,738.
    b. $175,088.
    c. $203,088.
    d. $325,088.
    e. $825,088.

3. Which of the following assets would be included in Kristi's probate estate if she died today?

    a. Savings.
    b. Life insurance policy.
    c. Fox stock.
    d. Personal residence.
    e. Kristi's IRA.

4. Paul is considering selling the Mutual Fund bond portfolio and expects to receive net proceeds of $136,000 from the sale. He is concerned, however, about the tax consequences of such a sale. What are the tax consequences of such a sale assuming that it takes place on April 15, 2008?

    a. No gain or loss.
    b. $9,000 long-term capital loss.
    c. $12,000 long-term capital loss.
    d. $15,000 long-term capital loss.
    e. $18,000 long-term capital loss.

5. Assume that Paul has a need for retirement income from Roth Printing and that he wants to ultimately avoid any capital gain taxation on any disposition of Roth. In addition, he wants to make sure it is not included in his estate and that there is no gift tax on the transfer. Which of the following devices or methods can be used to accomplish his goals?

    1. Private annuity.
    2. Charitable Remainder Annuity Trust (CRAT).
    3. Grantor Retained Annuity Trust (GRAT).
    4. Self-Canceling Installment Note (SCIN).

        a. 1 only.
        b. 2 only.
        c. 1, 2, and 3.
        d. 1, 2, and 4.
        e. 1, 2, 3, and 4.

6. Assuming they can earn their required rate of return, how much capital do they need when Paul is age 65 to provide for both of them in retirement? (Round to the nearest thousand and assume they are both living and expected to live to 95.)

        a. $2,583,000.
        b. $2,623,000.
        c. $2,707,000.
        d. $2,932,000.
        e. $3,073,000.

7. Concerning investment risk within the Bond Portfolio, which of the following statements is/are correct?

    1. All of the bonds are subject to reinvestment rate risk except the T-bills.
    2. None of the bonds are subject to foreign currency risk.
    3. All of the bonds are subject to interest-rate risk.
    4. Only Big Co. bonds and Weak Co. bonds are subject to default risk.
    5. All of the bonds, except the T-bills, are subject to liquidity risk.

        a. 1, 3, and 4.
        b. 2 and 3.
        c. 2, 3, and 5.
        d. 1, 2, 3, and 5.
        e. All of the above.

8. How could Paul protect his gain in Big Co. stock without selling the stock?

    1. Sell Big Co. short.

    2. Sell a put option on Big Co.

    3. Purchase a put option on Big Co.

    4. Purchase a call option on Big Co.

    5. Sell a call option on Big Co.

      a. 1 only.

      b. 3 only.

      c. 2 and 4.

      d. 3 and 5.

      e. 1 and 3.

9. Based on the value of the bonds in the bond portfolio, what have interest rates been doing during the holding period?

    a. Interest rates have been increasing.

    b. Interest rates have been stable.

    c. Interest rates have been decreasing.

    d. It is not possible to determine the answer based on the information provided.

10. According to the Jensen Model, rank the order of performance of the stocks in the brokerage account from highest to lowest. Assume that the actual returns are as follows:

	Actual Return
Big Co.	13.00%
Small Co.	13.50%
Oil Co.	9.00%
Auto Co.	10.50%

    a. Big Co., Small Co., Auto Co., Oil Co.

    b. Oil Co., Auto Co., Big Co., Small Co.

    c. Oil Co., Auto Co., Small Co., Big Co.

    d. Big Co., Oil Co., Auto Co., Small Co.

    e. Oil Co., Big Co., Small Co., Auto Co.

11. What is the weighted alpha of the entire stock portfolio (using the actual returns in Question 10)?

    a. (1.08).

    b. (0.99).

    c. 1.08.

    d. 2.00.

    e. 2.07.

12. Concerning the Roths' brokerage account, which of the following statements is (are) correct?

    1. 64% of the change in the account can be explained by the market.
    2. The entire account movement can be explained by the market.
    3. The portfolio is sufficiently diversified such that there is almost no unsystematic risk exposure within the portfolio.
    4. Unsystematic risk accounts for more than one-third of total risk.

        a. 2 only.
        b. 2 and 3.
        c. 1 and 4.
        d. 1 and 3.
        e. None of the above.

13. Roth Printing used a cross-purchase life insurance program to provide protection against the early and untimely death of a principal shareholder. Paul owns 80%; two other individuals (X and Y) own 10% each. How many policies did they have and for what amounts? Assume that Roth Printing is worth $350,000.

    1. Six (6) policies must be purchased.
    2. Paul must own two (2) policies of $140,000 each.
    3. X must own a policy on Paul for $280,000.
    4. Y must own a policy on Paul for $140,000 and on X for $17,500.
    5. Each must own a policy valued at $350,000.

        a. 5 only.
        b. 1 and 4.
        c. 2 and 3.
        d. 3 and 4.
        e. None of the above.

14. If Kristi were to sell the Fox stock today for the value on the Statement of Financial Position, what would be the income tax consequences?

        a. $800 short-term capital gain.
        b. $1,500 short-term capital gain.
        c. $2,900 long-term capital gain.
        d. $3,200 long-term capital gain.
        e. $3,250 long-term capital gain.

15. Since Paul has been diagnosed with diabetes, he has been concerned about his finances. With everything going on, he wants to wait to make an IRA contribution to his traditional IRA for 2007. Paul wants to know if he can make a 2007 contribution in 2008?

    a. No, a contribution for 2007 cannot be made after December 31, 2007.

    b. Yes, he can make a deductible contribution on or before April 15, 2008.

    c. Yes, he can make a contribution anytime in 2008 for 2007.

    d. Yes, he can make a contribution if he has not already filed his income tax return for 2007, but it is not deductible because he makes too much money.

    e. Yes, he can make a contribution if he has not already filed his income tax return for 2007, but it is not deductible because his wife is covered by a pension plan, and they make too much money.

16. Paul and Kristi have the following income and expenses from the rental of the condo during the year:

Rental Income	$2,100.00
Interest Expense	$7,733.41
Property Tax	$300.00
Depreciation	$4,800.00
Utilities Expense	$1,000.00

    What is the income tax treatment of the above items on their federal income tax return?

    a. Schedule E loss of $11,733.

    b. Schedule E loss of $11,733 suspended under the passive activity rules.

    c. No income, claim the interest and tax on Schedule A of Form 1040.

    d. $2,100 income (claimed as other income on the 1040).

    e. Claim the $2,100 in income but offset it by $2,100 exactly because it is a vacation home.

17. Paul had surgery in January 2007 to remove a small tumor from his arm and is hospitalized for several days. While in the hospital he incurs $5,200 in expenses. How much will Paul have to pay (i.e., how much is not covered by the health insurance policy)?

    a. $440.

    b. $1,040.

    c. $1,440.

    d. $1,840.

    e. $2,240.

18. How many option contracts should Paul buy/sell to fully hedge his position in Big Co. stock?

    a. He should buy 10 put option contracts to protect his long position.

    b. He should buy 1,000 put option contracts to protect his long position.

    c. He should sell 10 call option contracts to protect his position.

    d. He should sell 1,000 call option contracts to protect his position.

19. Blue Moon is considering setting up a health savings account (HSA) for its employees. Which of the following is (are) true regarding an HSA?

    1. Blue Moon does not qualify for an HSA because there are too many employees.

    2. Blue Moon qualifies for an HSA since its plan has high deductibles that meet the requirements of the Internal Revenue Code.

    3. Contributions by Kristi to an HSA would be deductible from her taxable income, and distributions used to pay qualified medical expenses are excludable from income.

    4. Any funds in Kristi's HSA account at her death are included in her gross estate.

    5. If Blue Moon elects to fund the HSA, contributions are deductible to the corporation and excludable from Kristi's income.

        a. 3 and 4.

        b. 2 and 4.

        c. 1 only.

        d. 2, 3, and 5.

        e. 2, 3, 4, and 5.

20. Which of the following statements are true regarding the High Tech Stock?

    1. The stock is overvalued in the market by approximately 46% using the constant growth dividend model.

    2. Since David and Paul are related parties, and the FMV of the stock exceeded the donor's basis on the date of the gift, Paul will have a basis of $13,500 for losses and $25,000 for gains.

    3. This is an inappropriate investment given their conservative risk tolerance.

        a. 1 only.

        b. 2 only.

        c. 1, 2, and 3.

        d. 1 and 3.

        e. None of the statements are true.

21. Before beginning a new venture for Roth Printing, Paul consults his CFP® practitioner about the net present value (NPV) and the internal rate of return (IRR) of the new project. Paul tells the planner that he has a ten percent required rate of return for the new project, and provides the planner with the expected inflows and outflows of the investment. After performing an internal rate of return analysis on the investment, the planner concludes that multiple IRRs exist for the project. What should the planner do?

        a. Run the analysis again because there must be an error in an input.

        b. Inform Paul not to make the investment.

        c. Inform Paul to make the investment as long as both IRRs are greater than 10 percent.

        d. Perform NPV analysis because it is the preferred method of investment valuation.

        e. Perform NPV analysis even though it is not the preferred method of investment valuation.

22. Before beginning a new venture for Roth Printing, Paul consults his CFP® practitioner about the net present value (NPV) and the internal rate of return (IRR) of the new project. Paul tells the planner that he has a ten percent required rate of return for the new project, and provides expected inflows and outflows of the investment. After performing a net present value analysis of the new project, the planner lets Paul know that the NPV turned out to be positive. What will the IRR equal for this project?

    a. Less than 0%.

    b. Between 0%–10%.

    c. Equal to 10%.

    d. Greater than 10%.

    e. Not enough information to solve the problem.

23. Paul is considering the purchase of a business overhead expense disability insurance policy for the printing business. The business will purchase the policy and pay the premiums. Which of the following statements is correct regarding this arrangement?

    a. Benefits will be paid during the disability period for the purchase of business equipment.

    b. These policies typically contain long elimination periods.

    c. Benefits are often paid until age 65, unless a lifetime option is selected.

    d. Benefits received from the policy are taxable.

PAUL AND KRISTI ROTH

Solutions

Paul and Kristi Roth

Answer Summary

1. d	6. e	11. a	16. c	21. d
2. c	7. c	12. c	17. e	22. d
3. c	8. e	13. b	18. a	23. d
4. e	9. c	14. d	19. e	
5. b	10. a	15. b	20. a	

Summary of Topics

1. Estates—Incapacity Planning and Minimization of Estate Taxes
2. Estates—Gross Estate
3. Estates—Probate Estate
4. Tax—Basis of Inherited Property
5. Estates—Minimization of Estate Taxes
6. Retirement—Needs Analysis
7. Investments—Types of Investment Risk
8. Investments—Option Strategies
9. Investments—Bond Valuation Concepts
10. Investments—Jensen Ratio
11. Investments—Jensen Ratio
12. Investments—Coefficient of Determination
13. Insurance—Business Uses of Insurance
14. Tax—Basis of Inherited Property
15. Tax—Traditional IRA
16. Tax—Itemized Deductions
17. Insurance—Health Insurance
18. Investments—Hedging Strategies
19. Employee Benefits—Health Savings Accounts
20. Investments—Dividend Growth Model and Client Risk Tolerance
21. Fundamentals—Time Value of Money
22. Fundamentals—Time Value of Money
23. Insurance—Entity Disability Insurance

SOLUTIONS

Estates—Incapacity Planning and Minimization of Estate Taxes

1. d

    - Life insurance is inappropriately owned.

    - Credit equivalency trust may not adequately take care of Kristi.

    - The will arrangement does not fully protect the children from a prior marriage, one of whom is older than Kristi. A QTIP trust would provide more protection for the children. Because of Kristi's young age, however, the children may not receive funds for many years.

    - No contingent beneficiaries named on retirement accounts.

    - No durable powers for health care.

    - No medical directives.

Estates—Gross Estate

2. c

    $203,088. See chart below for calculation.

	Gross Estate	Probate Estate
Savings (not checking)	$12,738	$0
Fox Stock	5,000	5,000
Personal Residence	90,000	0
Personal Property	50,000	0
Life Insurance Policy	28,000	0
IRA Kristi	17,350	0
Total	$203,088	$5,000

Estates—Probate Estate

3. c

    The Fox stock is included in the probate estate. The other assets will pass by contract or title.

Tax—Basis of Inherited Property

4. e

    Paul's adjusted taxable basis is $154,000, which consists of the fair market value at the date of death of Uncle Fred ($148,000) plus the reinvested income from 2007 of $6,000. If he sells the bond fund for $136,000, he will produce a long-term capital loss for 2008 of $18,000. (All inherited property is considered long term.)

Estates—Minimization of Estate Taxes

5.   b

The CRAT should only be used if Paul needs retirement income and has charitable intentions. The GRAT, Private Annuity, and Installment Sale (SCIN) all allow Paul to transfer the stock to his son, Anthony, and possibly avoid inclusion in his estate. Paul must outlive the GRAT to avoid inclusion in his estate, and he has made a taxable gift at the time of the creation of the GRAT. The Private Annuity is best suited for a person who is not in good health and does not need the extra security of notes that one would get in an installment sale. The SCIN solves the estate inclusion problem and allows the seller (Paul) some security (notes) beyond the basic contractual promise to pay.

Note: Neither the private annuity nor the SCIN allow for disposition without capital gains taxation.

Retirement—Needs Analysis

6.   e

Step 1: Adjust Retirement Needs for Inflation to Age 65.

PV   = $75,000

n = 20 (65 – 45)

i = 4%

FV   = ($164,334)

Step 2: Determine the Amount Needed for Paul.

PMT = $54,778 (1/3 × 164,334)

n = 30 (95 – 65)

i = 4.8077% [[(1.09 ÷ 1.04) – 1] × 100]

PV_{AD} = ($902,237) (rounded)

Step 3: Determine the Amount Needed for Kristi.

PMT   = $109,556 (2/3 of $164,334)

n =   51 (95 – (24 + 20))

i =   4.8077%

PV_{AD} =   ($2,170,526)

Total amount needed at age 65 is $3,072,763 ($902,237 + $2,170,526).

Investments—Types of Investment Risk

7. c

Statements 2, 3, and 5 are correct.

- Big Co., Weak Co., and Texas Municipal bonds are considered to have default risk.
- All of the bonds, except the T-bills and zero-coupon bonds, are subject to reinvestment-rate risk.
- None of the bonds are subject to foreign currency risk.
- All of the bonds are subject to interest-rate risk.
- All of the bonds, except the T-bills, are subject to liquidity risk.

Investments—Option Strategies

8. e

Paul has two choices: He can either sell the stock short, called "shorting against the box," or he can purchase a put option. Selling a call will not protect his gain, only limit a loss in the case that the stock price declines. The constructive sale rules have greatly limited the usefulness of the "short-against-the-box" technique for tax purposes.

Investments—Bond Valuation Concepts

9. c

It seems clear from the change in fair market value (FMV) and from the yield to maturity (YTM) compared to the coupon payments, that interest rates have been declining. The most likely reason the Weak Co. bonds have such a high YTM is that the company must be in poor financial condition and the bonds are no longer considered investment grade bonds.

Investments—Jensen Ratio

10. a

Stock	R_f	Market Return	Market Premium	Beta	Expected Return	Actual Return	Jensen's Alpha
Big Co.	3.70%	12.00%	8.30%	0.88	11.00%	13.00%	2.00%
Small Co.	3.70%	12.00%	8.30%	1.24	13.99%	13.50%	(0.49%)
Oil Co.	3.70%	12.00%	8.30%	1.00	12.00%	9.00%	(3.00%)
Auto Co.	3.70%	12.00%	8.30%	1.12	13.00%	10.50%	(2.50%)
Note: The risk-free rate of return is assumed to be the T-bill rate.							

Investments—Jensen Ratio

11. a

Weighted Alpha = -1.08%

Stock	FMV	Jensen's Alpha	Product
Big Co.	$14,500	2.00%	$290.00
Small Co.	$12,333	(0.49%)	($60.43)
Oil Co.	$15,150	(3.00%)	($454.50)
Auto Co.	$16,138	(2.50%)	($403.45)
	$58,121		($628.38)

Weighted alpha = ($628.38) ÷ $58,121 = -1.08%

OR

Stock	FMV	% of Portfolio	Jensen's Alpha	Weighted Alpha
Big Co.	$14,500	24.95%	2.00%	0.50%
Small Co.	$12,333	21.22%	(0.49%)	(0.11%)
Oil Co.	$15,150	26.07%	(3.00%)	(0.78%)
Auto Co.	$16,138	27.76%	(2.50%)	(0.69%)
	$58,121	100.00%		(1.08%)

Investments—Coefficient of Determination

12. c

The coefficient of determination explains the percent change in the dependent variable that can be explained by changes in the independent variable. It also represents the portion of total risk that is systematic risk.

Coefficient of Determination = (Correlation Coefficient)^2

<u>Systematic risk:</u>

$0.8^2 = 0.64$. Therefore, 64% of the change in the Roths' brokerage account can be explained by the market.

<u>Unsystematic risk:</u>

100% – 64% for systematic risk = 36%.

Insurance—Business Uses of Insurance

13. b

Paul's interest is 80% ($280,000) or $140,000 for each policy owned by persons X and Y. X would also own a policy on Y for $17,500 and Y would own a policy on X for $17,500. Paul would own a policy on X of $17,500 and on Y of $17,500. Total number of policies = 6.

	X	Y	Paul
Interest	$35,000	$35,000	$280,000
X's Policies	$0	$17,500	$140,000
Y's Policies	$17,500	$0	$140,000
Paul's Policies	$17,500	$17,500	$0

Tax—Basis of Inherited Property

14. d

1. First determine the adjusted taxable basis: fair market value at the date of death, determined as the average of the high and low of the day [($38 + $34) ÷ 2] = $36.

2. The stock has split (2 for 1), therefore, the adjusted taxable basis is equal to $18 per share.

3. All capital gains or losses from inherited stock are deemed to be long term.

4. Sales Price = $5,000
   Adjusted Taxable Basis (100 × $18) = (1,800)
   Long-Term Capital Gain = $3,200

Tax—Traditional IRA

15. b

Paul can make a contribution up until April 15, 2008, and it is deductible for 2007. A contribution made by April 15th will be deemed to be made in the previous year. Because Kristi is not participating in her 401(k) plan, she is not considered covered by a qualified plan (401(k) plan). Therefore, if Paul makes the IRA contribution by April 15, 2008, it will qualify as a 2007 deductible contribution regardless of their income.

Tax—Itemized Deductions

16. c

- Since the property is rented less than 15 days, it is considered a personal-use asset, not a mixed-use vacation home.

- The income does not have to be included in taxable income because the property was rented for less than 15 days.

- The interest and property taxes are deductible on Schedule A. None of the other expenses are deductible.

Insurance—Health Insurance

17. e

Expense	$5,200
Deductible	(1,500)
Net Expense	$2,200
Coinsurance (20%)	× 20%
Coinsurance Amount	$740

The total amount payable by Paul is $2,240 = ($1,500 + $740).

Investments—Hedging Strategies

18. a

Since option contracts are generally in denominations of 100 shares, he will need to buy 10 put option contracts (1,000 ÷ 100) to protect his long position in Big Co. stock.

Employee Benefits—Health Savings Accounts

19. e

Statement 1 is false. There is no limit on the number of employees for an employer to establish an HSA. Statement 2 is true. The limits for family coverage for 2007 are at least $2,200 annual family deductible and stop-loss limit not to exceed $11,000. Statements 3, 4, and 5 are true.

Investments—Dividend Growth Model and Client Risk Tolerance
Tax—Related Parties

20. a

Value of stock using constant growth dividend model:

$$\frac{\$0.40 \times (1.03)}{0.09 - 0.03} = \$6.87$$

Amount the stock is overvalued:

$$\frac{\$10.00 - \$6.87}{\$6.87} = 45.56\%$$

Statement 2 is false. Paul's basis is $13,500 for gains and losses. The basis would be higher, however, if David had paid gift tax on the gift. Statement 3 is false. This investment is not inappropriate given their moderate to moderate-aggressive risk tolerance.

Fundamentals—Time Value of Money

21. d

There exists the possibility of multiple IRRs. If large negative cash flows occur during the life of the project, then it is possible that more than one discount rate will equate the present value of future cash flows to the project's cost. The multiple IRR problem can lead to an incorrect interpretation regarding the profitability of a project.

NPV is generally preferred to IRR because the reinvestment rate assumption is more realistic for NPV than it is for IRR. The NPV assumes that cash flows are reinvested at the cost of capital, while the IRR assumes that cash flows can be and are reinvested each period at the IRR.

Fundamentals—Time Value of Money

22. d

A NPV greater than zero implies that the IRR of the cash flows is greater than the discount rate used to discount the future cash flows. A NPV of zero implies that the discount rate used is equal to the IRR for the cash flows. A NPV that is negative implies that the discount rate used is greater than the true IRR of the cash flows.

Insurance—Entity Disability Insurance

23. d

The company will receive an income tax deduction when paying premiums on a BOE policy. Therefore, the benefits will be taxable when received.

A is incorrect. Business overhead expense insurance will not provide a benefit for the purchase of business equipment.

B is incorrect. These policies typically contain very short elimination periods.

C is incorrect. Benefits are typically paid for 1–2 years.

TOM AND ERIN ACKERMAN

Case Scenario

Tom and Erin Ackerman

Tom and Erin Ackerman have come to you, a financial planner, for help in developing a plan to accomplish their financial goals. Assume today is December 31, 2007, and you have gathered the following information:

PERSONAL BACKGROUND AND INFORMATION

Tom Ackerman (Age 56)

Tom owns his own business, a coat store, with Schedule C net income of $50,000 in the current year. Tom has no employees other than his son, Justin, who works part-time.

Erin Ackerman (Age 51)

Erin is a professor of psychology at State University where she has been employed full-time for 17 years. Her W-2 income of $65,000, for 9 months of teaching, is paid ratably over 12 months at $5,416.67 per month.

The Ackermans

Tom and Erin have been married for five years. Both are in excellent health. They provide some support for Erin's father, Stanley, who is in a nursing home. Stanley is not a dependent for tax purposes.

The Children

Tom and Erin have 2 children (twins), Tom Jr. and Mary (age 5).

Tom has 2 children, Justin (age 17) and Riley (age 12) from a previous marriage.

Justin works part-time in the coat store (less than 20 hours per week).

PERSONAL AND FINANCIAL OBJECTIVES

1. To retire when Tom is 62 and Erin is 57.
2. To increase their tax-advantaged savings.
3. To be debt free of all mortgages at retirement.
4. To minimize estate taxes and avoid probate.
5. To transfer the coat business to Justin at death or retirement.

ECONOMIC INFORMATION

They expect inflation to average 4% over the long term.

The historical return on the market has been 12% and is expected to continue. The market has had a standard deviation of 14%, which is expected to continue.

T-bills are currently yielding 3% while T-bonds are yielding 5%.

INSURANCE INFORMATION

Life Insurance

	Policy #1	Policy #2
Person Insured	Tom	Erin
Face Amount	$200,000	$200,000
Cash Value	$0	$0
Type of Policy	Term	Group Term
Annual Premium	$1,600	Employer paid Erin pays $20/month
Beneficiary	Erin	Debra (Erin's mother)
Contingent Beneficiary	None	None
Policyowner	Tom	Erin
Settlement Option Clause	Life Annuity	None Chosen

Health Insurance

Persons Covered	Family
Type of Policy	Comprehensive Basic/State University Plan
Coverage	Major Medical 80/20, $2,500 stop loss
Deductible	$500 family deductible
Annual Premiums	Employer paid

Automobile Insurance

Type	Personal Auto Policy
Liability	$100,000/$300,000/$50,000
Medical payments	$3,000/person/accident
Uninsured motorist	$50,000/accident
Physical damage, own car	Actual cash value
Collision deductible	$200
Comprehensive deductible	$50
Annual premium for 2 cars	$1,000

Homeowners Insurance

Residence	
Type	HO-3 Special Form
Dwelling	$196,000
Personal property	$98,000
Personal liability	$100,000/occurrence
Medical payments	$5,000/person/occurrence
Deductible	$250
Premium (annual)	$1,000
Other	80/20 coinsurance clause

Condominium	
Type	HO-6 Personal property
Personal liability	$300,000
Medical payments	$2,000/person/occurrence
Deductible	$500
Premium (annual)	$850
Other	$15,000 covers renters with a rider

Disability Insurance (Long Term)

Disability Policy	
Insured	Erin
Definition	Own occupation
Premium	Employer pays 60%; Erin pays 40%; total of $600/year
Elimination period	90 days
Benefit	60% of gross pay (currently $3,250 per month)

Section 79 Costs for Group Term Insurance

(Costs per $1,000 of protection for one month)

Age	Cost
45 through 49	$0.15
50 through 54	$0.23
55 through 59	$0.43

INCOME TAX INFORMATION

The Ackermans file married filing jointly. They are in the 25% federal bracket. There is no state income tax. Justin and Riley are claimed as dependents by Tom's former wife.

RETIREMENT INFORMATION

Savings

The Ackermans are currently saving $15,700 annually, consisting of $10,000 of IRA contributions, $3,750 in reinvested dividends, and $1,950 in Erin's retirement plan.

Titling of Retirement Accounts	Beneficiary Designation
Tom's IRA	Erin
Erin's IRA	Tom
Erin's DC Retirement Plan	Tom

Social Security Benefits

Tom's Social Security benefits at full retirement age are estimated to be $12,000 per year (in today's dollars).

Retirement Plan

State University has a mandatory defined-contribution plan that contributes 7% of Erin's salary. Erin elected to contribute 3% after tax.

TSA 403(b) Plan

The university has a TSA plan for Erin. She can contribute 16% of her salary on a pretax basis. Erin currently does not participate in the 403(b) plan. The plan contains a loan provision.

GIFTS, ESTATES, TRUSTS, AND WILL INFORMATION

Tom's Will

Tom's will leaves his automobile and the coat business to his son Justin, and everything else to his wife Erin. Erin is the executrix for the estate. The residuary legatee is to pay all administrative expenses, costs, and taxes. Any indebtedness goes with the respective assets.

Erin's Will

Erin's will leaves everything to Tom.

STATEMENT OF CASH FLOWS
Tom and Erin Ackerman
Statement of Cash Flows
January 1, 2007–December 31, 2007

INFLOWS

Tom's Schedule C Net Income	$50,000	
Erin's Faculty Salary	65,000	
Dividend Income from Equity Portfolio	4,750	
Condo Rental Income (net of mgt. fees)	12,000	
Interest Income from Bonds	5,000	
Total Inflows		**$136,750**

OUTFLOWS

Savings and Investments	$15,700	
Fixed Outflows		
Alimony Payment	$6,000	
Mortgage—Principal Residence (P&I)	19,498	
Taxes—Principal Residence	1,800	
Insurance—Principal Residence	1,000	
Mortgage Condo—Rental (P&I)	14,591	
Condo Operating Costs	1,200	
Taxes—Condo	800	
Condo Association Dues	3,600	
Condo Insurance Premium	850	
Auto Note Payment	5,928	
Auto Insurance Premium	1,000	
Life Insurance Premium (Policy 1 and 2)	1,840	
Disability Insurance Premium	240	
Total Fixed Outflows	$58,347	
Variable Outflows		
Taxes	$24,093	
Food (including dining out)	4,800	
Transportation	2,600	
Clothing/Personal care	2,800	
Entertainment/Vacations	4,000	
Medical/Dental	2,000	
Utilities & Household Expenses	2,000	
Church Donations	520	
Miscellaneous	68	
Total Variable Outflows	$42,881	
Total Outflows		**$116,928**
Deficit		**$19,822**

Tax Detail:	Self-employment tax Tom	$6,120
	FICA Erin	$4,973
	Fed W/H	$13,000
		$24,093

STATEMENT OF FINANCIAL POSITION
Tom and Erin Ackerman
Balance Sheet
As of December 31, 2007

	ASSETS[1]			LIABILITIES & NET WORTH	
	Cash And Cash Equivalents			**Liabilities[4]**	
JTWROS	Cash and Checking	$15,000	JT	Automobile Notes Payable	$14,750
JTWROS	Money Market	20,000		Mortgage Condo[2]	99,330
	Total Cash and Equivalents	$35,000		Mortgage Personal Residence[3]	153,115
				Total Liabilities	$267,195
	Invested Assets				
H	Proprietorship	$400,000			
H	IRA—Tom	40,000			
W	IRA—Erin	50,000			
H	Equity Stock Portfolio	135,000			
W	Bond Portfolio	40,000			
JTWROS	Rental Real Estate Condo[2]	160,000			
W	Retirement Plan	80,000			
W	TSA 403(b) Plan	0			
	Total Invested Assets	$905,000		**Net Worth**	$1,057,805
	Use Assets				
JTWROS	Residence[3]—Dwelling	$260,000			
JTWROS	Residence[3]—Land	20,000			
W	Coin Collection	25,000			
JT	Automobiles	20,000			
JTWROS	Personal Property	60,000			
	Total Use Assets	$385,000			
	Total Assets	**$1,325,000**		**Total Liabilities & Net Worth**	**$1,325,000**

Notes to Financial Statements:

[1] Assets are stated at fair market value.

[2] Condo refinanced in 2004 at 10.5% for 15 years. The first payment was due January 15, 2005.

[3] Personal residence financed December 1, 2005 for $165,000 at 8.5% fixed for 15 years.

[4] Liabilities are stated at principal only.

H	=	Husband (sole owner)
W	=	Wife (sole owner)
JT	=	Joint tenancy/No survivorship
JTWROS	=	Joint Tenancy with Right of Survivorship

INFORMATION REGARDING ASSETS AND LIABILITIES

Proprietorship

This business was purchased by Tom 10 years ago for $100,000. There have been no additional capital contributions.

Equity Portfolio

Mutual Fund	Shares	FMV	Basis	Beta	Standard Deviation
A	1,000	$25,000	$10,000	1.3	25%
B	2,000	$40,000	$40,000	1.0	15%
C	6,000	$60,000	$45,000	0.9	20%
D	200	$10,000	$15,000	1.2	18%

Notes to Equity Portfolio:
- The portfolio of mutual funds has a correlation of 0.50 with the market.
- The portfolio has had a historical return of 14% with a volatility of approximately 18% as measured by standard deviation.

Bond Portfolio

The bond portfolio was a gift to Erin from her Uncle Stirling five years ago. The value of the portfolio at the time of the gift was $28,000. Stirling paid gift tax of $10,000 on the gift. The bonds currently earn 7.5% annually. Stirling had originally paid $33,000 for the bonds.

Rental Property (Condo)

The condo was purchased in January 1990 for $110,000. The current tax basis of the condo is $0 plus land cost of $10,000. The property is exclusively rental property. The Ackerman's have been depreciating the condo using the Modified Accelerated Cost Recovery System (MACRS) for federal income tax purposes.

Coin Collection

The coin collection was acquired from Erin's mother as a gift. At the time of the gift, Erin's mother's basis was $5,000 while the fair market value of the collection was $30,000. Erin's mother paid gift tax of $5,000 on this gift.

Divorce Decree and Alimony

Tom was divorced from Dorinda five years ago and remarried the same year. His divorce decree required payments to his former spouse (Dorinda) of $500 per month for support for 10 years, at which time Riley will be 18. The payments will then be reduced to $300 per month for five more years. In the event of Dorinda's early death, payments are to be made to her estate for the remainder of the 15-year period.

TOM AND ERIN ACKERMAN

---◼---

Questions

Tom and Erin Ackerman

QUESTIONS

1. What is the amount of alimony that Tom and Erin can deduct as alimony on their current federal income tax return?

    a. $0.

    b. $2,400.

    c. $3,600.

    d. $6,000.

2. What amount, if any, will be included in Erin's W-2 as a result of her group term insurance?

    a. $174.

    b. $240.

    c. $270.

    d. $414.

    e. $534.

3. Which of the following are the current insurance deficiencies of the Ackermans?

    1. Homeowners policy.

    2. Health policy.

    3. Disability insurance for Tom.

    4. Umbrella coverage.

    a. 3 only.

    b. 3 and 4.

    c. 2, 3, and 4.

    d. 1, 3, and 4.

    e. 1, 2, and 4.

4. If Erin were to become disabled March 31 of next year and remain disabled for the remainder of the year, how much would she collect in disability benefits?

    a. $0.

    b. $19,500.

    c. $22,750.

    d. $26,000.

    e. $29,250.

5. How much of Erin's disability benefits would be taxable if she were to become disabled March 31 of next year and remained disabled for the balance of the year?

    a. $0.
    b. $4,000.
    c. $7,800.
    d. $11,700.
    e. $17,550.

6. If the Ackermans were to have a fire in their personal residence that resulted in a loss of $20,000, how much of the loss would be paid by the insurance company?

    a. $14,827.
    b. $18,596.
    c. $18,611.
    d. $19,750.
    e. $20,000.

7. If Erin were to sell the bond portfolio today for the value on the Statement of Financial Position, what would be the tax consequences?

    a. No gain or loss.
    b. $3,000 short-term capital gain.
    c. $2,000 long-term capital gain.
    d. $7,000 long-term capital gain.
    e. $12,000 long-term capital gain.

8. What is Erin's adjusted taxable basis in the coin collection?

    a. $5,000.
    b. $9,167.
    c. $10,000.
    d. $30,000.
    e. $35,000.

9. Which of the following correctly describes the investment characteristics of the coin collection?

    a. Illiquid.
    b. Lack of marketability.
    c. Diverse investment.
    d. Appropriate hedge for stocks and bonds.
    e. Necessary for all balanced portfolios.

10. Assume the Ackermans made a $10,000 contribution ($5,000 each) to traditional IRA accounts for this year. What is the amount of their deductible IRA contributions?

    a. $0.

    b. $4,000.

    c. $5,000.

    d. $8,000.

    e. $10,000.

11. Which of the following retirement plans would you recommend for Tom's business?

    a.   A defined-benefit plan.

    b.   A money-purchase pension plan.

    c.   A SIMPLE.

    d.   A Simplified Employee Pension (SEP).

    e.   A profit-sharing plan.

12. Which of the following retirement plan alternatives would allow Tom the greatest deductible contribution while providing him with only a small cash flow commitment each year?

    a.   A defined-benefit plan.

    b.   A money-purchase plan.

    c.   A 401(k) plan.

    d.   A SEP.

    e.   A profit-sharing plan.

13. Which of the following are characteristics of Erin's TSA 403(b) plan?

    1.   Erin's maximum contribution is $15,500 for 2007.

    2.   10-year forward averaging is available for lump-sum distributions.

    3.   Rollovers to IRAs are permitted.

        a.   3 only.

        b.   1 and 2.

        c.   1 and 3.

        d.   2 and 3.

        e.   1, 2, and 3.

14. Assume Erin is hurt an auto accident, but Tom has sufficient disability coverage to cover her recovery period. Under what principle can she still collect from the negligent party?

    a.   Negligence Per Se.

    b.   Collateral Source Rule.

    c.   Vicarious Liability.

    d.   Constructive Receipt.

15. If Tom were to die today, what would be the value of his gross estate?

    a. $545,000.

    b. $718,902.

    c. $852,500.

    d. $918,902.

    e. $1,052,500.

16. If Tom were to die today, which of the following assets would be excluded from Tom's probate estate?

    a. Proprietorship.

    b. Stock portfolio.

    c. Automobile.

    d. Condo.

    e. All are included in the probate estate.

17. When Tom dies, he wants to have his son, Justin, take over the coat store business. Tom would like to enter into a buy-sell agreement for the coat store, but had a few questions with respect to the agreement. Which of the following is/are true?

    1. In a sole proprietorship, the proprietorship's personal assets and business assets are indistinguishable. The buy-sell agreement should, therefore, specify which assets will be sold to Justin.

    2. If arranged properly, the buy-sell agreement can be used to determine the estate tax value of the business at Tom's death.

    3. A trustee can be used to collect and pay premiums on the life insurance policy and to transfer the business upon Tom's death.

    4. Buy-sell agreements are not allowed for a sole proprietorship.

        a. 4 only.

        b. 1 and 2 only.

        c. 2 and 3 only.

        d. 1, 2, and 3 only.

        e. 1, 3, and 4 only.

18. Assuming Tom's last medical, funeral, and administrative expenses were $50,000, what would be the amount of Tom's marital deduction?

    a. $0.

    b. $466,277.

    c. $592,500.

    d. $642,500.

    e. $652,500.

19. Which of the following is proper criticism of the current estate plan of Tom?

    1. The will disinherits Riley.
    2. Each estate is currently overqualified.
    3. The insurance is improperly titled.
    4. No durable power of attorney exists for health care.
        a. 4 only.
        b. 3 only.
        c. 2, 3, and 4.
        d. 1, 3, and 4.
        e. 1, 2, 3, and 4.

20. Assume Tom wins the lottery next year receiving a lump-sum distribution of $2 million. Which of the following devices <u>could</u> be used to improve Tom Ackerman's estate plan?

    1. Use of an Irrevocable Life Insurance Trust (ILIT).
    2. Create a testamentary credit shelter trust.
    3. Start an annual gifting program.
    4. Change titling of insurance policies.
        a. 1 only.
        b. 1 and 2.
        c. 2, 3, and 4.
        d. 1, 2, and 4.
        e. 1, 2, 3, and 4.

21. What is the implied capitalization rate for the condo? Assume depreciation is $2,000 per year.

        a. 7.5%.
        b. 4.3%.
        c. 3.5%.
        d. 2.2%.
        e. 1.8%.

22. What is the Treynor index for the equity portfolio?

        a. 0.0818.
        b. 0.0877.
        c. 0.0100.
        d. 0.1072.
        e. 0.1365.

23. The Ackermans would like to evaluate how well their portfolio has performed on a risk-adjusted basis. Based on some previous analysis, they know that their portfolio has an alpha of +2.00%. Based on this information, which of the following statements is true?

   a. The Ackermans' equity portfolio has clearly outperformed the market since it has a positive alpha of 2.00%.

   b. Although alpha is positive and is an absolute measure of performance, the equity portfolio did not outperform the market when you consider total return and total risk as in the Sharpe ratio.

   c. Since both Alpha and Treynor of the equity portfolio are higher than that for the market, the equity portfolio is superior on a risk-adjusted basis.

   d. Since Alpha for the market is 3% and the Alpha for the equity fund is only 2%, the market portfolio is better.

   e. Since the Treynor is lower for the market, the return for the market is higher, on a risk-adjusted basis.

24. Which of the following statements is correct regarding the Ackerman's rental real estate condo?

   a. The loss from the condo can be deducted this year only to the extent of the Ackerman's investment income.

   b. There will be no alternative minimum tax consequences resulting from the Ackerman's ownership of the condo.

   c. If the Ackerman's sold the condo for its current fair market value any gain on sale would be taxed at a favorable 15% capital gain rate.

   d. The loss from the condo is not fully deductible this year against the Ackerman's ordinary income.

TOM AND ERIN ACKERMAN

Solutions

Tom and Erin Ackerman

1. a	6. b	11. c	16. d	21. c
2. a	7. d	12. c	17. d	22. d
3. d	8. b	13. a	18. b	23. b
4. b	9. a	14. b	19. e	24. d
5. d	10. c	15. e	20. e	

SUMMARY OF TOPICS

1.   Tax—Adjustments
2.   Employee Benefits—Group Term Life Insurance
3.   Insurance—Analysis of Risk Exposures
4.   Insurance—Disability Income Insurance
5.   Tax—Disability Income Benefits
6.   Insurance—Homeowners
7.   Tax—Basis of Gift Property
8.   Tax—Basis of Gift Property
9.   Investments—Collectibles
10. Retirement—Traditional IRA
11. Retirement—Plan Selection for Businesses
12. Retirement—Plan Characteristics
13. Retirement—403(b) Plans
14. Insurance—Liability
15. Estates—Gross Estate
16. Estates—Probate Estate
17. Estates—Buy-Sell Agreements
18. Estates—Marital Deduction
19. Estates—Minimization of Estate Taxes
20. Estates—Minimization of Estate Taxes
21. Investments—Capitalized Earnings
22. Investments—Treynor Ratio
23. Investments—Performance Measures
24. Tax—Rental Real Estate

SOLUTIONS

Tax—Adjustments

1. a

Alimony is deductible only if there must be no payments made or promised to be made after the death of the recipient spouse.

Employee Benefits—Group Term Life Insurance

2. a

Erin's W-2 will include the excess of $200,000 over $50,000, multiplied by the rate found in the schedule in Section 79 of the Internal Revenue Code, less any payments she makes toward the premium for the policy.

The Section 79 Schedule calls for $0.23 per $1,000 per month ($150 \times 0.23 \times 12 = \$414$).
$414 – $240 = $174.

The $240 = $20 per month payment by Erin × 12 months.

Insurance—Analysis of Risk Exposures

3. d

The Ackermans are deficient in disability insurance for Tom.

Health insurance appears to be adequate at present. Additional information is needed regarding health insurance after retirement.

The Ackermans need an umbrella policy of $1–$2 million.

The homeowners policy is deficient if the dwelling is worth $260,000 and they carry $196,000. They would need a policy with minimum coverage of $208,000 (80% of FMV) to avoid a coinsurance problem. The value of the land is $20,000. Additionally, they would need a rider for the coin collection.

Insurance—Disability Income Insurance

4. b

The elimination period is 90 days. She would begin collecting 60% of $5,416.67 per month on July 1 and collect for 6 months.

$3,250 × 6 months = $15,000.

Tax—Disability Income Benefits

5. d

Erin pays 40% of the premiums. That 40% would be nontaxable to Erin because she received no deduction for the premiums. The remainder (60%) would be taxable because the premiums were paid by her employer.

$2,250 × 40% = $1,300 × 6 = $7,800 nontaxable

$3,250 × 60% = $1,950 × 6 = $11,700 taxable

Comment: Because a portion of the benefit is taxable, the benefit of 60% of gross pay may be inadequate coverage.

Insurance—Homeowners

6. b

$18,596 of the loss would be paid by the insurance company.

Loss amount is $20,000.

$260,000 × 0.80 = $208,000 needed coverage to avoid coinsurance.

[($196,000 ÷ $208,000) × $20,000] − $250 = $18,596

Tax—Basis of Gift Property

7. d

First, Erin's adjusted taxable basis must be determined.

Sale Price	$40,000	
Basis for Gains	(33,000)	Basis for Losses $28,000
Long-Term Capital Gain	$7,000	

The basis of a gift to a donee is the donor's basis, except when the fair market value at the date of the gift is less than the donor's basis, in which case, the donee has a double basis (the fair market value for losses and the donor's basis for gains). Any gift tax paid on *appreciation* of the asset in the hands of the donor may be added pro rata to the basis of the donee. In this situation, there was no appreciation as of the date of the gift, and, therefore, the pro rata share of the gift tax cannot be added to basis. Stirling's original basis was $33,000.

Tax—Basis of Gift Property

8. b

The basis of a gift to a donee is generally the basis of the donor ($5,000). In addition, the donee can add the pro rata share of any gift tax paid by the donor on the portion of the fair market value that represents appreciation [(Appreciation ÷ FMV) × Gift Tax Paid] = Basis Adjustment.

$5,000 + (($25,000 ÷ $30,000) × $5,000) = $9,167   Erin's adjusted taxable basis

Investments—Collectibles

9. a

A coin collection is illiquid.

Retirement—Traditional IRA

10. c

Tom can make a deductible contribution of up to $5,000 for 2007 ($4,000 maximum deductible contribution plus $1,000 catch-up since he is 50+). A couple with one spouse who is an "active participant" in a qualified plan will not preclude deduction for the other spouse until their combined AGI exceeds $156,000. No deduction is allowed for the spouse of an active participant if their combined AGI exceeds $166,000. Erin's contribution is not deductible because she is an "active participant" in a qualified plan and their joint AGI exceeds $103,000 (the 2007 phaseout for taxpayers married filing jointly).

Retirement—Plan Selection for Businesses

11. c

Because Tom's business is relatively small, only generates $50,000 of income, and he has no other employees besides his son, it is not reasonable to incur the costs of a qualified plan, unless he is trying to maximize his deferred income.

A defined-benefit plan is too expensive. A money-purchase pension plan provides the same benefit as a profit-sharing plan or a SEP, but the money-purchase plan requires mandatory contributions each year.

Tom can, however, defer more in a SIMPLE than in the other plans. In the SIMPLE, he can defer $13,000 ($10,500 salary deferral, plus $2,500 as a catch-up contribution) plus receive a 3 percent match.

In a SEP, he would be limited to $9,235 as follows:

$50,000	Schedule C income
(3,825)	1/2 self-employment tax (FICA)
$46,175	Net
$9,235	20% of net Schedule C income (0.25 ÷ 1.25 = 20%)

Retirement—Plan Characteristics

12. c

The defined-benefit plan and the money-purchase pension plan both require annual funding. The SEP and the profit-sharing plan both provide the same contribution of 25 percent of earned income (converts to 20 percent because he is self-employed).

Although a SEP or profit-sharing plan provides tremendous flexibility, a 401(k) plan could provide the same flexibility and provide a significantly higher benefit.

Tom is self-employed and, therefore, must first reduce his Schedule C net income by half his self-employment tax and then take 20% of the result.

$50,000	Schedule C income
(3,825)	1/2 self-employment tax (FICA)
$46,175	Net
$9,235	20% of net Schedule C income (0.25 ÷ 1.25 = 20%)

Tom can contribute approximately $9,235 with either a SEP or a profit-sharing plan. With a 401(k) plan, he can increase the contribution by $20,500 ($15,500 salary deferral plus $5,000 as a catch-up contribution) to $29,735 for 2007. This dramatic change is a result of the plan limit no longer including salary deferrals.

Retirement—403(b) Plans

13. a

- For 2007, employee elective deferral contributions are deductible up to $15,500. Since Erin is over age 50, she will be allowed to contribute an additional $5,000 for 2007 as a "catch-up" adjustment. She is also eligible for a second $3,000 catch-up adjustment, since she has worked for the university for over 15 years and has not been making contributions to the 403(b) plan in past years.

- Rollovers are allowable.

- Ten-year averaging is not permitted for 403(b) plans.

Insurance—Liability

14. b

The collateral source rule holds that damages assessed against an individual should not be reduced by the existence of other sources of recovery available to the injured party, such as insurance.

Estates—Gross Estate

15. e

$1,052,500. See the explanation for Question 18.

Estates—Probate Estate

16. d

The condo would be excluded from the probate estate. See the following chart.

Estates—Buy-Sell Agreements

17. **d**

Buy-sell agreements can be established for sole proprietorships. All other statements are correct.

Estates—Marital Deduction

18. **b**

$466,277. See the following chart.

CHART FOR QUESTIONS 15, 16, AND 18

	Total	Gross Estate (Tom)	Probate Assets	Liabilities	Qualified for Marital Deduction	Comment
Cash & Cash Equivalents	$35,000	$17,500	$0	$0	$17,500	JTWROS
Proprietorship	400,000	400,000	400,000	0	0	
IRA Tom	40,000	40,000	0	0	40,000	Beneficiary
Stock Portfolio	135,000	135,000	135,000	0	135,000	
Condo	160,000	80,000	0	49,665	80,000	JTWROS
Personal Residence	280,000	140,000	0	76,558	140,000	JTWROS
Autos	20,000	10,000	10,000	7,375	0	JT only
Personal Property	60,000	30,000	0	0	30,000	JTWROS
Insurance	200,000	200,000	0	0	200,000	Beneficiary
		$1,052,500 (#15)	$545,000 (#16)	$133,598	$642,500	

Marital Deduction =

642,500	Amount qualifying for marital deduction
(50,000)	Administrative expenses
(126,223)	Liabilities for the property she is inheriting
466,277	Marital deduction

The marital deduction is limited to the amount of assets the spouse will actually receive.

Estates—Minimization of Estate Taxes

19. **e**

The overall estate plan is poor. Each estate is overqualified. If one spouse dies soon after the other, there will be an estate tax liability. In addition, the wills are not written consistent with the Ackermans' likely objectives (the wills disinherit Riley).

Estates—Minimization of Estate Taxes

20. e

1. Use an ILIT for each insurance policy. Make the current owner of the insurance a trust. The life-income beneficiary would be the spouse who could disclaim. The principal beneficiaries could be the children.

2. Leave sufficient assets in a credit shelter trust with power to invade for health, education, maintenance, and support for all beneficiaries. Life-income beneficiary is the spouse. Remainder beneficiaries are the children.

3. Annual gifting will reduce the value of the estate and can be completed without incurring gift tax.

4. Change the titling of insurance policies.

Investments—Capitalized Earnings

21. c

Rental Income (Net)		$12,000
Operation Costs	$1,200	
Taxes	800	
Association Dues	3,600	
Insurance Premiums	850	
Total Expenses		(6,450)
Net Operating Income		$5,550

FMV = $160,000 (from Balance Sheet)

$$\text{Implied Capitalization Rate} = \frac{\$5,550}{\$160,000} = 3.469\%$$

Note: Neither depreciation nor mortgage interest are used in determining the value of the real estate.

Investments—Treynor Ratio

22. d

$$\text{Treynor Index} = \frac{R_p - R_f}{B_p} = \frac{0.14 - 0.3}{1.02593} = 0.1072$$

Weighted Beta

Fund	FMV	Beta	FMV × Beta
A	$25,000	1.3	32,500
B	40,000	1.0	40,000
C	60,000	0.9	54,000
D	10,000	1.2	12,000
	$135,000		$138,500

$$\text{The Weighted Beta} = \frac{\$138,500}{\$135,000} = 1.02593$$

Note: The T-bill rate of 3% is used as the risk-free rate.

Investments—Performance Measures

23. b

R^2 (Coefficient of Determination) is an indication of the percentage of returns, which is attributable to the market, as well as the percentage of systematic risk within the portfolio. Since R^2 equals 25% $(0.5)^2$, systematic risk only represents about one-fourth of the total risk within the portfolio. Since R^2 is so low and beta only measures systematic risk, beta will not be a reliable measure of risk. Similarly, since Treynor and alpha both rely on beta as the risk measure, it would not be appropriate to use either performance measure. The Sharpe ratio uses standard deviation as the measure of risk. Since standard deviation measures total risk, the Sharpe ratio is the preferred measure.

$$\text{Sharpe Ratio for the Portfolio} = \frac{R_p - R_f}{\sigma_p} = \frac{14\% - 3\%}{18\%} = 0.6111$$

$$\text{Sharpe Ratio for the Market} = \frac{R_p - R_f}{\sigma_p} = \frac{12\% - 3\%}{14\%} = 0.6429$$

Since the Sharpe ratio for the market is higher than the portfolio, the market has a higher risk-adjusted rate of return.

Tax—Rental Real Estate

24. d

Up to $25,000 of rental real estate losses are deductible by a taxpayer against ordinary income. The $25,000 loss allowance is phased out one dollar for every two dollars that AGI (excluding the condo) exceeds $100,000. The Ackerman's AGI is more than $100,000 (excluding the condo), so the loss on the condo will not be fully deductible.

A is incorrect. Losses up to $25,000 from rental properties can be deducted directly against ordinary income, subject to AGI limits.

B is incorrect. Since the condo is being depreciated under the Modified Accelerated Cost Recovery system, there will be an AMT adjustment for depreciation.

C is incorrect. Since the condo is depreciable real property, the portion of any gain on sale of the condo that represents depreciation recapture will be taxed at a 25% rate.

BARRY AND KAY BLOCKER

Case Scenario

Barry and Kay Blocker

CASE SCENARIO

Today is December 31, 2007. Barry and Kay Blocker have come to you, a financial planner, for help in developing a plan to accomplish their financial goals. From your initial meeting together, you have gathered the following information:

PERSONAL BACKGROUND AND INFORMATION

Barry Blocker (Age 67)

Barry Blocker's date of birth is May 11, 1940. He has been employed for 20 years as a partner at Blocker Securities (Blocker). He participates in a Keogh plan at Blocker. He was previously employed for 20 years as a broker with Semper Investors, Inc., where he participated in the 401(k) plan.

Kay Blocker (Age 67)

Kay Blocker's date of birth is January 10, 1940. She has volunteered at the Boys and Girls Clubs of America and the Associated Charities for the past 15 years.

The Blockers

They have been married 42 years. Both Barry and his wife, Kay, are currently in good health, although Barry had knee replacement surgery 8 years ago. Barry's life expectancy is 17 years. Kay's life expectancy is 20 years. Their joint life expectancy is 26 years.

Children

Katie	Age 39	2 children
Denise	Age 36	5 children
Lauren	Age 30	4 children
Jessica	Age 29	3 children
Barry, Jr.	Age 18	No children

All of the girls are healthy, employed, married, and not living with Barry and Kay. Barry, Jr. is an unemployed, single, high school graduate, living with his parents.

PERSONAL AND FINANCIAL OBJECTIVES

- Barry plans to sell his share of the business.
  - He will sell half of his share of the business to his key employee, Andrew Byland.
  - He will sell the other half to his oldest daughter, Katie, who is the senior broker in the firm.
- Barry plans to retire now and begin his retirement by traveling around the world with his wife.
- After traveling around the world, Barry plans to return to the business as a self-employed consultant on a fee basis beginning January 1, 2009. He expects to earn $250,000 per year in consulting fees.
- Barry's grandchild, Beau (Katie's youngest child), was born with a serious physical disability; Barry plans to give Beau $2 million in trust.

ECONOMIC INFORMATION

- The couple expects inflation to average 4% annually.
- Expected stock market returns are 10% annually, as measured by the S&P 500 index, with a standard deviation of 10%.
- The 30-day T-bill is yielding 3.5%.
- The 30-year Treasury bond is yielding 7.5%.
- Current mortgage rates are 7.5% for 15 years and 8.0% for 30 years. In addition, closing costs (3% of the mortgage) are added to any refinancing loan.

INSURANCE INFORMATION

Life Insurance

Neither spouse has life insurance.

Health Insurance

Barry's business provides coverage for both Kay and himself during employment and retirement.
- Major medical 80/20.
- $250 deductible per person.
- $1,000,000 cap.
- $2,000 family stop loss provision.

Disability Insurance

Neither Barry nor Kay has disability insurance.

Homeowners Insurance

HO-3 on the primary residence and vacation homes.

	Residence	Vacation Home 1	Vacation Home 2
Dwelling	$975,000	$700,000	$600,000
Coinsurance	80/20	80/20	80/20
Deductible	$250	$250	$250

Umbrella Policy

$3 million.

Automobile Insurance

Maximum liability, $100,000/$300,000/$50,000, no comprehensive or collision.

Insurance Premiums

- Car insurance: $6,000 per year for all three automobiles.
- Homeowners insurance: $2,400 per year (includes all homes).
- Boat insurance: $1,200 per year (covered under the umbrella policy).
- Umbrella policy: $1,000 per year.

INVESTMENT INFORMATION

- The Blockers have a required rate of return of 8%.
- The Blockers have a medium-to-high-risk tolerance, but see little need to take excessive risks due to their net worth.
- Barry plans to sell 4,468 shares of Q-Mart stock to his daughter, Jessica, who is an employee of Q-Mart. Barry anticipates the stock will appreciate greatly in the upcoming years. (The stock was purchased four years ago for $26.66 per share, and is currently trading at $11.25 per share.)

INCOME TAX INFORMATION

- Barry and Kay are currently in the highest federal income tax bracket (35% marginal rate).
- They also pay state taxes of 9.5% for a total of 44.5%.
- For personal income tax reporting, Barry has a $700,000 salary.
- They do not reside in a community property state.

RETIREMENT INFORMATION

- The 401(k) plan has a balance of $600,000 consisting of a portfolio of small cap value stocks. This portfolio is projected to average a return of 16% over the next 20 years with a standard deviation of 8%.
- His scheduled Social Security retirement benefit is $15,000 next year and will increase at the expected CPI of 4%.
- Barry has a profit-sharing Keogh plan. His company contributes $12,000 per year into the profit-sharing plan. The contributions to this plan have been made out of the company's profits. The balance is a result of an annual contribution of $12,000, with a 7% average return since July 1, 1988.
- Barry and Kay will continue to collect $200,000 per year in rental proceeds from Commercial Property A.
- Barry will receive $50,000 per year from the Charitable Remainder Annuity Trust that owns Commercial Property B.

GIFTS, ESTATES, TRUSTS, AND WILL INFORMATION

Gifts

The following are Barry Blocker's only lifetime gifts (Kay has made no taxable gifts).

1. A 5% CRAT (Charitable Remainder Annuity Trust) was established by Barry this year by transferring to the CRAT an apartment building (Commercial Property B) that was inherited from Barry's grandfather. The initial valuation of the trust was $1,000,000, with the initial income in the first year projected to be $50,000 beginning next year. The charitable remainder beneficiary is the Chicago Art Institute.

2. Although the trust document has not been finalized, Barry is working with an attorney to draft an irrevocable trust for the benefit of his grandchild, Beau, who is the youngest child of Katie. Barry will contribute $2 million to the trust. Under the provisions of the trust, Katie will receive income from the trust for the rest of her life, with the remainder of the trust passing to Beau at Katie's death. The trustee will have the authority to make distributions of trust principal during Katie's lifetime to Beau as the trustee sees fit.

3. Kay has made no taxable gifts during her lifetime nor have any gifts been split.

Estates

For the purpose of estimating estate tax liability of both spouses:

- The last illness and funeral expenses are expected to be $250,000 each. (Terminal illnesses anticipated.)

- Estate administration expenses are estimated at $200,000 each.

Wills

Mr. and Mrs. Blocker have simple wills. They have left all probate assets to each other. Each will also include a 6-month survivorship clause. Debts and taxes are to be paid from the residue of the estate.

WILL

Excerpts from Barry's Statutory Last Will and Testament

I, BARRY BLOCKER, SR. being of sound mind and wishing to make proper disposition of my property in the event of my death, do declare this to be my Last Will and Testament. I revoke all of my prior wills and codicils.

1.1   I have been married but once, and only to Kay Blocker with whom I am presently living.

1.2   Out of my marriage to Kay Blocker, five children were born, namely, Katie Blocker, Denise Blocker, Lauren Blocker, Jessica Blocker, and Barry Blocker, Jr.

1.3   I have adopted no one nor has anyone adopted me.

3.1   I give my entire estate to Kay Blocker, my wife.

3.2   In the event that Kay Blocker predeceases me or fails to survive me for more than 6 months from the date of my death, I give my entire estate to my children Katie Blocker, Denise Blocker, Lauren Blocker, Jessica Blocker, and Barry Blocker, Jr., in equal and undivided 1/5 shares.

3.3   In the event that any of the named heirs or legatees should predecease me, die within six months from the date of my death, disclaim or otherwise fail to accept any property bequeathed to him or her and said legatee has no descendants, his or her share of all of my property of which I die possessed shall be given to the surviving named legatees.

5.1   I name Kay Blocker to serve as my executrix of my succession, with full seizin and without bond.

5.2   I direct that the expenses of my last illness, funeral, and the administration of my estate shall be paid by my executrix as soon as practicable after my death.

5.3   All inheritance, estate, succession, transfer, and other taxes (including interest and penalties thereon) payable by reason of my death shall be apportioned in accordance with the law.

STATEMENT OF CASH FLOWS
Barry & Kay Blocker
Annual Statement of Cash Flows
January 1, 2007—December 31, 2007

CASH INFLOWS:

Salary	Barry's Salary	$700,000	
	Kay's Salary	0	
	Total Salary		$700,000
Rental Income			200,000
Dividend Income	Barry	$5,000	
	Kay	1,500	
	Total Dividend Income		6,500
Interest Income[1]			1,000
Total Income			**$907,500**

CASH OUTFLOWS

Mortgage Payments	Primary Residence	$37,030	
	Vacation Home I	45,181	
	Vacation Home II	79,308	
	Total Mortgage Payments		$161,519
Insurance Premiums	Homeowners	$2,400	
	Auto	6,000	
	Boat	1,200	
	Umbrella	1,000	
	Total Insurance Premiums		$10,600
Miscellaneous Expenses	Credit Card Payments	$ 2,400	
	Entertainment	50,000	
	Food	14,400	
	Clothes	30,000	
	Utilities	24,000	
	Charity	90,000	
	Total Miscellaneous Expenses		$210,800
Tax	Property	$ 84,000	
	Income Tax	408,375	
	Total Tax		$492,375
Total Outflows			**$875,294**
Discretionary Cash			**$32,206**

Notes to Financial Statements:

[1]Income from the CRAT of $50,000 is not included from the Statement of Cash Flows.

STATEMENT OF FINANCIAL POSITION
Barry & Kay Blocker
Statement of Financial Position
As of December 31, 2007

ASSETS[1]			LIABILITIES AND NET WORTH		
			Liabilities[2]		
Cash/Cash Equivalents			**Current Liabilities**		
JT	Cash	$100,000	W	Credit Card 1	$1,000
			W	Credit Card 2	15,000
Total Cash/Cash Equivalent		$100,000	**Total Current Liabilities**		$16,000
Invested Assets			**Long-Term Liabilities**		
H	Blocker Securities	$5,000,000	JT	Mortgage—Primary	$258,630
W	Kay's Portfolio	500,000	JT	Mortgage—Vacation 1	369,428
H	Deferred Annuity	233,047	JT	Mortgage—Vacation 2	687,444
H	Retirement Plan 401(k)	600,000	**Total Long-Term Liabilities**		$1,315,502
H	Keogh	526,382	**Total Liabilities**		$1,331,502
H	Barry's Portfolio	4,000,000			
JT	Commercial Property A	1,500,000			
Total Investments		$12,359,429			
Personal Use Assets			**Net Worth**		$15,087,927
JT	Primary Residence	$1,300,000			
JT	Vacation Home 1	800,000			
JT	Vacation Home 2	700,000			
JT	Personal Property/Furniture	875,000			
H	Auto 1	80,000			
H	Auto 2	55,000			
W	Auto 3	40,000			
W	Yacht	110,000			
Total Personal Use		$3,960,000			
Total Assets		$16,419,429	**Total Liabilities and Net Worth**		$16,419,429

Notes to Financial Statements:

[1]Assets are stated at fair market value.

[2]Liabilities are stated at principal only.

Property Ownership:

JT = Joint tenancy with right of survivorship.

H = Husband separate property.

W = Wife separate property.

INFORMATION REGARDING ASSETS AND LIABILITIES

Blocker Security Investments

(Barry is a 50% partner)

- Market value of Barry's interest is $5 million.
- Adjusted tax basis $1 million.
- Transfer of business (sale).
  - 50%: Ten-year installment sale to Andrew Byland for a down payment of 20% on January 1, 2008, and monthly payments beginning February 1, 2008, at 10% interest.
  - 50%: Self-Canceling Installment Note (SCIN) to Katie.

Primary Residence

- Jointly owned—purchased 14 years ago.
- Market value $1,300,000.
- Original purchase price $300,000.
- Current mortgage @ 12% interest. Payment: $3,085.84 (30 year) per month.

Vacation Home 1

- Jointly owned—purchased last year.
- Market value $800,000.
- Original purchase price $400,000.
- Current mortgage @ 7.75% interest. Payment: $3,765.10 (15 year) per month.

Vacation Home 2

- Jointly owned—Purchased this year.
- Market value $700,000.
- Original purchase price $700,000.
- Current mortgage @ 7.8% interest. Payment: $6,608.99 (15 year) per month.

Commercial Property A

- Original site of business.
- Fair market value: $1,500,000.
- Adjusted basis $200,000.

Single Premium Deferred Annuity

- Barry purchased this annuity on July 1, 1981, for $60,000. The current fair market value is $233,047.
- Earnings rate of 6% compounded annually is expected in near term.
- Annuity start date is January 1, 2009, at which time the fair market value is projected to be $247,030 and will consist of monthly payments made over 180 payments (15 years).
- If Barry dies before the annuity start date, Kay is named beneficiary (100% Joint and Survivor Annuity).

Summary of Indebtedness

Asset	Date of 1st Pmt.	Mortgage Amount	Term/ Years	Interest	Monthly Payments	Remaining Payments	Remaining Balance
Primary Residence	4/1/93	300,000.00	30	12.00%	($3,085.84)	183	$258,629.77
Vacation Home 1	1/1/06	400,000.00	15	7.75%	($3,765.10)	156	$369,427.87
Vacation Home 2	7/1/07	700,000.00	15	7.80%	($6,608.99)	174	$687,443.57
Total							$1,315,501.21

Detailed Investment Portfolios

Barry's Portfolio

Description	Acquired	Shares	Adjusted Basis	Beta	Current FMV
Sears	8/00	16,325	$201,633	0.9	$830,214
Q-Mart	1/03	4,468	$119,117	1.2	$50,265
Canon Inc.	2/05	22,249	$400,188	1.4	$2,230,462
*RC Inc.	9/05	3,742	$67,181	1.5	$222,600
WW Grainger	10/07	4,257	$221,435	1.2	$311,293
Circuit City Stores	9/07	10,561	$304,062	1.2	$355,166
Total			$1,313,616		$4,000,000

* The RC Inc. stock is Section 1244 Small Business Stock.

Kay's Portfolio

Description	Acquired	Shares	Adjusted Basis	Beta	Current FMV
Tenet Health Care	1/01	2,542	$30,504	0.6	$50,209
Bay Bank Inc.	2/05	1,500	$120,000	0.5	$167,250
Microsoft	9/05	589	$53,010	0.7	$66,189
Zenith	10/06	22,190	$177,520	0.8	$216,352
Total			$381,034		$500,000

BARRY AND KAY BLOCKER

Questions

Barry and Kay Blocker

QUESTIONS

1. Assume that today Barry sells the Q-Mart stock to Jessica for the current fair market value. What are Barry's tax consequences that result from this transaction?

    a. LTCG of $50,265.

    b. STCG of $50,265.

    c. STCL of $68,852.

    d. LTCL of $68,852.

    e. No gain or loss.

2. Assume that Barry sells the Q-Mart stock to Jessica for the current fair market value as of December 31, 2007, and Jessica resells the Q-Mart stock at $16.50 per share in November of next year. What is the tax consequence to Jessica?

    a. No gain or loss.

    b. STCG of $23,457.

    c. LTCG of $23,457.

    d. STCL of $45,395.

    e. LTCL of $45,395.

3. If Barry sells all of his RC Inc. stock this year at the current fair market value, what will be the tax treatment?

    a. LTCG of $155,419.

    b. Ordinary income $100,000 and LTCG $55,419.

    c. Ordinary income $100,000 and STCG $55,419.

    d. Ordinary income $100,000 and carryover $55,419 ordinary income.

    e. Ordinary income $50,000 and carryover $105,419 ordinary income.

4. If Barry sells all of his RC Inc. stock this year at the current fair market value, what will the tax treatment be if the stock was 1202 stock instead of 1244 stock?

    a. LTCG of $55,419.

    b. LTCG of $77,710.

    c. LTCG of $105,419.

    d. LTCG of $116,564.

    e. LTCG of $155,419.

5. Which of the following techniques could be used to lower Barry's gross estate?

   1. Totten Trust.

   2. Revocable Living Trust.

   3. Qualified Personal Residence Trust (QPRT).

   4. Pay-on-Death Arrangements (POD).

      a. 1 and 3.

      b. 2 and 4.

      c. 2 only.

      d. 3 only.

      e. 2, 3, and 4.

6. Barry and Kay want you to evaluate their insurance situation. Which of the following statements correctly describe(s) their insurance situation?

   1. They have a serious disability insurance deficiency.

   2. The homeowners policy is appropriate and adequate.

   3. The umbrella policy is adequate.

   4. They are underinsured for life insurance.

      a. 3 only.

      b. 2 and 3.

      c. 1, 2, and 4.

      d. 2, 3, and 4.

      e. 1, 2, 3, and 4.

7. Assume Barry begins a consulting career, and he expects to have taxable earned income of $100,000 per year. Which of the following statements correctly describes the impact of his consulting activities?

      a. He will lose Social Security benefits of $1 for every $2 earned.

      b. He will lose Social Security benefits of $1 for every $3 earned over $34,440.

      c. He will lose Social Security benefits of $1 for every $2 earned over $12,960.

      d. He will lose all of his Social Security benefits.

      e. None of the above.

8. Which of the following investment planning recommendations would you make to Kay and Barry?

    1. Diversify their portfolio since a significant amount of wealth is invested in only a few stocks.

    2. Since they can tolerate high amounts of risk, their current portfolio is fine.

    3. Due to their tax bracket, they should consider investing in tax-free securities, such as municipal bonds.

    4. Since their basis in several stocks is so low, they should not sell any of these securities.

    5. Any investment with taxable income should be made in Barry's 401(k) or Keogh plan to avoid any additional tax liability.

        a. 1 and 5.

        b. 2 and 5.

        c. 1, 3, and 5.

        d. 2, 3, and 4.

        e. 1, 2, 4, and 5.

9. If Barry were to refinance his primary residence at current mortgage market rates for 15 years, how much would his monthly payment decline?

        a. $614.23.

        b. $616.38.

        c. $688.30.

        d. $2,397.54.

        e. $2,467.47.

10. Assume Barry began his consulting in 2009. Which of the following is/are correct regarding his ability to defer taxes utilizing a qualified retirement plan (assume plan limits will be the same as the current year)?

    1. He can contribute the maximum amount to a profit-sharing Keogh.

    2. A 401(k) plan will allow him to shelter more than a profit-sharing plan.

    3. A Tandem plan is a great choice because it will allow for a maximum contribution.

        a. 1 only.

        b. 2 only.

        c. 1 and 2.

        d. 1 and 3.

        e. 1, 2, and 3.

11. Which of the following transfers will not result in a taxable gift to Barry? For purposes of the annual exclusion and lifetime applicable credit amount, assume they take place in the year 2007.

   1. Barry pays each grandchild's private school tuition to the school ($6,000 each).
   2. Barry pays City Hospital for the hospital bill of a friend ($15,000).
   3. Barry gives a distant cousin money for law school tuition ($25,000).
   4. Barry pays the tuition for Barry Jr. to Horizon College ($30,000).

      a. 2 only.
      b. 1 and 3.
      c. 1, 2, and 4.
      d. 1, 3, and 4.
      e. 1, 2, 3, and 4.

12. With regard to the installment sale portion of Barry's interest in Blocker Securities to Andrew Byland, how much, if any, of the down payment is taxable to Barry in 2008, and what is the character of the down payment?

      a. No taxable income; a return of basis.
      b. Capital gain of $400,000.
      c. Ordinary income of $250,000 and capital gain of $150,000.
      d. Ordinary income of $500,000 and capital gain of $300,000.
      e. Capital gain of $800,000.

13. Calculate the total monthly installment payments that will be made to Barry by Byland during 2008.

      a. $288,329.
      b. $290,732.
      c. $314,541.
      d. $317,162.
      e. $363,415.

14. If Barry dies January 1 of next year, and Kay survives him by 6 months, which of the following is true regarding the installment sale to Andrew Byland?

      a. Because this is a SCIN, nothing will be included in Barry's gross estate.
      b. The summation of the remaining notes payable will be included in Barry's gross estate, but will qualify for the unlimited marital deduction.
      c. The summation of the remaining notes payable will be included in Barry's gross estate, but will not qualify for the unlimited marital deduction.
      d. The discounted present value of the notes will be included in Barry's gross estate and will qualify for the unlimited marital deduction.
      e. The discounted present value of the notes will be included in Barry's gross estate but will not qualify for the unlimited marital deduction.

15. Barry has paid his general liability insurance premiums for Blocker Securities for 2 years in advance (January 1, 2008–December 31, 2009). The premium for the 2 years was $144,000. At the time of his sale of the firm to Byland and Katie, there will be a prepaid insurance amount. Barry plans to assign the insurance policy to the new partnership of Katie and Byland and, thereby, wants them to pay him for the remaining prepaid insurance premiums. Regarding the validity and effectiveness of the assignment of the policy:

    a.   The assignment is effective and Katie and Byland each owe Barry $72,000.

    b.   The assignment is effective and Katie and Byland each owe Barry $36,000.

    c.   The assignment is effective and Katie and Byland each owe Barry $36,000 plus interest.

    d.   Barry cannot assign the remaining general liability insurance to Katie and Byland without consent of the insurer.

16. What is the likelihood that the investments in Barry's 401(k) plan will yield a return that is below the Blockers required rate of return?

    a.   0%.

    b.   8%.

    c.   16%.

    d.   24%.

    e.   34%.

17. Barry and Kay are considering the purchase of a joint and survivor (second-to-die) life insurance policy for the purpose of wealth replacement, for the assets that were transferred to the CRAT and to help to create estate liquidity. Which of the following is/are the most appropriate owner(s) for the policy?

    a.   The children should own the policy to have cash to pay estate taxes and/or loans to the estate.

    b.   Kay should own the policy since Barry's estate is overqualified.

    c.   An irrevocable life insurance trust should be created to own the policy to keep the proceeds outside both Kay's and Barry's estates.

    d.   Barry and Kay should own the policy jointly to keep control over the cash value build up.

18. If Barry dies December 31, 2008, how much of an annual Social Security benefit will Kay expect to receive for year 2009?

    a. $7,500.

    b. $7,800.

    c. $11,700.

    d. $15,000.

    e. $15,600.

19. Which of the following is/are true?

    a. As a result of setting up the CRAT, Barry will receive a charitable income tax deduction this year equal to the PV of the remainder interest in the trust.

    b. If Barry dies in March of next year (after the sale of his business), the value of the installment note and the SCIN will be included in his gross estate.

    c. Commercial Property B will be included in Barry's gross estate, if he dies next year.

    d. Payments received from the CRAT will be income tax free to Barry.

20. Barry recently attended an investment seminar and learned about the concepts of business risk and concentrated portfolios. The speaker discussed many topics that day, and Barry's head was spinning. He has already addressed the issue of Blocker Securities by entering into two transactions. However, he would like to consider minimizing the risk attributable to owning $2.2 million of Cannon, Inc. Which of the following would be a good method for dealing with his concentrated portfolio?

    1. Transfer the stock to an exchange-traded fund.

    2. Establish an employee stock ownership plan.

    3. Enter into a zero-cost collar.

        a. 1 only.

        b. 3 only.

        c. 1 and 3.

        d. 1 and 2.

        e. 1, 2, and 3.

21. Assuming the trust being established for the benefit of Beau is finalized, which of the following statements is correct?

    a. At the time the trust is finalized, Barry is considered to have made a direct skip for generation skipping tax purposes.

    b. If Katie died two years after the trust was created, the trust would be included in her gross estate at the full date of death value.

    c. If the trustee distributes $50,000 of principal to Beau during Katie's lifetime, a taxable distribution has occurred for generation skipping tax purposes.

    d. If Barry dies within three years of the establishment of the trust, the trust will be included in his gross estate at the full date of death value.

BARRY AND KAY BLOCKER

Solutions

Barry and Kay Blocker

ANSWER SUMMARY

1.	e	6.	a	11.	c	16.	c	21.	c
2.	a	7.	e	12.	b	17.	c		
3.	a	8.	c	13.	b	18.	e		
4.	e	9.	b	14.	d	19.	a		
5.	d	10.	a	15.	d	20.	b		

SUMMARY OF TOPICS

1.   Tax—Related-Party Transaction
2.   Tax—Related-Party Transaction
3.   Tax—Section 1244 Stock
4.   Tax—Section 1202 Stock
5.   Estates—Minimization of Estate Taxes
6.   Insurance—Analysis of Risk Exposures
7.   Retirement—Social Security Benefits
8.   Investments—Portfolio Diversifications
9.   Fundamentals—Mortgage Refinancing
10. Retirement—Qualified Retirement Plans
11. Estates—Gift Tax Compliance
12. Estates—Installment Note
13. Fundamentals—Time Value of Money
14. Estates—Installment Note
15. Insurance—Legal Aspects of Insurance
16. Investments—Normal Distribution
17. Estates—Use of Life Insurance in Estate Planning
18. Retirement—Social Security Benefits
19. Estates—Gross Estate
20. Investments—Strategies for Dealing With Concentrated Portfolios
21. Estates—GSTT

SOLUTIONS

Tax—Related-Party Transaction

1. **e**

Barry has an economic loss of $68,852 that would be realized but not recognized because this is a related party transaction. Thus, there would be no gain or loss associated with this transaction.

Tax—Related-Party Transaction

2. **a**

Jessica has an adjusted taxable basis for gains of $26.66 ($119,117 ÷ 4,468) per share and an adjusted taxable basis for losses of $11.25 ($50,265 ÷ 4,468) per share. There is no gain or loss because the stock was sold for a price that is between $26.66 and $11.25. This was a related-party sale loss of property, and, therefore, the double-basis rule applies.

Tax—Section 1244 Stock

3. **a**

Barry would have a long-term capital gain of $155,419. While this is Section 1244 stock (small business stock), the 1244 rules only apply to losses, not gains. The treatment of Section 1244 for gains is the same as any ordinary stock transaction.

Sale Price	$222,600
Adjusted Taxable Basis	(67,181)
Long-Term Capital Gain	$155,419

Tax—Section 1202 Stock

4. **e**

Although there is a 50% exclusion for stock that qualifies as Section 1202 stock, Barry has not met the five-year holding period. Therefore, the stock is taxed as a normal LTCG.

Estates—Minimization of Estate Taxes

5. **d**

Only the Qualified Personal Residence Trust (QPRT) will lower the gross estate. All of the other techniques are used to avoid probate. A Totten trust will not lower the gross estate because it is a *revocable* trust and the depositor can change the beneficiary at any time. A Totten trust is similar to a bank account except the depositor puts the money into an account under the depositor's name as trustee for the beneficiary. While a Totten trust will not decrease the gross estate, it will allow the funds to escape the probate estate, and will transfer to the listed beneficiary upon death of the depositor.

Insurance—Analysis of Risk Exposures

6. **a**

The homeowners policy has put them in a coinsurance position; thus, the policy is inappropriate and inadequate. They do not have a need for life insurance due to their net worth and liquidity. Since they are retired, they have no need for disability insurance. Their umbrella policy is adequate. The only correct statement is Statement 3.

Retirement—Social Security Benefits

7. e

The earnings test does not apply to individuals who have attained normal retirement age. Barry's normal retirement age is 65, and, therefore, he will not lose any of his Social Security benefits, even if he has earned income.

Investments—Portfolio Diversifications

8. c

Diversification of their portfolio, investment in tax-free securities, and investment of taxable income in Barry's 401(k) and Keogh plans are highly recommended. Statements 1, 3, and 5 are correct.

Fundamentals—Mortgage Refinancing

9. b

$3,085.84 (current payment) – $2,469.46 = $616.38 savings per month

		$258,629.77	Current mortgage balance
		× 1.03	For closing costs
PV	=	$266,388.66	New mortgage
n	=	180	Term
i	=	0.625 (7.5 ÷ 12)	Interest
PMT_{OA}	=	$2,469.46	Payment

Retirement—Qualified Retirement Plans

10. a

Barry can defer approximately 20% (because he is self-employed (0.25 ÷ 1.25 = 20%)). This will allow him to reach the maximum annual additions limit.

Because salary deferrals no longer count against the 25 percent plan limit, lower income earners can generally increase their overall contribution to a retirement plan by also contributing to a 401(k) plan. However, salary deferrals do count against the annual additions limit. Therefore, Barry will be maxed out with or without a 401(k) feature.

A tandem plan is not a good choice in retirement plans. Historically, its purpose was to maximize the contribution (25%) with minimal commitment (10%). Today, the profit-sharing plan alone does a better job than the old tandem plan. In addition, a tandem plan requires higher administrative costs due to maintaining multiple plans and having to file two Form 5500s.

Estates—Gift Tax Compliance

11. c

Statement 3 is not a qualified transfer and is subject to gift tax because the tuition was not paid directly to the law school. Statements 1, 2, and 4 are qualified transfers, and, therefore, none are taxable gifts.

Estates—Installment Note

12. b

There is a capital gain of $400,000.

	Value	−	Basis	=	Capital Gain
$5,000,000 value × 50% interest =	$2,500,000		$500,000		$2,000,000
	× 20%		× 20%		× 20%
The down payment is equal to:	$500,000	−	$100,000	=	$400,000

Fundamentals—Time Value of Money

13. b

n	=	120 (10 × 12)
i	=	0.8333 (10 ÷ 12)
PV	=	$2,000,000.00 (80% × $2,500,000)
PMT_{OA}	=	$ 26,430.15
		× 11 payments in 2008
Total payments =		$290,731.65

Estates—Installment Note

14. d

The discounted present value of the notes will be included in Barry's gross estate on a present value basis. The transfer of the installment notes to Kay will qualify for the unlimited marital deduction.

Insurance—Legal Aspects of Insurance

15. d

The assignment of insurance (except life insurance) is ineffective without the consent of the insurer because insurance contracts are personal. Thus, Barry cannot assign the remaining general liability insurance to Katie and Byland without the consent of the insurer.

Investments—Normal Distribution

16. c

- 68% of outcomes fall within one standard deviation.

- Because 8% is one standard deviation to the left of the mean, the probability of having a return below 8% will be 16% (50% – 34%).

- 50% represents one-half of the area under the curve.

- 34% represents one-half of the area within one standard deviation.

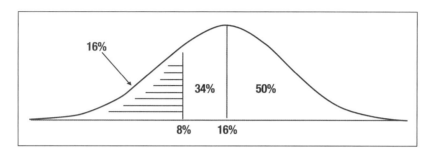

Estates—Use of Life Insurance in Estate Planning

17. c

While the children's owning the policy would keep the proceeds outside of Kay and Barry's estate, the best answer is the irrevocable life insurance trust. In the event a child was to die owning the policy, a portion of the policy's cash value would be includible in the child's estate.

Retirement—Social Security Benefits

18. e

Kay will step into Barry's place and receive $15,600 ($15,000 × 1.04). Kay is a nonworking, age-appropriate spouse and will, therefore, receive 100% of Barry's primary insurance amount. The 1.04 adjustment is made to increase the amount for inflation as stated in the scenario.

Estates—Gross Estate

19. a

Option (a) in correct because the grantor will receive an immediate income tax deduction when the CRAT is established.

Option (b) is incorrect because the SCIN will cancel upon Barry's death and, therefore, will not be included in his gross estate.

Option (c) is incorrect because the property was transferred to the CRAT and will be excluded from the gross estate.

Option (d) is incorrect because the CRAT payments will be taxable to Barry.

Investments—Strategies for Dealing With Concentrated Portfolios

20. b

Exchange-traded funds are like open-ended mutual funds that trade like closed-end funds. Examples include SPDRs, QQQ, and Diamonds. The Canon stock cannot be transferred to an exchange-traded fund.

There is no indication that Barry has control of Cannon to make a decision to establish an ESOP. There is also no indication that he owns a large portion of the stock.

A zero-cost collar is an effective method for limiting downside risk with minimal cost. A zero-cost collar is a strategy that is used to protect a gain in a long position of a stock. It consists of a long position in stock, a long put option, and a short call option. The investor purchases a put option to protect against downside risk and sells a call option to generate premium income to cover the cost of the premium for the put option.

Estates—GSTT

21. c

A "taxable distribution" has occurred for GSTT purposes.

A is incorrect. A direct skip can only occur when only skip persons are involved (a person two or more generations below the grantor). Since Katie is a non-skip person, a direct skip did not occur when the trust was established.

B is incorrect. Since Katie only possessed a life estate (terminable interest) at her death, the trust would be excluded from her gross estate at her death.

D is incorrect. Once the trust is established, the assets are out of Barry's gross estate. The three year inclusion rule only applies to life insurance and gift tax paid on gifts given within three years of death.

IDA KLAR

Case Scenario

Ida Klar

CASE SCENARIO

Today is December 31, 2007. Ida Klar has come to you, a financial planner, for help in developing a plan to accomplish her financial goals. From your initial meeting together, you have gathered the following information:

PERSONAL BACKGROUND AND INFORMATION

Ida Klar (Age 69)

Ida is a retired homemaker. She is a recent widow. Ida's 70th birthday will be March 1, 2008.

Gerard Klar (deceased)

Ida was married to Gerard Klar who died November 1 of this year at the age of 69 after a brief battle with cancer. His date of birth was June 1, 1938.

Gerard's estate is in probate. Gerard was employed 45 years as a supervisor at ABC Co., Inc., (ABC) before retiring at age 65.

The Children

Ida has two children from her marriage to Gerard: Robert (age 50) and Bryan (age 49). Robert and Bryan are each married, healthy, employed, and self-sufficient.

The Grandchildren

Robert and his wife, Gloria, have one daughter, Sharon (age 18). Sharon is currently a senior in high school and will be a freshman at Private University in the fall. The cost of tuition for Private University is currently $12,000. Ida would like to pay Sharon's tuition for this year. As a high school graduation present, Ida is paying for Sharon's trip to Europe this summer. The total cost of this trip is $3,000.

Bryan and his wife, Tara, have one son, Owen (age 17). Owen is a junior in high school. Owen is in need of orthodontic work that will cost $6,000. Ida would like to pay for Owen's orthodontic work. Ida is also considering gifting stock worth $9,000 to Owen because she wishes to treat each grandchild equally.

The Klars

They were married 50 years. Ida is currently in fair health.

PERSONAL AND FINANCIAL OBJECTIVES

- Generate sufficient income ($30,000 per year in today's dollars including any Social Security benefits).
- Consider acquiring a smaller residence.
- Explore long-term nursing care alternatives (annual cost in today's dollars $40,000).
- Donate to the American Cancer Society.
- Provide for her children and grandchildren.
- Pay Sharon's tuition ($12,000).
- Gift stock to Owen ($9,000).
- Pay for Owen's orthodontic work ($6,000).
- Send Sharon to Europe ($3,000).

ECONOMIC INFORMATION

- Inflation is expected to be 4% annually.
- No state income tax.
- Slow growth economy, stocks are expected to grow at 9.5%.

Bank lending rates are as follows:

- 15-year mortgages 7.5%.
- 30-year mortgages 8.0%.
- Secured personal loan 10.0%.

Minimum Distribution Divisors (Uniform Distribution Table)

Age	Distribution Period
70	27.4
71	26.5

INSURANCE INFORMATION

Life Insurance

Irrevocable Life Insurance Trust (ILIT)

Gerard created an ILIT 10 years ago. The only asset in the trust is a permanent life policy with a face value of $200,000. The income beneficiary of the ILIT is Ida. She is also the trustee and has a general power of appointment over the trust assets. The remainder beneficiaries are the grandchildren.

Health Insurance

Gerard and Ida were both covered under Medicare Part A.

INVESTMENT INFORMATION

Ida's investment risk tolerance is low.

INCOME TAX INFORMATION

The Klars filed federal income taxes as married filing jointly last year. Ida and Gerard have always lived in a community property state.

RETIREMENT INFORMATION

Gerard had a pension with ABC with Ida designated as the beneficiary. The pension has a lump-sum death benefit of $150,000 as one of its options. As the beneficiary, Ida can choose to receive a life annuity or a lump-sum payment from the pension.

Ida currently has an IRA with Gerard as her named beneficiary.

Ida is the named beneficiary on Gerard's IRA.

Both Gerard and Ida began receiving Social Security benefits on their respective 65th birthdays. Gerard's benefit for this year was $1,200 per month until his death in November, and Ida's benefit for this year is estimated to be $600 per month.

GIFTS, ESTATES, TRUSTS, AND WILL INFORMATION

Gerard's will left all of his probate assets to Ida. The grandchildren are named as equal contingent beneficiaries.

Ida does not have a will.

STATEMENT OF FINANCIAL POSITION
Gerard (deceased) and Ida Klar
Balance Sheet
As of December 31, 2007

	ASSETS[1]			LIABILITIES & NET WORTH	
	Cash and Equivalents			**Liabilities[2]**	
CP	Cash	$25,000		W Credit cards[3]	$20,000
CP	Savings Account	20,000			
	Total Cash and Equivalents	$45,000			
	Invested Assets				
H	Stocks	$20,000		*Total Liabilities*	$20,000
W	IRA	40,000			
H	IRA	50,000			
CP	Pension	150,000		**Net Worth**	$1,180,000
	Total Invested Assets	$260,000			
	Personal Use Assets				
CP	Primary Residence[4]	$600,000			
W	Vacation Home[5]	200,000			
CP	Auto	18,000			
CP	Furniture & Personal Property	77,000			
	Total Use Assets	$895,000			
	Total Assets	**$1,200,000**		**Total Liabilities & Net Worth**	**$1,200,000**

Notes to Financial Statements:

[1] Assets are stated at fair market value.

[2] Liabilities are stated at principal only. All liabilities are community property.

[3] Interest rate 18.3%.

[4] The primary residence was originally purchased for $110,000. There have been no additions or upgrades.

[5] The vacation home was inherited by Ida from her mother. Adjusted taxable basis is $125,000.

Other Notes to Financial Statements:

The income beneficiary of the ILIT is Ida. Remainder beneficiaries are the grandchildren. Ida has general power of appointment over trust assets. Trustee has power to invade for health, education, maintenance, and support for the grandchildren. The ILIT is not listed on the balance sheet.

INFORMATION REGARDING ASSETS AND LIABILITIES

Primary Residence

- Purchased April 1, 1970.
- Original purchase price $110,000.

Vacation Home

- Owned by Ida (fee simple).
- Inherited from her mother 17 years ago. (Fair market value at transfer to Ida of $125,000.)
- Current fair market value $200,000.
- Vacation home is located in a noncommunity property state. All payments for repairs and maintenance have been made using community property assets.

IDA KLAR

Questions

Ida Klar

1. Which of the following are appropriate for Ida's options with regard to Gerard's IRA?

    1. Ida can leave Gerard's IRA intact and receive distributions over her remaining single life expectancy, beginning in 2007.

    2. Ida can roll Gerard's IRA over to her own IRA and name the grandchildren as beneficiaries.

    3. Ida can take a complete distribution from Gerard's IRA with a step-up in basis to the fair market value at the date of death.

    4. Ida must withdraw the entire balance of Gerard's IRA over a period of time not to exceed 5 years.

        a. 1 and 2.

        b. 2 and 3.

        c. 2 and 4.

        d. 2, 3, and 4.

        e. 1, 3, and 4.

2. When must Ida receive her first distribution from her IRA account?

        a. April 1, 2008.

        b. December 31, 2008.

        c. April 1, 2009.

        d. December 31, 2009.

3. Calculate Ida's probate estate as of today assuming the pension plan is inheritable from Gerard.

        a. $960,000.

        b. $980,000.

        c. $1,000,000.

        d. $1,200,000.

        e. $1,400,000.

4. Calculate Ida's gross estate as of today assuming the pension plan is inheritable from Gerard.

        a. $960,000.

        b. $980,000.

        c. $1,000,000.

        d. $1,200,000.

        e. $1,400,000.

5. Which of the following estate planning devices should Ida consider regarding Gerard's estate?

    1. Effective disclaimer.
    2. Special use valuation election.
    3. Installment payment of estate tax election.
    4. Qualified Terminable Interest Property (QTIP) election.
        a. 1 only.
        b. 1 and 2.
        c. 2, 3, and 4.
        d. 1 and 4.
        e. 1, 2, 3, and 4.

6. Ida is considering selling her personal residence. What is Ida's adjusted taxable basis for the personal residence?

        a. $110,000.
        b. $355,000.
        c. $490,000.
        d. $500,000.
        e. $600,000.

7. Which of the following is correct regarding the titles of the vacation home property upon Gerard's death?

        a. Fee simple property of Ida.
        b. Jointly held property with survivorship rights.
        c. Community property due to commingling of funds.
        d. Fee simple, but Gerard's estate is entitled to reimbursement for one-half the expenditures for repairs, and so forth.

8. Ida would like to set up Qualified Tuition Plans (QTPs) for college tuition expenses for both Sharon and Owen. If Ida did not want to use any of her applicable credit amount in making the transfer, what is the total amount she could contribute to the plan this year and still avoid all gift and generation-skipping transfer taxes?

        a. $2,000.
        b. $12,000.
        c. $24,000.
        d. $48,000.
        e. $120,000.

9. Ida is considering making a charitable contribution for the American Cancer Society and wants the grandchildren to receive income from the property for an extended period. Which of the following charitable devices may be appropriate to meet Ida's objective?

    1. Charitable Remainder Annuity Trust.

    2. Charitable Remainder Unitrust Trust.

    3. Pooled Income Fund.

    4. Charitable Lead Trust.

        a. 1 only.

        b. 1 or 2.

        c. 1, 2, and 3.

        d. 2, 3, and 4.

        e. 1, 2, 3, and 4.

10. If Ida exercised her right to take a lump-sum cash distribution from Gerard's pension plan, how much money will she actually receive as a distribution from the plan?

        a. $60,000.

        b. $75,000.

        c. $120,000.

        d. $150,000.

        e. $180,000.

11. Which of the following Social Security benefits does Ida currently qualify for?

    1. $255 death benefit.

    2. Widow's share of retirement benefit.

    3. Caretaker's benefit.

    4. Medicare.

        a. 1 and 4.

        b. 1, 2, and 4.

        c. 2 and 3.

        d. 1, 2, 3, and 4.

12. What happens to Ida's IRA account upon her death, assuming she makes no changes to the account?

    1. The heirs get a step-up in basis.

    2. The IRA is in her gross estate.

    3. The IRA is in her probate estate.

    4. The IRA is subject to income tax upon distribution.

        a. 1 and 2.

        b. 2 and 3.

        c. 2, 3, and 4.

        d. 1, 3, and 4.

        e. 1, 2, 3, and 4.

13. Assuming that Ida has taken a lump-sum distribution from Gerard's pension plan, which combination of the following investments is appropriate for Ida?

1. Long-term bonds (average maturity 23 years).
2. Short-term bonds (average maturity 3 years).
3. Money markets.
4. T-bills.
5. Growth stocks.
6. Treasury notes.
7. Intermediate bonds (average maturity 10 years).
    a. A combination of 2, 5, 6, and 7.
    b. A combination of 1, 2, 6, and 7.
    c. A combination of 2, 3, 6, and 7.
    d. A combination of 2, 4, 5, and 6.

14. How could Ida benefit each grandchild without incurring any transfer taxes or utilizing her applicable credit amount?

1. Pay Sharon's tuition directly to the school.
2. Transfer $15,000 to Owen and use a split gift election.
3. Give Sharon the money for her trip to Europe.
4. Pay for Owen's orthodontic work directly to the dentist.
    a. 1 only.
    b. 1 and 4.
    c. 1, 3, and 4.
    d. 2, 3, and 4.
    e. 1, 2, and 3.

15. What is Ida's federal income tax filing status for the years 2007, 2008, 2009, and 2010?

	2007	2008	2009	2010
a.	MFJ	S	S	S
b.	MFJ	QW	QW	S
c.	MFJ	QW	QW	HH
d.	QW	QW	HH	HH

MFJ = Married filing jointly
QW = Qualifying widow
HH = Head of household
S = Single

16. How much will Ida's monthly Social Security benefit be next year?

    a. $600.

    b. $900.

    c. $990.

    d. $1,200.

17. On November 1, 2008, Ida decides to sell the personal residence for the fair market value as of December 31, 2007. What will be her tax consequences?

    a. No gain or loss.

    b. $240,000 long-term capital gain.

    c. $345,000 realized gain, but exempt from tax.

    d. $490,000 long-term capital gain.

18. Ida is very concerned about her long-term health and is considering enrolling in Medicare Part B. Which of the following benefits are covered under Medicare Part B?

    1. Hospice care.

    2. Medical supplies.

    3. Outpatient hospital services for diagnosis.

    4. Physicians' fees.

        a. 4 only.

        b. 1, 2, and 3.

        c. 2, 3, and 4.

        d. 1 and 2.

19. Ida has enrolled in Medicare Part B but is still concerned about the deductibles and co-pay requirements. She is considering either purchasing a Medigap policy or joining a Medicare HMO. What are the advantages of an HMO over a Medigap policy in Ida's situation?

    1. Costs are less in the HMO.

    2. She can keep her own doctors.

    3. Referrals to specialists are easier under the HMO.

    4. Limitations in coverages are generally much higher and broader under the HMO.

        a. 1 only.

        b. 2 and 4.

        c. 1, 3, and 4.

        d. 1, 2, 3, and 4.

20. Ida is worried that she will need long-term custodial care, because while her mother lived at home until age 95 she needed assistance in bathing, dressing, and toileting once she became 75 years old. Ida is worried that there will be no family member around to care for her. Which of the following would provide Ida with such continued assistance in her home?

   1. Medigap.
   2. Medicare Part A and Part B.
   3. Medicare HMO.
   4. Long-term care insurance.

      a. 4 only.
      b. 1 and 2.
      c. 3 and 4.
      d. 1, 3, and 4.

21. At her death Ida wants to maximize her benefit to the American Cancer Society and at the same time maximize benefits to her children and grandchildren. Which of the following assets would be best left to the American Cancer Society?

      a. The IRAs.
      b. The vacation home.
      c. The stocks.
      d. The primary residence.

IDA KLAR

Solutions

Ida Klar

ANSWER SUMMARY

1. a	6. e	11. b	16. d	21. a
2. c	7. d	12. c	17. a	
3. d	8. e	13. c	18. c	
4. e	9. c	14. c	19. a	
5. a	10. c	15. a	20. a	

SUMMARY OF TOPICS

1. Retirement—IRA
2. Retirement—Minimum Distributions
3. Estates—Probate Estate
4. Estates—Gross Estate
5. Estates—Postmortem Elections
6. Tax—Personal Residence
7. Fundamentals—Property Classification
8. Estates—Gifting and Educational Funding
9. Estates—Charitable Trust
10. Retirement—Pension Distribution
11. Retirement—Social Security Benefits
12. Retirement—IRA Beneficiary
13. Investments—Selection
14. Estates—Gifting
15. Tax—Filing Status
16. Retirement—Social Security Benefits
17. Tax—Sale of Personal Residence
18. Insurance—Medicare
19. Insurance—Medicare
20. Insurance—Long-Term Care
21. Estates—Charitable Giving

SOLUTIONS

Retirement—IRA

1. a

Statements 1 and 2 are correct. Since Gerard died before beginning minimum required distributions, Ida (spousal beneficiary) has the following choices with respect to Gerard's IRA:

- Ida can receive distributions over her remaining life expectancy, using the Uniform Distributions Table each year. Distributions must begin in the year in which Gerard would have reached age 70½.

- Ida can roll the IRA balance over, and wait until she attains age 70½ to begin taking minimum distributions.

- Ida can *elect* to distribute the entire account balance within five years after the year of the owner's death (5-year rule). This election can only be made if the plan provisions allow the 5-year rule.

Statement 3 is incorrect. There is no step-up in basis to fair market value at death for IRAs, because assets held in an IRA at death are considered to be income in respect of a decedent (IRD) assets. Statement 4 is incorrect, because Ida is not <u>required</u> to withdraw the entire account balance over 5 years or less.

Retirement—Minimum Distributions

2. c

Since her 70th birthday is March 1, 2008, she will be 70½ on September 1, 2008. Therefore, her first distribution must be made by April 1, 2009.

Estates—Probate Estate

3. d

See the following calculation. (Keep in mind that she does not have a will.)

Estates—Gross Estate

4. e

Assets	Gross Estate	Probate Estate	
Cash	$25,000	$25,000	
Savings	20,000	20,000	
Stocks	20,000	20,000	
IRA	50,000	50,000	No subsequent or contingent beneficiary
IRA (wife)	40,000	40,000	No subsequent or contingent beneficiary
Pension	150,000	150,000	
Personal Residence	600,000	600,000	
Vacation Home	200,000	200,000	
Auto	18,000	18,000	
Furniture	77,000	77,000	
ILIT*	200,000	0	
Total	**$1,400,000 #4**	**$1,200,000 #3**	

* Since she has a general power of appointment, the ILIT will be included in her gross estate.

Estates—Postmortem Elections

5. a

Disclaim an amount equal to the applicable exclusion amount of $2 million (for 2007) or any amount or fraction up to that amount in favor of the grandchildren. None of the other elections are appropriate.

The special-use valuation election and installment payment of estate tax election are offered to owners of farms or closely held businesses.

The QTIP election is unnecessary because there are not any children from a previous marriage or a need to control the assets "from the grave." There is no real benefit here, and it would limit Ida's control over the assets.

Gerard's gross estate equals one-half the community property ($445,000) plus his separate property ($70,000). She can disclaim any assets, amount, or fraction.

Tax—Personal Residence

6. e

$600,000. Ida receives a step-up in basis on both halves of community property at Gerard's death.

Fundamentals—Property Classification

7. d

Fee simple with debt owed to community of one-half the expenditures made from community property.

Estates—Gifting and Educational Funding

8. e

For gift tax purposes, contributions to a QTP can be treated as though they were made ratably over a five-year period, allowing an individual to use five year's worth of annual exclusions on an initial contribution. Since the annual exclusion for 2007 is $12,000, Ida can contribute up to $120,000.

[($12,000 × 5) × 2].

The Generation-Skipping Transfer Tax (GSTT) does not apply to the gift as long as it does not exceed the annual exclusion amount.

Estates—Charitable Trust

9. c

Statements 1, 2, and 3 are correct. CRATs and CRUTs both provide for income to be paid to the beneficiaries and the remainder interest to charity. A pooled income fund works similarly to both CRATs and CRUTs but is managed by the charity. A CLT is designed to pay the income produced to the charity with the remainder interest being transferred to a family member or the grantor. The pooled income fund can only provide a life interest, not for a term certain.

Retirement—Pension Distribution

10. c

$120,000. There is a mandatory 20% withholding on distributions from qualified plans.

$150,000 × 0.80 = $120,000.

Retirement—Social Security Benefits

11. b

Ida is not a caretaker of a dependent child under the age of 16; therefore, Statement 3 is incorrect. The remaining statements (1, 2, and 4) are correct.

Retirement—IRA Beneficiary

12. c

Statements 2, 3, and 4 are correct. The IRA is her own property and, therefore, will be included in her gross estate. It will also be included in her probate estate because she has no living named beneficiary. IRAs are subject to federal income tax upon distribution and do not get a step-up to FMV at death. The assets in an IRA are considered to be income in respect of a decedent.

Investments—Selection

13. c

The process of elimination should be used to answer this question. Long-term bonds (Statement 1) are inappropriate for her age, so Option (b) is incorrect. Growth stocks (Statement 5) are inappropriate for her risk tolerance, so Options (a) and (d) are incorrect. Therefore, the best combination of investments is Option (c) short-term bonds, money markets, Treasury notes, and intermediate bonds. T-bills (Statement 4) may have been an appropriate investment selection; however, Option (d) includes T-bills in combination with other inappropriate investments (5 growth stocks).

Estates—Gifting

14. c

Statements 1, 3, and 4 are all appropriate.

Statement 2 is incorrect. Because Gerard has died, the split gift election is not available. The amount transferred to Owen exceeds the annual exclusion and is, therefore, a taxable gift, requiring Ida to use some of her applicable exclusion amount.

Statement 3 is correct. The cost of the trip to Europe is less than the annual exclusion and, therefore, is not a taxable gift.

Tax—Filing Status

15. a

Ida's filing status is married filing jointly for the 2007 tax year (the year of the death of the spouse). After 2007, she will be required to file as single, as she has no qualifying dependent child.

Retirement—Social Security Benefits

16. d

Ida will receive 100% of Gerard's primary insurance amount (PIA) as a result of his death. Essentially, she steps into his place. If he had begun benefits before normal retirement age, she would have been subject to a reduced amount. If she were not age appropriate (under 65), she would receive a reduced benefit.

Tax—Sale of Personal Residence

17. a

No gain or loss. The basis of a community property asset is the fair market value at the death of the first spouse, thus $600,000.

Insurance—Medicare

18. c

Hospice care is covered under Medicare Part A, not Part B.

Insurance—Medicare

19. a

Cost savings is the major advantage. All of the other items are false. Note: Medigap is designed to cover deductibles and coinsurance associated with Medicare and cannot contain exclusions, limitations, or reductions that are not consistent with Medicare.

Insurance—Long-Term Care

20. a

Only long-term care insurance will provide the kind of coverage that Ida seeks.

Estates—Charitable Giving

21. a

The IRAs would not be taxable to the charity, but would be income taxable to other beneficiaries. The other assets would receive a step-up to fair market value at Ida's death and, therefore, would be better left to the children/grandchildren.

BILLY JO AND DANIELLE HOBERT

Case Scenario

Billy Jo and Danielle Hobert

Billy Jo and Danielle Hobert have come to you, a financial planner, for help in developing a plan to accomplish their financial goals. From your initial meeting together, you have gathered the following information. Assume today is December 31, 2007.

PERSONAL BACKGROUND AND INFORMATION

Billy Jo Hobert (Age 60)

Billy Jo is employed as a vice president for a large spice manufacturer and has been with the company 25 years. He participates in the company's defined-benefit plan. Billy Jo's first wife died several years ago.

Danielle Hobert (Age 29)

Danielle owns Shape Spa and Enchanted Flower Garden.

Billy Jo and Danielle Hobert

Billy Jo and Danielle married July 4, 2005, but do not have any children together.

Billy Jo's Children

Taylor—Age 34
Kennedy—Age 33
McKenzie—Age 32
Samantha—Age 31

All are healthy, employed, married, and not living with Billy Jo and Danielle. Taylor has two children, Tom and Melissa.

PERSONAL AND FINANCIAL GOALS

1. Danielle plans to sell her businesses.

2. Billy Jo plans to retire on January 1 of next year (life expectancy 25.75 years).

3. They plan to sell their primary residence.

4. They plan to refinance their vacation home.

5. They plan to travel extensively before deciding where to permanently relocate.

ECONOMIC INFORMATION

- They expect inflation to average 3% (CPI) annually over both the short term and the long term.
- Expected stock market return of 11% on the S&P 500 Index.
- T-bills are currently yielding 5%.
- Current mortgage rates are:

    15-year, fixed   6.75%

    30-year, fixed   7.25%
- Closing costs are expected to be 3% of any mortgage.
- They will finance closing costs in any refinance.

INSURANCE INFORMATION

Life Insurance

	Policy 1	Policy 2
Insured	Billy Jo	Danielle
Owner	Billy Jo	Danielle
Beneficiary	In equal shares to the surviving children of the insured and to the surviving children of any deceased children of the insured, per stirpes.	Billy Jo Hobert, husband of the insured.
Face Amount	$150,000	$150,000
Cash Value	0	0
Type of Policy	Term	Term
Settlement Options	Lump Sum	Lump Sum
Premium (Annual)	$450	$150

Health Insurance

Billy Jo's employer currently provides health insurance for both Billy Jo and Danielle. The employer will continue to provide the health insurance during retirement.

Disability Insurance

Neither Billy Jo nor Danielle has disability insurance.

Homeowners Insurance

HO-3 on both primary residence and vacation home.

	Residence	Vacation Home
Dwelling	$200,000	$150,000
Coinsurance	80/20	80/20
Deductible	$250	$250

Umbrella Policy

$3 million.

Automobile Insurance

Maximum liability, no comprehensive or collision.

INVESTMENT DATA

- Emergency fund is adequate at $40,000.

- They can accept moderate risk.

- Billy Jo's IRA investment portfolio is worth $200,000 with $100,000 invested in low-to-medium risk equity mutual funds. Danielle is the beneficiary.

- The remaining $100,000 is invested in staggered maturity short-term Treasury notes.

- Billy Jo expects to use the income and some of the principal from the $100,000 to make up any shortfall between his retirement needs and his defined-benefit plan annuity for the period of time until Social Security benefits are received (2 years at age 62).

- Billy Jo is currently earning 6.5% on the $100,000 invested in Treasury notes and expects the earnings rate to continue until the notes mature.

INCOME TAX INFORMATION

(Also see Assets)

- Billy Jo and Danielle file a joint federal income tax return and are both average and marginal 25% federal income taxpayers but pay no state income tax.

RETIREMENT INFORMATION

Billy Jo

- Has an employer-provided defined-benefit plan that will pay him a joint and survivor annuity equal to 80% of single life annuity at any retirement age 60 or older. No reduction for retirement at 60 or older.

- The defined-benefit formula is 1.25% per year multiplied by the number of years multiplied by the last salary with no offset for Social Security (Billy Jo's final salary for this year was $100,000).

- The present value of his projected annual Social Security benefits at 66 is $13,500 per year or 75% of that amount at age 62. Social Security benefits are expected to increase directly with the inflation rate.

- Billy Jo is expected to retire January 1 of next year. He has three options from which to select regarding the form of benefits from his defined-benefit plan:

1. Take a lump sum of $400,000.

2. Take a single life annuity beginning January 1 of next year of $2,865 per month.

3. Take a joint and survivor annuity beginning January 1 of next year of $2,200 per month.

GIFTS, ESTATES, TRUSTS, AND WILL INFORMATION

Gifts

Lifetime taxable gifts made are as follows:

- Ten years ago, Billy Jo gifted $200,000 to each of his four children. The $800,000 was put in an irrevocable trust. During the same year he gave $10,000 to each child (total $40,000) to utilize the annual exclusion. He paid gift tax of $75,000 at the time. He inherited the $915,000 ($800,000 + $40,000 + $75,000) as the primary legatee from his mother ten years ago. The successor legatees were the four grandchildren (children of Billy Jo).

- Danielle has made no taxable gifts during her lifetime.

Estates

For purposes of estimating estate tax liability (of either spouse):

- Last illness and funeral estimated at $20,000.
- Estate administration expense estimated at $30,000.

Wills

Billy Jo and Danielle have simple wills leaving all probate assets to each other. Debts and taxes are to be paid from the inheritance of the surviving spouse.

STATEMENT OF FINANCIAL POSITION
Billy Jo and Danielle Hobert
Statement of Financial Position
As of December 31, 2007

ASSETS[1]

LIABILITIES & NET WORTH[2]

Cash/Cash Equivalents

JTHW	Cash (Money Market)	$40,000
	Total Cash/Cash Equivalents	$40,000

Invested Assets

W	Shape Spa	$300,000
W	Enchanted Flower Garden	100,000
W	Danielle's Investment Portfolio	90,000
H	SPDA	110,801
H	Billy Jo's Investment Portfolio—IRA	200,000
H	Defined-Benefit Plan (vested benefits)	400,000
	Total Investments	$1,200,801

Personal Use Assets

JTHW	Primary Residence	$300,000
JTHW	Vacation Home	180,000
JTHW	Personal Property & Furniture	100,000
H	Auto 1	20,000
W	Auto 2	22,000
	Total Personal Use	$622,000
Total Assets		**$1,862,801**

Liabilities

Current:

H	Bank Credit Card 1	$5,000
W	Bank Credit Card 2	7,000
W	Bank Credit Card 3	8,000
H	Auto Note 1 Balance	10,000
W	Auto Note 2 Balance	10,000
	Current Liabilities	$40,000

Long-Term:

Mortgage—Primary Residence		$150,000
Mortgage—Vacation Home		120,000
Long-Term Liabilities		$270,000
Total Liabilities		$310,000

Net Worth	**$1,552,801**

Total Liabilities & Net Worth	**$1,862,801**

Notes to Financial Statements:

[1] All assets are stated at fair market value.

[2] Liabilities are stated at principal only.

Titles and Ownership Information:

H   = Husband separate

W   = Wife separate

JTHW = Joint husband and wife (with survivorship rights)

INFORMATION REGARDING ASSETS AND LIABILITIES

Assets

1. *Shape Spa* (Danielle 100% shareholder of C corporation)

    *   Fair market value $300,000.

    *   Original and present tax basis $75,000 (acquired by purchase seven years ago).

    *   Danielle has agreed to sell the company for $300,000 on April 1, 2008. Terms are 20% down on April 1st and the balance paid in equal monthly installments over 10 years at 11% interest beginning May 1, 2008.

2. *Enchanted Flower Garden* (Danielle 100% shareholder of C corporation—Section 1244 stock)

    *   She started the business ten years ago, and her tax basis is $250,000.

3. *SPDA (Single Premium Deferred Annuity)* (Billy Jo's)

    *   Acquired January 1, 1981 for $25,000 current fair market value is $110,801.

    *   Contract has back and surrender charges of 5% for first 7 years.

    *   Fixed earnings rate of 6% compounded quarterly.

    *   Annuity start date is October 1, 2008, and will consist of quarterly payments over Billy Jo's life (Billy Jo's life expectancy is 25 years as of October 1, 2008).

    *   Danielle is the named beneficiary if Billy Jo dies before the annuity start date.

4. *Defined-Benefit Plan*

    *   Vested benefits are valued at $400,000.

    *   In the event of Billy Jo's death before retirement benefits begin, the entire balance is paid directly to Danielle as his named beneficiary.

5. *Primary Residence*

    *   Was originally owned by Billy Jo but one-half was given to Danielle when they were married.

    *   Fair market value is $300,000 with a cost basis of $140,000.

    *   Expect to pay 6% real estate commission on sale.

6. *Vacation Home*

    *   Fair market value is $180,000.

    *   Original mortgage was for a period of 15 years at 9%.

    *   Current payment is $1,522 per month (principal and interest).

    *   Current mortgage balance is $120,000 with a remaining term of 120 months.

7. *IRA Investments* (Billy Jo)

    *   Beneficiary is Danielle.

DANIELLE'S DETAILED INVESTMENT PORTFOLIO

Description	Quantity	FMV	Beta	Maturity (Duration)	Coupon	Yearly Returns '07	'06	'05	'04	'03
ABC Fund	200	$6,000.00	1.15			10%	15%	12%	6%	(5%)
Texaco	500	$10,000.00	0.90			5%	6%	3%	7%	(6%)
Warner Brothers	1,250	$10,000.00	0.85			5%	9%	8%	8%	(1%)
Silicon Graphics	400	$20,000.00	1.20			11%	15%	12%	10%	3%
Growth Fund	1,400	$21,000.00	1.15			5%	11%	14%	9%	2%
Treasury A (1 Bond)	1	$929.64		2 (1.95)	$50					
Treasury B (2 Bonds)	2	$2,050.62		3 (2.74)	$100					
Treasury C (2 Bonds)	2	$2,272.28		5 (4.07)	$125					
Cash		$17,747.46								
Total		$90,000.00								

Note: The correlation coefficient between Danielle's portfolio and the market is 0.9. All bonds have a par value of $1,000. The coupon amount represents the amount per bond.

BILLY JO AND DANIELLE HOBERT

Questions

Billy Jo and Danielle Hobert

QUESTIONS

1. Billy Jo and Danielle have decided to refinance their vacation home over the remaining life of their existing current mortgage. What will be the monthly P & I payment necessary to do so assuming they refinance?

   a. $1,061.89.
   b. $1,093.75.
   c. $1,370.18.
   d. $1,377.89.
   e. $1,419.23.

2. Assume Billy and Danielle have sold their personal residence with a realized gain. They want to invest $100,000 of the gain while they are traveling abroad, with the intent of using the investment towards the purchase of their next principal residence expected shortly. Given their moderate risk tolerance, which of the following asset allocations would be the most appropriate for this investment?

   a. $50,000 Growth Fund, $25,000 Balanced Fund, $25,000 International Fund.
   b. $50,000 Money Market, $25,000 Balanced Fund, $25,000 Bond Fund.
   c. $50,000 Balanced Fund, $25,000 Growth Fund, $25,000 Bond Fund.
   d. $50,000 Growth Fund, $30,000 Small Cap Fund, $20,000 Bond Fund.
   e. $75,000 Money Market, $25,000 Bond Fund.

3. In the event of a $25,000 loss due to fire on the personal residence, how much will the homeowners insurance company pay of such a loss?

   a. $20,000.
   b. $20,583.
   c. $20,833.
   d. $25,000.

4. Considering Danielle's current Bond Portfolio, which of the following risks is she <u>not</u> subject to, if she holds the bonds to maturity?

    1. Purchasing power risk.

    2. Reinvestment rate risk.

    3. Exchange rate risk.

    4. Default risk.

    5. Financial risk.

        a. 1 and 2.

        b. 1, 3, and 4.

        c. 2, 4, and 5.

        d. 3, 4, and 5.

        e. 1, 3, 4, and 5.

5. Is Danielle's portfolio of common stocks (including the mutual fund) subject to unsystematic risk?

        a. Yes, because unsystematic risk includes business risk, and common stocks naturally contain this risk.

        b. Yes, because the coefficient of determination of the portfolio is not at its maximum level.

        c. Yes, because unsystematic risk includes market risk, and all common stock and common stock portfolios are subject to market risk.

        d. No, because the portfolio certainly contains enough stocks to be completely diversified.

        e. No, because the market and the portfolio will not move precisely together as the market changes.

6. Which of the following is correct regarding the installment sale of Shape Spa?

    1. The installment payments received by Danielle could cause a portion of Billy Jo's Social Security benefits to be taxable.

    2. If Danielle sells the spa to a related party, Danielle must recognize any remaining gain on the sale if the related party sells the spa within two years of purchase.

    3. If Billy Jo dies during the note term, the present value of the remaining installment payments will be included in his gross estate.

    4. The down payment on the note will be taxed as part capital gain and part return of basis.

        a. 1 and 3.

        b. 2 and 4.

        c. 1, 2, and 4.

        d. 1, 2, 3, and 4.

7. Assume Billy Jo decides to withdraw $15,000 from his SPDA on January 1 of next year. The insurance company has informed him that his quarterly annuity payment will be reduced. What is the income tax effect of Billy Jo's proposed withdrawal?

   a. $15,000 is ordinary income.

   b. $3,384 is ordinary income.

   c. $11,615.55 is ordinary income.

   d. $11,615.55 is ordinary income, and there is a 10% early withdrawal penalty.

   e. $15,000 is return of basis, not taxable.

8. Assume Billy Jo decides to work as a consultant during 2009. Which of the following statements is/are correct?

   1. Billy Jo will qualify for retirement benefits from Social Security during the year.

   2. Consulting income above a certain level will reduce his Social Security benefits by $1 for every $3 of earnings.

   3. Consulting income will allow him to create a self-employed qualified plan.

   4. Regardless of his consulting income, 85% of his Social Security benefits are likely to be included in taxable income.

   a. 1 and 2.

   b. 1, 2, and 4.

   c. 1, 3, and 4.

   d. 2, 3, and 4.

9. Under what conditions can Billy Jo select a single life annuity from his defined-benefit plan?

   a. Only if he has adequate life insurance.

   b. Only if Danielle waives her rights.

   c. He cannot select a single life annuity.

   d. He must be a US citizen.

10. Excluding the down payment, what is the total of the expected installment payments to be received by Danielle next year from the sale of Shape Spa? (Round to nearest dollar.)

   a. $26,208.

   b. $26,448.

   c. $29,484.

   d. $29,754.

   e. $39,672.

11. Which of the following is true regarding the SPDA, if Billy Jo dies before the annuity starting date?

   a. The annuity will be included in his gross estate.

   b. The annuity will be included in his probate estate.

   c. The annuity will not be eligible for the marital deduction because it is a terminable interest.

   d. If Billy Jo borrowed $10,000 from the annuity, he will be taxed on the amount borrowed, but will not be subject to an early withdrawal penalty.

12. Assume Billy Jo elects to take the lump-sum benefit from his defined-benefit plan. He believes that his after-tax earnings rate on such a portfolio would be 10% and that inflation would be equal to the projected CPI. What real amount of a single life monthly annuity could he create assuming the payments were made at the beginning of each month and began October 1 of next year?

    a. $2,083.33.

    b. $2,604.17.

    c. $2,759.68.

    d. $2,775.31.

    e. $3,604.76.

13. Assume Billy Jo died today, what is the total of his probate estate?

    a. $0.

    b. $20,000.

    c. $190,000.

    d. $440,000.

    e. $590,000.

14. What is the modified duration of Danielle's bond portfolio?

    a. 2.8580.

    b. 2.9133.

    c. 3.1755.

    d. 3.3333.

15. Assuming Billy Jo and Danielle sell their primary residence for the fair market value today, what are the recognized tax consequences, assuming they have no plans to reinvest in a new residence and they take advantage of any available elections?

    a. $35,000 LTCG.

    b. $142,000 LTCG.

    c. $142,000 gain excluded.

    d. $160,000 LTCG.

    e. $160,000 gain excluded.

16. Billy Jo is contemplating gifting his life insurance policy to his children who are the current beneficiaries. What is the correct valuation for gift tax purposes of such a gift?

    a. The interpolated terminal reserve.

    b. The replacement cost.

    c. The interpolated terminal reserve plus unearned premiums.

    d. The unearned premiums at the date of the gift.

17. You review the insurance coverage on Danielle and Billy Jo for catastrophic coverage and estate planning. Which of the following show(s) deficiency in the insurance arrangement considering catastrophic coverage and estate planning?

   1. Disability insurance for Danielle.
   2. Lack of comprehensive and collision auto insurance.
   3. Insufficient umbrella coverage.
   4. Life insurance for estate liquidity at Billy Jo's death.
      a. 1 and 4.
      b. 1, 2, and 3.
      c. 1, 2, and 4.
      d. 1, 2, 3, and 4.
      e. 4 only.

18. Which of the following risks should Danielle be concerned about with regard to her investment portfolio?

   1. Systematic risk.
   2. Unsystematic risk.
   3. Market risk.
   4. Reinvestment rate risk.
   5. Interest rate risk.
   6. Default risk.
      a. 1, 2, and 6.
      b. 3, 4, 5, and 6.
      c. 1, 2, 3, 4, 5, and 6.
      d. 1, 3, 4, 5, and 6.
      e. 1, 2, 3, 4, and 5.

19. Determine which of the following bonds Danielle could purchase if she wants to increase the duration of her bond portfolio.

   1. Bond 1: Three-year, zero-coupon bond selling for $772.18 (Duration = 3 years).
   2. Bond 2: Four-year bond selling for $1,923.32 with an annual coupon of $375 (Duration = 2.985 years).
   3. Bond 3: Four-year bond selling for $983.80 with an annual coupon of $85 (Duration = 3.55 years).

   Note: All bonds have a maturity of $1,000.

      a. 1 only.
      b. 2 only.
      c. 3 only.
      d. 2 or 3.
      e. 1, 2, or 3.

20. Billy Jo is interested in purchasing some Treasury securities. Which of the following is true with regard to the original issue of Treasury securities?

    a. T-bills are sold in denominations of $1,000 and T-notes are sold in denominations of $10,000.

    b. T-notes may be issued at a discount.

    c. T-notes have semiannual coupon payments.

    d. Both T-bills and T-notes have semiannual coupon payments.

21. What is the tax treatment next year of the down payment made on April 1 of next year when Danielle sells Shape Spa, assuming that she treats the sale as an installment sale?

    a. Long-term capital gain of $225,000.

    b. Return of capital of $60,000.

    c. Long-term capital gain of $45,000.

    d. Ordinary income of $6,600.

    e. Long-term capital gain, return of basis, and ordinary income.

22. Assume that Danielle sells Enchanted Flower Garden for the fair market value on December 31 of this year. What is the impact of such a transaction on the joint tax return for the Hoberts this year?

    a. $50,000 ordinary loss.

    b. $100,000 ordinary loss.

    c. $150,000 ordinary loss.

    d. $150,000 long-term capital loss.

    e. $100,000 ordinary loss and a $50,000 long-term capital loss.

23. Assume that Danielle sells Shape Spa on an installment sales basis. What are the investment risks associated with the installment notes?

    1. Default risk.

    2. Reinvestment risk.

    3. Interest rate risk.

    4. Purchasing power risk.

        a. 1 and 2.

        b. 2, 3, and 4.

        c. 1, 2, and 3.

        d. 1, 2, 3, and 4.

        e. None of the above.

24. Assume Billy's oldest child, Taylor, has a 5-year-old son. Billy and Danielle want to contribute a lump sum of $20,000 towards the child's higher education expenses. All of the following are correct regarding this investment, except:

    a. A Coverdell Education Savings Account can be utilized and it allows tax-deferred growth.

    b. The contribution is considered a completed gift, and with Billy and Danielle utilizing the split gift annual exclusion, no gift tax is owed.

    c. A QTP would be appropriate and does allow the contributor to select among different investment strategies when the initial contribution is made.

    d. GSTT would not apply on this gift as long as the gift does not exceed the exclusion amount.

25. Danielle is considering adding XYZ Company stock to her investment portfolio. She just read the annual report for the XYZ Company. What form of the efficient market hypothesis supports this?

    a. Weak form.

    b. Semistrong form.

    c. Strong form.

    d. Super strong form.

    e. None of the above.

26. Assuming Billy Jo decides to take Social Security retirement benefits beginning on his birthday in 2009, calculate his expected monthly Social Security benefit for 2009.

    a. $843.75

    b. $895.13

    c. $1,010.08

    d. $1,125.00

    e. $1,193.50

27. If Billy Jo died today, what would be the total of his gross estate?

    a. $440,051.

    b. $640,051.

    c. $1,040,051.

    d. $1,139,801.

    e. $1,190,801.

28. What could Billy Jo have done in 1997 to avoid his current estate situation and still have achieved the same result as his initial gifting?

    a. He could have orally disclaimed the inheritance from his mother.

    b. He could have given a written disclaimer to the executor directing that the monies should be paid to the successor legatees in trust.

    c. He could have accepted the money and used it until the filing date on the 706. Then he could have given the remainder to the successor legatees, and it would not have been a taxable gift.

    d. He could have given a written disclaimer, which would have been due six months after death.

    e. None of the above.

29. If Taylor predeceased Billy Jo, which of the following situations would represent the correct life insurance payout from Billy Jo's term policy upon Billy Jo's subsequent death?

    a. Taylor—$37,500; Kennedy—$37,500; McKenzie—$37,500; Samantha—$37,500.

    b. Kennedy—$37,500; McKenzie—$37,500; Samantha—$37,500; Tom—$18,750; Melissa—$18,750.

    c. Kennedy—$30,000; McKenzie—$30,000; Samantha—$30,000; Tom—$30,000; Melissa—$30,000.

    d. Taylor—$37,500; Danielle—$37,500; McKenzie—$37,500; Samantha—$18,750; Melissa—$18,750.

BILLY JO AND DANIELLE HOBERT

Solutions

Billy Jo and Danielle Hobert

1.	e	6.	c	11.	a	16.	d	21.	c	26.	b
2.	e	7.	e	12.	c	17.	e	22.	e	27.	e
3.	b	8.	c	13.	b	18.	e	23.	d	28.	e
4.	d	9.	b	14.	b	19.	c	24.	a	29.	b
5.	b	10.	b	15.	c	20.	c	25.	a		

SUMMARY OF TOPICS

1. Fundamentals—Time Value of Money
2. Investments—Asset Allocation
3. Insurance—Coinsurance
4. Investments—Bonds and Risk
5. Investments—Coefficient of Determination
6. Tax—Installment Sale
7. Retirement—Annuities
8. Retirement—Social Security
9. Retirement—Single Life Annuity
10. Fundamentals—Installment Sale
11. Estates—Valuation of Annuities
12. Fundamentals—Time Value of Money\Annuities
13. Estates—Probate Estate
14. Investments—Modified Duration
15. Tax—Sale of Personal Residence
16. Estates—Gifts
17. Insurance—Deficiencies
18. Investments—Risks
19. Investments—Bond Duration
20. Investments—Treasury Bonds
21. Tax—Installment Sale
22. Tax—Property Disposition
23. Investments—Installment Notes
24. Fundamentals—Educational Funding
25. Investments—Efficient Market Hypothesis
26. Retirement—Social Security

27. Estates—Gross Estate
28. Estates—Planning
29. Estates—Life Insurance

SOLUTIONS

Fundamentals—Time Value of Money

1. e

They would pay 3% closing costs and pay over a period of 120 months at a 15-year fixed rate of 6.75%.

n	=	120 (10 × 12)
i	=	0.5625 (6.75 ÷ 12)
PV	=	$123,600 ($120,000 × 1.03)
PMT_{OA}	=	$1,419.23

Investments—Asset Allocation

2. e

Because they need the funds relatively soon, they need to invest in assets that are very liquid. Options (a), (b), (c), and (d) are too aggressive given the Hobert's risk tolerance and time horizon. Therefore, Option (e) is the best answer.

Insurance—Coinsurance

3. b

$300,000 × 0.80 = $240,000

$$\left[\$25,000 \left(\frac{\$200,000}{\$240,000} \right) \right] - \$250^* = \$20,583$$

*$250 is the deductible.

Investments—Bonds and Risk

4. d

The Bond Portfolio consists entirely of Treasury securities; therefore, it will not have any default risk. Exchange rate risk involves foreign bonds, and financial risk relates to common stock, not bonds. She would certainly be subject to purchasing power risk and reinvestment risk.

Investments—Coefficient of Determination

5. b

The coefficient of determination is the square of the correlation coefficient. Therefore, because the correlation coefficient is 0.9, the coefficient of determination is 0.81. Thus, 81% of the changes in Danielle's investment portfolio can be explained by changes in the market. However, 19% (100% − 81%) is explained by some other source. Because this other source is not systematic risk, which would have been explained by the changes in the market, it must be unsystematic risk. Therefore, **b** is the correct answer.

Tax—Installment Sale

6. c

Statement 1 is correct. Installment payments are included in modified adjusted gross income, which will cause a portion of Billy Jo's Social Security benefits to be taxable (when he starts receiving benefits).

Statement 2 is correct.

Statement 3 is incorrect. The note is Danielle's property.

Statement 4 is correct.

Retirement—Annuities

7. e

Annuity contracts entered into before August 14, 1982 use the FIFO basis recovery rule (basis recovered first). He may withdraw amounts up to his adjusted taxable basis ($25,000) tax free.

Retirement—Social Security

8. c

Statements 1, 3, and 4 are correct. Statement 2 is false because the reduction is $1 for every $2 of earnings above a certain threshold.

Retirement—Single Life Annuity

9. b

Danielle must waive her marital rights.

Fundamentals—Installment Sale

10. b

n	= 120 (10 × 12)	Sale Price	$300,000
i	= 0.9167 (11 ÷ 12)	Down Payment	(60,000)
PV	= $240,000	Balance of Installment Note	$240,000
PMT_{OA}	= $3,306.00		
x 8*	= $26,448		

*Only 8 payments are received next year.

Installment payments are ordinary annuities following the down payment.

Estates—Valuation of Annuities

11. a

While the annuity will be included in the gross estate, it will avoid the probate estate.

Fundamentals—Time Value of Money\Annuities

12. c

Correct
PV = $400,000
$i = 0.5663 \ [((1.10 \div 1.03) - 1.00) \times 100] \div 12$
$n = 300 \ (25 \times 12)$
$PMT_{AD} = \$2,759.68$

Estates—Probate Estate

13. b

$20,000

Assets	%	Probate Estate
Cash	50%	$0
SPDA	100%	0
IRA investments	100%	0
Defined benefit	100%	0
Residence	50%	0
Vacation home	50%	0
Personal property	50%	0
Auto1	100%	20,000
Subtotal		$20,000
Life insurance proceeds		0
Total		$20,000

Investments—Modified Duration

14. b

The modified duration of the bonds is equal to the portfolio duration divided by one plus the Yield to Maturity. Thus, the modified duration is 2.9133. The calculations are as follows:

Step 1: Calculate the Yield to Maturity.

	Treasury A	Treasury B	Treasury C
PV	$929.64	$1,025.31	$1,136.14
FV	$1,000.00	$1,000.00	$1,000.00
n	2	3	5
PMT	$50	$100	$125
i	9.00%	9.00%	9.00%

Note: *i* above represents the YTM.

All of the bonds have a YTM of 9%.

Step 2: Calculate the duration of the bond portfolio.

FMV	Duration	Weighted Duration
$929.64	1.95	$1,812.80
$2,050.62	2.74	$5,618.70
$2,272.28	4.07	$9,248.18
$5,252.54		$16,679.68

Portfolio Duration = $16,679.68 ÷ $5,252.54 = 3.1755

Step 3: Calculate the modified duration.

$$\text{Modified duration} = \frac{\text{Portfolio duration}}{1 + \text{YTM}} = \frac{3.1755}{1.09} = 2.9133$$

Tax—Sale of Personal Residence

15. c

	Correct
Sale Price	$300,000
Less: Commission	(18,000)
Amount realized	$282,000
Basis	(140,000)
Realized Gain	$142,000

Note: They can exclude up to $500,000 of gain from the sale of a personal residence that was owned and used for a period of two years. The Hoberts are not required to reinvest in a new residence to take advantage of the gain exclusion.

Estates—Gifts

16. d

This is a term policy. The value of the policy as a gift is equal to the unearned premium at the date of the gift.

Insurance—Deficiencies

17. e

Since Billy Jo is retiring and there is no indication that Danielle earns a salary, disability insurance is not necessary. Their net worth is strong and umbrella insurance is sufficient. Because they have such a strong net worth and good liquidity, the absence of collision and comprehensive auto coverage is not cause for concern. However, the life insurance is insufficient for estate liquidity. Billy Jo's life insurance is paid to his children and the Statement of Financial Position only shows $40,000 of liquid assets. Estimated administrative and funeral expenses are $50,000.

Investments—Risks

18. e

All risks apply, except default risk, because Treasury bonds are considered default risk free. The other investments are equities and are not subject to default risk.

Investments—Bond Duration

19. c

FMV	Duration	Weighted Duration
$929.64	1.95	$1,812.80
$2,050.62	2.74	$5,618.70
$2,272.28	4.07	$9,248.18
$5,252.54		$16,679.68

Portfolio Duration = $16,679.68 ÷ $5,252.54 = 3.1755

Since the duration for this portfolio equals 3.1755 years, Danielle should purchase a bond with a duration greater than 3.1755 to increase the duration of the current portfolio. Thus, Option (c) is correct because Bond 3 is the only bond with duration greater than the current portfolio.

Investments—Treasury Bonds

20. c

Option (c) is correct because T-notes have semiannual coupon payments.

Option (a) is incorrect because T-notes are not sold in denominations of $10,000.

Option (b) is incorrect because unlike T-bills, T-notes are not issued at a discount.

Option (d) is incorrect because T-bills do not make coupon payments (they are essentially zero-coupon securities). T-bills are issued at a discount and mature at face value.

Tax—Installment Sale

21. c

The down payment does not include any ordinary income. The $60,000 down payment is 75% LTCG and 25% return of taxable basis.

Sales Price	$300,000	100%	Down Payment	$60,000	100%
Basis	(75,000)	(25%)	Return of Basis	(15,000)	(25%)
Capital Gain	$225,000	75%	LTCG	$45,000	75%

Tax—Property Disposition

22. e

Sales Price	$100,000
Tax Basis	(250,000)
Realized Loss	($150,000)
Ordinary Portion	(100,000)
Capital Loss	($50,000)

Note: Section 1244 stock entitles the owner to receive up to $100,000 (for married filing jointly) in ordinary losses instead of capital losses (per year); the remaining $50,000 is a long-term capital loss.

Investments—Installment Notes

23. d

All the risks identified are associated with installment notes. Installment notes have the same basic characteristics as fixed-income securities.

Fundamentals—Educational Funding

24. a

Option (a) is not correct because the Coverdell Education Savings Account currently allows annual contributions of $2,000.

Investments—Efficient Market Hypothesis

25. a

Reading an annual report is a type of fundamental analysis. Fundamental analysis is only supported by the weak form of the efficient market hypothesis.

Retirement—Social Security

26. b

Billy Jo receives 75% of $14,322, because he will be 62 in 2009.

PV	=	$13,500
i	=	3
n	=	2
FV	=	$14,322.15 × 0.75 = $10,741.61

$10,741.61 ÷ 12 = $895.13 monthly

Estates—Gross Estate

27. e

$1,190,801.

Assets	Gross Estate
Cash	$20,000
SPDA	110,801
IRA Investments	200,000
Defined Benefit	400,000
Residence	150,000
Vacation home	90,000
Personal property	50,000
Auto 1	20,000
Subtotal	$1,040,801
Life insurance proceeds	150,000
TOTAL	$1,190,801

Estates—Planning

28. e

An effective disclaimer has four elements:

1. It must be in writing.
2. It must be made within nine months of the interest arising.
3. The disclaimant cannot have benefited from the interest he is now disclaiming.
4. He cannot direct the interest that is disclaimed.

Estates—Life Insurance

29. b

Since the life insurance is to be distributed in equal shares to the surviving children of the insured, and to the surviving children of any deceased children of the insured, per stirpes, Tom and Melissa will receive Taylor's portion.

Therefore, the $150,000 life insurance payout will be as follows:

Kennedy—$37,500

McKenzie—$37,500

Samantha—$37,500

Tom—$18,750

Melissa—$18,750

JEFF AND ROSA MARTIN

Case Scenario

Jeff and Rosa Martin

Today is December 31, 2007. Jeff and Rosa Martin have come to you, a financial planner, for help in developing a plan to accomplish their financial goals. From your initial meeting together, you have gathered the following information:

PERSONAL BACKGROUND AND INFORMATION

Jeff Martin (Age 60)

Jeff is the executive vice president of Postal Accidents, Inc. He has been at Postal for 25 years.

Rosa Martin (Age 45)

Jeff's wife, Rosa, age 45, taught college courses at State University for 14 years. Three years ago, she retired to devote more time to her family.

The Children

Jeff and Rosa have two children, 18-year-old Steven and 11-year-old Mary.

Jeff also has a 30-year-old son, Tom, from a previous marriage. Tom is an aspiring actor living in Los Angeles. Two years ago, Tom was arrested for drug possession and is currently on probation.

The Martins

Jeff and Rosa have been married for 19 years.

PERSONAL AND FINANCIAL GOALS

- Save for college tuition.
- Pay off all debt by Jeff's retirement.
- Retire at the age of 65 with 70% of salary at the time of Jeff's retirement.
- Prepare a proper will and estate plan.
- Evaluate both investment and insurance risk.

ECONOMIC INFORMATION

- They expect inflation to average 4.0% annually, both currently and for the long term.
- They expect salaries and net income to increase at 4.0% annually, both currently and long term.
- They believe the S&P 500 is a good measure of the market's performance. Its historical rate of return is 12%. The equities market is expected to remain at historical levels.

INCOME TAX INFORMATION

Their marginal income tax rate is currently 35% for federal taxes, and the state income tax rate is a flat 5%.

RETIREMENT INFORMATION

Jeff plans to retire in 5 years, at the age of 65. The Martins would like to have a standard of living equal to 70% of their preretirement income. They expect to be in retirement for 30 years.

Jeff has a 401(k) plan through Postal Accidents, Inc. He has been contributing the maximum allowable amount to the 401(k). He has averaged an annual return of 7% over the past eight years. Rosa has a 403(b) plan through her former employer, State University.

Jeff expects to collect $14,000 in Social Security benefits for full retirement at age 65 or 80% of that amount at age 62 (in today's dollars). Rosa expects to collect $7,000 in Social Security benefits at age 66 and 70% at age 62 (in today's dollars). Jeff will begin collecting benefits as soon as he reaches normal retirement age. Rosa has been considering the possibility of receiving her Social Security benefits at age 62.

GIFTS, ESTATES, TRUSTS, AND WILL INFORMATION

Gifts

Five years ago, Jeff bought 5,000 shares of stock at $20 per share in Jedco Pharmaceutical Company. He immediately gifted 1,500 shares of the stock to Steven and another 1,500 shares of the stock to Mary. Today, the stock is worth $40 per share and is paying a dividend of $2 per share. Jeff feels that the stock will appreciate at a rate of 9% per year, including the dividend. These were the only gifts given by Jeff. Rosa has never given any gifts.

Estates

Jeff and Rosa estimate that funeral expenses will be $25,000 each and administrative expenses will be $50,000 for each of them.

Trusts

Jeff is considering the creation of an irrevocable trust for the benefit of his older son, Tom. Jeff would like income from the trust to be paid to Tom each year, and would like for the trustee to have the discretionary power to distribute trust principle to Tom in the case of hardship. Since Tom has experienced drug problems in the recent past, Jeff would like to prevent Tom from having any additional access to the trust assets, and he does not want Jeff to be able to pledge his interest in the trust as collateral for a loan.

STATEMENT OF CASH FLOWS

Jeff and Rosa Martin
Annual Statement of Cash Flows
January 1, 2007—December 31, 2007

CASH INFLOWS:

Salary:	Jeff's Salary	$260,000	
	Rosa's Salary	0	
	Total Salary	$260,000	
Unearned Income:	Rental Prop Loss	(30,000)	
	Dividends	$25,000	
	Interest Income	55,000	
		$50,000	
Total Income:			$310,000

CASH OUTFLOWS:

Mortgage Payments:	Primary Residence	$30,000	
Insurance Premiums:	Homeowners	$1,400	
	Life	8,500	
	Auto	2,400	
	Umbrella—Liability	800	
	Total Insurance Premiums	$13,100	
Misc. Expenses:	Credit Card payments	$3,400	
	Entertainment	22,000	
	Food	8,400	
	Clothes	12,000	
	Utilities	6,000	
	Charity	15,000	
	Total Misc. Expenses	$66,800	
Tax:	Property	$ 19,000	
	Income Tax	125,000	
	Total Tax	$144,000	
Total Outflows:			$253,900
Discretionary Cash			$56,100

STATEMENT OF FINANCIAL POSITION
Jeff and Rosa Martin
Statement of Financial Position
As of December 31, 2007

ASSETS [1]

Cash/Cash Equivalents

JT	Savings Account	$38,000
H	Cash Value of Universal Life Policy	25,000
W	Cash Value of Whole Life Policy	40,000
Total Cash/Cash Equiv.		**$103,000**

Invested Assets

H	Postal Accidents Stock	$600,000
H	Traditional IRA	150,000
H	401(k) Plan	550,000
W	403(b) Plan	55,000
JT	Investment Portfolio	2,000,000
JT	Office Building	800,000
Total Investments		**$4,155,000**

Personal-Use Assets

JT	Primary Residence	$450,000
JT	Personal Property/Furniture	100,000
H	Sports Utility Vehicle	55,000
W	Jeep	40,000
Total Personal-Use		**$645,000**
Total Assets		**$4,903,000**

LIABILITIES AND NET WORTH

Liabilities [2]

Current Liabilities

H	Visa Credit Card	$6,000
W	Mastercard Credit Card	10,000
Total Current Liabilities		**$16,000**

Long-Term Liabilities

JT	Mortgage—Primary Residence	$200,000
Total Long-Term Liabilities		**$200,000**
Total Liabilities		**$216,000**

Net Worth	**$4,687,000**

Total Liabilities and Net Worth	**$4,903,000**

Notes to Financial Statements:

[1] Assets are stated at fair market value (rounded to even dollars).

[2] Liabilities are stated at principal only (rounded to even dollars).

Property Ownership

JT—Joint tenancy with right of survivorship.

H—Husband separate property.

W—Wife separate property.

INSURANCE INFORMATION

Life Insurance

	Universal Life	Whole Life
Insured	Jeff	Rosa's Father
Face Amount	$500,000	$300,000
Cash Value	$25,000	$40,000
Annual Premium	$6,000	$2,500
Premium Payer	Jeff	Rosa
Beneficiary	Tom	Rosa
Policyowner	Jeff	Rosa
Comments	Jeff's niece, Janice, is contingent beneficiary.	Rosa purchased this policy from her father for $30,000 and has paid $5,000 in premiums.

Health Insurance

Jeff and Rosa are covered under Jeff's employer plan which is an indemnity plan with a $500 deductible per person per year and an 80/20 major medical coinsurance clause with a family annual stop loss of $1,500.

Long-Term Disability Insurance

Jeff is covered by an "own occupation" policy with premiums paid by his employer. The benefits equal 60% of gross pay after a 180-day elimination period. The policy covers both sickness and accidents.

Rosa is not covered by disability insurance.

INVESTMENT INFORMATION

Detailed Investment Portfolio

Description	Acquired	Shares	Adjusted Basis	Beta	Current FMV
Altria	6/00	14,000	$201,633	0.9	$450,000
Jedco Pharmaceutical	4/01	2,000	$40,000	1.3	$80,000
Wal-Mart	2/02	4,000	$119,000	1.2	$250,000
JDS Uniphase	3/03	22,249	$400,188	1.4	$130,000
T-Bills			$1,000,000	1.2	$1,090,000
			$1,760,821		$2,000,000

Jeff's 401(k) Plan

Jeff currently has a balance in his 401(k) plan of $550,000. This balance is comprised of mutual fund investments, as well as $250,000 of Postal Accidents stock. The Postal stock was contributed to the account by Jeff's employer over Jeff's career. The total cost of the stock contributed was $120,000.

Jeff has elected not to participate in his firm's deferred-compensation plan. He has the option of deferring up to 30% of his compensation. Any compensation deferred would be automatically paid as an annuity at retirement.

Office Building

Four years ago, Jeff and Rosa purchased an office building for $600,000. They spent $50,000 renovating the building, and are currently renting the offices to several doctors. Their annual rental income is $80,000 per year, but they are actually losing money on the property due to taxes, maintenance, and depreciation expenses. For tax purposes, they have taken $65,000 in depreciation deductions over the years.

JEFF AND ROSA MARTIN

Questions

Jeff and Rosa Martin

QUESTIONS

1. Jeff and Rosa have decided to begin setting aside funds for their children's education. Which of the following education planning vehicles could they establish if their goal is to eventually receive tax-free distributions from the account to pay for the education costs?

    1. Roth IRA.
    2. Qualified Tuition Plan.
    3. Series EE Savings Bonds.
    4. Coverdell Education Savings Account.

        a. 2 only.
        b. 3 and 4.
        c. 1, 2, and 3.
        d. 2 and 4.
        e. 1, 2, 3, and 4.

2. Which of the following education savings vehicles would allow Jeff and Rosa to change the beneficiary from one child to another?

    a. A Section 2503(c) trust.
    b. UTMA account.
    c. 529 plan.
    d. Series EE savings bond.

3. Which of the following is an income tax ramification of Jeff's employer-sponsored long-term disability?

    a. The benefit would be taxable to Jeff.
    b. The benefit would be income tax free.
    c. The cost of the disability coverage would be taxable to Jeff.
    d. The cost of the disability coverage exceeding $50,000 would be taxable to Jeff.

4. When Jeff purchased the universal life insurance policy, he elected to include an automatic premium loan provision in the policy. Which of the following statements is (are) correct regarding this provision?

    1. The automatic premium loan provision provides a better option for Jeff than reinstatement of a lapsed policy.

    2. The automatic premium loan provision will not only keep the policy in force, it will also keep any policy riders in force, such as accidental death and disability.

    3. An automatic premium loan will reduce the policy's cash value and may cause the policy to terminate early.

    4. The automatic premium loan can occur for up to 30 days beyond the grace period in most policies.

        a. 1 and 4.

        b. 1 and 3.

        c. 2 and 3.

        d. 1, 2, and 3.

        e. 2, 3, and 4.

5. Jeff is considering transferring his universal life insurance policy to an irrevocable life insurance trust (ILIT). Proceeds from the policy will be included in Jeff's gross estate if

    1. Jeff is allowed to use the policy as collateral for a loan.

    2. The trust purchases assets from Jeff's estate upon Jeff's death.

    3. Jeff dies within three years of transferring the policy to the trust.

    4. The ILIT terms indicate that a contingent beneficiary will replace Rosa as the beneficiary in the event of divorce.

        a. 3 only.

        b. 1 and 3.

        c. 1, 3, and 4.

        d. 1, 2, and 4.

        e. 1, 2, 3, and 4.

6. With respect to the Jedco Pharmaceutical stock Jeff gifted to Mary and Steven, which of the following statements is true?

    a. All dividends from Mary's shares will be taxed at her income tax rate.

    b. If Steven sold the stock for its fair market value, and the proceeds were contributed to a Qualified Tuition Plan for the benefit of Steven, the gain on the sale of the stock would be income tax free.

    c. If Steven sold the stock for its fair market value, a portion of the capital gain would be taxed at Jeff's 15% rate.

    d. A portion of the dividends received by Mary will be taxed at Jeff and Rosa's income tax rate.

7. Jeff has accumulated a significant amount of his company's stock. About which of the following risks should he be most concerned?

    a. Interest rate risk.

    b. Purchasing power risk.

    c. Market risk.

    d. Foreign exchange risk.

    e. Default risk.

8. Assuming that Jeff and Rosa actively participate in the administration of the office building, how much of the loss could they deduct on their joint income tax return for the current year?

    a. $0.

    b. $3,000.

    c. $15,000.

    d. $25,000.

    e. $30,000.

9. When Jeff retires, which of the following options is/are available with respect to the funds in his 401(k) retirement plan?

    1. Roll the funds into a Traditional IRA.

    2. Take a lump-sum distribution and elect 10-year averaging.

    3. Distribute the stock from the 401(k) plan as part of a lump-sum distribution and receive the net unrealized appreciation (NUA) in the stock without immediate income tax consequences.

    4. Roll the funds into a Traditional IRA, then distribute the stock from the IRA and receive the net unrealized appreciation (NUA) in the stock without immediate income tax consequences.

    a. 1 and 2.

    b. 1 and 3.

    c. 2 and 4.

    d. 2, 3, and 4.

    e. 2 and 3.

10. Assume that while Jeff and Tom were driving to Texas, they crashed into an 18-wheeler in Oklahoma, killing them both instantly. Under the Uniform Simultaneous Death Act, which one of the following would receive the proceeds of Jeff's universal life insurance policy?

    a. Jeff's estate.

    b. Tom's estate.

    c. Jeff's children, per stirpes.

    d. Janice.

11. All of the following would be potential advantages of Jeff's participation in his company's deferred compensation plan EXCEPT:

    a. He would reduce his current income tax liability.

    b. The earnings within the plan would not be taxed to Jeff.

    c. The benefit would be income tax free to Jeff when received at retirement.

    d. Jeff could defer compensation greater than the defined-contribution plan limit.

12. Jeff is considering the creation of a charitable remainder annuity trust (CRAT) that would provide him a fixed payment for the rest of his life. If created, Jeff would contribute a portion of his Postal Accidents stock. Which of the following is a correct statement regarding the trust?

    a. Jeff would receive an immediate charitable contribution deduction, equal to the fair market value of the stock transferred to the trust.

    b. The stock will be excluded from Jeff's gross estate upon his death.

    c. The stock could be sold within the trust, without recognizing capital gain upon the sale.

    d. A private foundation could not be named as the beneficiary of the CRAT.

13. Jeff and Rosa have requested information regarding the characteristics of a 2503(c) trust. Which of the following statements concerning such a trust is/are correct?

    1. Any remaining trust corpus must be paid to the beneficiary upon attainment of age 21.

    2. The income earned by the trust assets must be paid out to the beneficiary each year.

    3. Transfers to the trust will qualify for the gift tax annual exclusion.

    4. Income accumulated by the trust will be taxed at trust income tax rates.

    a. 1 and 4

    b. 2 and 3

    c. 2 and 4.

    d. 1, 2 and 4.

    e. 1, 3, and 4.

14. Which of the following is the biggest weakness in the Martin's investment portfolio?

    1. Marginal equity diversification.

    2. Insufficient current income.

    3. Inadequate tax advantage.

    4. Excessive liquidity.

    a. 1 and 2.

    b. 2 and 3.

    c. 1 and 4.

    d. 1, 3, and 4.

    e. 1, 2, 3, and 4.

15. If Rosa's father died, what would be the income tax ramifications of the life insurance proceeds paid to Rosa?

   a. The entire $300,000 of proceeds would be income tax free.

   b. $260,000 would be taxable as ordinary income, and $40,000 would be income tax free.

   c. $260,000 would be taxable as capital gain, and $40,000 would be taxable as ordinary income.

   d. $265,000 would be taxable as ordinary income, and $35,000 would be income tax free.

   e. The entire $300,000 of proceeds would be taxable at ordinary income tax rates.

16. If Jeff died today, how much would be included in his gross estate?

   a. $2,774,000.

   b. $3,074,000.

   c. $3,549,000.

   d. $4,256,000.

17. If Jeff died today, what amount of deductions could Jeff take against his gross estate in arriving at his adjusted gross estate?

   a. $0

   b. $75,000.

   c. $81,000.

   d. $181,000.

18. Jeff and Rosa are considering selling the office building. It's causing administrative headaches, and losing money each year. If they sold the office building today for its fair market value, what would be the income tax ramifications?

   a. $150,000 would be taxed at ordinary income tax rates.

   b. $215,000 would be taxed at the 15% capital gain rate.

   c. $65,000 would be taxed at ordinary income tax rates, and $150,000 would be taxed at the 15% capital gain rate.

   d. $65,000 would be taxed at the 25% capital gain rate, and $150,000 would be taxed at the 15% capital gain rate.

   e. $215,000 would be taxed at the 25% capital gain rate.

19. How could Jeff protect his gain in Postal Accidents stock without selling the stock?

    1. Sell Postal Accidents short.

    2. Sell a put option on Postal Accidents.

    3. Purchase a put option on Postal Accidents.

    4. Purchase a call option on Postal Accidents.

    5. Sell a call option on Postal Accidents.

       a. 1 only.

       b. 3 only.

       c. 2 and 4.

       d. 3 and 5.

       e. 1 and 3.

20. Rosa is considering the purchase of mortgage-backed securities for her portfolio. These securities contain which of the following risks?

    1. Prepayment risk.

    2. Inflation risk.

    3. Business risk.

    4. Interest rate risk.

       a. 1 only.

       b. 3 only.

       c. 2 and 4.

       d. 1, 2, and 4.

       e. 1, 2, 3, and 4.

21. Which of the following trusts would be the best type of trust for Jeff to establish for the benefit of his son, Tom?

       a. Special Needs Trust

       b. Section 2503(c) Trust

       c. Spendthrift Trust.

       d. Grantor Retained Annuity Trust.

JEFF AND ROSA MARTIN

Solutions

Jeff and Rosa Martin

1.	a	6.	d	11.	c	16.	c	21.	c
2.	c	7.	c	12.	c	17.	d		
3.	a	8.	a	13.	e	18.	d		
4.	d	9.	b	14.	d	19.	e		
5.	b	10.	d	15.	d	20.	d		

SUMMARY OF TOPICS

1. Fundamentals—Education Savings
2. Fundamentals—Education Savings
3. Insurance—Long-term Disability
4. Insurance—Policy Provisions
5. Estate Tax—Life Insurance
6. Income Tax—Kiddie Tax
7. Investments—Risk
8. Income Tax—Passive Activities
9. Retirement—Plan Distributions
10. Insurance—Life Insurance Provisions
11. Retirement—Deferred-Compensation
12. Estate Planning—Charitable Remainder Annuity Trust
13. Estate Tax—2503(c) Trusts
14. Investments—Portfolio Weaknesses
15. Income Tax—Life Insurance Proceeds
16. Estate Tax—Gross Estate
17. Estate Tax—Adjusted Gross Estate
18. Income Tax—Section 1250 Property
19. Investments—Options
20. Investments—Risks
21. Estates—Trusts

SOLUTIONS

Fundamentals—Education Savings

1. **a**

Option 1 is incorrect. The Martins' income level precludes them from contributing to a Roth IRA.

Option 2 is correct. Distributions from Qualified Tuition Plans used for qualified education costs are income tax free.

Option 3 is incorrect. At Jeff and Rosa's AGI level, they will be taxed on earnings when the Series EE Bonds are redeemed.

Option 4 is incorrect. Jeff and Rosa are not eligible to contribute to a Coverdell Education Savings Account due to their AGI level.

Fundamentals—Education Savings

2. **c**

A is incorrect. A 2503(c) trust is an irrevocable trust and is considered a completed gift.

B is incorrect. Gifts made to an UTMA account are also completed gifts.

C is correct. The owner of the 529 plan can change the beneficiary.

D is incorrect. Savings bonds have non-transferable ownership and do not list beneficiaries. Jeff or Rosa could cash in the bond and use the proceeds for their children's education.

Insurance—Long-term Disability

3. **a**

Since the premiums were paid by the employer, the disability benefits will be taxable to Jeff.

Insurance—Policy Provisions

4. **d**

Option 1 is correct. If Jeff allowed the policy to lapse, he would be required to show evidence of insurability to reinstate the policy. An automatic premium loan does not require evidence of insurability.

Option 2 is correct. Riders would be continued in force with the automatic premium loan provision. Nonforfeiture options in a lapsed policy do not keep the riders in force.

Option 3 is correct. The automatic premium loan will reduce the policy's cash value and will increase the cost of maintaining the policy by the amount of interest owed on the loan.

Option 4 is incorrect. The automatic premium loan must occur by the end of the grace period, or the policy will lapse.

Estate Tax—Life Insurance

5. b

Option 1 is correct. If the insured is allowed to use the policy as collateral for a loan, the insured will have incidents of ownership in the policy, causing inclusion in the gross estate.

Option 2 is incorrect. The purchase of assets from the decedent's estate by the trust will not cause inclusion of the proceeds in the decedent's gross estate.

Option 3 is correct. If a policy is transferred by the insured within three years of death, the proceeds are included in the insured's gross estate.

Option 4 is incorrect. A contingent beneficiary can be named in the case of divorce, without causing incidents of ownership.

Income Tax—Kiddie Tax

6. d

A is incorrect. Mary is under age 18, and as a result, some of her dividend income will be taxed at her parents' rate.

B is incorrect. The gain would still be taxable.

C is incorrect. Steven is age 18, and the kiddie tax does not apply. The entire gain will be taxed at Steven's rate.

D is correct. The kiddie tax will apply.

Investments—Risk

7. c

Market risk would be his main concern. Since he holds equities, default risk and purchasing power risk are not a primary concern. Since Postal Accidents is a domestic corporation, foreign exchange risk is not an issue. Interest rate risk could be of concern, but market risk is the most influential.

Income Tax—Passive Activities

8. a

None of the loss would be deductible. Losses on rental real estate are limited to $25,000. This loss allowance, however, is phased out at AGI of $100,000–$150,000. Since Jeff and Rosa's AGI is well above $150,000, none of the loss will be deductible.

Retirement—Plan Distributions

9. b

Option 1 is correct. Jeff could roll the 401(k) into a traditional IRA.

Option 2 is incorrect. 10-year averaging is only available for individuals born before 1936.

Option 3 is correct. If he receives employer stock in a lump-sum distribution from a qualified plan, only the original cost basis of the stock is taxable at the time of distribution. The net unrealized appreciation (NUA) would not be taxed until the stock was subsequently sold.

Option 4 is incorrect. Favorable NUA treatment only applies to distributions from a qualified plan, not an IRA.

Insurance—Life Insurance Provisions

10. d

Under the Uniform Simultaneous Death Act, the insured (Jeff) is considered to survive the beneficiary. Therefore, the proceeds would automatically pass to the contingent beneficiary, Janice.

Retirement—Deferred-Compensation

11. c

Jeff would be taxed on the deferred compensation when he received the money (at retirement).

Estate Planning—Charitable Remainder Annuity Trust

12. c

A is incorrect. The deduction would be equal to the present value of the remainder interest in the trust.

B is incorrect. Since the trust will last for his life, the value of the trust will be included in his gross estate at Jeff's death. It should be noted that his estate will receive an estate tax charitable deduction.

C is correct. A CRAT is a tax-exempt trust. Therefore, the stock could be sold within the trust, without an immediate capital gain.

D is incorrect. Private foundations can be named as the beneficiary of a CRAT.

Estate Tax—2503(c) Trusts

13. e

Option 1 is correct. Any remaining trust principal must be distributed when the beneficiary attains age 21.

Option 2 is incorrect. Income can be accumulated in the trust until the beneficiary attains age 21.

Options 3 and 4 are correct.

Investments—Portfolio Weaknesses

14. d

Option 2 is not a weakness due to the high amount of income generated by the T-Bills.

Income Tax—Life Insurance Proceeds

15. d

Since Rosa purchased the policy from her father, a transfer-for-value has occurred. Therefore, Rosa will be taxed on the life insurance proceeds at ordinary income tax rates. Rosa can reduce the taxable amount by her basis in the policy. Her basis in the policy is the sum of the amount paid for the policy, plus the premiums paid.

Proceeds	$300,000
Less Basis	35,000 ($30,000 paid for policy plus $5,000 of premiums paid)
Taxable amount	$265,000

Estate Tax—Gross Estate

16. c

Description	Gross Estate Inclusion
Savings Account	$ 19,000
Universal Life Insurance (Jeff is owner)	500,000
Postal Stock	600,000
Traditional IRA	150,000
401(k) Plan	550,000
Investment Portfolio	1,000,000
Office Building	400,000
Residence	225,000
Furniture	50,000
SUV	55,000
Total	$3,549,000

Estate Tax—Adjusted Gross Estate

17. d

The Adjusted Gross Estate is the Gross Estate less:

Funeral expenses	$25,000
Administrative expenses	$50,000
Casualty Losses	$0
Debts	$106,000 (credit card plus 50% mortgage)

The total deduction is $181,000.

Income Tax—Section 1250 Property

18. d

The office building is Section 1250 property. The gain on Section 1250 property is taxed at the 25% capital gain rate to the extent of depreciation taken. Any additional gain is taxed at the 15% capital gain rate.

Proceeds	$800,000	
Basis	(585,000)	[$650,000 cost less $65,000 accumulated depreciation]
Gain	$215,000	

Of the $215,000 gain, only $65,000 would be taxed at the 25% capital gain rate. The remaining $150,000 of gain will be taxed at the 15% capital gain rate.

Investments—Options

19. e

Jeff has two choices. He can either sell the stock short, called "shorting against the box," or he can purchase a put option. Selling a call will not protect his gain, only limit a loss in the case that the stock price declines. The constructive sale rules have greatly limited the usefulness of the "short-against-the-box" technique for tax purposes.

Investments—Risks

20. d

Option 3 is incorrect, since mortgage-backed securities are pooled funds. The risk inherent in individual businesses is diversified away.

Estates—Trusts

21. c

C is correct. A spendthrift trust is a trust that restricts the beneficiary from transferring any of his or her future interest in the corpus or income.

A is incorrect. A special needs trust is a discretionary trust used for the benefit of a developmentally disabled child after the parent's death.

B is incorrect. A Section 2503(c) trust is a minor's trust in which the principal and income must be distributed to the beneficiary upon attainment of age 21.

D is incorrect. A GRAT is a trust that pays the grantor an annuity each year for a term of years (usually 2-5 years), at which point the assets in the trust are transferred to the beneficiary.

SUSAN WOOD

Case Scenario

Susan Wood

Today is December 31, 2007. Susan Wood has come to you, a financial planner, for help in developing a plan to accomplish her financial goals. From your initial meeting together, you have gathered the following information:

PERSONAL BACKGROUND AND INFORMATION

Susan Wood (Age 50)

Susan and her brother, Glen East, along with their mother Maude own EastWood Architectural, a C corporation. Susan is divorced with one daughter, Audrey (age 30), and a grandson, Billy (age 2).

Glen East (Age 45)

Glen is Susan's brother and a co-owner of EastWood Architectural. He is age 45 and married to Ruth, age 42. Ruth is a stay-at-home mom. They have two children, Matt, age 11 and Sarah, age 8.

Maude East (Age 74)

Maude is 74 years old. Maude's home is worth $120,000, and there is no longer a mortgage on it. She receives a modest pension benefit of $12,000 per year from her late husband's employer. She also receives Social Security benefits of $15,000 per year. Her most significant source of income has been CDs and government bonds. With the decline in interest rates, her discretionary income has decreased significantly, and she is concerned about having sufficient funds to take care of herself. Her 20% interest in the business is her single largest investment.

EastWood Architectural

Susan, Glen, and Maude own EastWood Architectural, a C corporation. Susan and Glen each own 40% of the stock, while Maude owns the remaining 20%. Susan and Glen formed the company 15 years ago with their funds and a capital contribution from Maude.

EastWood drafts architectural plans for several different venues, including small office complexes, small to medium retail centers and small resorts. Susan and Glen both believe the business has significant growth potential. The firm has been approached for other projects, such as a local government office complex and an upscale retail center.

Today EastWood employs a total of 15 people—Susan, Glen, 7 architects, and 6 administrative office personnel. The firm grossed $3,000,000 last year and had a profit of $700,000. Susan and Glen have not had the firm appraised, but believe a reasonable value is $4,500,000. The firm does not pay any dividends. Maude has indicated to both Susan and Glen she would like to start receiving income from the business or sell her stock to Susan or Glen.

Susan and Glen each receive a base salary of $250,000 per year. The other 7 architects receive salaries ranging from $75,000 to $175,000. Salaries for the remaining office personnel range between $18,000 and $50,000.

Susan and Glen are interested in providing additional benefits that would help them retain their current employees and attract the additional talent they need to remain competitive. They are also interested in creating a market for their stock. Neither Susan nor Glen is particularly interested in acquiring a bigger stake in the firm, but they do not want to see stock sold to individuals outside the firm. Susan's daughter has no interest in the firm.

SUSAN'S PERSONAL AND FINANCIAL GOALS

- Leave the company within five years, while maintaining her desired level of income and lifestyle.
- Establish an exit strategy for the business.
- Ensure her mother, Maude, has adequate income, possibly through the acquisition of the mother's stock in the company.
- Evaluate both investment and insurance risk.
- Spend $50,000 on the purchase of new bedroom and living room furniture for her home.

ECONOMIC INFORMATION

- Susan expects inflation to average 3.5% annually, both currently and for the long term.
- She expects her salary to increase 10.0% annually.
- Interest rates are very low and expected to rise in the near future.
- Slow growth economy; stocks are expected to grow at 9.5% annually.

INCOME TAX INFORMATION

Her marginal income tax rate is currently 35% for federal income taxes. The state income tax rate is a flat 5%.

RETIREMENT INFORMATION

Susan plans to retire in 5 years at the age of 55. She would like to have a standard of living equal to 80% of her preretirement income. She expects to be in retirement for 35 years.

The company implemented a profit-sharing plan several years ago. Last year, the company contributed 15% of each eligible employee's salary to the plan. The plan incorporates a 5-year cliff vesting schedule, and employees are eligible to participate after completing one year of service. The plan offers loan provisions, subject to Internal Revenue Code limits. Susan's account has a current balance of $350,000.

Susan expects to collect $13,500 in Social Security benefits at her normal retirement age. She has been considering the possibility of receiving her Social Security benefits at age 62.

DIVORCE INFORMATION

Susan and her ex-husband, Mark, were divorced two years ago. Mark works in the marketing department of a Fortune 500 company, and his salary is $75,000. Pursuant to the divorce arrangement, Susan is required to pay Mark alimony in the amount of $45,000 each year for the next seven years. If Susan dies during the next seven years, payments must be made from her estate.

Susan and Mark purchased a house several years ago for $280,000. They owned the house together as JTWROS until the divorce. Per the divorce agreement, the house was titled in Mark's name only. The value of the house at the time of divorce was $350,000, and the value of the house today is $375,000.

Susan was also required to transfer her $800,000 whole life insurance policy to Mark pursuant to the divorce agreement. The cash value of the policy is currently $40,000, and the divorce agreement requires Susan to pay the annual $10,000 premium.

GIFTS, ESTATES, TRUSTS, AND WILL INFORMATION

Gifts

Susan has not given any taxable gifts.

Estates

Susan's will leaves everything to her ex-husband, Mark. She has not updated the will since the divorce.

STATEMENT OF CASH FLOWS
Susan Wood
Annual Statement of Cash Flows
January 1, 2007—December 31, 2007

CASH INFLOWS:

Salary:	Susan's Salary	$250,000	
	Susan's Bonus	$100,000	
	Total	$350,000	
Unearned Income:	Dividends	$2,000	
	Interest Income	$30,000	
		$32,000	
Total Income:			**$382,000**

CASH OUTFLOWS:

Mortgage Payments:	Primary Residence	$50,000	
Insurance Premiums:	Homeowners	$2,500	
	Auto	3,000	
	Life (Alimony)	10,000	
	Total Insurance Premiums	$15,500	
Misc. Expenses:	Alimony	$45,000	
	Entertainment	20,000	
	Food	8,400	
	Clothes	15,000	
	Utilities	10,000	
	Charity	20,000	
	Total Misc. Expenses	$118,400	
Tax:	Property	$ 35,000	
	Income Tax	135,000	
	Total Tax	$170,000	
Total Outflows:			**$353,900**
Discretionary Cash			**$28,100**

STATEMENT OF FINANCIAL POSITION
Susan Wood
Statement of Financial Position
As of December 31, 2007

ASSETS[1]

Cash/Cash Equivalents

S	Savings Account	$8,000
S	Cash Value of Universal Life Policy	20,000
M	Cash Value of Whole Life Policy	40,000
Total Cash/Cash Equiv.		**$68,000**

Invested Assets

S	EastWood Stock	$1,800,000
S	Profit-Sharing Plan	350,000
S	Investment Portfolio	900,000
Total Investments		**$3,050,000**

Personal-Use Assets

S	Primary Residence	$750,000
S	Personal Property/Furniture	200,000
S	Cadillac	85,000
S	Ford Explorer	50,000
Total Personal Use		**$1,085,000**
Total Assets		**$4,203,000**

LIABILITIES AND NET WORTH

Liabilities[2]

Current Liabilities

S	Visa Credit Card	$35,000
S	Mastercard Credit Card	20,000
Total Current Liabilities		**$55,000**

Long-Term Liabilities

A	Auto Loan[3]	$200,000
S	Mortgage—Primary Residence	$600,000
Total Long-Term Liabilities		**$800,000**
Total Liabilities		**$855,000**

Net Worth — $3,348,000

Total Liabilities and Net Worth — **$4,203,000**

Notes to Financial Statements:

[1] Assets are stated at fair market value (rounded to even dollars).

[2] Liabilities are stated at principal only (rounded to even dollars).

[3] The auto loan was used for the purchase of a car by Audrey. Susan is a cosigner on the loan. Audrey has made all payments to date on a timely basis.

Property Ownership
S—Susan's property.
M—Mark's property.
A—Audrey's property.

INSURANCE INFORMATION

Life Insurance

	Universal Life	Whole Life
Insured	Glen	Susan
Face Amount	$500,000	$800,000
Cash Value	$20,000	$40,000
Annual Premium	$6,000	$10,000
Premium Payer	Glen	Susan
Beneficiary	Susan	Mark
Policyowner	Susan	Mark
Comments	Susan is a revocable beneficiary.	Policy transferred to Mark pursuant to the divorce.

Health Insurance

Susan is covered by the company's health plan, which is an indemnity plan with a $1,000 deductible per person per year and an 80/20 major medical coinsurance clause.

Long-Term Disability Insurance

Susan is covered by an *own occupation* policy with premiums paid by the company. The benefits equal 60% of gross pay after a 180-day elimination period. The policy covers both sickness and accidents.

INVESTMENT INFORMATION

Detailed Investment Portfolio

Description	Expected Return	Current FMV
Taxable Zero-Coupon Bonds	7%	$200,000
Zero-Coupon Municipal Bond Fund	6%	$300,000
Long-Term Municipal Bond Fund	5%	$200,000
International Stocks	10%	$10,000
Precious Metals Mutual Fund	4%	$90,000
Treasury Bills	2%	$100,000
Total		$900,000

Susan is willing to take reasonable investment risk if appropriate, but she does not want to invest aggressively.

She is interested in investing in more equity securities. She was recently told by a broker that Rett Manufacturing Company stock would be a wise purchase. The stock is currently trading at $45 per share and pays a dividend of $2 per share, with an estimated 4% growth rate of the dividend. The stock has a beta of 1.04.

SUSAN WOOD

■

Questions

Susan Wood

1. Susan's financial adviser has indicated that Susan and Glen have several alternatives to choose from that would address their mother's desire for income and need for greater liquidity. These alternatives could include all the following EXCEPT:

   a. Private annuity.

   b. Installment sale.

   c. Rights offering.

   d. Company stock redemption.

2. Susan and Glen have been considering the use of a private annuity to purchase Maude's business interest. Which of the following statements reflect the disadvantage of a private annuity?

   1. Payments must continue to Maude, even if she lives significantly longer than her projected life expectancy.

   2. If Maude dies sooner than her projected life expectancy, Susan and Glen may have a taxable gift.

   3. Susan's interest expense on the private annuity payments will not be deductible for income tax purposes.

   4. If Maude dies within three years of the transaction, the stock will be included in her gross estate.

      a. 1 only.

      b. 1 and 3.

      c. 2 and 4.

      d. 2, 3, and 4.

      e. 1, 2, 3, and 4.

3. Glen is considering converting the business to an S corporation when Susan retires. If this takes place EastWood may be subject to all of the following EXCEPT:

   a. Built-in Gains Tax.

   b. LIFO Recapture Tax.

   c. Excess Net Passive Income Tax.

   d. Depreciation Recapture Tax.

4. Glen is willing to consider a 10- or 15-year installment sale, but only if Susan will also participate in the purchase of Maude's stock. Is an installment purchase appropriate for Susan's situation?

   a. Yes, it allows her to purchase the stock in small amounts over time.

   b. No, the time frame of the purchase falls within Susan's planned retirement time horizon.

   c. Yes, it allows her to maintain an ownership percentage equal to Glen's.

   d. No, Susan may not be able to fully deduct the interest expense associated with the purchase.

5. What type of plan benefits could EastWood establish that not only would provide a means for Maude to liquidate her stock, but eventually could be used to help Susan and Glen liquidate their own holdings?

    a. Restricted stock plan.

    b. ESOP.

    c. 412(i) plan.

    d. Corporate owned life insurance (COLI).

6. Glen and Susan have agreed to implement cross purchase buy-sell agreements between the two of them in the event of death or disability. They have chosen not to implement one between them and Maude. Which of the following statements is true regarding the buy-sell agreement?

    a. Maude could only be included in the buy-sell agreement if she were an active participant in the business.

    b. Premiums will be deductible by the corporation, because the S Corporation election was not made.

    c. The cost to insure Maude's life would be significantly more expensive if she were included in the buy-sell agreement.

    d. Provisions in Maude's will could bind Susan and Glen to purchase her shares upon her death.

7. A Section 303 stock redemption provides which of the following?

    a. A method to transfer shares to grandchildren, with the amount transferred being excluded from the transferor's gross estate.

    b. A method to fully fund a marital trust with no tax implications for the surviving spouse.

    c. A method for redeeming sufficient stock to pay estate taxes and deductible funeral and administrative costs, with the redeemed stock being taxed at ordinary income tax rates.

    d. A method for redeeming sufficient stock to pay estate taxes and deductible funeral and administrative costs with the redeemed stock being taxed at capital gains rates.

8. Susan's daughter is married to a wealthy businessman and is financially secure. Susan would prefer that the bulk of her estate go to her grandson. Which of the following would be the best technique to accomplish her goal?

    a. Make annual gifts to her grandson that do not exceed the annual exclusion amount.

    b. Include generation-skipping transfer provisions in her will.

    c. Title her assets as JTWROS with her grandchild.

    d. Make a lifetime gift of the GST exemption amount to her grandson.

9. Susan would like to help fund the college education costs for her grandson. Assuming she does not want to give up control of the assets and wants tax deferral, which of the following would be an appropriate vehicle to consider?

    a. 2503(b) Trust.

    b. Roth IRA.

    c. UGMA.

    d. 529 plan.

10. Which of the following investments would be appropriate to diversify Susan's investment portfolio?

    1. Zero-coupon municipal bond fund.

    2. International stocks.

    3. S & P 500 Index fund.

    4. Leveraged commercial real estate.

        a. 1 only.

        b. 1 and 4.

        c. 2 and 3.

        d. 2, 3, and 4.

        e. 1, 2, 3, and 4.

11. Given the current economic environment, which of the following strategies would be the best for Susan?

        a. Sell the Treasury Bills.

        b. Buy convertible bonds.

        c. Sell the long-term municipal bond fund.

        d. Buy intermediate term bonds.

12. Assuming that Susan has a required rate of return of 7%. Would the purchase of Rett Manufacturing Company stock be advisable for her portfolio?

        a. Yes, because the stock is undervalued.

        b. No, because the stock is overvalued.

        c. Yes, because the required rate of return is greater than the expected growth rate.

        d. No, because the stock is not within her risk tolerance.

13. Which of the following benefits could EastWood install on a discriminatory basis, without adverse tax consequences for any covered individuals?

    1. A group term life insurance plan that provides up to $50,000 of tax-free coverage.

    2. A disability income plan that provides benefits that are subject to income tax.

    3. A supplemental executive retirement plan (SERP).

    4. Section 125 cafeteria plan.

        a. 1 only.

        b. 2 and 3.

        c. 1 2, and 3.

        d. 2, 3, and 4.

        e. 1, 3, and 4.

14. If Susan and Glen entered into a stock redemption buy-sell agreement with EastWood, which of the following would be a disadvantage?

    a. The possible transfer-for-value problem that could occur upon Susan's death if Glen survives her.

    b. More policies will be required with a redemption agreement than with a cross-purchase agreement.

    c. Both the value of the stock and the life insurance proceeds will be included in Susan's estate upon her death.

    d. The possible income taxation of the insurance proceeds to EastWood upon the death of Susan or Glen.

15. Maude is covered by both Medicare Part A and B. Which of the following expenses are not covered under Medicare?

    a. Hospice costs for terminally ill patients.

    b. Mammograms.

    c. Annual flu shots.

    d. Coverage for custodial care.

16. Marvin, a long-time employee at EastWood Architectural, resigned during the year to pursue other opportunities. How many months of medical insurance COBRA continuation coverage will be available to Marvin?

    a. No coverage will be available.

    b. 18 months.

    c. 29 months.

    d. 36 months.

17. Per the divorce agreement, Susan and Mark's house was transferred to Mark. Which of the following statements is true regarding the income tax consequences of the transfer?

    a. Since the transfer occurred after the couple was no longer married, a gift occurred from Susan to Mark.

    b. Mark will have a basis in the home of $280,000.

    c. Mark's basis in the home will be increased by any gift tax paid upon the transfer.

    d. Mark will have a basis in the home of $350,000.

18. Which of the following statements is/are true regarding the whole life insurance policy on Susan's life?

    1. If Susan died today, the entire $800,000 death benefit would be included in her gross estate.
    2. The cash value of the policy, less the annual exclusion, was considered a taxable gift from Susan to Mark.
    3. Susan is entitled to an income tax deduction for the premiums paid on the life insurance policy.
    4. A transfer of a life insurance policy pursuant to a divorce agreement is considered a transfer-for-value for income tax purposes, and therefore the death benefit will be taxable to Mark when Susan dies.

       a. 1 and 2.
       b. 1 and 3.
       c. 2 and 4.
       d. 1, 3, and 4.
       e. 2, 3, and 4.

19. Which of the following statements is (are) correct regarding Susan's financial statements?

    1. Susan should not include the whole life policy on her Statement of Financial Position.
    2. Susan has an inadequate emergency fund.
    3. Susan should not include the auto loan on her Statement of Financial Position.
    4. If Susan purchases the new bedroom and living room furniture for her home, this purchase would appear as a variable outflow on her cash flow statement.

       a. 1 and 4.
       b. 2 and 3.
       c. 2, 3, and 4.
       d. 1, 3, and 4.
       e. 1, 2, 3, and 4.

20. Susan has inquired about the possibility of taking a loan from the profit-sharing plan. Which of the following statements is true regarding loans from qualified plans?

       a. Because the plan is a Keogh plan, loans to Susan, a business owner, will be limited to 20% of her salary.
       b. The interest paid on the loan will be deductible for income tax purposes to the extent Susan has taxable investment income.
       c. Susan is not permitted to take a loan from the plan because she is a more-than-10% owner.
       d. The maximum loan Susan can take from the plan is $50,000.

SUSAN WOOD

―――――――――――― ■ ――――――――――――

Solutions

Susan Wood

ANSWER SUMMARY

1.	c	6.	c	11.	c	16.	a
2.	b	7.	d	12.	a	17.	b
3.	d	8.	b	13.	b	18.	b
4.	b	9.	d	14.	d	19.	e
5.	b	10.	c	15.	d	20.	d

SUMMARY OF TOPICS

1. Estate Planning—Business Continuation
2. Estate Planning—Private Annuity
3. Fundamentals—S Corporations
4. Estate Planning—Business Succession Planning
5. Retirement—Qualified Plans
6. Estate Planning—Buy-Sell Agreement
7. Estate Planning—Section 303 Redemption
8. Estate Planning—Gifting Techniques
9. Fundamentals—Education Funding
10. Investments—Diversification
11. Investments—Portfolio Management
12. Investments—Constant Dividend Growth Model
13. Retirement—Employee Benefits
14. Estate Planning—Buy-Sell Agreement
15. Insurance—Medicare
16. Insurance—Health Insurance
17. Income Tax—Property Transfer
18. Income Tax—Life Insurance
19. Fundamentals—Financial Statements
20. Retirement—Qualified Plan Rules

SOLUTIONS

Estate Planning—Business Continuation

1. c

A rights offering would not provide the mother with income.

Estate Planning—Private Annuity

2. b

Statement 1 is correct. The payments will continue to Maude for life.

Statement 2 is incorrect. There is no gift with a private annuity.

Statement 3 is correct. Interest expense paid by the buyer is nondeductible with a private annuity.

Statement 4 is incorrect. This is a sale technique, so the stock is immediately out of Maude's estate.

Fundamentals—S Corporations

3. d

Options (a), (b), and (c) are taxes S corporations may be subject to if they were previously C corporations.

Estate Planning—Business Succession Planning

4. b

Susan is planning on retiring in five years. Therefore, a 10- to 15-year installment note payable is probably not a wise idea. Option (a) is incorrect since all of the stock is purchased at one time. Only the payments are made over time. Option (c) is incorrect because Susan wishes to retire soon. Option (d) is incorrect because interest expense is deductible in installment sales.

Retirement—Qualified Plans

5. b

Option (a) is incorrect. A restricted stock plan would provide more shares to the owners. This plan would not help in the liquidation of the owners' interests.

Option (b) is correct. An employee stock ownership plan (ESOP) may be appropriate. This plan, which is a qualified plan, could purchase the stock from the shareholders. ESOPs have other tax advantages as well.

Option (c) is incorrect. A 412(i) plan is a defined-benefit plan that is funded with life insurance.

Option (d) is incorrect. COLI is a good planning strategy, but will not solve their liquidation goals.

Estate Planning—Buy-Sell Agreement

6. c

Maude is older, and, therefore, premiums on a life insurance policy on her life would be more expensive. Buy-sell agreements are not limited to active participants. The premiums are not deductible. Maude's will cannot require Susan and Glen to purchase her shares.

Estate Planning—Section 303 Redemption

7. d

A 303 redemption would provide for capital gain treatment when a decedent's estate sells company stock back to the company. To qualify for Section 303, the redemption proceeds must be used for federal estate taxes, state death taxes, funeral or administrative costs.

Estate Planning—Gifting Techniques

8. b

Although most of the strategies have merit, strategies (a), (c), and (d) all involve giving up some control over the assets right now.

Fundamentals—Education Funding

9. d

Option (a) is incorrect. A 2503(b) trust would cause Susan to give up control of the assets and does not provide tax deferral.

Option (b) is incorrect. Susan does not qualify for a Roth IRA due to her income.

Option (c) is incorrect. An UTMA account would cause Susan to give up control of the assets and does not provide tax deferral.

Option (d) is correct.

Investments—Diversification

10. c

Susan has relatively no equity exposure in her portfolio other than the stock in the closely held company.

Statement 1 is incorrect. The municipal bond fund would not provide the needed growth component.

Statement 4 is incorrect. Leveraged commercial real estate is outside her risk tolerance.

Investments—Portfolio Management

11. c

When interest rates are expected to rise, an investor should sell long-term bonds and reinvest the proceeds at a higher coupon rate once interest rates rise.

Investments—Constant Dividend Growth Model

12. a

Under the constant dividend growth model, the stock is worth $69.33.

Value = ($2 × 1.04) / (.07 − .04) = $69.33

The stock is undervalued at $45 per share.

Retirement—Employee Benefits
13. b

Statement 1 is incorrect. If a group term life insurance plan is discriminatory, the key employees will lose the $50,000 income tax exclusion.

Statement 2 is correct. If the disability benefits are taxable, the employees will not be taxed on the payment of premiums by the employer, even if the plan discriminates.

Statement 3 is correct. A SERP is a nonqualified plan that can discriminate.

Statement 4 is incorrect. If a cafeteria plan is discriminatory, the key employees will have adverse tax consequences.

Estate Planning—Buy-Sell Agreement
14. d

Option (a) is incorrect. A transfer of a life insurance policy from a shareholder to a corporation will not be considered a transfer-for-value.

Option (b) is incorrect. A cross purchase agreement will typically require the purchase of more policies.

Option (c) is incorrect. Only the stock would be included in Susan's estate.

Option (d) is correct. Life insurance proceeds received by a corporation are subject to corporate alternative minimum tax.

Insurance—Medicare
15. d

Custodial care is not covered under Medicare.

Insurance—Health Insurance
16. a

COBRA coverage only applies to employers with 20 or more employees.

Income Tax—Property Transfer
17. b

When a recipient receives property pursuant to a divorce, the basis in the property will always be carryover basis.

Income Tax—Life Insurance

18. b

Statement 1 is correct. The policy was transferred to Mark pursuant to the divorce two years ago. Transfers of life insurance within three years of death will cause gross estate inclusion.

Statement 2 is incorrect. A transfer of a life insurance policy pursuant to a divorce is considered a property transfer and is not subject to gift tax.

Statement 3 is correct. Since Susan transferred ownership of the policy, and she is required to pay premiums on the life insurance policy, the premium payments will be considered deductible alimony. Note: Mark will be required to include the amount of the premium payments in his gross income.

Statement 4 is incorrect. Transfers incident to a divorce are not subject to the transfer-for-value rule.

Fundamentals—Financial Statements

19. e

Statement 1 is correct. Susan is not the owner of the policy.

Statement 2 is correct. Susan's emergency fund should be equal to 3-6 months worth of nondiscretionary expenses.

Statement 3 is correct. The auto loan should only be included on the Statement of Financial Condition if Audrey defaults on the loan (Susan is only a cosigner).

Statement 4 is correct. The purchase is a variable outflow. This purchase would also appear as a Personal-Use Asset on her net worth statement.

Retirement—Qualified Plan Rules

20. d

Option (a) is incorrect. The plan is not a Keogh plan, because the company is a C Corporation. In addition, there is no such rule for loans.

Option (b) is incorrect. Interest on loans from qualified plans is considered personal interest and is not deductible for income tax purposes.

Option (c) is incorrect. While there were previously restrictions on loans for business owners, those restrictions have been eliminated. The previous restrictions only applied to Keogh plans.

Option (d) is correct. The maximum loan that can be taken from a profit-sharing plan is $50,000.

WILLIAM AND MARILYN MATHEWS

Case Scenario

William and Marilyn Mathews

CASE SCENARIO

Released as of November 1994

© Certified Financial Planner Board of Standards, Inc., Reprinted with permission

*Questions marked with an asterisk (*) are no longer accurate due to changes in the Federal Tax Code.

Your clients, Bill and Marilyn Mathews, have asked you to help them with a number of issues facing them as Bill prepares to sell his business and formally retire. Marilyn will also retire, having worked as the company bookkeeper for twenty years. Negotiations for the sale of Bill's business, Calculator City, are almost concluded, pending resolution of a number of questions Bill raised regarding installment payments for the business as well as a request from the proposed owner that Bill continue to provide consulting services.

PERSONAL INFORMATION

	Age	Health	Occupation
William Mathews	65	Excellent	Business Owner
Marilyn Mathews	63	"	Bookkeeper
John Mathews (son)	32	"	Engineer
James Mathews (son)	30	"	CPA
Grandchildren	3, 4, 5, and 7	"	

Neither son has any intention of becoming involved in the business. The Mathews file a joint tax return. Client and spouse have simple wills leaving all to each other.

ECONOMIC ENVIRONMENT

The current economic environment exhibits low real short-term rates, high real long-term rates, little economic growth, and high unemployment.

CLIENT OBJECTIVES

- Maintain current lifestyle, including frequent travel.

- Revise estate plan to minimize taxes, take advantage of opportunities in various elections available in the Internal Revenue Code, and maximize amounts passing to children and grandchildren.

- Review investment portfolio and make changes as necessary to reflect different priorities and risk tolerance levels during retirement. Initial indications are that the clients are willing to take normal investment risks, desirous of adequate current income, reasonable safety of principal, inflation protection, tax advantage, and some modest long-term appreciation, in that order of priority.

- Review and revise total risk management and insurance situation as necessary to provide adequate protection and eliminate gaps and overlaps.

- Determine the most advantageous method of taking distributions from the 401(k) accounts.

FINANCIAL STATEMENTS
WILLIAM AND MARILYN MATHEWS
Statement of Financial Position
12/31/92

ASSETS		LIABILITIES AND NET WORTH	
Invested Assets			
Cash/Cash Equivalents	$8,000	Auto Loan	$6,000
Marketable Securities[a]	1,580,000	Mortgage [b]	12,000
Business Interest [c]	1,500,000	Mortgage[d]	74,000
Life Insurance Cash Value[e]	60,000		$92,000
Annuity	120,000		
	$3,268,000		
Use Assets			
Primary Residence	$188,000		
Summer Home	126,000		
Personal Property	60,000		
Automobiles	26,000	Net Worth	$3,951,000
	$400,000		
Retirement Plan Assets[f]			
IRA (H)	$27,000		
IRA (W)	28,000		
401(k) (H)	280,000		
401(k) (W)	40,000		
	$375,000		
Total Assets	**$4,043,000**	**Total Liabilities & Net Worth**	**$4,043,000**

a. See separate Investment Portfolio Supplement.

b. Principal residence; originally, 30 years @ 7%.

c. Business is to be sold for $1.5 million. Purchase price was $700,000 in 1982. Terms of sale include $300,000 down payment on July 1, 1993, with the balance to be paid over 120 months starting August 1, 1993, at 10% interest.

d. Summer home; originally, 15 years @ 9%.

e. Face Amount: $200,000; Bill is insured, Marilyn is beneficiary.

f. Spouse is beneficiary for IRA and 401(k). The IRAs are invested in a common stock growth mutual fund. The 401(k) plans are invested in 3-year Treasury notes.

PROJECTED MONTHLY CASH FLOW STATEMENT
WILLIAM AND MARILYN MATHEWS
1/1/93 through 12/31/93
(Incomplete)

Cash Inflows

Social Security (H)	$820
Social Security (W)	$410
Installment Payments (120 pmts @ 10%)	?
Interest Income (tax-exempt)	$600
Dividend Income	$540
Interest Income (taxable)	?
Other Investment Income	?

Outflows

Savings and Investment	?
Mortgage (residence: PITI)	$600
Mortgage (summer home: PITI)	$1,100
Food	$300
Utilities	$400
Transportation (gas, oil, maintenance)	$200
Car Payment	$600
Clothing	$250
Entertainment	$450
Travel	$1,680
Family Gifts	$1,666
Charitable Gifts	$500
Life Insurance	$300
Hospitalization (Medigap/Medicare)	$100
Automobile Insurance	$150
Miscellaneous	?
Federal Income Tax	$5,800
State Income Tax	$900
Other	?

INSURANCE AND ANNUITY INFORMATION

Life Insurance

Person Insured/Owner	Bill
Type of Policy	Whole Life
Face Amount	$200,000
Dividend Option	Paid Up Additions
Issue Date	2/13/77
Beneficiary	Marilyn
Current Cash Value	$60,000
Premium	$300 per month

Person Insured/Owner	Bill
Type of Policy	Single Premium Deferred Annuity
Fixed or Variable	Fixed
Current Value	$120,000
Current Interest Rate	6.5%
Issue Date	1/1/81
Purchase Price	$40,000

Homeowners Policy

Type	HO-3
Amount on Dwelling	$175,000
Personal Property Coverage	$ 87,500
Personal Liability	$100,000

Automobile Policy

Type	Personal Auto Policy
Bodily Injury/Property Damage	$300,000 Combined Single Limit
Collision	$250 Deductible
Comprehensive	Full, with $100 Deductible
Uninsured Motorist	$300,000 Single Limit

INVESTMENT PORTFOLIO SUPPLEMENT

These securities were accumulated over a period of years and are essentially unmanaged.

Common Stocks	FMV
AT&T	$30,000
Bell South	10,000
Bell Atlantic	9,000
Ameritech	8,500
NYNEX	7,000
Pacific Telesis	8,000
Southwestern Bell	8,000
US West	7,000
Canon	22,000
Comerica Bank	29,000
Danko	7,000
de Beers	8,000
du Pont	29,000
Disney	12,000
Dow Chemical	9,000
Detroit Edison	24,000
General Motors	8,000
GM E	10,500
D&T, Inc.*	25,000
Common Stock Mutual Fund (IRAs)	55,000

Municipal Bonds

Franklin Intermediate Tax Exampt Fund	$100,000

Annuities & Insurance

Cash Value Life Insurance	$60,000
Single Premium Deferred Annuity	120,000

(Continued on next page)

Bonds

Treasury Notes (401(k))	$320,000
US EE Savings Bonds	75,000

Cash and Equivalents

Cash	$8,000
Cash Equivalents incl. Money Markets	134,000
Treasury Securities (T-Bills)	1,000,000
TOTAL	**$2,143,000**

*Small Business Corp. (1244 stock) solely owned by Bill and originally purchased for $76,000 on 1/1/87.

WILLIAM AND MARILYN MATHEWS

Multiple-Choice Questions

William and Marilyn Mathews

*Questions marked with an asterisk (*) are no longer accurate due to changes in the Federal Tax Code.

1. The tax treatment of the down payment made to Bill for the sale of his business is:

    a. <u>Not</u> taxable as a return of basis.

    b. Fully taxable as a capital gain.

    c. Partially a return of basis and partially taxable as ordinary income.

    d. Partially a return of basis, partially a capital gain, and partially ordinary income.

    e. Partially a return of capital and partially a capital gain.

2. How much will Bill receive from the monthly installment payments during 1993 (rounded to the nearest dollar)?

    a. $79,290.

    b. $95,149.

    c. $190,297.

    d. $379,290.

    e. $395,149.

3. The amount of interest income from the installment sale for the year ending 12/31/93 is approximately:

    a. $49,000.

    b. $59,000.

    c. $60,000.

    d. $72,000.

    e. $120,000.

4. How will Bill's receipt of installment payments for the sale of his business affect his Social Security benefits?

    a. His Social Security benefits will be reduced because of his installment payments.

    b. His Social Security benefits will <u>not</u> be taxable because installment payments are <u>not</u> wages.

    c. Receipt of installment payments will increase the amount of Modified Adjusted Gross Income, causing some of the Social Security benefits to be taxable.

    d. Because Bill is 65, his Social Security benefits will be subject to the excess earnings test applied to the installment payments. Benefits will be reduced $1 for every $2 earned over the base amount.

    e. Because Bill is 65, his Social Security benefits will be subject to the excess earnings test applied to the installment payments. Benefits will be reduced $1 for every $3 earned over the base amount.

5. * Bill and Marilyn both have account balances in the 401(k) Plan, and they want to determine what options they can pursue.

    Which of the following statements describe options available for Bill and Marilyn?

    1. Bill can make an IRA Rollover with his account; Marilyn can elect 10-Year Special Averaging for hers.

    2. Both Bill and Marilyn can make IRA Rollovers.

    3. Bill can elect a partial rollover and use 5-Year Special Averaging on the balance; Marilyn can roll over her entire amount.

    4. Both Bill and Marilyn can elect either 5-Year or 10-Year Special Averaging for their respective distributions.

        a. 1, 2 and 4.

        b. 1 and 3.

        c. 2 only.

        d. 2 and 3.

        e. 1, 2, 3 and 4.

6. The Mathews family is considering the purchase of a survivorship life insurance policy, payable on the second death of either Bill or Marilyn, for the primary purpose of providing liquidity for the payment of the federal estate tax. The ownership and beneficiary arrangements are being studied for the best overall result.

    Which of the following options for ownership and beneficiary arrangements are viable?

    1. Bill and Marilyn can purchase the policy and retain ownership; the proceeds will not be includible in either estate because of the unlimited marital deduction.

    2. Bill and Marilyn can purchase the policy, and then transfer ownership to one or both of their sons, so that the proceeds avoid inclusion in either Bill's or Marilyn's estate no matter when death occurs because they do not have any incidents of ownership.

    3. Ownership can be vested immediately in an irrevocable life insurance trust, with appropriate "Crummey" provisions, to avoid inclusion of the proceeds in either estate.

    4. The Mathews family Revocable Living Trust can be the initial owner and beneficiary, in order to avoid estate taxes in either estate, because life insurance death proceeds retain their tax-free character in the trust.

        a. 1, 3 and 4.

        b. 2 and 4.

        c. 3 only.

        d. 2 only.

        e. 1 and 4.

7. If Bill decides to make a partial withdrawal from his Single Premium Deferred Annuity, what income tax result will ensue?

    a. The withdrawal will be taxed as long-term capital gain, subject to a maximum rate of 28%.

    b. The withdrawal will be subject to ordinary income tax, since there is <u>no</u> preference for long-term capital gain.

    c. The withdrawal will be taxed according to the annuity rules, so that a portion will be taxable as ordinary income and the balance will be a tax-free recovery of capital.

    d. The withdrawal will be tax free up to Bill's cost basis, since FIFO treatment applies to this annuity.

    e. The withdrawal will be taxable on a LIFO basis to the extent of earnings in the contract.

8. Bill is contemplating selling his D&T, Inc. stock for the fair market value. Assuming he sold D&T on 12/31/92, the tax impact would be:

    a. A fully deductible capital loss of $51,000.

    b. A capital loss limited to $3,000 assuming no other investment transactions; carryover $48,000 long-term capital loss.

    c. An ordinary loss of $50,000 with a $1,000 loss carryover.

    d. An ordinary loss of $51,000.

    e. A short-term capital loss of $51,000 because of Sec. 1244 status.

9. In view of the combined estate values for Bill and Marilyn, which of the following estate planning techniques may be appropriate?

    1. Placing life insurance in an irrevocable trust.

    2. Making use of annual gift tax exclusion.

    3. Establishing a revocable living trust, using the unlimited marital deduction and the full unified credit.

    4. Arranging for a preferred stock recapitalization for Bill's business interest.

        a. 2 and 3.

        b. 1, 2 and 3.

        c. 1, 3 and 4.

        d. 1, 2 and 4.

        e. 1, 2, 3 and 4.

10. The Mathews currently own a number of tax-advantaged financial instruments. Which of the following statements is/are true with respect to these various instruments?

    1. Interest income and capital appreciation from the municipal bond fund is federally tax exempt.

    2. An initial partial withdrawal from the single premium deferred annuity is fully taxable.

    3. When redeemed, the return on the savings bonds is <u>not</u> subject to state income taxes.

    4. The Treasury bills are federally taxed only upon maturity.

      a. 1, 2 and 3.

      b. 2 and 4.

      c. 3 only.

      d. 3 and 4.

      e. 1, 2, 3 and 4.

11. If Bill and Marilyn wish to limit the growth of their combined estate, which techniques may be advisable?

    1. Use of the annual gift tax exclusion and split gift election.

    2. Current use of both unified credits.

    3. Payment of tuition for grandchildren.

    4. Payment of direct medical expenses for children and grandchildren.

      a. 1 and 2.

      b. 2, 3 and 4.

      c. 1 only.

      d. 1, 2 and 3.

      e. 1, 2, 3 and 4.

12. The CFP Board of Examiners has eliminated this question and answer.

13. Assume Bill provides consulting services for the new owner and is properly classified as an independent contractor. Which statements properly describe Bill's ability to shelter current taxable income?

    1. Bill may take a nondeductible IRA for $2,000.

    2. Bill may set up a profit-sharing Keogh.

    3. Bill can set up a money-purchase plan.

    4. Bill can set up a combined money-purchase and profit-sharing plan, but his contributions will be limited to 20% of Schedule C income.

      a. 2 and 3.

      b. 1, 2 and 3.

      c. 2, 3 and 4.

      d. 1, 2, 3 and 4.

      e. 1 and 3.

14. In reviewing Bill and Marilyn's cash flow projections as well as the investment portfolio supplement, you question the appropriateness of some of the holdings. Which combination of portfolio weaknesses best summarizes a valid critique of their investments?

    a. Excessive liquidity, inadequate tax advantage, marginal equity diversification.

    b. Inadequate tax advantage, excessive growth orientation, marginal equity diversification.

    c. Excessive liquidity, excessive growth orientation, inadequate tax advantage.

    d. Excessive reliance on Treasury Bills, insufficient growth opportunities, inadequate current income.

    e. Insufficient growth opportunities, inadequate liquidity, excessive tax advantage.

15. Assuming that Bill reaches agreement with the new owner as to the installment payments for the business interest, what are the estate tax ramifications if Bill dies at the end of the third year of the ten-year payout schedule?

    a. The remaining value of the installments is <u>not</u> includible in Bill's estate, because the payments continuing to Marilyn qualify for the marital deduction.

    b. Seventy percent of the original cash purchase price upon which the installments were based is includible in Bill's estate but qualifies for the marital deduction because payments will continue to Marilyn.

    c. The present value of the future income stream to Marilyn is included in Bill's estate, but the continuing payments qualify for the marital deduction.

    d. The present value of the future income stream to Marilyn is included in Bill's estate, but the continuing income payments do <u>not</u> qualify for the marital deduction because it is a terminable interest.

    e. Nothing is included in the estate because the installment payments are <u>not</u> guaranteed.

16. The inadequacies in their estate planning can be summarized as follows:

    1. Failure to take full advantage of each unified credit.

    2. Failure to avoid probate.

    3. Lack of proper documents to address the potential problem of incapacity.

    4. Failure to coordinate titling of assets with documentation.

        a. 1 and 2.

        b. 1, 2 and 3.

        c. 2, 3 and 4.

        d. 2 and 4.

        e. 1, 2, 3 and 4.

Regarding questions 17 and 18 and given the current economic conditions, you recommend allocating the Mathews' investment funds into three asset categories: equity, debt, and cash.

17. Which of the following statements describe(s) action(s) that you would recommend in order to meet the Mathews' goals?

1. Because of the economic environment, the Mathews should immediately increase the proportion of equity investments to provide for growth for the estate.

2. This is the opportune time to lengthen the maturity of the fixed-income proportion of the portfolio.

3. Because of the current economic scenario and their retired status, the Mathews should liquidate the equity portion of the portfolio.

4. The Mathews should gradually increase the equity proportion of the portfolio over the next 3 years to provide for growth in their estate.

    a. 3 and 4.

    b. 1 and 2.

    c. 2 and 4.

    d. 4 only.

    e. 2, 3 and 4.

18. In order to meet their goals, the Mathews should:

1. Reduce cash level, expand fixed-income securities.

2. Expand fixed-income securities.

3. Increase cash level, decrease equities.

4. Expand fixed-income securities, decrease equities.

    a. 1 only.

    b. 1 and 4.

    c. 2 and 3.

    d. 2, 3 and 4.

    e. None of the above.

19. You are considering liquidating the individual equity holdings and moving this amount into equity mutual funds. The following alternative allocations have been proposed:

Choice A		Choice B	
Market index fund	40%	Growth fund	33%
Growth fund	20%	International equity fund	33%
Value-oriented fund	20%	Value-oriented fund	34%
International equity fund	20%		
Choice C		**Choice D**	
Market index fund	30%	Small company fund	25%
Gold stock fund	50%	Aggressive growth fund	45%
Equity-income fund	20%	Growth fund	30%

    a.   Choice A is preferred because it includes multiple management styles and market diversification.

    b.   Choice B is preferred because it employs both active and passive funds.

    c.   Choice C is preferred because it best meets the Mathews' goals.

    d.   Choice D is preferred because it maximizes growth while meeting the Mathews' goals.

    e.   Do <u>not</u> liquidate the current portfolio.

WILLIAM AND MARILYN MATHEWS

Multiple-Choice Solutions

William and Marilyn Mathews

ANSWER SUMMARY

*Questions marked with an asterisk (*) are no longer accurate due to changes in the Federal Tax Code.

1. e	6. c	11. e	16. e
2. a	7. d	12. deleted	17. d
3. a	8. d	13. c	18. e
4. c	9. b	14. a	19. a
5. a*	10. d	15. c	

SUMMARY OF TOPICS

1. Tax—Installment Sale
2. Fundamentals—Time Value Calculations
3. Tax—Installment Sale
4. Retirement—Social Security
5. Retirement—401(k) Distributions
6. Estates—Life Insurance in Estates
7. Insurance—Annuities
8. Tax—Section 1244 Stock
9. Estates—Planning
10. Tax—Bonds
11. Estates—Gross Estate
12. Deleted
13. Retirement—Plans
14. Investments—Integration
15. Estates—Installment Sales
16. Estate—Weaknesses
17. Investments—Asset Allocation
18. Investments—Asset Allocation
19. Investments—Asset Allocation

SOLUTIONS

Tax—Installment Sale

1. **e**

The return of capital portion is determined by the gross profit percentage of this installment sale. Since it is the down payment, there is no income component. There is, however, a portion of capital gain.

Selling Price	$1,500,000
Basis	$700,000
Capital Gain	$800,000

$700,000 ÷ $1,500,000 = 46.67% return of capital

$800,000 ÷ $1,500,000 = 53.33% capital gain

Fundamentals—Time Value Calculations

2. **a**

N	= 120 (10 ×12)
i	= 0.8333 (10 ÷ 12)
PV	= $1,200,000
PMT	= $15,858 × 5 = $79,290 ordinary annuity as of July 1, 1993 for 5 months.

Note: Installment payments are generally ordinary annuities not annuities due. Below is the CFP Board of Examiners' response to a candidate's question regarding this exam item: #2 is based on a sale price of $1.5 million with a down payment of $300,000, leaving a balance of $1.2 million. Payments are for 120 months at an interest rate of 0.83% per month (10% divided by 12). By the end of 1993, Bill will have received five payments. The answer to the question can be arrived through normal annuity calculation. I would agree that it probably should be calculated as an annuity due, in which case, the answer would have been slightly different, the amount of $78,635. Even if calculated this way, clearly the closest and best answer would be A.

Tax—Installment Sale

3. a

Total 1993 payments $15,858.09 × 5 = $79,290.45

Balance of Liability as of 12/31/93

Interest is $49,507.74 (See Amortization table)

Principal reduction was $29,782.71

Balance	Principal	Interest	Payment
$1,200,000.00	$5,858.09	$10,000.00	$15,858.09
$1,194,141.91	$5,906.91	$9,951.18	$15,858.09
$1,184,235.00	$5,956.13	$9,901.96	$15,858.09
$1,182,278.87	$6,005.77	$9,852.32	$15,858.09
$1,176,273.10	$6,055.81	$9,802.28	$15,858.09
$1,170,217.29	$29,782.71	$49,507.74	$79,290.45

Below is the CFP Board of Examiners' response to a candidate's question regarding this exam item:

Installment Note—$1,200,000

Monthly payment—$15,858.09

# of payments in 1993—5

Installment note balance as of 12-31-93—$1,170,217.29

Total 1993 Principal payments—$29,782.71

Total 1993 interest payments—$49,507.74

Retirement—Social Security

4. c

The interest income from the installment sale will increase modified AGI. The sale of an asset or an installment basis is not earned income and, therefore, will not affect the collection of Social Security retirement benefits. The test is earned income. A, D, and E are incorrect. B is incorrect, because his Social Security benefits will be taxed. C is correct.

Retirement—401(k) Distributions

5. a*

Bill and Marilyn can make rollovers, so statement #2 is correct. They can also elect 10-year averaging making statement #1 correct. They also could elect 5-year averaging making statement #4 correct. Bill cannot use 5-year averaging and have a partial rollover.

Note: 5-year averaging was repealed for distributions made after 1999.

Estates—Life Insurance in Estates

6. c

The objective is to provide estate liquidity at the death of the second spouse. Obviously inclusion in the estate of the second to die is undesirable. Statement #1 is incorrect, making A and E incorrect. Statement #2 is incorrect because of the 3-year throwback rule, making B and D incorrect. Statement #4 is a revocable trust and, therefore, would cause inclusion due to incident of ownership.

Insurance—Annuities

7. d

The annuity starting date is unknown.

This withdrawal would appear to be a nonperiodic payment.

D is correct if this contract was entered into before August 14, 1982. It is clear when the annuity was purchased January 1, 1981.

Below is the CFP Board of Examiners' response to a candidate's question regarding this exam item:

See IRS publication 575, which is on point.

Tax—Section 1244 Stock

8. d

Sale of Section 1244 stock will result in an ordinary loss of $51,000 assuming married filing jointly.

Estates—Planning

9. b

Statements #1, #2, and #3. Bill has already agreed to sell the business on an installment basis. Any of statements #1, #2 or #3 could be effective for estate planning. Preferred stock recapitalization is a technique that must be planned carefully under transfer tax laws.

Tax—Bonds

10. d

T-Bills only pay income at maturity because they are bought at a discount. Therefore, statement #4 is correct. Statement #1 is incorrect because appreciation of a municipal bond is taxable. Those two eliminate A and E. Savings bonds are not subject to state income tax; therefore, B is eliminated. D must be chosen. Statement #2 is false because the SPDA is a pre-'82 SPDA.

Estates—Gross Estate

11. e

This does not even require a reading of the case except to verify that children and grandchildren exist. Statements #1–#4 will each reduce their gross estate.

12. deleted

The CFP Board of Examiners has eliminated this question and answer.

Retirement—Plans

13. c

Statement #1 is wrong, because it does not shelter current taxable income except to the extent of earnings on such an IRA. Statements #2, #3, and #4 are correct, except statement #4 should be modified to read "Schedule C income less 1/2 Social Security".

Investments—Integration

14. a

A review of the balance sheet and investment portfolio supplement reveals excessive liquidity (T-Bills), a lack of growth orientation (common stocks), a lack of marginal diversification and low tax advantaged investments. E, C, and B can be quickly eliminated. D fails due to large income. A is the answer by deduction.

Estates—Installment Sales

15. c

The question could have stated "gross estate" instead of just "estate", but the value of the installment notes is the present value and would be included in the gross estate. It would then qualify for the marital deduction based on the simple wills.

Estate—Weaknesses

16. e

Statement #1 is correct, because they have simple wills. Statement #2 is correct due to titling of assets. Statement #3 is correct due to lack of durable powers, trusts, and living wills. Statement #4 is correct, because financials do not indicate clear ownership interest.

Below is the CFP Board of Examiners' response to a candidate's question regarding this exam item:

(4) would be correct since there is <u>no</u> indication on the statement of financial position as to who holds title to many of the assets. This is what is meant by "failure to coordinate titling of assets with documentation."

Investments—Asset Allocation

17. d

The current economic environment is not conducive to substantive growth in equities. However, the Mathews should begin to increase their equity positions to provide additional growth. Review the economic environment. Nominal interest rates are low while real long-term rates are high. This would not be a good time to invest in long-term bonds.

Investments—Asset Allocation

18. e

The Mathews need to increase their equity holdings. None of the answers are consistent with this strategy. Long-term fixed income securities should not be bought at this time.

Investments—Asset Allocation

19. a

A is the only one that meets the needs of the Mathews. B is incorrect because none of the funds are passive. C has too much risk with 50% in gold. D contains 70% in very aggressive funds—too risky for the Mathews.

STUART AND MARILYN KINCAID

Case Scenario

Marilyn and Stuart Kincaid

CASE SCENARIO

Released as of December 1996

© Certified Financial Planner Board of Standards, Inc., Reprinted with permission

*Questions marked with an asterisk (*) are no longer accurate due to changes in the Federal Tax Code.

PERSONAL DATA

Marilyn Kincaid

- 53 years old, physician.

- For the past 17 years Marilyn has been a staff physician and employee of Nopaine Hospital where she currently earns $200,000/year.

- She also operates a private practice clinic with Schedule C net income of $100,000. The practice has three employees.

Stuart Kincaid

- 55 years old, recently taken his company's early retirement option.

Stuart and Marilyn Kincaid

- Married 31 years, have always lived in a state that is <u>not</u> a community property state.

- Marilyn plans to retire in 7 years.

- Four daughters, ages 28 (married, 1 child); 26 (married, 2 children); 24 (single) and 22 (single); the two youngest children are <u>not</u> living at home and have just started working as independent consultants.

- Own a vacation home in another noncommunity property state.

- Have simple wills. Stuart leaves his estate to Marilyn and Marilyn leaves her estate to Stuart. After the death of the survivor, the estate is left to their issue in per stirpes (by right of representation). The Kincaids estimate they save $2,000 per month (after retirement plan contributions).

INSURANCE DATA

- Marilyn's health insurance provided by Blue Cross/Blue Shield. Monthly $600 premium paid by Nopaine Hospital. Deductible of $250 per person, Kincaid family copayment of 20%, and out-of-pocket per family cap is $1,000/year. Lifetime maximum on major medical is $500,000 per person.

- Marilyn's disability coverage is a group disability contract provided by Nopaine Hospital that pays a $5,000 monthly benefit for two years. The contract has a liberal "own occupation" definition. The elimination period is 30 days.

- Marilyn has a $500,000 universal life policy with XYZ Insurance Co. She pays the annual premium. Stuart is the primary beneficiary and Marilyn is the owner. At the time of the purchase, policy projections were based on the 5-year Treasury rates of 6%.

- Marilyn has a $350,000 annual renewable group term through the American College of Physicians. The $760 annual premium is paid through the Kincaids' personal checking account. Stuart is the beneficiary and Marilyn is the insured and has all incidents of ownership.

- Marilyn has a $100,000 group term policy provided by the hospital. The hospital pays the entire premium. The beneficiary is Marilyn's estate.

- Stuart has a $200,000 whole life policy converted at retirement from his former group term; annual premium is $4,000, and there is no cash value at this time. Stuart is the owner and Marilyn is the beneficiary.

OTHER FINANCIAL DATA

- Nopaine Hospital sponsors a 403(b) tax-sheltered annuity (TSA) program but does not contribute to the plan.

- Marilyn makes the maximum contributions from her salary to the TSA.

- The current TSA account balance is $375,000. Marilyn has chosen a fixed-rate option with these funds, and the present rate is 8%.

- Marilyn has a self-employed retirement plan which incorporates both a 10% money-purchase program with a profit-sharing option. Marilyn has chosen fixed-rate investments for these assets, and the total for the plan equals $800,000.

- Stuart is the beneficiary of all Marilyn's qualified retirement plans.

- The average after-tax rate of return on invested assets is 7%.

- The Kincaid's current annual disposable income is $55,000.

- Additional investment data is included on the attached balance sheet.

- The Kincaids are in the marginal 31% federal tax bracket and a 4% state bracket.

- The Kincaids rent their vacation home for $2,000 to their neighbors for ten days during December each year. The Kincaids spend every weekend, outside of December, at the home.

- Marilyn and Stuart recently completed a refinancing of their vacation residence and obtained a $400,000 mortgage amortized at 10% for 30 years. The financing was arranged through an independent mortgage broker for two points.

FINANCIAL OBJECTIVES IN ORDER OF PRIORITY

1. Marilyn wants to retire in seven years, and they expect to retain both residences.

2. They would like to be able to spend $10,000 (after-tax) per month in today's dollars during retirement years.

3. They want to reduce income and estate taxes.

BALANCE SHEET
Stuart and Marilyn Kincaid

ASSETS AT FAIR MARKET VALUE		LIABILITIES AND NET WORTH	
Cash /Cash Equivalents			
Checking Account (J)[1]	$5,000	Vacation home mortgage (J)	$400,000
Bank X Money Market (W)	110,000		
Bank X Money Market (H)	90,000		
Credit Union Acct (H)[2]	175,000		
Savings Bank Acct (H)	50,000		
XYZ Insurance Cash Value (W)	50,000		
TOTAL Cash/Cash Equivalents	$480,000	**Total Liabilities**	$400,000
Invested Assets			
Clinic Bank Account (W)[3]	$150,000		
Bank X CD (H)	82,000		
Stocks—six companies (W)	99,000		
Muni Bonds (H)[4]	235,000		
Series E Bonds (W)	3,000		
SPDA Annuity One (purchased in 1981) (W)[5]	175,000		
SPDA Annuity Two (purchased in 1988) (W)[5]	85,000		
IRA Bank X Money Market (W)	3,000		
IRA Growth Mutual Fund (W)	12,000		
Retirement Plan Bank X CD (W)	125,000		
Retirement Plan Bank Z CD (W)	75,000		
Retirement Plan US T-Bill (W)	300,000		
Retirement Plan Bank X CD (W)	50,000		
Retirement Plan Bank X Money Market (W)	50,000		
Retirement Plan Bank Z CD (W)	100,000		
Retirement Plan US T-Note (W)	100,000		
403(b) TSA (W)	375,000		
TOTAL Invested Assets	$2,019,000	**Net Worth**	$3,549,000

(Continued next page)

Personal Use Assets

Personal residence (J)	$1,000,000
Vacation home (J)	400,000
Automobiles (W)	25,000
Personal property (J)	25,000
TOTAL Personal Use Assets	$1,450,000

Total Assets	$3,949,000	**Total Liabilities and Net Worth**	$3,949,000

1 J = joint tenancy with right of survivorship, W = Marilyn as owner, H = Stuart as owner

2 Stuart's distribution from his former company's qualified retirement plan.

3 Consists of $20,000 Bank X checking account and $130,000 Bank X money market.

4 Double-tax exempt.

5 Single premium deferred annuity, current rate is 7½%; the beneficiaries are the children
   SPDA 1 cost: $50,000; SPDA 2 cost: $50,000

STUART AND MARILYN KINCAID

Multiple-Choice Questions

Stuart and Marilyn Kincaid

QUESTIONS

*Questions marked with an asterisk (*) are no longer accurate due to changes in the Federal Tax Code.

1. The Kincaids would like to retire in seven years. Excluding assets devoted to personal use, if their current portfolio can earn an annual rate of return of 7% (after-tax), what is the closest estimate of the value of that portfolio at retirement?

    a. $3,300,000.
    b. $3,500,000.
    c. $3,700,000.
    d. $4,000,000.
    e. $5,700,000.

2. If the Kincaids expect to earn 7% (after-tax) annually and anticipate annual inflation to be 5%, what future monthly income will the Kincaids need when they retire in 7 years to meet their first-year retirement expenditures? (rounded to the nearest $100)

    a. $11,400.
    b. $11,500.
    c. $14,100.
    d. $15,000.
    e. $16,100.

3. * Which combination of the following estate planning actions or techniques is most appropriate for the Kincaids at this time assuming that their marriage is stable?

    1. Transfer additional assets from Marilyn to Stuart to equalize estates.
    2. Create demand trusts (Crummey) for the children.
    3. Inclusion of a bypass/credit shelter trust for both.
    4. Irrevocable life insurance trust.

    a. 1 and 3.
    b. 1 and 4.
    c. 2, 3 and 4.
    d. 1, 2 and 3.
    e. 2 and 4.

4. Which of the following is the nearest estimate of Marilyn Kincaid's <u>gross</u> estate, if she were to die at this time?

    a. $2,600,000.

    b. $3,300,000.

    c. $3,500,000.

    d. $3,800,000.

    e. $4,300,000.

5. If Marilyn Kincaid were to die at this time, what is the total value of her <u>probate</u> estate?

    a. $387,000.

    b. $487,000.

    c. $1,002,000.

    d. $1,202,000.

    e. $1,337,000.

6. Upon initial review of the Kincaids' situation, what are the three most apparent areas of concern?

    1. Too much deposited in Bank X.

    2. Too much life insurance on Marilyn.

    3. Investment portfolio provides a poor inflation hedge.

    4. Too few assets owned by Stuart.

    5. Underutilization of available estate tax savings opportunities.

    a. 1, 2 and 3.

    b. 2, 3 and 4.

    c. 1, 4 and 5.

    d. 1, 3 and 5.

    e. 2, 4 and 5.

7. * The Kincaids are concerned that they are paying too much tax. Dr. Kincaid is contributing $20,000 of her Schedule C net income to the combination qualified retirement plan and she is contributing $9,500 to the 403(b) TSA plan. What is the most significant step the Kincaids can take to defer tax on current income?

    a. Marilyn increases the self-employed plan contribution to 25% or $30,000.

    b. Stuart can open a deductible IRA.

    c. Marilyn can increase the 403(b) contribution to $12,500.

    d. Marilyn can establish a Rabbi Trust to defer an additional 12.5% of income.

    e. The Kincaids can prepay real estate and state income taxes.

8. With respect to Stuart's need for life insurance, he should:

    a. Purchase additional whole life insurance to provide estate liquidity.

    b. Purchase <u>no</u> additional life insurance because the asset will be included in his gross estate.

    c. Purchase single premium whole life insurance because it provides inflation protection.

    d. Purchase <u>no</u> additional life insurance because he has <u>no</u> need for additional coverage.

    e. Purchase variable life insurance to reduce the overall risk level of his current portfolio.

9. Dr. Kincaid agrees with your recommendation that she needs to supplement her group disability program with a separate policy. Which combination of the following provisions are the most appropriate for any additional disability coverage?

    1. A presumption of total disability if the policyholder tests positive for HIV.

    2. A 4% COLA rider on the benefit.

    3. Lifetime benefit versus one that terminates at age 65.

    4. A proportionate partial disability benefit that does not first require total disability.

    5. A contract that is guaranteed renewable.

        a. 1 and 5.

        b. 3 and 5.

        c. 2 and 4.

        d. 2 and 3.

        e. 4 and 5.

10. The other major weaknesses of the Kincaids' insurance program are:

    1. The medical insurance out-of-pocket cap of $1,000 is too high.

    2. The lifetime maximum on the major medical is inadequate.

    3. The Kincaid's liability coverage is inadequate.

    4. A portion of the premium for medical insurance paid by the hospital is taxable to Marilyn.

        a. 1 and 2.

        b. 1, 2 and 4.

        c. 2 and 3.

        d. 2, 3 and 4.

        e. 3 and 4.

11. Which combination of the following statements supports the Kincaids' current portfolio allocation in the qualified plans?

    1. Since the Kincaids have a very small percentage of their present total portfolio in equities, it would <u>not</u> be appropriate to emphasize equities in their pension funds.

    2. Since fixed-income assets held to maturity have low correlation with equities, a portion of fixed-income assets is appropriate.

    3. A projection of higher income tax in 7 years reduces the benefit of investing in high potential growth assets in a tax-deferred account.

    4. Retirement will necessitate the Kincaids making major changes in their asset allocation in seven years.

       a. 1, 2 and 3.

       b. 1 and 3.

       c. 2 and 4.

       d. 2 only.

       e. 1, 2, 3 and 4.

12. Dr. Kincaid's SPDA Annuity One has <u>no</u> surrender charges. What should she do?

    a. Cash in the annuity and pay taxes and reinvest the net proceeds.

    b. Exchange the annuity under Section 1035 of the Internal Revenue Code to another annuity paying a similar rate.

    c. Annuitize over her life with a 10-year certain and continuous payment.

    d. Annuitize over a joint life expectancy.

    e. Leave the annuity intact.

13. If the Kincaids had a personal emergency need for $50,000 in excess of their cash/cash equivalents, their best source of funds from invested assets would be to draw from the:

    a. Retirement plan Treasury bills.

    b. SPDA Annuity One.

    c. Stock portfolio.

    d. SPDA Annuity Two.

    e. 403(b) TSA.

14. The Kincaids wish to reduce the overall purchasing power risk of their portfolio. Which of the following investment vehicles is best suited for this purpose?

    1. International equity funds.

    2. Precious metal funds.

    3. Treasury Bills.

    4. Municipal bonds.

    5. Variable annuities.

        a. 1, 2 and 5.

        b. 1, 3 and 4.

        c. 1, 4 and 5.

        d. 2, 3 and 5.

        e. 3, 4 and 5.

15. Which of the following is/are correct concerning the vacation home?

    1. The $2,000 must be included as rental income.

    2. The mortgage interest is deductible as an itemized deduction except that $10/365^{ths}$ is deductible as an itemized deduction subject to 2% of adjusted gross income (AGI).

    3. All the interest is deductible as an itemized deduction on Schedule A.

    4. The mortgage interest and rental income offset each other on Schedule E.

        a. 1 only.

        b. 1 and 2.

        c. 1 and 3.

        d. 3 only.

        e. 4 only.

STUART AND MARILYN KINCAID

Multiple-Choice Solutions

Stuart and Marilyn Kincaid

ANSWER SUMMARY

*Questions marked with an asterisk (*) are no longer accurate due to changes in the Federal Tax Code.

1. d	6. d	11. d
2. c	7. e*	12. e
3. c*	8. d	13. b
4. c	9. e	14. a
5. b	10. c	15. d

SUMMARY OF TOPICS

1. Fundamentals—Time Value of Money
2. Retirement—Needs Analysis
3. Estates—Minimization of Estate Taxes
4. Estates—Gross Estate
5. Estates—Probate Estate
6. Fundamentals—Determining the Client's Financial Status
7. Retirement—Taxation of Retirement Plans
8. Insurance—Analysis of Risk Exposure
9. Insurance—Disability Insurance
10. Insurance—Analysis of Risk Exposures
11. Investments—Asset Allocation
12. Insurance—Annuities
13. Insurance—Taxation of Annuities
14. Investments—Purchasing Power Risk
15. Tax—Itemized Deductions

SOLUTIONS

Fundamentals—Time Value of Money

1. d

PV = $2,499,000 ($480,000 + $2,019,000) (Invested assets plus cash equivalent)

$i = 7$

$n = 7$

FV = $4,012,848 ≈ $4,000,000

Retirement—Needs Analysis

2. c

$n = 7$

$i = 5$ (inflation rate)

PV = $10,000 (provided in the case)

FV = $14,071 (round to $14,100)

The earnings rate is irrelevant to the question. The question asks for the future monthly income needed in 7 years.

Estates—Minimization of Estate Taxes

3. c*

There is no reason to equalize the estates. The other suggestions are obviously correct. Also note there is no answer containing statements #1, #2, #3, and #4.

Note: Below is the CFP Board of Examiner's response to a candidate's question regarding this exam item:
Concerning why technique (1) [estate equalization] is <u>not</u> appropriate in this situation:

- Stuart's estate already is large enough to take advantage of the unified credit without the necessity of Marilyn transferring assets to him. (Kaplan note: This statement is no longer applicable because of the increase in the unified credit applicable to estate taxes.)

- Many of Marilyn's solely owned assets are in her IRAs, her 403(b) plan, and other qualified plans. Those assets could not be transferred to Stuart without first distributing them, thus incurring a taxation and a penalty tax.

- The two SPDAs owned by Marilyn name the children as beneficiaries, so would <u>not</u> be included in Stuart's gross estate in any event, even if Marilyn predeceases him.

- The value of <u>other</u> assets owned solely by Marilyn and the value of the assets owned solely by Stuart is fairly equal already.

Estates—Gross Estate

4. **c**

Take total assets from the balance sheet, less Stuart's assets, less the cash value of the life insurance, plus $950,000 of insurance on her life = $3,502,000 rounded to $3.5 million. ($3,949,000 – $12,500 – $200,000 – $500,000 – $235,000 – $82,000 – $50,000 – $175,000 – $90,000 – $2,500 – $50,000 + $950,000)

Estates—Probate Estate

5. **b**

All retirement assets have named beneficiaries; all joint assets have survivorship rights (add $110,000 + $150,000 + $99,000 + $3,000 + $25,000 + $100,000 [term insurance] = $487,000).

Note: Below is the CFP Board of Examiner's response to a candidate's question regarding this exam item: *(To calculate the amount of Marilyn's probate estate as $487,000, Stuart is the beneficiary of Marilyn's IRAs and retirement plans. The Series E bond does not have a POD (pay on death) beneficiary specified.)*

Fundamentals—Determining the Client's Financial Status

6. **d**

The deposits in Bank X for Marilyn exceed FDIC coverage, so statement 1 is correct. Reviewing the Kincaid's portfolio reveals a large proportion devoted to short-term investments, so statement 3 is correct. Statement 5 is clearly true, so d is the only possible answer.

Retirement—Taxation of Retirement Plans

7. ***e**

At the time this case was released by CFP Board, A, C and D were not allowed. Stuart cannot open a deductible IRA because they are covered by a qualified plan and have too high of a level of income, and he is not employed. E is the answer, and they can get a deduction for current income tax.

Insurance—Analysis of Risk Exposure

8. **d**

Stuart has no life insurance needs. They have substantial net worth and no dependents. Income replacement is not an issue; D is the correct answer.

Note: Below is the CFP Board of Examiner's response to a candidate's question regarding this exam item. *Because there is no objective concerning preserving the assets for children given in the case information, there is no specific support for additional insurance on the husband's life for the purpose of paying death taxes.*

Insurance—Disability Insurance

9. **e**

The question asks for the combination (of two items) that is the most appropriate. Note that only two answers can be correct. Statement #4 is the best choice since she will work for 7 more years and partial disability is a possibility; statement #5 is also true. The correct answer is E.

Insurance—Analysis of Risk Exposures

10. **c**

Statement #1 is false, thus eliminating A and B. Statement #2 is true, which eliminates E. Statement #3 is true; statement #4 is false. The answer is C.

Investments—Asset Allocation

11. **d**

Statement #1 is false. Even small allocations of equities in a retirement portfolio will help protect against purchasing power risk. However, a larger percentage would certainly be appropriate. Statement #2 is true. Statement #3 is false; high potential growth assets are always good for tax-deferred accounts. Statement #4 is false; they may need small but not major changes in asset allocation in 7 years.

Insurance—Annuities

12. **e**

Since Marilyn is not planning to retire and has no immediate need for cash, she should leave the SPDA intact.

Insurance—Taxation of Annuities

13. **b**

The SPDA annuity is a pre-1982 annuity, which means that amounts up to her adjusted basis can be withdrawn on a FIFO basis resulting in no tax implications. All of the other options have negative tax implications.

Investments—Purchasing Power Risk

14. **a**

International equity funds, precious metal funds, and variable annuities are the best-suited vehicles to reduce purchasing power risk. T-bills and municipal bonds do not provide protection against purchasing power risk.

Tax—Itemized Deductions

15. **d**

Statement #1 is false because the vacation home was rented for less than 14 days, therefore the income need not be claimed. Statement #2 is false because all mortgage interest is deductible as an itemized deduction not subject to 2%. Statement #3 is true because this is technically a second home not rental property and not a "vacation home". Statement #4 is false because the property is not rental property and Schedule E does not apply.

JAMES AND PAT CLARKE

■

Case Scenario

James and Pat Clarke

CASE SCENARIO

Released as of January 1999

© Certified Financial Planner Board of Standards, Inc., Reprinted with permission

*Questions marked with an asterisk (*) are no longer accurate due to changes in the Federal Tax Code.

PERSONAL DATA

Husband: James Clarke, age 44, college professor

Wife: Pat Clarke, age 43, college professor

Child: Kim Clarke, age 14

James' parents: In good health, in mid to late 70s

Pat's parents: Deceased

FINANCIAL DATA

James and Pat Clarke have the following assets at fair market value (FMV):

- Single premium deferred annuity (Pat) $50,000
- Cash (JTWROS*) $250,000
- Stock in the XYZ Corporation** (JTWROS) $50,000
- IRAs
  Pat $20,000
  James $30,000
- Home (JTWROS) $100,000
- Their simplified income statement is presented as follows:
  Salary (combined) $82,500
  Interest income $12,500
  Living expenses and taxes $90,000

- They have <u>no</u> liabilities and <u>no</u> company-sponsored retirement plans.

- They have <u>no</u> wills and they live in a noncommunity property state.

- James' parents can meet all current expenses from current cash flow but have very limited reserve funds and still live in their own paid-for mobile home.

*Joint tenancy with right of survivorship.

**XYZ Corporation is an S-corporation for which James worked before he started teaching.

OTHER PERTINENT DATA

- The tax basis of the home is $90,000; the tax basis of the stock is $55,000.

- The Clarkes are in a 30% marginal combined state and federal tax bracket.

- They are inexperienced investors, but they are willing to take reasonable and normal   investment risk if appropriate, but they do <u>not</u> wish to invest aggressively.

- Both James and Pat have purchased term life insurance policies with $250,000 death benefit on each; they own their own policies, and Kim is the contingent beneficiary on both policies.

- James is the primary beneficiary of Pat's single premium deferred annuity; Kim is the contingent beneficiary.

- You have found their disability insurance inadequate. The Clarkes have indicated they could fit your proposed $1,600 annual premium for an adequate policy into their living expenses.

- You have reviewed their auto, homeowner's, liability, and life insurance and found their policies adequate. James and Pat are responsible for their medical expenses.

- Kim is a trustworthy high school honor student who earns $2,000 annually and has a $500 savings account.

- The "cash" is invested in a variety of money market funds and insured savings accounts.

- Their IRAs are invested in money market funds. James and Pat are the primary beneficiaries on each other's IRA account; Kim is the contingent beneficiary.

- They do <u>not</u> plan additional children and they have <u>no</u> other dependents.

- The Clarkes currently can save $5,000 per year out of current salary and can continue to do so (in inflation-adjusted dollars) until they retire in 20 years. This savings rate assumes that all planned asset acquisition and replacements are paid out of income before savings (except the three goals shown below).

GOALS (IN ORDER OF PRIORITY)

1. College education for Kim. They expect to spend a total of $50,000 (present value) for her entire education.

2. Retirement in 20 years, which maximizes their standard of living at retirement. Their IRAs, Social Security, and personal retirement savings form a basis for retirement.

3. Pat and James plan to take 6 months off from work ("sabbatical") in 4 years for travel and research and to spend $50,000 (after tax and in current dollars).

ECONOMIC ENVIRONMENT

The economy has been in a period of modest economic growth for about 2 years. Inflation, as measured by the CPI, was at a 4.9% annual rate over the last year. Ninety-day T-bill rates are currently 6%, while the yield to maturity on 20-year government bonds is 7.5%. During the last quarter, unemployment was at 4.8% and real economic growth was about 0.75%. Most forecasts call for little change in these conditions over the short and long term.

PLANNER'S ASSUMPTIONS

Investment	Pretax Expected Return	Beta with S & P 500
Biotech mutual fund	20.0%	1.75
Leveraged commercial real estate	8.5%	1.40
Small cap stock mutual fund	10.0%	1.10
S&P 500	9.0%	1.00
Taxable zero-coupon bonds	9.0%	1.00
Zero-coupon municipal bond fund	7.5%	0.80
Treasury bonds (30-year)	7.5%	0.70
Long-term municipal bond fund	5.0%	0.70
International stocks	11.0%	0.40
Treasury notes (7-year)	7.0%	0.25
Treasury bills	6.0%	0.10
Precious metals	5.0%	(0.25)
R&D partnership	14.0%	N/A
Certificate of deposit	7.0%	N/A

You are doubtful anyone can "beat the market" through asset selection or timing.

JAMES AND PAT CLARKE

Multiple-Choice Questions

James and Pat Clarke

*Questions marked with an asterisk (*) are no longer accurate due to changes in the Federal Tax Code.

1. Which one of the following statements most accurately describes the risk exposure of the Clarkes' portfolio?

    a. The portfolio has excessive market risk.

    b. The portfolio should be unaffected by changes in interest rates.

    c. The portfolio contains an excessive level of business risk.

    d. The portfolio contains excessive liquidity risk.

    e. The portfolio contains excessive purchasing power risk.

2. With respect to the Clarkes' risk tolerance, which of the following statements is true?

    a. Because of their lack of investment experience, equity investments are inappropriate.

    b. Because of their stated risk preferences, investment in an R&D partnership is inappropriate.

    c. Regardless of their specific goals, a portfolio with a weighted average beta close to 1 is appropriate.

    d. Because of their stated risk preferences, a biotech mutual fund is appropriate.

    e. Regardless of their risk tolerance, leveraged commercial real estate is appropriate.

3. To diversify the Clarkes' investment portfolio, which of the following investments would be most appropriate?

    1. S&P 500 Index Fund.
    2. Zero-coupon municipal bond fund.
    3. International stocks.
    4. Leveraged commercial real estate.

    a. 1 and 3.

    b. 1 and 4

    c. 2 and 3.

    d. 2 and 4.

4. What would you advise James and Pat regarding James' parents' estate planning documents?

    a. Transfer the parents' assets to a pooled income fund.

    b. Establish a charitable remainder annuity trust.

    c. Transfer the parents' assets to a rcvocable trust.

    d. Set up durable power of attorney for healthcare.

5. * With regard to funds earmarked for the education goal, which type of investment makes the most sense and why?

    a.   A series of taxable zero-coupon bonds owned by Kim because they can provide appropriate funds at the correct times and are taxed at the child's rate.

    b.   A variable life insurance policy owned by Kim because it saves taxes and it contains life insurance.

    c.   A certificate of deposit owned by James and Pat because CDs are very safe.

    d.   A small cap stock mutual fund owned by Kim because it provides the best return at a modest level of risk consistent with the time horizon.

    e.   Treasury notes with a 7-year maturity owned by James and Pat because the 7-year maturity Treasury notes have little interest rate risk.

6. Which type(s) of investment(s), to be held in their IRA accounts, would be consistent with their retirement goal and why?

    1.   A small cap mutual fund, because it provides growth with reasonable risk.

    2.   A municipal bond fund, because it provides tax advantages and relative safety.

    3.   An international stock fund, because it provides an element of diversification and growth.

    4.   Precious metals, because they provide diversification and tax advantages.

        a.   1 only.

        b.   1 and 3.

        c.   2 and 4.

        d.   1, 2 and 3.

        e.   1, 3 and 4.

7. With regard to the funds earmarked for the Clarkes' "sabbatical" goal, which type of investment is most appropriate?

    a.   S&P 500 index fund.

    b.   Zero-coupon municipal bond.

    c.   7-year Treasury notes.

    d.   Biotech mutual fund.

    e.   Small cap stock mutual fund.

8. Assume the following additional facts:

The Clarkes have purchased a homeowner's policy (HO-3-comprehensive) covering 100% of the replacement cost of their residence. This policy has a $500 deductible. Also, they have purchased a disability income policy with a 30-day elimination period and an any-occupation definition of disability. What actions should the Clarkes consider in order to improve the quality of the insurance program described above?

1. Purchase an endorsement to the homeowner's policy providing all risk/replacement cost (all perils) coverage for personal property.
2. Decrease the homeowner's policy deductible to $250.
3. Reduce the homeowner's policy coverage to 75%.
4. Purchase an own-occupation disability policy.

    a. 1 and 4.

    b. 2 and 4.

    c. 1, 2 and 4.

    d. 1, 3 and 4.

9. One commonly used method of calculating the total retirement fund necessary on the first day of retirement is to use the present value of an annuity due. The Clarkes anticipate that their annual retirement income will need to increase each year at the rate of inflation. Based on the following assumptions, calculate the total amount needed to be in place when James and Pat retire. (Round to the nearest $1,000.)

First-year annual income	$90,000
Social Security annual income, assumed to increase at the rate of inflation	$45,000
Annual after-tax rate of return on invested assets	7%
Joint life expectancy during retirement	25 years

    a. $878,000.

    b. $887,000.

    c. $896,000.

    d. $1,773,000.

    e. $1,792,000.

10. Assume that James has predeceased Pat by 1 year. If Pat died yesterday, which combination of the following financial assets would be included in her probate estate?

    1. James' life insurance policy.

    2. Pat's SPDA.

    3. XYZ stock.

    4. Home.

    5. Pat's life insurance policy.

        a. 4 only.

        b. 1 and 5.

        c. 3 and 4.

        d. 1, 2 and 5.

        e. 2, 3, 4 and 5.

11. Which of the following tax forms or schedules will XYZ Corporation provide to James and Pat on an annual basis?

        a. Schedule E.

        b. Form 1099-S.

        c. Form 1099.

        d. Form W-2.

        e. Schedule K-1.

JAMES AND PAT CLARKE

Multiple-Choice Solutions

James and Pat Clarke

ANSWER SUMMARY

*Questions marked with an asterisk (*) are no longer accurate due to changes in the Federal Tax Code.

1. e	6. b	11. e
2. b	7. b	
3. a	8. a	
4. d	9. c	
5. a*	10. c	

SUMMARY OF TOPICS

1. Investments—Types of Investment
2. Investments—Asset Allocation
3. Investments—Modern Portfolio Theory
4. Estates—Estate Planning Documents
5. Investments—Asset Allocation
6. Investments—Asset Allocation
7. Investments—Asset Allocation
8. Insurance—Analysis and Evaluation of Risk Exposures
9. Retirement—Needs Analysis
10. Estates—Probate Estate
11. Tax—Business Entities

SOLUTIONS

Investments—Types of Investment

1. e

The Clarkes have $300,000 in cash/cash equivalents on the balance sheet that make up 60% of total assets and 75% of invested assets. There is a significant amount of exposure to purchasing power risk in their portfolio.

Investments—Asset Allocation

2. b

Investment in R&D partnership is clearly an inappropriate investment based on their level of risk tolerance.

Investments—Modern Portfolio Theory

3. a

The Clarkes have no equity exposure in their portfolio (except XYZ Corporation); it would be appropriate to emphasize equities in their portfolio to provide a growth component and inflation hedge. The municipal bond fund would not provide the needed growth component. Leveraged commercial real estate is outside their risk tolerance at this point. Therefore, the best choice would include the S&P 500 Index fund and international stocks.

Estates—Estate Planning Documents

4. d

The only answer that related to "documents" is D.

Investments—Asset Allocation

5. a*

Funds for education must meet the appropriate time horizon; therefore, E, which relates to investments that have mature beyond the time horizon, is wrong. D is wrong, because small cap stocks are too risky of an investment for such a short period of time. B does not match the investment vehicle to the time horizon of the investment. The zero-coupon bond allows the Clarkes to match the time horizon of the investments to the duration of the bonds and avoid reinvestment rate risk. Kim is 14; consequently, the Kiddie tax does not apply. (Kaplan note: When this case was written, the kiddie tax age threshold was under 14. Option (a) was the better answer. Because the kiddie tax age threshold is now under 18, the kiddie tax would apply to any bonds maturing or redeemed before Kim is 18.)

Investments—Asset Allocation

6. b

Municipal bonds should not be held in a tax-advantaged account. Precious metals are more risky than the Clarkes' risk tolerance would allow. Small cap stocks and international stocks provide growth and diversification and would be appropriate choices for a retirement account with a long-term time horizon.

Investments—Asset Allocation
7. b

The sabbatical is only 4 years away; therefore, equities would not be appropriate (A, D, E). A 7-year treasury (C) does not match the time horizon of the goal. The only possible choice would be the zero-coupon municipal bond.

Insurance—Analysis and Evaluation of Risk Exposures
8. a

The objective of the question is to improve the Clarkes' insurance program. Statement #4 clearly improves the program but is remarkably in all answers. Statement #1 is generally a good planning idea. Statement #2 does little to improve the quality of the program. Statement #3 is clearly incorrect, because it would cause the Clarkes to be in a co-insurance situation.

Retirement—Needs Analysis
9. c

$$n = 25$$

$$i = 2.0019 \ [[(1.07 \div 1.049) - 1] \times 100]$$

$$PMT_{AD} = \$45,000 \ (\$90,000 - \$45,000)$$

$$PV_{at\ Ret} = (\$895,942.85)$$

Estates—Probate Estate
10. c

The question asks for assets included in the probate estate. Generally, assets that transfer by law or contract avoid the probate estate. Pat's SPDA and life insurance policy have named beneficiaries and will, therefore, avoid probate. The proceeds from James' insurance policy, but not his policy, would likely be included in the probate estate. The XYZ stock will certainly be included in the probate estate.

Tax—Business Entities
11. e

Owners of S corporations will receive an annual Schedule K-1. Owners who work for the S corporation will also receive a Form W-2. Since neither James nor Pat works in the business, they will only receive Schedule K-1.

SUSAN DAVIS

Case Scenario

Susan Davis

CASE SCENARIO

Released as of August 2004

©Certified Financial Planner Board of Standards Inc., Reprinted with permission.

Susan Davis, a new client, has requested that a CFP® certificant assist her in evaluating her personal and business financial situation. Susan is the founder and sole stockholder of Exclusively Unique Gifts, Inc., a C corporation. Her children work part-time in the shop as permitted by state law. Susan is a recent divorcee and realizes that her finances may need to be revised now that her divorce has been settled. Her former husband, Richard, is the father of her two children and the major stockholder of Davis Manufacturing, Inc. Davis Manufacturing has been in business 15 years, is financially stable, and currently has a book value in excess of $1,400,000.

PERSONAL INFORMATION

Name	Age	Health	Occupation
Susan Davis	39	Good	President—Exclusively Unique Gifts, Inc.
Mary Beth Davis	14	Excellent	Student
Nathaniel Davis	9	Excellent	Student
Richard Davis	42	Excellent	President—Davis Manufacturing, Inc.

Wills were last completed 5 years ago. They live in a common-law state.

ECONOMIC ENVIRONMENT

Currently, the economy is in a recovery phase with decreasing unemployment and increasing economic growth. Inflation and interest rates are currently low. It currently costs $12,000 per year to attend college, and this cost is expected to increase at 5% each year. Susan prefers to save monthly and can earn 9% (after taxes) on the college account.

CLIENT OBJECTIVES

1. Ensure financial security for herself and her children by:

   - Planning for her portion of the 4-year funding for the children's college education.
   - Retiring at age 55.
   - Using direct deposit from her paycheck at the end of each month to fund education and retirement.

2. Develop a plan that will provide for the care of her children without passing any of her assets to Richard.

3. Review all insurance coverages and make adjustments necessary to provide proper risk management.

4. Review and develop proper strategies for her business to provide both current and retirement income for herself. Susan tends to be conservative and prefers to assume only moderate risks. Safety of principal and risk diversification are primary concerns now that she is divorced. The reduction of taxes is of secondary importance.

5. Retain and reward current full-time employees of the business while maintaining cash flow flexibility.

STATEMENT OF FINANCIAL POSITION
Susan Davis
12/31 Prior Year

ASSETS		LIABILITLIES AND NET WORTH	
Invested Assets		Credit cards[1]	$ 6,000
Cash/Cash equivalents	$ 2,000	Mortgage[2]	60,000
Business interest	286,000	Auto loan	3,000
Total	$288,000	**Total Liabilities**	$ 69,000
Use Assets			
Residence[3,4]	$330,000		
Personal property	50,000		
Auto	15,000		
Total	$395,000	**Net Worth**	$638,000
Retirement Plan Assets			
IRA (growth mutual funds)	$ 24,000		
		Total Liabilities	
Total Assets	$707,000	**and Net Worth**	$707,000

[1] Variable rate, currently 16.9% APR.

[2] Fixed rate of 9.5% in the name of Richard and Susan Davis; 4 years, 7 months are remaining on the loan.

[3] Originally purchased 15 years, 5 months ago for $110,000. Excellent condition with no major repairs foreseen in the near future.

[4] Lot valued at $50,000; dwelling valued at replacement cost, which is approximately the same as fair market value.

PROJECTED MONTHLY CASH FLOW STATEMENT
Susan Davis
Current Year

Cash Inflows

Gross salary	$4,300
Child support	1,400
Total	$5,700

Cash Outflows

Savings and investments	$0
Mortgage (P & I)	1,350
Property taxes	300
Homeowners insurance	100
Insurance (other insurance)	50
Maintenance and repairs on the home	100
Food and supplies	500
Utilities	350
Transportation (gas, oil, repairs)	200
Car payment	150
Clothing	200
Travel and entertainment	250
Credit card payments	250
State and local income tax (flat 4%)	160
Federal income tax[1]	800
FICA	300
Total	$5,060
Surplus/(Deficit) Cash Flow	$640

[1] Susan is in the 25% federal marginal tax bracket.

INSURANCE INFORMATION

Homeowners Policy

Type	HO-3 (open-peril)
Amount on dwelling	$270,000
Personal property coverage	$145,000
Personal liability	$100,000

Automobile Policy

Type	Personal auto policy
Bodily injury/property damage	$300,000 combined single limit
Collision	$300 deductible
Comprehensive	$250 deductible
Uninsured motorist	$300,000 single limit

Employee Benefits Provided by Exclusively Unique Gifts, Inc.

Life insurance	Employee—two times earnings Dependents—$2,000
Medical	$300 deductible, 80/20 coinsurance Out-of-pocket maximum—$5,000 Lifetime limit—$500,000 Coverage on employees only
Disability	Company pays 50% of salary for 6 months Waiting period—5 working days

EXCLUSIVELY UNIQUE GIFTS, INC.[1]
Year-End Balance Sheet
12/31 Prior Year

Assets		Liabilities	
Cash/Cash equivalents	$33,000	Accounts payable	$128,000
Accounts receivable	110,000	Loan[2]	150,000
Inventory	250,000		
Furniture and fixtures, net of depreciation	127,000	**Total liabilities**	$278,000
Prepaid expenses and other	44,000		
Total Assets	$564,000		
		Stockholder Equity[3]	$286,000
		Total Liabilities and Shareholder Equity	$564,000

[1] All assets are listed at fair market value (FMV)

[2] $4,000 a month payable to Richard Davis at 10% interest, which is the going market rate on similar loans.

[3] The company has experienced increasing profits over the last 7 years.

EXCLUSIVELY UNIQUE GIFTS, INC.
Projected Monthly Income and Expenses
Current Year

Total Sales[1]	$125,000
Expenses	
Cost of goods sold	$75,000
Advertising and promotion	1,500
Depreciation	2,400
Interest on loan	1,250
Insurance—business	250
Payroll taxes and benefits	3,400
Rent	4,700
Salaries[2]	16,300
Supplies and miscellaneous	3,500
Utilities	1,200
Income taxes, fed and state (estimated)	5,600
Total Expenses	$115,100
Net Income	$9,900

[1]Sales vary directly with the local economy and are projected to increase/decrease at twice the rate of change in the local economy. This year's sales and economic growth was estimated at 8%.

[2] Employee data:

Name	Monthly Salary	Date of Hire	Age	Status
Susan Davis	$ 4,300	1/01/94	39	100% stockholder/full-time employee
Kate Jackson*	$ 3,000	6/01/95	28	Full-time employee
Cindi Smith	$ 2,500	2/15/97	47	Full-time employee
Sandy Wise	$ 2,500	8/15/97	34	Full-time employee
Tom Mitcham	$ 2,200	3/01/99	36	Full-time employee
Jack Young	$ 500	7/15/01	20	Part-time employee less than 1,000 hours
Steve Jones	$ 500	7/15/02	17	Part-time employee less than 1,000 hours
Sue Jackson	$ 500	8/01/02	19	Part-time employee less than 1,000 hours
Amy DeLong	$ 300	8/15/02	22	Part-time employee less than 1,000 hours
Mary Beth Davis	$ 200	1/01/03	14	Part-time employee less than 1,000 hours
Nathanial Davis	$ 200	1/01/03	9	Part-time employee less than 1,000 hours

* Kate has expressed an interest in investing up to $100,000 in the business at this time and would like to acquire 100% ownership should Susan ever decide to sell. If Kate did acquire partial ownership, she would become the corporate secretary and vice-president.

SUMMARY OF DIVORCE AGREEMENT, INCORPORATED INTO THE DIVORCE DECREE
Richard and Susan Davis
Prior Year

Custody	Joint, with the children residing primarily with their mother. Both children will reside with their father in the event of their mother's death.
Tax Returns	Susan will claim the children as dependents.
Child Support	Richard is to pay $700 per month per child until each child reaches age 18.
College Support	College costs are to be divided evenly in thirds, with 1/3 being paid by Richard, 1/3 by Susan, and 1/3 by the student.
Insurance	Richard is to provide adequate health insurance on the children until after their graduation from college and also $10,000 of life insurance on each child. In addition, Richard must carry $175,000 life insurance on himself with the children named as the beneficiaries until the younger child reaches age 23.
Assets	Susan is granted 100% equity in both the residence and Exclusively Unique Gifts, Inc., while Richard receives all of the invested assets and also 100% equity in Davis Manufacturing, Inc. and his retirement plan. Susan is to refinance the mortgage on the personal residence to remove Richard's name as a debtor. Richard will continue to hold the business loan for Exclusively Unique Gifts, Inc., provided that no additional loans are acquired.
Alimony	Five-year payment schedule to Susan from Richard:

Year 1	$10,000
Year 2	$30,000
Year 3	$15,000
Year 4	$15,000
Year 5	$15,000

SUSAN DAVIS

■

Multiple-Choice Questions

Susan Davis

QUESTIONS

1. Which of the following is the most appropriate strategy to improve Susan's financial security?

    a. Establish and borrow on a home equity line of credit.

    b. Sell her current residence, buy a less expensive home, and invest the net proceeds in municipal bonds.

    c. Increase her salary for personal debt reduction and investments.

    d. Sell 50% of the business to Kate for $100,000 in cash.

2. Which of the following statements regarding Susan's insurance coverages is correct?

    1. The disability insurance on Susan is adequate.

    2. The property section of her homeowners insurance is adequate at the present levels of coverage.

    3. Susan's personal liability coverage is adequate.

    4. Susan needs additional life insurance.

    5. The medical insurance is inadequate since Susan does not have dependent coverage on her policy.

        a. 2 and 4 only.

        b. 1, 2 and 3 only.

        c. 2, 3 and 4 only.

        d. 3, 4 and 5 only.

3. Susan wants to start investing $600 monthly to achieve her stated objectives. Which of the following monthly investments is most appropriate for Susan at this time?

    a. $200 in a money market account, $200 in a Roth IRA account funded with short-term Treasury bills, and $200 in a Roth IRA international growth fund.

    b. $500 in a growth mutual fund and $100 in a municipal bond fund.

    c. $100 in a money market account and $500 in a long-term US Government bond fund.

    d. $100 in a money market account, $150 in a Roth IRA global balanced mutual fund, and $350 in a short-term bond fund.

4. Which of the following statements about investment risks is true?

    a. Susan's investment liquidity is appropriate for her goals.

    b. Susan's current investments are subject to unsystematic risk.

    c. Richard's risk exposure would benefit from having the business loan paid off early if interest rates decrease.

    d. Susan will reduce her interest rate exposure if she refinances her home with a 30-year, 9.5% fixed-rate mortgage.

5. Susan has asked the CFP® certificant to recommend an employee benefit plan to fulfill her objectives. Which of the following types of plans would be most appropriate?

    a. SIMPLE IRA.

    b. Simplified employee pension (SEP).

    c. Profit sharing.

    d. Target benefit.

6. Susan has decided to improve the benefits provided to all full-time employees of Exclusively Unique Gifts, Inc. Due to financial constraints, she can implement only three of the following options over the next 3 years. Which three of the following options should the CFP® certificant recommend as the most beneficial?

    1. Increasing the life insurance to a maximum of five times earnings.

    2. Decreasing the medical out-of-pocket maximum to $2,500.

    3. Increasing the medical insurance lifetime limit to $1,000,000.

    4. Increasing the disability benefit to 70% of salary for 6 months.

    5. Providing long-term disability coverage equal to 50% of earnings.

        a. 1, 2 and 5.

        b. 2, 3 and 4.

        c. 2, 3 and 5.

        d. 3, 4 and 5.

7. If Susan decides to move into a less expensive home and has approximately $200,000 to invest from the sale proceeds of her home, which of the following portfolios would be most appropriate for her, given her goals and current investments?

    a. $50,000 certificate of deposit, $50,000 money market account, and $100,000 Treasury bill.

    b. $50,000 money market account, $50,000 Standard & Poor's 500 (S&P 500) index fund, and $100,000 balanced mutual fund.

    c. $120,000 aggressive-growth stock fund and $80,000 US Government long-term bond fund.

    d. $150,000 growth mutual fund and $50,000 Standard & Poor's 500 (S&P 500) index mutual fund.

8. Which of the following actions would be most appropriate for Susan to take now to plan for her estate liquidity?

    a. Purchase a life insurance policy.

    b. Establish an unfunded IRC Section 303 corporate stock redemption plan.

    c. Arrange for a 10-year installment sale of the business to Kate.

    d. Use a grantor retained income trust (GRIT) to remove assets from the taxable estate.

9. * Susan's company adopts a profit sharing plan for the company with the following characteristics: the plan requires 1 year of service and attainment of age 21 and, in practice, is not top heavy. True statements about the plan include which of the following?

    1. Both Susan and Kate would be classified as highly compensated employees.

    2. The plan would meet the minimum eligibility requirements.

    3. This year, all part-time employees would be excluded.

    4. A 7-year, graded vesting schedule would best fulfill Susan's objectives.

        a. 4 only

        b. 2 and 3 only

        c. 1, 2 and 4 only

        d. 2, 3 and 4 only

10. True statements regarding Susan and Richard's 5-year alimony payment schedule include which of the following?

    1. To qualify as alimony, payments must be made as part of a written divorce agreement, signed by Susan and Richard.

    2. To qualify as alimony for income tax purposes, payments must be in cash, the couple must live in separate households, and payments must cease upon Susan's death.

    3. The alimony payment schedule constitutes excess alimony.

        a. 1 only.

        b. 3 only.

        c. 1 and 2 only.

        d. 2 and 3 only.

11. Susan wants to establish a trust to provide for her children in case of her death. Which of the following should the CFP® certificant recommend as the most appropriate trust given Susan's overall situation and objectives?

        a. An irrevocable life insurance trust granting Crummey powers to the children.

        b. A grantor retained income trust (GRIT) with Mary Beth and Nathaniel named as beneficiaries.

        c. A revocable living trust naming a third party as successor trustee, with Susan as the primary beneficiary while living and the children listed as contingent beneficiaries.

        d. A revocable living trust naming the children as beneficiaries and Richard as the trustee.

12. If Susan sells her current residence for $367,000 and she purchases a new residence for $180,000 in the same calendar year, the amount of proceeds subject to capital gains tax is:

        a. $0.

        b. $7,000.

        c. $187,000.

        d. $257,000.

SUSAN DAVIS

Multiple-Choice Solutions

Susan Davis

ANSWER SUMMARY

1. c	6. c	11. c
2. a	7. b	12. b
3. d	8. a	
4. b	9. d*	
5. c	10. c	

SUMMARY OF TOPICS

1. Retirement—Profit-Sharing Plan
2. Insurance—General
3. Investments—Asset Allocation
4. Investments—Risk
5. Retirement—Plan Types
6. Tax—Employee Benefit
7. Investment—Asset Allocation
8. Estates—Planning
9. Retirement—Profit-Sharing Plan
10. Tax—Alimony
11. Estates—Trust
12. Tax—Personal Residence

SOLUTIONS

Fundamentals—Planning

1. c

Susan is running a profitable business that shows a net profit of approximately $120,000 on an annual basis. Her current annual salary is only $51,600. She should increase her salary (which would provide an additional deduction for the business) and use the additional money to pay down her debt. A is incorrect. Additional borrowing is not necessary. She has a profitable business that she can take additional salary from to generate cash flow. B is incorrect. Although Susan could sell her home to generate cash, this may not be a desirable option. Taking a larger salary from the business would be a more appropriate strategy. D is incorrect. Nothing indicates that Susan is ready to sell 50% of the business. The business book value is $564,000. Therefore, it would be unwise to sell 50% of the business for only $100,000.

Insurance—General

2. a

1 is incorrect. Susan does not have a long-term disability policy. She is only covered for 6 months. 2 is correct. The value of the dwelling is $280,000 ($330,000 – $50,000 land value). The 80% coinsurance amount is only $224,000, and Susan has $270,000 in coverage. 3 is incorrect. Susan only has $100,000 of personal liability coverage under the homeowner's policy. She needs an umbrella policy. 4 is correct. Susan has inadequate life insurance coverage. The only insurance coverage she has is the company-provided policy, which is $103,200 (2 times earnings). 5 is incorrect. Per the divorce agreement, Richard is to provide adequate health insurance coverage on the children.

Investments—Asset Allocation

3. d

A is incorrect. Under this scenario, Susan would invest $400 into a Roth IRA each month, for a total of $4,800 for the year. This exceeds the maximum allowable Roth IRA contribution for a calendar year. B is incorrect. This scenario provides for no liquidity of her investments. C in incorrect. Interest rates are low, so the long-term fixed income investment would probably not be appropriate.

Investments—Risk

4. b

Susan's main investment asset is her business. She is not diversified, and has a high business risk exposure. Business risk is a type of unsystematic (diversifiable) risk. A is incorrect. Susan only liquid investment asset is $2,000 of cash. Her business is illiquid. C is incorrect. Richard is currently receiving 10% interest from the note receivable. If the note were paid off early, and interest rates decreased, Richard would have increased exposure to reinvestment rate risk. D is incorrect. The current mortgage will be paid off in less than five years. If Susan refinances for 30 years at 9.5%, she will be locking herself into a high interest rate for a long-term period.

Retirement—Plan Types

5. c

Susan would like to retain and reward current full time employees of the business while maintaining cash flow flexibility. A profit-sharing plan would allow her to make discretionary contributions, and would allow her to exclude part-time employees working less than 1,000 hours.

A is incorrect. A SIMPLE IRA would place the burden of retirement savings predominately on the employees. Susan wants to retain and reward the employees. Also, since many of the part-time employees earn more than $5,000, they would be eligible to participate. B is incorrect. Although a SEP allows discretionary contributions, part-time employees would most likely be included in the plan. Susan wants to reward full-time employees only. D is incorrect. A target-benefit plan is a pension plan that would require an actuary and mandatory contributions.

Tax—Employee Benefit

6. c

1 is incorrect. Susan already offers life insurance coverage equal to two times earnings. Although increasing the insurance coverage would be a good benefit, it is not in the top three benefits given Susan's cost constraints. Susan should purchase a separate policy on her life. 2 and 3 are correct. Both of these adjustments to the medical plan would be cost effective, needed changes. 4 is incorrect. Susan currently provides short-term disability coverage equal to 50% of salary, which is adequate coverage. 5 is correct. Susan currently offers no long-term disability benefits to her employees. She also does not have a long-term disability policy for herself, which is needed.

Investment—Asset Allocation

7. b

This portfolio provides liquidity (money market account), growth (index fund), and income (balanced fund). In addition, this portfolio is consistent with her moderate risk tolerance.

A is incorrect. This entire portfolio consists of cash and cash equivalents. Susan would have a very low rate of return and a high exposure to purchasing power risk. C is incorrect. Susan is a conservative investor and prefers only moderate risks. Investing the majority of the portfolio in an aggressive growth stock fund would be inappropriate for her risk tolerance. D is incorrect. This portfolio is illiquid, and does not have a fixed income component.

Estates—Planning

8. a

Susan has a small amount of life insurance, but needs additional life insurance. The most appropriate strategy for her to take *now* would be to purchase life insurance. B is incorrect. A Section 303 stock redemption is a postmortem planning technique that could be used to generate liquidity for her estate. The executor could initiate a Section 303 redemption plan after Susan's death. Susan need not take any action with respect to a Section 303 redemption at this time. C is incorrect. Susan does not plan on retiring until age 55. She did not express any desire to sell the business now. D is incorrect. In most situations, a GRIT will not remove assets from the estate. Typically, the grantor retains income from the GRIT for life. This retained life estate will cause gross estate inclusion.

Retirement—Profit-Sharing Plan

9. *d

1 is incorrect. A highly compensated person is an individual who owns more than 5% of the company, or earns compensation in excess of $90,000. Susan is highly compensated because she owns 100% of the company. However, Kate is not highly compensated, because she has no ownership in the company, and her salary is less than $90,000. 2 is correct. A qualified plan, such as a profit-sharing plan, can restrict participation in the plan to those individuals who have attained age 21 and have completed one year (1,000 hours) of service. Susan's profit-sharing plan has implemented these exact eligibility requirements. 3 is correct. All of the part-time employees would be excluded from the plan because they will not have 1,000 hours, which is the qualified plan threshold for eligibility. 4 is correct. A graded vesting schedule, which is allowed in a profit-sharing plan, would help Susan meet her goal of retaining employees. Beginning in 2007, the only defined-contribution plan vesting schedule available is the 2–6 year graded; the Pension Protection Act of 2006 eliminated the 7-year graded schedule for defined-contribution plans.

Tax—Alimony

10. c

1 is correct. To qualify as alimony for income tax purposes, the payments must be made pursuant to a written divorce agreement. 2 is correct. The following are requirement for tax-deductible alimony:

- The agreement must be in writing.

- The payments must be made in cash.

- The former spouses must live apart.

- The agreement cannot specify that the payments are not alimony for income tax purposes.

- The payments must cease upon the death of the recipient.

3 is incorrect. The payments do not constitute excess alimony. Excess alimony occurs when the payments decrease by MORE THAN $15,000 from the first to second year or second to third year after a divorce. From year 1 to year 2, the payments actually increase. From year 2 to year 3, the payments decrease by exactly (not more than) $15,000. Years 4 and 5 can be ignored.

Estates—Trust

11. c

A revocable living trust with a third-party trustee would be the most appropriate strategy. The trust would avoid probate, and would provide for her children in the event of her death. A is incorrect. Susan's net worth is $707,000. She does not have an estate tax problem. A life insurance trust is probably not necessary because the inclusion of the life insurance in her gross estate would not cause an estate tax liability. If she established an ILIT, she would be required to give up control of the life insurance policy. B is incorrect. A GRIT is a trust in which the grantor (Susan) retains income for life. Since Susan will be retaining a life estate, the GRIT will be included in her gross estate upon her death. In addition, Susan may be subject to unfavorable gift tax consequences when establishing the GRIT. D is incorrect. Although a revocable living trust is an appropriate strategy, Richard should not be named the trustee.

Tax—Personal Residence

12. **b**

Susan will have a recognized gain of $7,000, calculated as follows:

Sales price	$367,000
Basis (from net worth statement)	(110,000)
Realized (economic) gain	$257,000
Exclusion for sale of residence	(250,000)
Capital gain	$ 7,000

The purchase of the new residence is irrelevant.

ITEM SETS

∎

Problems

Item Set Scenarios

Bob and Ann Crow wish to begin saving for their child's education. The child, Lee Schan, is born today. The first payment will be made today, and she will start college on her eighteenth birthday. Lee Schan will attend college for four years with the annual payment due at the beginning of the school year. The current cost of the college education is $25,000 per year. It is expected that the cost of a college education will increase at an average rate of 7% per year during the projection period and that the general rate of inflation will be 4%. The Crows have the option of investing in the following funds: 1) a stock mutual fund expected to earn 12.0% during the projection period, and 2) a bond fund expected to earn 8.5% during the projection period.

1. Calculate the sum total of the projected withdrawals. (round to the nearest dollar)

    a. $350,623.

    b. $375,168.

    c. $401,429.

    d. $206,792.

    e. $215,063.

2. Calculate the annual payment required to fund the cost of college education assuming the Crows invest in the bond fund and make deposits on every birthday, exclusive of Lee Schan's 18th birthday. (round to the nearest dollar)

    a. $9,373.

    b. $7,759.

    c. $8,419.

    d. $8,793.

    e. $8,638.

3. If Bob and Ann make a contribution to a Qualified Tuition Plan, which of the following statements is true?

    a. The plan is not subject to market risk.

    b. The plan assets would not be included in Bob or Ann's gross estate.

    c. A portion of the interest and dividends that the plan earns will be taxed at the parents' highest marginal tax rate.

    d. Making similar periodic contributions to the plan is considered an active investment strategy.

ITEM SET SCENARIO 2

Al and Irma Dell have resided in New Orleans for several years. During the current year, a fire damaged their home, automobiles, and personal property as follows:

Description	RC Prior to Fire	RC After Fire
Dwelling	$100,000	$60,000
Personal Property	$50,000	$25,000
Honda Accord	$18,000	$14,500
Toyota Camry	$20,000	$18,000

RC = Replacement Cost.

Fortunately, the Dells had insurance on the house, automobiles, and personal property.

HOMEOWNERS INSURANCE			AUTOMOBILE INSURANCE	
Policy Type	HO-3		Honda Accord	Toyota Camry
Coverage	$75,000			
Deductible	$500	Premium	$1,200	$950
Premiums (amount)	$1,025	Coverage	$50,000/$100,000	$50,000/$100,000
Liability	$100,000	Comprehensive	$250	$500
Medical Payments	$1,000	Collision	$300	$550

They also have an endorsement for personal property to be valued at replacement value.

1. How much will the insurance company pay to have the dwelling repaired?

    a. $40,000.

    b. $37,500.

    c. $37,000.

    d. $32,000.

    e. $30,000.

2. How much will the Dells have to pay personally to have the automobiles fixed?

    a. $5,500.

    b. $4,750.

    c. $4,650.

    d. $850.

    e. $750.

3. Assume the Dell's adjusted gross income for the current year is $60,000, and assume that they receive the following amounts of insurance proceeds:

Dwelling	$30,000
Personal Property	$20,000
Honda Accord	$1,000
Toyota Camry	$1,000

How much of a casualty loss can the Dells deduct on their current federal income tax return?

    a. $12,400.
    b. $12,500.
    c. $18,400.
    d. $18,500.
    e. $64,400.

ITEM SET SCENARIO 3

John, a single man, had the following stock transactions during 2007:

1. Sold 1,000 shares of Bachelor, Inc. for $15,000 on 6/1/07. The stock was originally purchased on 1/1/07 for $12,000.

2. Purchased 500 shares of Bachelor, Inc. on 6/15/07 for $16/share.

3. Sold 200 shares of Freedom Corp. stock (Sec. 1244 stock) for $35,000 on 9/1/07. The stock was originally purchased for $125,000 on 12/15/05.

4. Sold 500 shares of Footloose, Inc. on 6/1/07 for $12,000. Stock was inherited from his uncle on 3/1/07. Uncle's basis was $2,000 and the fair market value on the uncle's date of death was $11,000.

5. Shares of Clueless, Inc. became worthless on 9/1/07. John originally purchased the stock on 10/1/06 for $5,000.

6. On 7/15/07, John sold 200 shares of Wild'n'Crazy for $3,000. John had received the stock on 12/31/06 in exchange for 300 shares of Diddly stock (Diddly FMV at date of exchange was $3,700). John originally purchased Diddly on 6/15/05 for $3,000.

1. What is the capital gain/loss on the sale of Bachelor, Inc.?

    a. $3,000 LTCG.

    b. $3,000 STCG.

    c. $4,500 LTCG.

    d. $2,500 STCG.

    e. No gain or loss currently recognized.

2. What is the nature of the gain/loss on the sale of Freedom Corp.?

    a. $90,000 STCL.

    b. $90,000 LTCL.

    c. $90,000 ordinary loss.

    d. $50,000 ordinary loss and $40,000 STCL.

    e. $50,000 ordinary loss and $40,000 LTCL.

3. Regarding all of the stock sales, which of the following statements are incorrect?

    1. John's maximum deductible capital loss for the current year is $3,000.

    2. How John's uncle acquired Footloose stock is irrelevant for the purpose of determining John's capital gain/loss from sale of the stock. (Transaction #4).

    3. The sale of Bachelor, Inc. (Transaction #1) falls under the wash sale rules.

    4. John's basis in Wild' n' Crazy stock was $3,700 (Transaction #6).

    a. 2 only.

    b. 2 and 3.

    c. 2, 3, and 4.

    d. 1 and 4.

    e. 3 and 4.

---

4. What is John's long-term capital gain/loss for the current year (before netting with short-term gains/ losses)?

    a. $35,000 LTCL.

    b. $38,000 LTCL.

    c. $39,000 LTCL.

    d. $44,000 LTCL.

    e. $94,000 LTCL.

5. What is John's short-term capital gain/loss for the current year (before netting with long-term gains/ losses)?

    a. No short-term gains or losses.

    b. $2,800 STCL.

    c. $2,300 STCG.

    d. $3,000 STCG.

    e. $3,800 STCG.

ITEM SET SCENARIO 4

Harold is a 55-year-old corporate executive employed with one of the Fortune 500 companies. He is planning to retire at age 65 and has accumulated the assets listed below for his retirement. Harold is willing to accept enough risk to meet his goals, but he does not want to accept additional risk, nor does he ever want to die with less than $1,000,000 (in today's dollars) in his account (i.e., he hopes to have at least this much in his estate at the end of the 25-year retirement period).

	Stock Portfolio Various Stocks	Bond Portfolio Various Bonds
Market Value	$572,160	$143,040
Average Historic Return	12%	7%
Standard Deviation	15%	9%
Current YTM	N/A	7%
Duration	N/A	5 yrs.
Correlation to the Stock Market	77.5%	N/A

Note: The correlation coefficient between stocks and bonds is +40%.

1. Harold is concerned about the volatility of his portfolio and would like some help in assessing the risk. Based on his current allocation between his bond portfolio and his stock portfolio, what is the standard deviation of his entire portfolio (stock and bond portfolio together)?

    a. 12.0%.

    b. 12.4%.

    c. 12.8%.

    d. 13.4%.

    e. 13.8%.

2. Harold has taken an active role in developing his financial goals by reading Money Magazine. After reading about diversification, he has become concerned about the diversity of his stock portfolio. What portion of the risk in his stock portfolio is inherent to a specific business or industry?

    a. 20%.

    b. 40%.

    c. 60%.

    d. 80%.

    e. 100%.

3. With recent changes in the economy, there has been significant talk about the Federal Reserve raising interest rates. What would be the approximate decline in the value of Harold's bond portfolio if interest rates increase to 7.43%?

   a. 1.0%.

   b. 2.0%.

   c. 3.0%.

   d. 5.8%.

   e. 6.1%.

4. Harold knows that the bond market has been performing well and would like to know what is the probability of having a return of at least 17% from his bond portfolio.

   a. 9%.

   b. 16%.

   c. 22%.

   d. 28%.

   e. 34%.

5. Harold's previous financial planner told him that he should allocate 45% of his portfolio to stocks and 55% to bonds. How much would his portfolio be worth when he retired, if he followed this advice? Assume the portfolio retains this 45%/55% asset allocation.

   a. $1,732,375.

   b. $1,772,428.

   c. $1,773,385.

   d. $1,813,313.

   e. $1,872,385.

ITEM SET SCENARIO 5

During the year 2007, Smallco, Inc. has 3 employees as indicated below:

Employee	Age	Status	401(k) Deferral	Compensation	Coverage in Health Plan
Aaron	30	Single	$3,000	$34,000	Single coverage
Barbara	65	Married	$6,000	$60,000	Family coverage
Charlie	45	Married	$4,000	$47,500	Family coverage

Smallco has a health plan that has the following annual deductibles:

- For single coverage $2,000
- For family coverage $4,000

Smallco pays the health insurance premiums.

Barbara is also employed by ABC Corporation, where she is covered under a health plan as an employee with single coverage. The employer pays the premiums, and the annual deductible for single coverage is $500.

1. What is the maximum limit that Aaron can contribute to a Health Savings Account (HSA) for the year 2007?

    a. $0.
    b. $1,000.
    c. $1,800.
    d. $2,000.
    e. $2,850.

2. Assume that in 2006 and 2007, Aaron made a contribution to an HSA. In 2007, he married Doris who is employed with XYZ Corporation and covered under the XYZ health care plan. In late 2007, Doris became sick and Aaron took a distribution from his HSA to cover her deductible and her coinsurance from major medical. What are the tax consequences to Aaron of such a transaction?

    a. The withdrawal was medically related; therefore, there are no tax consequences.
    b. The withdrawal was medically related; therefore, it is included as ordinary income for the withdrawal amount, but there is no penalty.
    c. The withdrawal is treated as ordinary income and is subject to a 10% penalty tax.
    d. None of the above.

3. Barbara would like to open her own HSA. How much may she deduct from her taxes and contribute to the HSA for 2007?

    a. $0.

    b. $1,000.

    c. $2,000.

    d. $2,700.

    e. $3,400.

4. Assume that in 2007 Barbara establishes an HSA, contributes $500, and makes no withdrawals during 2007. What are the tax consequences to Barbara related to the establishment of the HSA account during 2007?

    a. There are no tax consequences.

    b. She can deduct $500 from income.

    c. She cannot deduct the $500 from income.

    d. She has no deduction and a $30 penalty.

5. Barbara has a working spouse who is 61 years old and is not an active participant in a qualified plan. What is the maximum deductible traditional IRA contribution that Barbara's husband can make for 2007, assuming he earns $50,000 in compensation?

    a. $0.

    b. $1,000.

    c. $4,000.

    d. $4,500.

    e. $5,000.

6. Charlie has a 42-year-old, nonworking spouse and wishes to establish an IRA for his wife. What is the maximum deductible IRA contribution that Charlie can make for himself and his wife for year 2007?

    a. $0.

    b. $4,000.

    c. $5,000.

    d. $8,000.

    e. $9,000.

ITEM SET SCENARIO 6

Margaret believed that she and her husband, Steve, were America's most happily married couple. Margaret was a full-time housewife and mother while Steve owned a retail paper goods store. Quite by accident, Margaret discovered that one week while Steve was supposed to be attending a paper goods convention, he was actually spending the week in the unoccupied half of their rental duplex with his young and beautiful secretary. Margaret has no intention of getting a divorce and plans to file a joint tax return with her husband for 2007. She does, however, feel that Steve needs to suffer as a result of his thoughtless behavior. Therefore, the next Monday (October 7, 2007) she embarks on a program of charitable giving as follows:

1. She donates all of his custom tailored leisure suits to the Salvation Army.

   Cost basis = $4,000.
   Fair market value = $50.

2. She donates paper plates, cups, and napkins from Steve's store to a Democratic Fundraiser. Steve is a staunch Republican.

   Cost basis = $300.
   Fair market value = $600.

3. She donates the rental duplex to their church to be used as a home for wayward girls.

   Cost basis = $55,000 on September 1, 1998.
   Fair market value = $155,000.

4. She donates Steve's favorite picture, a Leroy Neiman lithograph of "Harry's Bar" to the Boy Scouts of America who hang it in the lobby of their headquarters.

   Cost basis = $2,500 on January 1, 1986.
   Fair market value = $17,500.

5. The young and beautiful secretary is a faux blonde. Consequently, Margaret donates all of their Clairol stock to the University of Troy's Department of Accounting.

   Cost basis = $900 on June 2, 2006 (date of purchase).
   Fair market value = $1,100 (date of contribution).

6. Margaret donates Steve's new white Toyota Supra with leather interior to a private nonoperating foundation that is not a 50% organization.

   Cost basis = $40,000 on January 1, 2007.
   Fair market value = $34,000.

1. Which of the following statements is (are) correct?

    1. The paper plates, cups, and napkins are ordinary income property; therefore, the charitable contribution deduction is limited to $300 (cost).

    2. The Clairol stock is capital gain property; therefore the charitable contribution deduction is the FMV at the date of the contribution.

    3. The donation of the duplex to the church will be an adjustment for AMT.

    4. Since Steve had only held his car for nine months, he can only deduct the basis of $40,000 as a charitable contribution.

        a. 1 and 2.

        b. 1, 2, and 3.

        c. 2 and 3.

        d. 3 and 4.

        e. None of the statements are correct.

2. Steve and Margaret's charitable deduction for the rental duplex is:

        a. $55,000 with a 50% of AGI ceiling.

        b. $55,000 with a 30% of AGI ceiling.

        c. $155,000 with a 50% of AGI ceiling.

        d. $155,000 with a 30% of AGI ceiling.

        e. Either a or d (their choice).

3. Which of the following statements is (are) correct?

    1. The charitable deduction for the car will be limited to 20% of AGI.

    2. The duplex can either be subject to the 50% or the 30% of AGI ceiling.

    3. The suits are subject to a 50% of AGI ceiling.

        a. 1 only.

        b. 2 only.

        c. 2 and 3 only.

        d. 1, 2, and 3.

        e. None of the above.

4. The deduction for the Leroy Neiman lithograph contribution to the Boy Scouts would be equal to the fair market value if:

        a. The organization had used it as part of an art appreciation program for the Boy Scouts.

        b. Margaret believed they were going to use it as part of an education program for the Boy Scouts, but they did not.

        c. The organization had sold the painting and used the proceeds for scouting programs.

        d. Both (a) and (b).

ITEM SET SCENARIO 7

Mrs. Anna Bartoromo, age 64, died September 8, 2007. She had been employed with the XYZ Corporation, where she had a vested retirement account and a completely vested 401(k) account. In addition, she had an IRA and other property listed below. She had not started any distributions.

Valuation of Her Interest					
Asset	9/08/07	Date of Disposition 1/1/08	3/08/08	Adjusted Cost Basis	Titling or Beneficiary *
Qualified Plan	$1,000,000		$800,000	$0	Beneficiary D
401(k)	750,000		600,000	0	Beneficiary S
IRA	2,000,000		1,700,000	0	Beneficiary H
½ personal residence	400,000		450,000	280,000	JTWROS with H
Annuity (10-year certain)(8%)	300,000		290,000	200,000	Beneficiary H
Installment note (5 year/9%)	200,000		183,789	160,000	Willed to H
Other property	250,000	$300,000	250,000	80,000	Willed to H

*H = Husband
 S = Son
 D = Daughter

1. How much is included in Mrs. Bartoromo's gross estate? Assume any appropriate election is made.

   a. $4,273,789.

   b. $4,323,789.

   c. $4,350,000.

   d. $4,900,000.

2. How much is Mrs. Bartoromo's approximate probate estate?

   a. $450,000.

   b. $750,000.

   c. $1,150,000.

   d. $2,150,000.

3. Which of the following are Mr. Bartoromo's options regarding Mrs. Bartoromo's individual retirement account (IRA)?

    1. He can roll over her balance into his IRA account and begin distributions by his age 70½.

    2. He can maintain the same account and begin distribution when Mrs. Bartoromo would have attained 70½.

    3. He can take a distribution from the account immediately, and will not be subject to the 10% early withdrawal penalty, even if he is under age 59½.

        a. 1 only.

        b. 2 only

        c. 1 and 2.

        d. 1 and 3.

        e. 1, 2, and 3.

4. Mrs. Bartoromo's 35-year-old son is the beneficiary of her 401(k) plan. Which of the following are the son's options regarding the 401(k) balance?

    1. Son could leave the balance in Mrs. Bartoromo's name and take a distribution from the account immediately. He will not be subject to the 10% early withdrawal penalty.

    2. Son could leave the balance in Mrs. Bartoromo's name and begin distribution over the son's life expectancy in the year following the year of death.

    3. Son could roll over the 401(k) to his own IRA and delay distributions until son is 70½.

        a. 1 only.

        b. 2 only

        c. 1 and 2.

        d. 1 and 3.

        e. 1, 2, and 3.

ITEM SET SCENARIO 8

Mrs. Keri Mayer, age 64, died September 8, 2007. She had been employed with the Reed Corporation, where she had a vested retirement account and a completely vested 401(k) account. In addition, she had an IRA and other property listed below. She had not started any distributions. Assume her executor makes any appropriate elections.

Valuation of Her Interest					
Asset	9/08/07	Date of Disposition 1/1/08	3/08/08	Adjusted Cost Basis	Titling or Beneficiary *
Qualified retirement account	$1,000,000		$800,000	$0	Beneficiary H
401(k)	750,000		600,000	0	Beneficiary S
IRA	2,000,000		1,700,000	0	Beneficiary D
½ personal residence	400,000		450,000**	280,000***	JTWROS with H
Annuity (10-year certain)(8%)	300,000		290,000	200,000	Beneficiary H
Installment note (5 year/9%)	200,000		183,789	160,000	Willed to H
Other property	250,000	$300,000	250,000	80,000	Willed to H

* H = Husband
  S = Son
  D = Daughter

** Represents 50% of value of personal residence
*** Represents 50% of total basis

1. What is her husband's adjustable taxable basis in the installment note?

    a. $0.

    b. $160,000.

    c. $183,789.

    d. $200,000.

2. What is her husband's adjusted taxable basis in the "other property"?

    a. $0.

    b. $80,000.

    c. $250,000.

    d. $300,000.

3. What is her husband's basis in the annuity?

    a. $0.

    b. $200,000.

    c. $290,000.

    d. $300,000.

4. What is her husband's basis in the personal residence?

    a. $450,000.

    b. $560,000

    c. $705,000.

    d. $730,000.

    e. $900,000.

5. What is her son's basis in the 401(k) plan?

    a. $0.

    b. $300,000.

    c. $600,000.

    d. $350,000.

    e. $700,000.

ITEM SET SCENARIO 9

On August 23, 2007, Fred, a single taxpayer, gave his son, Sammy, a gift of ABC stock with a fair market value of $100,000, as of the date of the gift. This was the only gift made this year. Fred had an adjusted taxable basis (cost) in the ABC stock of $160,000 and had acquired the stock on July 31, 1999. Fred had made only one previous taxable gift in his lifetime, and that gift was to Sammy in the amount of $600,000, made August 23, 2005. Fred has a remaining net worth of $1,300,000.

1. What was Fred's gift tax to be paid on the gift of the ABC stock?

    a. $0.

    b. $24,050.

    c. $33,300.

    d. $37,000.

    e. $225,730.

2. Assume that on December 31, 2007, Sammy sold the ABC stock for $140,000. What are the income tax consequences to Sammy for this sale?

    a. No gain or loss.

    b. Short-term capital gain of $40,000.

    c. Long-term capital gain of $40,000.

    d. Short-term capital loss of $20,000.

    e. Long-term capital loss of $20,000.

3. Assume that Sammy sold the ABC stock on December 31, 2007 for $90,000. What are the income tax consequences to Sammy for this sale?

    a. No gain or loss.

    b. Short-term capital loss of $10,000.

    c. Long-term capital loss of $10,000.

    d. Short-term capital loss of $70,000.

    e. Long-term capital loss of $70,000.

4. Regardless of what Sammy does with the stock, what are the income tax consequences to Fred in 2007 with respect to the gift of ABC stock?

    a. No gain or loss.

    b. Short-term capital loss of $60,000 fully deductible.

    c. Long-term capital loss of $60,000 fully deductible.

    d. Short-term capital loss of $60,000 limited to $3,000 deductible.

    e. Long-term capital loss of $60,000 limited to $3,000 deductible.

---

5. Assume that Fred died December 31, 2007. How much, if any, of the ABC stock transaction and other gifts would be included in Fred's gross estate?

    a. $0.
    b. $24,050.
    c. $89,000.
    d. $689,000.
    e. $700,000.

6. Assume Fred died December 31, 2007, with $1,300,000 in cash, no debts and no life insurance. Utilizing all of the information in the original statement and the following information:

Funeral and administrative expenses	$50,000
Charitable contributions	$150,000

    What is Fred's tentative tax base?

    a. $800,000.
    b. $888,000.
    c. $900,000.
    d. $1,300,000.
    e. $1,788,000.

ITEM SET SCENARIO 10

Robert DuCharm, age 65, is planning to retire and wants to transfer his 100% ownership interest in the XYZ Corporation to his daughter, Veronica. The current fair market value of XYZ is $1,000,000. Robert's adjusted basis in the property is $300,000. Robert is married to Kelly Spyhawk, a citizen of Peru, who is also 65 and does the morning local radio show on traffic from her helicopter. Veronica is 32 and works full-time as the vice president of XYZ. Robert is in excellent health and has a family history of long life. His table life expectancy is 17 years and his joint life expectancy with Kelly is 25 years. Any installment sale would be made over the life expectancy of Robert. An appropriate market rate of interest is 9%. Assume interest rates remain stable.

1. Assuming that it is Robert's intention that neither the property nor the balance of indebtedness be included in his gross estate if he were to die prior to his life expectancy, which of the following devices would be appropriate in this situation?

    1. Private annuity.
    2. Installment sale.
    3. Grantor Retained Annuity Trust (GRAT) for 17 years.
    4. Self-canceling installment notes (SCIN).

        a. 1 only.
        b. 2 and 3.
        c. 2 and 4.
        d. 1 and 4.
        e. 1, 2, 3, and 4.

2. Robert has decided to use a traditional installment sale to transfer the property to Veronica. The terms of the sale are 20% down on July 31 of the current year, and the balance paid in equal monthly installments beginning August 31 of the current year, over a period of 12 years at 9% interest. How much cash does Robert expect to receive in the current year?

    a. $45,521.
    b. $236,417.
    c. $245,521.
    d. $254,625.
    e. $309,251.

3. Of the amount received from the down payment and the periodic payments, how much ordinary income does Robert have in the current year?

    a. $14,195.
    b. $17,743.
    c. $21,292.
    d. $29,765.
    e. $30,000.

---

4. If Robert dies after receiving 48 installment note payments, what amount, if any, should be included in his gross estate as a result of the installment sale?

    a. $0.

    b. $565,865.

    c. $621,442.

    d. $800,000.

    e. $874,008.

5. Robert has a simple will leaving all of his assets to his wife, Kelly Spyhawk. Which one of the following statements is correct regarding the installment notes?

    a. The present value of the notes will qualify for the unlimited marital deduction.

    b. The full amount of the remaining payments will qualify for the unlimited marital deduction.

    c. The adjusted taxable basis to Kelly on the inherited installment notes is the fair market value at the date of death.

    d. Kelly will continue to receive a partial return of basis, part capital gain, and part ordinary income from the continuing installment payments.

    e. None of the above.

ITEM SET SCENARIO 11

You invest $5,000,000 in investment A and it is worth $6,500,000 at the end of year one. You invest $8,000,000 in investment B and it is worth $10,000,000 at the end of year one.

1. Your after-tax hurdle rate is 10%. Which of the following investments has a net present value of $909,090.90 and an IRR of 30%?

    a. Investment A.

    b. Investment B.

    c. Both investment A and investment B.

    d. Neither.

2. Your after-tax hurdle rate is 10%. Which of the following investments has a net present value of $1,090,909.09 and an IRR of 25%?

    a. Investment A.

    b. Investment B.

    c. Both investment A and investment B.

    d. Neither.

3. Your after-tax hurdle rate is 10%. Which of the following investments has a net present value of $909,090.90 and an IRR of 100%?

    a. Investment A.

    b. Investment B.

    c. Both investment A and investment B.

    d. Neither.

4. Your after-tax hurdle rate is 10%. Which of the following investments has a net present value of $1,090,909.09 and an IRR of 100%?

    a. Investment A.

    b. Investment B.

    c. Both investment A and investment B.

    d. Neither.

5. Your after-tax hurdle rate is 10%. Which of the following investments has an IRR of 25%?

    a. Investment A.

    b. Investment B.

    c. Both investment A and investment B.

    d. Neither.

ITEM SET SCENARIO 12

Doris buys 1,000 shares of ABC stock for $100 per share with an initial margin of 55% and a maintenance margin of 30%.

1. At what price will Doris receive a margin call?

      a. $45.00.

      b. $55.00.

      c. $64.29.

      d. $69.23.

      e. $78.57.

2. If the stock drops to $70 per share, how much cash per share will Doris be required to deliver?

      a. $5.00.

      b. $6.00.

      c. $6.54.

      d. $8.57.

      e. No cash will be required.

3. If the stock drops to $50 per share, how much cash per share will Doris be required to deliver per share?

      a. $2.00.

      b. $5.00.

      c. $10.00.

      d. $19.22.

      e. $78.57.

ITEM SET SCENARIO 13

You have a two-asset portfolio with equal weighting with the following characteristics:

	Return	Risk (Standard Deviation)
A	5%	20%
B	15%	40%

1. If the correlation coefficient between asset A and B is 0.6, where does the standard deviation of the two-asset portfolio fall?

    a. Below 15%.

    b. 15–30%.

    c. 30–50%.

    d. Over 50%.

    e. Cannot calculate.

2. If the correlation coefficient between asset A and B is equal to 1, where does the standard deviation of the two-asset portfolio fall?

    a. 15–29%.

    b. 30%.

    c. 31–50%.

    d. Cannot determine.

ITEM SET SCENARIO 14

Jennifer is in the process of purchasing a house for $175,000 with a down payment of 20%. She will finance the balance over 30 years at 8%.

1. Assuming she purchases the above house, what will be Jennifer's monthly payment?

   a. $1,020.47.
   b. $1,027.27.
   c. $1,275.58.
   d. $1,284.09.

2. Assume Jennifer buys the house on January 1st of the current year. If payments are due the first of each month, how much qualified residence interest can she deduct for the current year on her tax Form 1040?

   a. $10,266.67.
   b. $10,231.53.
   c. $11,157.74.
   d. $11,299.97.

3. If Jennifer financed the house over 15 years instead of 30, how much interest would she save over the life of the loan (assuming the same interest rate)?

   a. $0.
   b. $55,915.20.
   c. $89,175.60.
   d. $128,993.40.

ITEM SET SCENARIO 15

Diana, a US citizen, has a portfolio of $1,000,000 and has AGI of $200,000 per year. She is 40 years old and is very concerned about her disabled child, Kevin, who is 8 years old. Diana is well off and wants to provide an inflation-protected life income for Kevin beginning when he reaches the age of 21. In addition, Diana wants to leave the principal of her portfolio to the New Orleans Museum of Art. She has a cost basis in the portfolio of $800,000. Her AGI is expected to remain constant for the next 10 years. If sold, the portfolio would result in long-term capital gains.

1. Which of the following parties could Diana name as a replacement remainder beneficiary for the New Orleans Museum of Art (NOMA), assuming that she no longer wanted to benefit NOMA, and she had a properly drafted trust?

    1. Loyola University.
    2. Kevin himself.
    3. Diana herself.
    4. Buffy, the friend of Diana's husband.

        a. The trust is irrevocable and she cannot change the remainderman.
        b. 1 only.
        c. 2 only, because he is already the beneficiary.
        d. 3 only, because she is the grantor.
        e. 1, 2, 3, and 4.

2. Suppose that Diana changes her mind and considers donating the entire portfolio directly to the charity with no income to Kevin. How much is the maximum charitable deduction that she can take in the current year?

    a. $60,000.
    b. $100,000.
    c. $800,000.
    d. $1,000,000.

3. What is the maximum total amount of charitable contributions she can deduct over the next 10 years from this contribution, if Kevin is not a beneficiary, and this is a straight charitable contribution of the $1,000,000 portfolio?

    a. $300,000.
    b. $360,000.
    c. $500,000
    d. $600,000.
    e. $1,000,000.

ITEM SET SCENARIO 16

1. The Guffins refinanced their home exactly two years ago on January 1st, at a 30-year rate of 7.5%. If the remaining mortgage balance at the time of refinancing was $104,000 and the closing costs of 3% of the amount being financed was added to the mortgage balance, how much do they owe today? (Assume they made all payments as agreed, including today's payment.)

    a. $103,922.

    b. $105,068.

    c. $105,160.

    d. $106,133.

    e. $107,120.

2. The Guffins refinanced their home two years ago on January 1st, at a 30-year rate of 7.5%. The initial 30-year loan was for $112,820 and was paid as agreed until refinancing. The balance at refinancing was $104,200 with a remaining term of exactly 22 years. Closing costs of 3% were financed. Assuming the old loan was at an interest rate of 9%, how much total cash will they save if they refinance and pay equal monthly payments over the remaining life of the old loan?

    a. $20,204.

    b. $26,748.

    c. $32,109.

    d. $36,400.

    e. $41,538.

ITEM SET SCENARIO 17

Matching: You may use an answer more than once or not at all.

Auto Coverage

a. Uninsured Motorist (bodily injury).

b. Collision.

c. Comprehensive (other than collision).

d. None of the above.

Event

1. _____ Bird collides with your windshield.

2. _____ You back your car into a tree on your property.

3. _____ An uninsured motorist damages your automobile but does not hurt you.

4. _____ An uninsured motorist strikes you while you are walking.

ITEM SET SCENARIO 18

Matching: You may use an answer more than once or not at all.

a. Charitable Remainder Annuity Trust (CRAT).

b. Charitable Remainder Unitrust (CRUT).

c. Both CRAT and CRUT.

d. Neither CRAT nor CRUT.

1. _____ Charitable deduction, fixed amount of annuity payment regardless of income.

2. _____ Charitable deduction, revocable.

3. _____ Estate tax advantage, variable amount of annuity depending on annual revaluation of trust assets.

4. _____ Charitable deduction, remainder interest paid to charity.

ITEM SET SCENARIO 19

Brett has invested 40% in Portfolio A and 60% in Portfolio B. The correlation between Portfolio A and Portfolio B is 0.4, and the respective standard deviations are 15.5% and 13.5%.

1. What is the standard deviation of Portfolio A and B together?

    a. 11.0%.

    b. 12.0%.

    c. 14.3%.

    d. 14.5%.

    e. 16.0%.

2. How would the answer to the above question change if there was no correlation between Portfolios A and B?

    a. 10.2%.

    b. 11.0%.

    c. 12.0%.

    d. 14.3%.

    e. 14.5%.

ITEM SET SCENARIO 20

Marleen, who turned age 70½ on June 30th of the current year, owns 12% of ABC Company. She has amassed $5,000,000 in her qualified plan account as of December 31st of the previous year and $5,500,000 as of December 31st of the current year. Distribution periods per IRS tables are as follows:

Age	Distribution Period
70	27.4
71	26.5
72	25.6

1. What is the minimum distribution for the current tax year?

   a. $0.

   b. $182,482.

   c. $188,680.

   d. $195,313.

   e. $286,458.

2. If she receives a distribution of $190,000 during the current year, how much is her income tax penalty?

   a. $0.

   b. $4,500.

   c. $30,000.

   d. $34,500.

   e. $60,000.

3. Which of the following statements is/are true regarding Marleen?

   1. If Marleen continues to work for ABC Company, she is permitted to defer her minimum distribution until after she retires.

   2. Marleen can roll over her account balance into an IRA rollover account if she is no longer employed by ABC Company.

   3. If she rolls over her account balance into an IRA rollover account and she does not commingle the funds with other IRA funds, then she will be permitted to use 5-year forward averaging on the entire balance.

   4. If Marleen leaves ABC Company and chooses to roll over her plan balance to an IRA via a direct trustee-to-trustee rollover, she will be subject to 20% withholding on the plan balance.

   a. 2 only.

   b. 1 and 2.

   c. 2 and 4.

   d. 3 and 4.

   e. 1, 2, and 4.

ITEM SET SCENARIO 21

Bob Pruit, the CEO of Tango, Inc. was awarded the following stock options from his company:

Stock Option	Grant Date	Type	Exercise Price	# Shares
A	2004 Feb. 1	ISO	$20	100
B	2005 July 1	NQSO	$25	100
C	2006 Aug.1	ISO	$30	100
D	2007 May 1	NQSO	$30	100

During 2007, Bob had the following transactions regarding the above stock options:

Stock Option	Date	Action	# Shares	Market Price on Action Date
A	2/1	Exercised	100	$42
A	2/1	Sold	100	$42
B	2/14	Exercised	100	$45
C	2/14	Exercised	100	$45
D	5/1	Exercised	100	$50
D	6/1	Sold	100	$60

1. Which of the following is correct regarding Stock Option A for 2007?

    a. Bob has a long-term capital gain of $2,200.

    b. Bob has a short-term capital gain of $2,200.

    c. Bob has ordinary income of $4,200.

    d. Bob has W-2 income of $2,200.

2. Which of the following is correct regarding Stock Option B for 2007?

    a. There are no tax consequences to exercising Stock Option B in 2007 because it was not sold.

    b. $2,000 of LTCG.

    c. $2,000 of STCG.

    d. $2,000 of W-2 income subject to payroll taxes.

    e. AMT income of $2,000 but no ordinary income.

3. Which of the following is correct regarding Stock Option C for 2007?

    a. Bob has LTCG of $1,500.

    b. Bob has AMT income of $1,500 but not regular taxable income.

    c. Bob has STCG of $1,500.

    d. Bob has W-2 income of $1,500.

    e. Bob has ordinary income of $1,500 but not W-2 income.

4. Which of the following is correct regarding Stock Option D for 2007?

    a. Bob must recognize $3,000 of STCG and $2,000 LTCG.

    b. Bob must recognize $3,000 of LTCG and no STCG.

    c. Bob must recognize $3,000 of ordinary income (not W-2).

    d. Bob must recognize $1,000 of STCG and $2,000 of W-2 income.

    e. Bob must recognize $1000 of LTCG and $2,000 ordinary income (not W-2).

ITEM SET SCENARIO 22

Steve, who had never married, died in the curent year. One year before his death he paid gift tax of $18,000 as a result of making the following gifts to friends (the only gifts he made that year):

  a. Bonds worth $40,000 to Tom;

  b. A $400,000 (proceeds value) life insurance policy on his life to Andrea. (The policy was worth $8,000 at the time of transfer.)

At Steve's death, the bonds had increased in value to $90,000 and the life insurance company paid the $400,000 to Andrea. Consider the two transfers and the gift taxes paid when answering the following questions.

1. What effect will the gifts made last year have on Steve's gross estate?

     a. His gross estate will include the gift tax paid but not the value of the gifts.

     b. His gross estate will include the FMV of the bonds on the date of gift and the gift tax paid, but not the value of his life insurance policy.

     c. His gross estate will include the gift tax paid and the face value of the life insurance but not the value of the bonds.

     d. His gross estate will include the fair market value of the bonds and the face value of the life insurance policy but not the gift tax paid.

2. The taxable gifts included in the estate tax base will be:

     a. $0.

     b. $28,000.

     c. $40,000.

     d. $440,000.

3. If the two gifts had been made four years before Steve's death, what amount of the gift tax paid and value of the gifts would be included in his gross estate?

     a. $0.

     b. $18,000.

     c. $28,000.

     d. $400,000.

ITEM SET SCENARIO 23

Smith invests in a limited partnership that requires an outlay of $9,200 today. At the end of years 1 through 5, he will receive the after-tax cash flows shown below. The partnership will be liquidated at the end of the fifth year. Smith is in the 28% tax bracket.

Years	Cash Flows	
0	($9,200)	CF0
1	$600	CF1
2	$2,300	CF2
3	$2,200	CF3
4	$6,800	CF4
5	$9,500	CF5

1. The after-tax IRR of this investment is:

    a. 17.41%.

    b. 19.20%.

    c. 24.18%.

    d. 28.00%.

    e. 33.58%.

2. Which of the following statements are correct?

    1. The IRR is the discount rate that equates the present value of an investment's expected costs to the present value of the expected cash inflows.

    2. The IRR is 24.18% and the present value of the investment's expected cash flows is $9,200.

    3. The IRR is 24.18%. For Smith to actually realize this rate of return, the investment's cash flows will have to be reinvested at the IRR.

    4. If the cost of capital for this investment is 9%, the investment should be rejected because its net present value will be negative.

    a. 2 and 4.

    b. 2 and 3.

    c. 1 only.

    d. 1, 2, and 3.

    e. 1 and 4.

ITEM SET SCENARIO 24

Matching: You may use an answer more than once or not at all.

a.   401(k) plan.

b.   Stock bonus plan.

c.   Target-benefit plan.

d.   Cash-balance plan.

e.   Both (a) and (b).

f.   Both (c) and (d).

1. _____ Requires PBGC insurance.

2. _____ Features employee elective deferrals.

3. _____ Pension plan.

4. _____ Permits greater-than-10% investment in employer stock.

ITEM SET SCENARIO 25

Matching: You may use an answer more than once or not at all.

a. Included in the gross estate only.

b. Included in the probate estate only.

c. Included in both the gross estate and the probate estate.

d. Included in neither the gross estate nor the probate estate.

1. _____ Real estate owned Joint Tenants with Right of Survivorship.

2. _____ SEP with a named beneficiary who is deceased.

3. _____ Community property consisting of a personal residence.

4. _____ POD account with a balance of $400,000.

ITEM SET SCENARIO 26

Matching: You may use an answer more than once or not at all.

a. Subrogation.

b. Assumption of the Risk.

c. Collateral Source Rule.

d. Attractive Nuisance.

1. _____ Scott builds a new home with a large pool and diving board. He does not fence the yard as it would distract from the aesthetics.

2. _____ John is injured and has health insurance which pays for his damage, but he can still sue Jack, the negligent party.

3. _____ Mary was hit in the head by a foul ball at a baseball game.

4. _____ A contractual provision designed to prevent the insured from making a profit.

ITEM SET SCENARIO 27

Matching: You may use an answer more than once or not at all.

a.   FIFO tax treatment.

b.   LIFO tax treatment.

c.   Specific Identification.

d.   Either (a) or (c).

e.   None of the above.

1.   _____   Loan from Modified Endowment Contract (MEC).

2.   _____   Distribution from Roth IRA.

3.   _____   Sale of 300 shares of Sysko Sistems stock.

4.   _____   Distribution from a Traditional IRA.

ITEM SET SCENARIO 28

Aaron Young is 62 and preparing to retire. Aaron has three adult children. He has asked you to help him determine the implications of transferring, surrendering, or borrowing from his whole life insurance policy. The policy information is as follows:

Description	Amount
Death Benefit of Policy	$1,000,000
Cash Value of Policy	$90,000
Outstanding Loan on Policy	$35,000
Net Premiums Paid	$58,000
Surrender Value	$84,000

1. If Aaron terminates the policy, how much cash will he receive from the insurance company?

    a. $32,000.

    b. $35,000.

    c. $49,000.

    d. $55,000.

    e. $90,000.

2. How much will be included in Aaron's taxable income if he terminates the policy?

    a. $26,000.

    b. $35,000.

    c. $49,000.

    d. $55,000.

    e. $90,000.

3. If Aaron decided to transfer the policy to an Irrevocable Life Insurance Trust, with his oldest child as the trust beneficiary, which of the following statements is/are true?

    1. If Aaron dies two years after the transfer, the entire death benefit will be included in Aaron's gross estate.

    2. If Aaron dies two years after the transfer, the entire death benefit will be included in Aaron's probate estate.

    3. Aaron can be the trustee of the Irrevocable Life Insurance Trust without any negative estate tax ramifications.

    4. Aaron can make annual gifts to the trust to pay future premiums. These gifts may be eligible for the gift tax annual exclusion.

        a. 1 only.

        b. 1 and 4 only.

        c. 2, 3, and 4 only.

        d. 1, 2, and 4 only.

        e. 1, 3, and 4 only.

ITEM SET SCENARIO 29

Marshall Orangewhite is a 58-year-old employee of ABC Company. Marshall is married, and he and his wife have a 30-year-old son. A review of his net worth statement reveals the following retirement plans and values:

Description	Current Value	Beneficiary
401(k) plan from ABC Company (his current employer)	$1,000,000	Spouse
401(k) plan from Johnson Industries (former employer – separated from service 10 years ago)	$90,000	Spouse
Roth IRA (established in 1999 with a $2,000 initial contribution; no additional contributions made)	$10,000	Spouse
Traditional IRA (established several years ago with $10,000 of after-tax contributions)	$58,000	Son

1. Marshall plans on retiring in March of this year, and he and his wife would like to take a vacation to the Bahamas in November. He would like to pay for the $10,000 of travel and hotel costs of the vacation by taking a distribution from one of his retirement plans. Which of the following plans would allow Marshall to take a penalty-free withdrawal to fund his vacation (ignoring any mandatory tax with-holding)?

    a. 401(k) plan from ABC Company.

    b. 401(k) plan from Johnson Industries.

    c. Roth IRA.

    d. Traditional IRA.

    e. None of the plans will be exempt from the penalty because Marshall has not attained age 59½.

2. Which statement below is false regarding the beneficiary designations of Marshall's retirement plans?

    a. Marshall can change the beneficiary designation of his Roth IRA without obtaining prior consent from his spouse.

    b. If Marshall changes the beneficiary designation of his Traditional IRA to his grandson, his minimum required distributions at age 70½ will not be affected.

    c. Marshall must have spousal consent to change the beneficiary of his Johnson Industries 401(k) plan.

    d. Marshall can change the beneficiary designation of his ABC Company 401(k) plan to his son without obtaining prior consent from his spouse.

ITEM SET SCENARIO 30

Use the following client information to answer the questions below.

Description	Amount
Bank loan balance	$30,000
Alimony payment	$10,000
Dividend income	$2,000
Wages	$60,000
Federal income taxes owed (< 3 years old)	$18,000
Government student loans (< 5 years old)	$22,000
Monthly mortgage payments	$2,000
Muni Bonds	$20,000
Tax-exempt interest from muni bonds	$1,000
Auto loan balance	$12,000

1. Which one of the following items would NOT be included in the client's cash flow statement?

    a. Wages.

    b. Mortgage payments.

    c. Alimony payment.

    d. Tax-exempt interest.

    e. Auto loan balance.

2. If the client filed for bankruptcy under Chapter 7, how much can be discharged?

    a. $42,000.

    b. $44,000.

    c. $52,000.

    d. $60,000.

    e. $72,000.

3. Assume that the client borrowed money on margin to purchase the muni bonds. The client paid $1,500 of margin interest expense during the current year. How much of the margin interest expense is deductible for federal income tax purposes?

    a. $0.

    b. $1,000.

    c. $1,500.

    d. $2,000.

    e. $3,000.

ITEM SET SCENARIO 31

On August 30th, the SmoothCo December 55 call option has a premium of $6.50. The stock's market price is currently $58 per share. The stock is publicly traded, and has a current P/E ratio of 15.

1. Based on the information above, what is the intrinsic value of the call option?

    a. $0.
    b. $2.00.
    c. $3.00.
    d. $3.50.
    e. $6.50.

2. Based on the information above, what is the time value of the call option?

    a. $0.
    b. $2.00.
    c. $3.00.
    d. $3.50.
    e. $6.50.

3. The accounting firm of Bumble, Stumble, and Fumble used the Black/Scholes option valuation model to value the above option. Which of the following factors will cause the value of the option to increase?

    a. A decrease in the variance of the stock.
    b. A decrease in the price of the stock.
    c. A decrease in general interest rates.
    d. A decrease in the exercise price of the option.

ITEM SET SCENARIO 32

Matching: You may use an answer more than once or not at all.

a. Capital Asset.

b. Ordinary Asset.

c. Section 1231 Asset.

d. None of the above.

1. _____ Copyright.

2. _____ Welding machinery used by Roche Welding in its business.

3. _____ Personal automobile.

4. _____ Electric razors sold by the Razor Company, who manufactures them.

ITEM SET SCENARIO 33

Mary has become very wealthy due to business dealings. In 2007, she established an irrevocable trust with Crummey provisions for her 33-year-old daughter, Rianna. The trust document provides that the income from the trust will be paid to Rianna each year, with the remainder passing to Mary's granddaughter at Rianna's death. In 2007, Mary contributed $100,000 of nondividend paying stock to the trust.

1. If Rianna exercises her demand right, how much can she withdraw from the trust during the first 30 days?

    a. $0.

    b. $5,000.

    c. $12,000.

    d. $100,000.

    e. 5% of the trust value.

2. If no other money is gifted to the trust, how much can Rianna withdraw in the second year?

    a. $0.

    b. $5,000.

    c. $12,000.

    d. $100,000.

    e. 5% of the trust value.

3. If Mary dies two years after making the gift, how much of the $100,000 gift will be included in her gross estate?

    a. $0.

    b. $5,000.

    c. $89,000.

    d. $100,000.

    e. 5% of the trust value.

ITEM SET SCENARIO 34

Roger is a 35-year-old attorney, taxed in the 35% income tax bracket. He has the following assets in his investment portfolio:

Description	Holding Period	Fair Market Value	Basis
Rare stamp collection	18 Months	$25,000	$10,000
Small business (Section 1202) stock	6 Years	$25,000	$7,000
Philip Morris common stock	11 Months	$25,000	$13,000
Investment land	3 Years	$25,000	$3,000

1. Roger needs $22,000 in cash to pay for a new car. Which one of the assets listed above should he sell to raise the money?

   a. Rare stamp collection.

   b. Section 1202 stock.

   c. Common stock.

   d. Investment land.

   e. None of the above will result in enough after-tax cash to fund the purchase.

2. If Roger decided to donate the rare stamp collection to the Boy Scouts, which one of the following statements is true (ignore AGI limits)?

   a. He will receive a charitable deduction of $10,000 because the stamp collection is considered a collectible.

   b. He will receive a charitable deduction of $25,000 because the stamp collection is capital gain property.

   c. He will receive a charitable deduction of $10,000 because the property is unrelated use.

   d. He will receive a charitable deduction of $25,000 because the stamp was held long term.

   e. None of the above.

3. Which one of the following statements regarding Roger's investments is true?

   a. Since the Section 1202 stock receives favorable income tax treatment, the stock will not receive a step-up in basis at the owner's death.

   b. A portion of the excluded gain on the sale of the Section 1202 stock is a tax preference item for purposes of alternative minimum tax.

   c. If Roger transfers his rare stamps to his traditional IRA, he could sell the stamps and pay no income tax until amounts are withdrawn from the IRA.

   d. If Roger exchanges his investment land for his friend's principal residence, which he plans on using for his own personal use, Roger will be eligible for like-kind exchange treatment.

ITEM SET SCENARIO 35

Cathy Nguyen is 55 years old, and in the financial distribution/gifting phase of her life. She wants to gift some of her assets and is seeking the professional assistance of her financial planner to decide to which donees she should gift certain assets. The assets she is currently considering gifting have all been held for more than one year and one day and are as follows:

Asset	Type	Fair Market Value	Yield	Adjusted Tax Basis	Expected Future Appreciation
A	Stock	$25,000	1%	$5,000	2%
B	Bond	$25,000	8%	$25,000	0%
C	Stock	$25,000	2%	$20,000	6%
D	Stock	$25,000	4%	$32,500	2%
E	Stock	$25,000	0%	$21,000	12%

1. Cathy wants to assist her mother, in need of income, by gifting her one of the listed assets. Which of the assets would be the most appropriate choice?

    a. Stock A.
    b. Bond B.
    c. Stock C.
    d. Stock E.

2. Cathy's son is 32 years old and is established in his career as a public television program director. Cathy wants to gift either Stock A or Stock E to her son because she is concerned with the consequences of asset appreciation. Which of the following statements indicates the best choice?

    1. Stock A should be gifted to Cathy's son so she can avoid the tax consequences associated with the large capital appreciation that has occurred.
    2. Considering the expected future appreciation for Stock E, Cathy should gift this stock to her son.
    3. Because Stock E currently has 0% yield, appreciation of this stock is not a concern of Cathy's.

    a. 1 only.
    b. 2 only.
    c. 3 only.
    d. None of the above.

3. Cathy wants to gift one of her assets to her favorite public charity. Ignoring the choices made in the previous questions, which of the following assets should she gift to the charity?

    a. Stock A.
    b. Bond B.
    c. Stock D.
    d. Stock E.

4. If Cathy is planning on selling one of the assets, which asset should she sell? Assume her objective is based on income tax benefits and she is also making gifts to her mother, son, friend, and charity.

    a. Stock A.

    b. Bond B.

    c. Stock C.

    d. Stock D.

    e. Stock E.

ITEM SET SCENARIO 36

Your client made the following stock purchases on January 1 of the current year:

Stock	Number of shares purchased on January 1 of current year	Original Purchase price per share	Ending price on 12/31 of current year	Dividends paid per share on 12/31 of the current year
ABC	200	$16	$8	None
XYZ	200	$18	$15	$0.75
THE	200	$14	$16	$1.00

On July 1 of the current year, the XYZ stock split 2-for-1. Use this information to answer the following questions:

1. What would be the total value of the stocks on the client's Statement of Financial Position on December 31?

    a. $6,300
    b. $7,800.
    c. $9,600.
    d. $10,800.
    e. $15,600.

2. What is the net cash flow from the stock for the current year, assuming the client did not sell any of the stock this year?

    a. $9,100 net cash inflow.
    b. $9,100 net cash outflow.
    c. $9,600 net cash inflow.
    d. $9,600 net cash outflow.
    e. $10,300 net cash outflow.

3. Assume that the XYZ stock has a P/E ratio of 15 on December 31 of the current year. What is the dividend payout ratio of the XYZ stock?

    a. 15%.
    b. 47%.
    c. 53%.
    d. 65%.
    e. 75%.

ITEM SET SCENARIO 37

Tom, age 48, is single, and is an active participant in his employer's 401(k) plan. He has the following income and loss items for the current year:

- $85,000 salary as an investment adviser from Bank of Texas Capital Management.
- $800 of dividends from XYZ company preferred stock.
- $300 of interest income from a corporate B-rated bond.
- $1,000 of interest income from a private activity bond.
- ($3,000) loss from an 8% limited partnership interest in Realty Capital Partners, a limited partnership.
- ($5,000) loss from a 25% interest in ABC Partnership. He does not materially participate in the partnership.
- ($2,000) loss from an interest in an S Corporation in which he does materially participate.
- Mortgage interest expense of $8,000.
- Margin interest expense of $4,000.

Use the above information to answer the following questions:

1. What is Tom's adjusted gross income (AGI)?

       a. $64,000.

       b. $64,100.

       c. $78,100.

       d. $84,100.

       e. $86,100.

2. Assuming Tom itemizes his deductions this year, how much of his margin interest expense will be deductible?

       a. $0.

       b. $300.

       c. $1,100.

       d. $2,100.

       e. $4,000.

3. Which of the following retirement planning options would be available to Tom?

    1. Tom could contribute to a Roth IRA for the current year.

    2. Tom could contribute to a deductible traditional IRA this year.

    3. Tom could contribute to a non-deductible traditional IRA this year.

    4. Tom could convert his existing traditional IRA to a Roth IRA this year.

        a. 1 and 4 only.

        b. 2 and 3 only.

        c. 1, 3, and 4 only.

        d. 2, 3, and 4 only.

        e. 1, 2, and 4 only.

4. What is Tom's passive loss carryforward to next year?

        a. $0.

        b. $3,000.

        c. $5,000.

        d. $8,000.

        e. $10,000.

ITEM SET SCENARIO 38 CFP® CERTIFICATION EXAMINATION, Released 08/2004

Ana, an unmarried resident of the state of New Mexico, is concerned about the costs and delays that could be caused by the probate process. She went to an estate planning attorney to discuss possible ways to avoid probate. The attorney recommended that Ana create a revocable living trust to hold some of her assets. She heeded the attorney's advice, and created the revocable trust.

In the current year, Ana transferred the following assets to the trust:

- Portfolio of dividend-paying stocks, with a standard deviation of 10%, and a dividend payout ratio of 25%.

- Apartment complex located in North Carolina. Ana has rented the property to tenants for the last few years, and has taken appropriate MACRS depreciation deductions on her tax return.

- An installment note receivable, with a 9% interest rate and a remaining term of 7 years.

Use the above information to answer the following four questions.

1. Which of the following is/are true with respect to the revocable living trust?

    1. Ana can be the trustee of the revocable living trust.

    2. The assets transferred to the living trust will be excluded from Ana's gross estate upon her death.

    3. Ana could use the trust to assist in managing the property if she becomes incapacitated.

    4. Upon Ana's death, the assets remaining in the trust will be distributed as directed by Ana's will.

        a. 1 and 2.

        b. 1 and 3.

        c. 2, 3, and 4.

        d. 2 and 4.

        e. 1, 3, and 4.

2. The following clause was placed in Ana's revocable living trust:

    "No interest in the principal or income of this trust shall be anticipated, assigned, encumbered, or subject to any creditor's claim or to legal process before its actual receipt by the beneficiary."

    Which of the following would best describe this clause?

        a. Rule against perpetuities.

        b. Attestation clause.

        c. Crummey clause.

        d. Disposition of property provision.

        e. Spendthrift provision.

---

3. Which of the following income tax ramifications are correct with respect to the revocable living trust?

   1. Since Ana transferred an installment note to the trust, she will be required to recognize any remaining deferred gain on her tax return.

   2. Since Ana transferred depreciable real property to the trust (apartment complex), she will be required to recapture all excess prior years' depreciation deductions on her tax return.

   3. Ana will be required to report the dividends from the stocks on her personal income tax return.

   4. At Ana's death, all of the assets in the trust, except for the installment note, will receive a step-up in basis.

      a. 1 and 2.

      b. 3 and 4.

      c. 1, 2, and 3.

      d. 2, 3, and 4.

      e. 1, 2, 3, and 4.

4. Which of the following assets would be the most appropriate for Ana to transfer to the revocable living trust?

      a. Traditional IRA.

      b. 401(k) plan.

      c. Annuity

      d. Personal residence, located in New Mexico.

      e. Life insurance policy on Ana's life.

ITEM SET SCENARIO 39 CFP® CERTIFICATION EXAMINATION, Released 08/2004

James and Susan Hansen, a happily married couple, live in a common-law state. James has asked for help with estate planning. Soon after their marriage, they executed simple Wills to name guardians for their children and to leave all assets to each other in the event of death.

James wants to be sure that they have enough money for retirement. He does not want to "spoil" his children by giving them too much money, and he wants to pay as little as possible in taxes. Susan wants to make life easier for their three children by making generous gifts of assets to them. She would also like to make major gifts to her church and a favorite charity. James hesitantly agrees to start contributing some family assets to charity.

James: age 55, business executive, $120,000 annual salary
Susan: age 53, homemaker
David: age 30, a physician, divorced, 2 children (ages 3 and 2)
Kristin: age 27, computer programmer, widowed, 1 child (age 1)
Todd: age 18, college freshman, $20,000 tuition per year, single

Federal income tax bracket is 28%.

No inheritances are anticipated.

Asset	Value	Related Liability	Monthly Invest-ment	Estimated Annual Total Return	Ownership	Income Tax Basis
Checking	$5,000				JTWROS	$5,000
Savings	6,000			3%	JTWROS	$6,000
Certificates of Deposit	380,000			5%	Susan	$380,000
Home	280,000	$50,000			JTWROS	$130,000
Vehicles, furniture, and so forth.	90,000				JTWROS	
Stocks[1]	300,000		$2,000	10%	James	$100,000
Apartments(4-plex)[2]	260,000	$90,000		4%	JTWROS	$125,000
401(k)[3]	600,000		$700	10%	James	
Total Assets	$1,921,000					

Life Insurance	Cash Value	Death Benefit	Insured	Owner	Beneficiary
Group Term Life Insurance		$120,000	James	James	Susan
Life Insurance[4]	$30,000	$250,000	James	James	Susan
Life Insurance	$5,000	$50,000	Susan	Susan	James

[1]Purchased over a 20-year period.

[2]Cost of $180,000 less straight-line depreciation of $55,000.

[3]All in equity mutual funds, Susan is the beneficiary.

[4]A total of $20,000 of premiums have been paid.

1. Which of the following recommendations would result in the most significant reduction of transfer taxes for the Hansens?

   a. Assign ownership of James $250,000 life insurance policy to Susan.

   b. Equalize their estates by changing ownership of each separately owned asset to joint tenancy with right of survivorship (JTWROS).

   c. Establish and make regular gifts to custodial accounts for their children and grandchildren.

   d. Establish revocable living trusts with by-pass provisions.

2. If James were to die today, the value of the assets included in his probate estate would be:

   a. $300,000.

   b. $900,000.

   c. $1,270,000.

   d. $1,590,500.

3. If James were to die today, the amount of his gross estate would be:

   a. $1,220,500.

   b. $1,520,500.

   c. $1,590,500.

   d. $1,911,000.

4. If the $250,000 life insurance policy on James life is not needed to provide income for Susan upon his death, which of the following would be best from a tax perspective?

   a. Transfer the policy to an irrevocable life insurance trust with the children as trust beneficiaries.

   b. Surrender the policy to receive the cash surrender value.

   c. Assign ownership of the policy to Susan and name the children as beneficiaries of the policy.

   d. Assign ownership of the policy to Susan and name James estate as beneficiary of the policy.

5. If Susan were to die today, which of the following amounts would be allowable as a marital deduction on her estate tax return?

    a. $380,000.

    b. $430,000.

    c. $680,500.

    d. $750,500.

ITEM SETS

■

Solutions

Item Set Solutions

Item Set 1	Item Set 2	Item Set 3	Item Set 4	Item Set 5
1. b	1. c	1. b	1. c	1. e
2. b	2. e	2. e	2. b	2. a
3. b	3. a	3. b	3. b	3. a
		4. d	4. b	4. d
		5. c	5. a	5. e
				6. d

Item Set 6	Item Set 7	Item Set 8	Item Set 9	Item Set 11
1. e	1. c	1. b	1. a	1. d
2. e	2. a	2. d	2. a	2. c
3. d	3. e	3. b	3. b	3. d
4. d	4. e	4. d	4. a	4. c
		5. a	5. a	5. d
			6. e	

Item Set 11	Item Set 12	Item Set 13	Item Set 14	Item Set 15
1. a	1. c	1. b	1. b	1. b
2. b	2. e	2. b	2. b	2. b
3. d	3. c		3. d	3. d
4. d				
5. b				

Item Set 16	Item Set 17	Item Set 18	Item Set 19	Item Set 20
1. b	1. c	1. a	1. b	1. c
2. a	2. b	2. d	2. a	2. a
	3. b	3. b		3. c
	4. a	4. c		

Item Set 21	Item Set 22	Item Set 23	Item Set 24	Item Set 25
1. d	1. c	1. c	1. d	1. a
2. d	2. b	2. d	2. a	2. c
3. b	3. a		3. f	3. c
4. d			4. e	4. a

Item Set 26	Item Set 27	Item Set 28	Item Set 29	Item Set 30
1. d	1. b	1. c	1. a	1. e
2. c	2. a	2. a	2. d	2. a
3. b	3. d	3. b		3. a
4. a	4. e			

Item Set 31	Item Set 32	Item Set 33	Item Set 34	Item Set 35
1. c	1. b	1. c	1. b	1. b
2. d	2. c	2. a	2. c	2. b
3. d	3. a	3. a	3. b	3. a
	4. b			4. d

Item Set 36	Item Set 37	Item Set 38	Item Set 39	
1. d	1. d	1. b	1. d	
2. b	2. b	2. e	2. a	
3. e	3. c	3. b	3. c	
	4. d	4. d	4. a	
			5. c	

ITEM SET SOLUTION 1

Fundamentals—Future Value

1. b

		Tuition Yr.1	Tuition Yr. 2	Tuition Yr. 3	Tuition Yr. 4
PV	=	$25,000	$25,000	$25,000	$25,000
n	=	18	19	20	21
i	=	7	7	7	7
PMT	=	$0	$0	$0	$0
FV	=	$84,498.31 v	$90,413.19 v	$96,742.11 v	$103,514.06 v

Σ v = $375,167.67

Fundamentals—Education Planning and Time Value of Money

2. b

Step 1:

FV	=	$0
PMT_{AD}	=	$25,000
i	=	1.402 [((1.085 ÷ 1.07) −1) × 100]
n	=	4
$PV_{AD@18}$	=	$97,945.13

Step 2:

$FV_{@18}$	=	$97,945.13
n	=	18
i	=	1.402
PMT	=	$0
$PV_{@0}$	=	$76,233.43

Step 3:

$PV_{@0}$	=	$76,233.43
n	=	18
i	=	8.5
FV	=	$0
PMT_{AD}	=	$7,758.98

Fundamentals—Educational Funding

3. b

Qualified Tuition Plan (529s) assets are included in the gross estate of the beneficiary and not of the contributors. Market risk is a systematic risk and inherent to all investment markets. Qualified Tuition Plan earnings grow tax deferred and distributions are tax free for qualified education expenses. Active investment strategies involve security selection and market timing. Dollar cost averaging is the process of purchasing securities over a period of time by investing a predetermined amount.

ITEM SET SOLUTION 2

Insurance—Homeowners Insurance

1. c

80% of replacement cost is required to avoid a co-insurance position.

80% of $100,000 = $80,000. Since they only have $75,000, they are in a co-insurance position.

$$\frac{\$75,000}{\$80,000} = 93.75\% \text{ (insurer's portion)}$$

Loss	$40,000
Insurer %	0.9375
	$37,500 Rounded
Deductible	(500)
	$37,000 Will be paid by the insurance company

Insurance—Automobile Insurance

2. e

	Honda	Toyota	Total
Total loss	$3,500	$2,000	$5,500
Less deductible	(250)	(500)	(750)
Loss payable by insurance company	$3,250	$1,500	$4,750

Amount payable by the Dells is $750 for the two deductibles.
Note: This is comprehensive, not collision.

Tax—Itemized Deductions

3. a

Total loss	$70,500	(40,000 + 25,000 + 3,500 + 2,000)
Less insurance proceeds	(52,000)	(30,000 + 20,000 + 1,000 + 1,000)
Unreimbursed loss	$18,500	
Less 10% AGI floor	(6,000)	(60,000 × 10%)
Less $100	(100)	(casualty and loss reduction −$100 per occurrence)
Deductible loss	$12,400	

ITEM SET SOLUTION 3

Tax—Capital Assets

1. b

The gain on the stock is $3,000. The gain is short-term (held for five months).

Tax—Section 1244 Stock

2. e

John incurred a $90,000 loss ($125,000 − $35,000). The stock had been held long term, and so the loss would normally be treated entirely as long-term capital loss. The stock, however, is Section 1244 stock, so John (who is single) will have a $50,000 ordinary loss and a $40,000 long-term capital loss.

Tax—Tax Consequences of the Disposition of Property

3. b

Statement 2 is incorrect. If the uncle received Footloose stock as a gift from John within a year of his death, John would not get a stepped up basis. Thus, it is relevant how the uncle acquired the stock. Statement 3 is incorrect because the wash sale rules apply only to losses, not gains, so repurchase in Transaction #2 within 30 days has no effect on Transaction #1. John's basis in Wild' n' Crazy is $3,700. Transaction #6 cannot be a like-kind exchange (securities do not qualify for like-kind exchange treatment), thus the basis of the shares acquired is equal to the FMV at the date of acquisition.

Tax—Capital Assets

4. d

$40,000 LTCL (Transaction #3).

$1,000 LTCG (Transaction #4).

$5,000 LTCL (Transaction #5).

Net $44,000 LTCL.

Regarding Transaction #4: John's basis in the inherited stock is the FMV at the date of death, $11,000. John has a gain of $1,000 on the transaction ($12,000 − $11,000). Inherited property automatically gets a long-term holding period.

Regarding Transaction #5: Worthless securities are deemed to have become worthless on the last day of the year, in this case, 12/31/07. Therefore, John will have a long-term capital loss of $5,000.

Tax—Capital Assets

5. c

$3,000 STCG (Transaction #1).

$700 STCL (Transaction #6).

Net $2,300 STCG.

Regarding Transaction #6: Securities do not qualify as a like-kind exchange.

When John exchanged his Diddly stock it had an adjusted basis of $3,000 plus a long-term gain of $700. The new basis for Wild'n'Crazy was $3,700, but John sold it for $3,000. This resulted in a short-term capital loss of $700.

ITEM SET SOLUTION 4

Investments—Standard Deviation

1. **c**

Percent of stock = 80%

Percent of bonds = 20%

$$\sigma^2 = x_s^2\sigma_s^2 + y_b^2\sigma_b^2 + 2x_sy_b[(\sigma_s)(\sigma_b)(r_{sb})]$$

$$\sigma^2 = (0.8)^2(0.15)^2 + (0.2)^2(0.09)^2 + 2(0.8)(0.2)[(0.15)(0.09)(0.40)]$$

$$\sigma^2 = 0.0144 + 0.00032 + 0.001728$$

$$\sigma^2 = 0.016448$$

$$\sigma = (0.016448)^{1/2} = 12.825\%$$

Investments—Coefficient of Determination

2. **b**

Correlation coefficient = 0.775

Coefficient of determination = $(0.775)^2 = 0.60$

Thus, 60% of the performance of Harold's stock portfolio is directly attributable to the performance of the market. Therefore, 40% of the returns of his portfolio are related to risk of a particular stock or industry.

Investments—Bond Duration

3. **b**

$$\frac{\Delta P}{P} = \left(\frac{-D}{(1 + YTM)}\right)(\Delta YTM)$$

$$\frac{\Delta P}{P} = \left(\frac{-5}{1.07}\right)(0.0743 - 0.07)$$

$\Delta P = (0.02)$ or (2%) Therefore, there is a decline in value of two (2) percent in Harold's bond portfolio if interest rates increase to 7.43%.

Investments—Normal Distribution

4. b

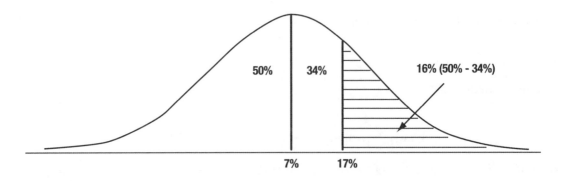

The probability of a return falling within one standard deviation (in this case, -3% to 17%) is 68%. Thus, the probability of a return between 7% and 17% must be 34% (one-half of 68%). Since 50% of returns will fall below and above the mean of 7%, it follows that the probability of a return above 17% is 16% (50% − 34%).

Investments—Investment Returns and Rebalancing

5. a

Weighted return = (0.45)(0.12) + (0.55)(0.07) = 0.0925 or 9.25%

The weighted return represents the return for a set of securities, such as a portfolio, where each return is weighted by the proportion of the security to the entire group or portfolio. The weighted return must be used instead of determining the FV of stocks and bonds separately because of the assumption that the 45%/55% allocation will be maintained throughout the holding period.

PV	=	$715,200
n	=	10 years
i	=	9.25%
PMT	=	$0
FV	=	$1,732,375

ITEM SET SOLUTION 5

Employee Benefits—Health Savings Account

1. e

1/12 of $2,850 is the maximum monthly contribution.

Employee Benefits—Health Savings Account

2. a

Since Aaron used his HSA distribution for qualified medical expenses of his spouse, there is no tax consequence.

Employee Benefits—Health Savings Account

3. a

Barbara is not eligible for an HSA, because she is covered under a health plan that is not a high deductible health plan.

Employee Benefits—Health Savings Account

4. d

There is a 6% excise tax penalty for over-funding an HSA. Barbara is covered by a health plan that's not a high deductible health plan, so she cannot establish an HSA. The entire contribution has a penalty of 6% × $500 = $30.

Retirement—Traditional IRA

5. e

Barbara is an active participant in a 401(k) plan, which is a qualified plan. The couple's AGI is under the threshold of $156,000 that applies when one spouse is not an active participant. Therefore, her husband is eligible for a deductible IRA contribution of $5,000 ($4,000 + $1,000 catch-up for individuals who have attained the age of 50 by the close of the tax year).

Retirement—Traditional IRA

6. d

The maximum deductible contribution is a total of $8,000 for both spouses for 2007. Charlie is an active participant in a 401(k) plan, which is a qualified plan, but he is under the deduction phase-out threshold of $83,000 for the year 2007. In 2007, the maximum IRA contribution is $4,000 ($5,000 for individuals who have attained the age of 50 by the close of the tax year).

ITEM SET SOLUTION 6

Tax—Charitable Contribution

1. e

None of the statements are correct. The Democratic Party contribution is not deductible at all. The stock is not held long term; thus, the adjusted basis is the deduction. No adjustment for AMT is necessary. Steve's holding period for the car is irrelevant.

Tax—Charitable Deduction

2. e

Either A or D. When donating long-term capital gain property to a 50% organization, the taxpayer has the choice of taking a deduction of adjusted basis up to 50% of AGI or FMV up to 30% of AGI.

Tax—Charitable Contribution

3. d

All three statements are correct. The car is given to a 20% charity (private nonoperating). The duplex can either be subject to the 50% or 30% of AGI ceiling, depending on the election. All other donations have 50% of AGI ceilings.

Tax—Charitable Deduction

4. d

If appreciated capital gain personal property is put to a related use, the deduction is the FMV. If the property is put to an unrelated use, the deduction is the adjusted basis. Answer A is correct because the use would be related to the charitable purpose of the organization. Answer B is also correct. If the taxpayer has reason to believe that the property will be put to a related use, even though the property was not put to that use, the FMV will be used. Answer C is incorrect, since this use would be considered an unrelated use.

ITEM SET SOLUTION 7

Estates—Gross Estate

1. c

The alternate valuation date should be elected, because it would result in a lower gross estate. The annuity and installment note are valued on the date of death because they are so-called "wasting assets." The other property is valued on the date of disposition. All remaining property is valued on the alternate valuation date.

Qualified Retirement Account	$800,000	Alternate valuation date
401(k)	600,000	Alternate valuation date
IRA	1,700,000	Alternate valuation date
Personal Residence	450,000	Alternate valuation date
Annuity	300,000	Date of death
Installment Note	200,000	Date of death
Other Property	300,000	Date of disposition
Gross Estate	$4,350,000	

Estates—Probate Estate

2. a

Probate is determined at the date of death (includes the "note" and the "other property") ($200,000 + 250,000) = $450,000. All other assets are non-probate assets.

The qualified plan, 401(k), IRA, and annuity all have a designated beneficiary, and will therefore avoid probate. The personal residence is titled Joint Tenancy With Rights of Survivorship (JTWROS) with the husband. Therefore, her share of the residence will automatically pass to her husband by operation of law at her death, thus avoiding probate.

Retirement—Traditional IRA

3. e

All of the options are available for a spouse beneficiary of an Individual Retirement Account (IRA).

Retirement—401(k) Plan

4. e

The son can rollover the 401(k) account into his own account. Beginning in 2007, a nonspouse beneficiary can rollover a qualified plan or IRA into their own IRA.

ITEM SET SOLUTION 8

Tax—Basis of Inherited Property

1. b

    $160,000—There is no step-up to fair market value at death for installment notes.

Tax—Basis of Inherited Property

2. d

    $300,000—The fair market value on the date of disposition. Even though the executor could elect the alternate valuation date, the basis in the property will be on the date of disposition.

Tax—Basis of Inherited Property

3. b

    $200,000—The carryover basis. There is no step to FMV for annuities.

Tax—Basis of Inherited Property

4. d

    He owned one-half already ($280,000 + 450,000 = $730,000). Step to FMV at death for decedent's half.

Tax—Basis of Inherited Property

5. a

    The son has a zero basis in the 401(k) since it is a qualified plan. There is no step to FMV at death for qualified retirement plans. **Note:** There is also no step-up to FMV for IRAs.

ITEM SET SOLUTION 9

Estates—Gift Tax Calculation

1. a

$88,000	Taxable gift ($100,000 –12,000 annual exclusion for 2007)
+ 600,000	Prior adjusted taxable gifts
$688,000	Total taxable gifts

$225,360	Total tax ($155,800 + (0.37 × $188,000)) (from Unified Tax Rate Schedule)
(345,800)	Applicable credit amount for gift tax (2007)
$0	Gift tax liability

Tax—Basis of Property Received By Gift

2. a

The son's adjusted tax basis for gain is $160,000. His basis for losses is $100,000. The sale was in-between the gain basis and the loss basis, therefore, there is no recognized gain or loss. Note: The double-basis rule applies to this gift because the fair market value was less than the donor's adjusted tax basis on the date of the gift (loss property).

Tax—Basis of Property Received By Gift

3. b

The basis for losses is $100,000. Because this sale results in a loss (i.e., the loss basis of $100,000 is used), the holding period starts on the date of the gift. Therefore, this is a short-term capital loss of $10,000. The holding period of the son would tack to the father's holding period only if the gain basis was used.

Estates—Tax Implication of Gifting

4. a

This is a gift. There are no income tax consequences to Fred.

Estates—Gross Estate

5. a

Gift tax paid on gifts made within three years of death is included in the gross estate. Fred paid no gift tax on the gift (see question 1), and therefore does not have to include any gift tax in his gross estate.

The taxable gift of $88,000 (see question 1) will be added back as a prior taxable gift, but is not included in Fred's gross estate.

Estates—Tentative Tax Base

6. e

	$1,300,000	Gross estate ($1,300,000)
−	200,000	Deductions (funeral, administrative, and charitable contributions)
=	$1,100,000	Taxable estate
+	688,000	Post-'76 taxable gifts ($600,000 + $88,000)
=	$1,788,000	Tentative tax base

ITEM SET SOLUTION 10

Estates—Exclusion of Property from the Gross Estate

1. d

If Robert dies early, the installment notes (at remaining present value) would be included in his gross estate. The SCIN would not be included in his gross estate because it cancels at the death of the seller. The GRAT would cause inclusion in the gross estate if the grantor dies during the trust term. The private annuity would not cause inclusion.

Fundamentals—Time Value of Money

2. c

$1,000,000	Sale price	PV	=	$800,000
(200,000)	Down payment	FV	=	$0
$800,000	Present value	n	=	144 months
		i	=	0.75 (9 ÷ 12)
		PMT_{OA}	=	$9,104.25

$245,521 = $200,000 + 45,521 [$9,104.25 (pmt) × 5]

Estates—Installment Notes

3. d

n	=	5 months
PV	=	$800,000
PMT	=	($9,104.25)
i	=	0.75 (9 ÷ 12)
FV	=	$784,244.18

Total payments $45,521 = [$9,104.25 × 5] less principal reduction.

Original debt	$800,000	Total payment	$45,521
Remaining debt at 12/31	(784,244)	Principal reduction	(15,756)
Principal reduction	$15,756	Ordinary income from interest	$29,765

Shortcut—Amortization (HP-12c)

PV	=	$800,000	Mortgage amount
i	=	9 ÷ 12	Interest per month
n	=	144	Term in months
PMT	=	$9,104.2456	Payment of an ordinary annuity
5f AMORT	=	$29,765	Portion of 1st year's payments applied to interest
$x_{<}^{>}y$	=	15,756	Portion of 1st year's payments applied to principal

Estates—Installment Notes

4. c

The gross estate will include the present value of the future installment note payments.

n = 96 (144 months − 48 months)
FV = $0
PMT_{OA} = $9,104.25
i = 0.75 (9 ÷ 12)
PV = $621,442

Estates—Marital Deduction

5. d

Installment notes do not receive a step to FMV at death. Because Kelly is a non-citizen, the property does not qualify for the unlimited marital deduction.

ITEM SET SOLUTION 11

Solutions to Questions 1–5.

		Investment A		Investment B	
IRR:	PV	($5,000,000)		($8,000,000)	
	n	1		1	
	PMT	$0		$0	
	FV	$6,500,000		$10,000,000	
	IRR(i)	30%		25%	#5
NPV:	CF_0	($5,000.000)		($8,000,000)	
	CF_1	$6,500,000		$10,000,000	
	i	10		10	
	(f)NPV	$909,090.90	#1	$1,090,909.09	#2

Fundamentals—TVM

1. a

Fundamentals—TVM

2. b

Fundamentals—TVM

3. d

Fundamentals—TVM

4. d

Fundamentals—TVM

5. b

ITEM SET SOLUTION 12

Investments—Use of Leverage

1. c

$$\frac{Loan}{(1 - Maintenance\ Margin)} = Margin\ Call$$

Loan = (0.45) × $100 = $45 per share

Therefore, a margin call will occur at $64.29 ($45 ÷ 0.7).

Investments—Use of Leverage

2. e

	Current Equity	Required Equity
Stock price	$70	$70
Loan	(45)	× 30%
Equity	$25	$21

Equity is required to be $21 = (30% of $70). Since equity is $25 = ($70 − 45), no margin call will occur.

Investments—Use of Leverage

3. c

	Current Equity	Required Equity
Stock Price	$50	$50
Loan	(45)	× 30%
Equity	$5	$15

Difference = $10

Required equity = $15 = (30% of $50)

Equity = $5 = ($50 − $45)

Difference = $10

Alternative method:

```
 64.29
(50.00)
 14.29
×  .70
$10.00
```

ITEM SET SOLUTION 13

Investments—Standard Deviation

1. b

$$\sigma^2 = W_A^2\,\sigma_A^2 + W_B^2\,\sigma_B^2 + 2W_AW_B\,[\sigma_A\sigma_B r_{AB}]$$

$$\sigma^2 = (0.5^2)(0.2^2)\ + (0.5^2)(0.4^2) + 2(0.5)(0.5)[(0.2)(0.4)(0.6)]$$

$$\sigma^2 = 0.01 + 0.04 + 0.024$$

$$\sigma^2 = 0.074$$

$$\sigma\ = 27.2\%$$

Note: The weighting is 50% for A and B.

Investments—Standard Deviation

2. b

$$\sigma^2 = W_A^2\,\sigma_A^2 + W_B^2\,\sigma_B^2 + 2W_AW_B\,[\sigma_A\sigma_B r_{AB}]$$

$$\sigma^2 = (0.5^2)(0.2^2) + (0.5^2)(0.4^2) + 2(0.5)(0.5)[(0.2)(0.4)(1.0)]$$

$$\sigma^2 = 0.01 + 0.04 + 0.04$$

$$\sigma^2 = 0.09$$

$$\sigma\ = 30\%$$

Note: The weighting is 50% for A and B.

ITEM SET SOLUTION 14

Fundamentals—TVM

1. **b**

FV	=	$0
n	=	360
i	=	0.6667 (8 ÷ 12)
PV	=	$140,000 (175,000 × 80%)
PMT_{OA}	=	($1,027.27)

Fundamentals—TVM

2. **b**

Beginning amount ($140,000)

n	=	11
i	=	0.6667 (8 ÷ 12)
PMT_{OA}	=	$1,027.27
FV	=	$138,931.55

Principal reduction $140,000 − 138,931.55 = $1,068.45.

Total payments ($1,027.27 × 11) − 1,068.45 = $10,231.53 interest expense.

Note: If you get a figure that is slightly off, it may be due to a failure to round to a monthly payment of $1,027.27.

Fundamentals—TVM

3. **d**

$1,027.27 × 360	=	$369,817.20
$1,337.91 × 180	=	−240,823.80
		$128,993.40 Savings

ITEM SET SOLUTION 15

Estates—Charitable Transfers

1. b

She can reserve the right to change the name of the charitable remainder beneficiary to some other *charitable remainder beneficiary.* She cannot name 2, 3, or 4, nor can she reserve that right and still qualify as an irrevocable charitable remainder trust.

Tax—Charitable Deduction

2. b

She can elect to deduct the basis and is then limited to 50% of AGI or $100,000. If she elects to deduct the FMV, she is limited to 30% of AGI or $60,000.

Tax—Charitable Deduction

3. d

She gets the deduction this year and a carryover for 5 years (total 6 years × $100,000 or $600,000 if she elects to deduct the basis, as opposed to the FMV). If the FMV were chosen, she would get to deduct a total of $360,000.

ITEM SET SOLUTION 16

Fundamentals—TVM

1. **b**

PV	=	$107,120 ($104,000 × 1.03)	PV	=	($107,120)	
n	=	360	n	=	24 months	
i	=	0.625 (7.5 ÷ 12)	PMT_{OA}	=	$749	
PMT_{OA}	=	$749.00 (rounded)	i	=	0.625 (7.5 ÷ 12)	
			FV	=	$105,068	

Fundamentals—TVM

2. **a**

Old payment	$907.78 × 22 × 12	=	$239,654
New payment	$831.25 × 22 × 12	=	$219,450
			$20,204

Old Payment			New Payment		
n	=	360	n	=	264 (22 × 12)
PV	=	$112,820	PV	=	$107,326 ($104,200 × 1.03)
i	=	0.75 (9 ÷ 12)	i	=	0.625 (7.5 ÷ 12)
PMT	=	$907.78	PMT	=	$831.25

ITEM SET SOLUTION 17

Insurance—Automobile Coverage

1. c

Contact with a bird or animal is specifically excluded from the category of collision and, therefore, will be covered as comprehensive.

Insurance—Automobile Coverage

2. b

Backing your car into a tree would fall within the definition of collision.

Insurance—Automobile Coverage

3. b

Damage to your automobile would fall under the definition of collision.

Insurance—Automobile Coverage

4. a

This is an example of uninsured motorist coverage.

ITEM SET SOLUTION 18

Estates—Charitable Remainder Trusts

1. a

CRATs pay a fixed annuity; whereas, CRUTs will pay an amount that varies based on the valuation of the assets in the trust.

Estates—Charitable Remainder Trusts

2. d

Both CRUTs and CRATs are irrevocable trusts.

Estates—Charitable Remainder Trusts

3. b

Only CRUTs will have a variable annuity.

Estates—Charitable Remainder Trusts

4. c

Both CRATs and CRUTs provide for the remaining property (remainder interest) to be left to charity.

ITEM SET SOLUTION 19

Investments—Standard Deviation

1. **b**

Based on a correlation of 0.4, the standard deviation of the two portfolios is approximately 12%.

$$\sigma^2 = W^2_A\sigma^2_A + W^2_B\sigma^2_B + 2W_A W_B [\sigma_A\sigma_B r_{AB}]$$
$$\sigma^2 = (0.4)^2(0.155)^2 + (0.6)^2(0.135)^2 + 2(0.4)(0.6)[(0.155)(0.135)(0.4)]$$
$$\sigma^2 = 0.00384 + 0.00656 + 0.00402 = 0.01442$$
$$\sigma = 12.009\%$$

Investments—Standard Deviation

2. **a**

The key to this question is to understand that the correlation between two assets that have no relationship is zero. The correlation of zero is then used in the formula for the standard deviation of a two-asset portfolio.

$$\sigma^2 = W^2_A\sigma^2_A + W^2_B\sigma^2_B + 2W_A W_B [\sigma_A\sigma_B r_{AB}]$$
$$\sigma^2 = (0.4)^2(0.155)^2 + (0.6)^2(0.135)^2 + 2(0.4)(0.6)[(0.155)(0.135)(0)]$$
$$\sigma^2 = 0.00384 + 0.00656 + 0 = 0.01040$$
$$\sigma = 10.2\%$$

ITEM SET SOLUTION 20

Retirement—Required Minimum

1. c

The minimum distribution for the current tax year is found by dividing the balance at December 31 of the previous year by the factor for age 71 (since she will be age 71 on December 31). The result is $188,680 ($5,000,000 divided by 26.5). The minimum distribution does not have to be received until April 1st of the year after Marleen turns 70½. The distribution is received *for* the year in which she is 70½, but not *in* the year in which she is 70½.

Retirement—Distribution Rules

2. a

No penalties will be assessed for the current year because Marleen received more than the minimum required distribution.

Retirement—Rules Distribution

3. a

Because Marleen is a 5% or greater owner, she is not allowed to defer her minimum distribution until April 1 of the year following the year she retires. Marleen is permitted to roll her account balance into an IRA rollover account. Five-year forward averaging has been repealed. The 20% withholding does not apply to direct trustee-to-trustee rollovers.

ITEM SET SOLUTION 21

Employee Benefits—ISOs

1. d

Bob has W-2 income of $2,200, the difference between the exercise price and the sale price. Because this option is an ISO, and he has not held it for longer than 2 years from the date of the grant and one year from the exercise date, the result is ordinary income. Because he has sold it within the same year as he exercised it, the ordinary income is reportable on the W-2, but it is not subject to payroll taxes.

Employee Benefits—NQSOs

2. d

Bob must recognize $2,000 of W-2 income upon exercising the NQSO.

Employee Benefits—ISOs

3. b

Bob recognizes AMT income at the exercise date of $1,500 but does not recognize any regular taxable income until he sells the stock.

Employee Benefits—NQSOs

4. d

Bob must recognize $2,000 as W-2 income on exercise date then $1,000 STCG on sale date.

ITEM SET SOLUTION 22

Estates—Gross Estate

1. **c**

    Gift tax paid on gifts made within three years of death are included in the gross estate. In addition, life insurance proceeds on policies transferred by the decedent within three years of death are included in the gross estate.

Estate—Taxable Gift

2. **b**

$40,000	Bonds to Tom
(12,000)	Annual exclusion
$28,000	Adjusted taxable gift

    Note: The value of the life insurance given to Andrea was offset by the annual exclusion, resulting in a taxable gift of zero.

Estates—Gross Estate

3. **a**

    The correct answer is zero because neither the life insurance proceeds nor the gift tax would be included in the gross estate, because Steve lived more than three years after the transfer.

ITEM SET SOLUTION 23

Fundamentals—Uneven Cash Flows

1. c

(9,200)	CF_o
600	CF_j
2,300	CF_j
2,200	CF_j
6,800	$[F_j$
9,500	CF_j
	IRR = 24.18%

Fundamentals—Uneven Cash Flows

2. d

Statement 4 is false, because, if the cost of capital is less than the IRR, then the project should be accepted (NPV > $0). Thus, A and E are incorrect. Statements 1, 2, and 3 are correct.

ITEM SET SOLUTION 24

Retirement—Qualified Plan Characteristics

1. d

Of the plans listed, only a cash balance plan requires PBGC insurance.

Retirement—Qualified Plan Characteristics

2. a

Of the plans listed, only the 401(k) plan allows employee elective deferral contributions (salary reduction contributions).

Retirement—Qualified Plan Characteristics

3. f

Both a target benefit plan and a cash balance plan are pension plans.

Retirement—Qualified Plan Characteristics

4. e

The 401(k) plan and stock bonus plan both permit unlimited investment in employer stock. Pension plans, such as the target benefit plan and a cash balance plan, are limited to 10% investment in employer stock.

ITEM SET SOLUTION 25

Estate—Gross and Probate Estate

1. a

Property owned Joint Tenants with Rights of Survivorship passes by operation of law, and therefore the property will avoid probate at the first spouse's death. However, one-half of the value of the property will be included in the decedent spouse's gross estate.

Estate—Gross and Probate Estate

2. c

A SEP with no named beneficiary will be included in the probate estate as well as the gross estate.

Estate—Gross and Probate Estate

3. c

Community property does not have rights of survivorship to a surviving spouse. Therefore, the property will be included in the decedent's gross estate and probate estate.

Estate—Gross and Probate Estate

4. a

A pay-on-death arrangement avoids probate. However, it will be included in the decedent's gross estate.

ITEM SET SOLUTION 26

Insurance—Legal Aspects

1. d

This is an attractive nuisance. If someone comes into the yard and drowns in the pool, Scott may be liable.

Insurance—Legal Aspects

2. c

Under the collateral source rule, damages assessed against the tort feasor (negligent party) are not reduced just because the injured party is insured.

Insurance—Legal Aspects

3. b

Mary assumed the risk by attending the baseball game. If the baseball team is sued, they can use this defense to free themselves of liability.

Insurance—Legal Aspects

4. a

Subrogation holds that if the insured party collects from the insurer, the insured party relinquishes the right to collect damages from the negligent party (the insurer can collect from the negligent party).

ITEM SET SOLUTION 27

Tax—Cost Recovery

1. b

Loans (or distributions) from a MEC are always taxed as though the earnings are distributed first. Therefore, basis is recovered last, or LIFO (last-in, first-out) tax treatment.

Tax—Cost Recovery

2. a

When amounts are distributed from a Roth IRA, they are treated first as a return of basis. Therefore, FIFO tax treatment would apply.

Note: Qualified distributions from a Roth IRA are completely income tax free.

Tax—Cost Recovery

3. d

When selling stock, the seller can use either the specific identification method to determine basis, or can use FIFO (first shares purchased are first shares sold) to determine basis of shares sold.

Tax—Cost Recovery

4. e

Basis (after-tax contributions) in a traditional IRA is recovered pro rata when the owner receives a distribution from the IRA.

ITEM SET SOLUTION 28

Insurance—Life Insurance

1. c

Aaron will receive $49,000 from the insurance company ($84,000 surrender value less $35,000 outstanding loan).

Insurance—Income Taxation of Life Insurance

2. a

Aaron must include $26,000 in his taxable income ($84,000 surrender value less the $58,000 premiums paid). The premiums paid represent Aaron's basis in the policy.

Estate—Irrevocable Life Insurance Trust

3. b

Statement 1 is correct. If a life insurance policy is transferred to an ILIT, the insured must live at least three years to avoid inclusion of the death benefit in his or her gross estate.

Statement 2 is incorrect. The life insurance proceeds will not be subject to probate, regardless of when death occurs due to the beneficiary designation.

Statement 3 is incorrect. If Aaron is the trustee, he will have "incidents of ownership" over the policy, causing the entire death benefit to be included in his gross estate.

Statement 4 is correct. If the trust contains appropriate Crummey provisions, the annual exclusion will be available for the gifts.

ITEM SET SOLUTION 29

Retirement—Distribution Rules

1. a

Option (a) is correct. The 401(k) plan from ABC company will be exempt from the 10% early withdrawal penalty. If a participant separates from service after the attainment of age 55, he or she can take a penalty-free withdrawal from the employer's qualified plan without incurring the early withdrawal penalty.

Option (b) is incorrect. Marshall is less than 59½ years old and separated from service from Johnson Industries at the age of 48 (10 years ago). Therefore, he had not attained age 55 and therefore will be subject to the penalty.

Options (c) and (d) are incorrect. The exception to the penalty for separation from service after attainment of age 55 does not apply to IRAs.

Retirement—Beneficiary Considerations

2. d

Option (a) is correct. Spousal consent is not required when changing the beneficiary of an IRA.

Option (b) is correct. The required minimum distribution is calculated using a prescribed IRS table. The table must always be used to calculate the minimum required distributions, unless the beneficiary is the spouse, and the spouse is more than 10 years younger than the participant. If the beneficiary is the son or the grandson, the IRS table must be used, and therefore the minimum distribution will be the same in either case.

Option (c) is correct. A participant of a qualified plan must have spousal consent to change the beneficiary.

Option (d) is incorrect. A participant of a qualified plan must have spousal consent to change the beneficiary.

ITEM SET SOLUTION 30

Fundamentals—Statements of Cash Flows

1. e

The auto loan balance would be included in the client's net worth statement as a liability. All of the other items would be included in the client's cash flow statement (even the tax-exempt interest).

Fundamentals—Bankruptcy

2. a

The federal income taxes (less than 3 years old), alimony, monthly mortgage payments, and government student loans cannot be discharged. Student loans can only be discharged if paying then would cause an undue hardship. Personal debt, such as bank loans and auto loan debt, may be discharged. Thus, $42,000 is the total amount that may be discharged.

Tax—Itemized Deductions

3. a

None of the margin interest expense can be deducted. Since the amounts borrowed were used to purchase tax-exempt securities, none of the margin interest expense is deductible.

ITEM SET SOLUTION 31

Investments—Derivatives

1. c

    The intrinsic value of a call option is the excess (if any) of the stock's fair market value over the exercise price of the option. The intrinsic value of this option is $3 ($58 stock value less $55 option price).

Investments—Derivatives

2. d

    The time value, or time premium, of a call option is the excess of the option's price over the option's intrinsic value. The time value of this option is $3.50 ($6.50 option price less $3 intrinsic value).

Investments—Black-Scholes Option Valuation

3. d

    A decrease in the exercise price of an option will increase, the option's value is under the Black/Scholes option valuation model.

ITEM SET SOLUTION 32

Tax—Taxable Assets

1. b

   Copyrights are ordinary assets.

Tax—Taxable Assets

2. c

   Machinery used in a trade or business is depreciable Section 1231 property.

Tax—Taxable Assets

3. a

   A personal auto is not used in a trade or business, and is therefore a capital asset.

Tax—Taxable Assets

4. b

   Razors sold by a company that manufactures razors would be considered inventory, which is an ordinary asset.

ITEM SET SOLUTION 33

Estates—Crummey Powers

1. c

Rianna can withdraw $12,000, the annual exclusion for 2007.

The Crummey clause provides a right of withdrawal equal to the lesser of 1) the annual exclusion, or 2) the value of the gift transferred.

Estates—Crummey Powers

2. a

Since there was no additional contribution to the trust, Rianna cannot withdraw any amounts from the trust in the second year.

The Crummey clause provides a right of withdrawal equal to the lesser of 1) the annual exclusion, or 2) the value of the gift transferred.

Estates—Gross Estate Inclusion

3. a

Mary will not be required to include the gift in her gross estate, regardless of when she died. The gift to an irrevocable trust is a complete gift, and will be out of Mary's gross estate. The taxable gift of $100,000 less the annual exclusion will be added back to the gross estate for purposes of determining the tentative tax base for post-76 gifts.

If Mary paid gift tax on the gift, her gross estate will include any gift taxes paid on the gift. Gift tax paid on gifts within three years of death are included in the gross estate.

ITEM SET SOLUTION 34

Tax—Capital Assets

1. b

Option (a) is incorrect. Rare stamps are collectibles, and are therefore taxed at a maximum capital gains rate of 28%. The total tax on the gain would be $4,200 ($15,000 gain × 28% tax rate), resulting in only $20,800 ($25,000 − $4,200) of after-tax proceeds.

Option (b) is correct. If Section 1202 stock is held for more than five years, only 50% of the gain is taxed. The recognized gain is taxed at a rate of 28%. Therefore, the tax due will be $2,520 ($18,000 gain × 50% × 28% tax rate). Roger will have $22,480 ($25,000 − $2,520) cash remaining after taxes, which is more than enough to fund the purchase.

Option (c) is incorrect. Since the stock was held short term, the gain on the common stock will be taxed at Roger's 35% ordinary income tax rate. Therefore, the tax on the gain will be $4,200 ($12,000 gain × 35% tax rate), resulting in only $20,800 ($25,000 − $4,200) of after-tax proceeds.

Option (d) is incorrect. The investment land was held long term, resulting in a 15% capital gain rate. However, the basis is so low that the tax on the gain will be $3,300 ($22,000 gain × 15% tax rate). Roger will only have $21,700 ($25,000 − $3,300) of cash remaining.

Tax—Charitable Contribution

2. c

Roger will only be allowed a charitable deduction for his tax basis in the stamps, because the property is use-unrelated.

Tax—Tax Consequences

3. b

Option (a) is incorrect. Section 1202 stock does receive a step-up in basis at the owner's death.

Option (b) is correct. A taxpayer may exclude 50% of the gain on the sale of Section 1202 stock, if certain conditions are met. However, a portion of the excluded gain is a tax preference item for purposes of alternative minimum tax.

Option (c) is incorrect. Collectibles are prohibited investments in IRAs.

Option (d) is incorrect. Personal use assets, such as a principal residence, are not considered like-kind property. Therefore, Roger would be required to recognize gain on the exchange. If Roger used the personal residence as a rental (investment) property, then the transaction could qualify for like-kind treatment.

ITEM SET SOLUTION 35

Estates—Gifting Strategies

1. **b**

Bond B is the best answer because Cathy's mother, who is probably 75-80 years old would benefit from the coupon payments from the bond.

Estates—Gifting Strategies

2. **b**

Stock E is the best answer because Cathy can remove the stock from her assets before large appreciation becomes an issue. Her son is young, thus, he will be able to take advantage of appreciating property. Statement 1 is not the best choice because the stock has appreciated the most and her son would be responsible for the capital gains tax when he sells the stock.

Estates—Gifting Strategies

3. **a**

By selecting Stock A, Cathy can remove the highly appreciated asset from her estate, have no capital gain consequences, and take a charitable income tax deduction based on the fair market value of the asset.

Estates—Gifting Strategies

4. **d**

Cathy should sell Stock D because it is currently valued at a loss. Assets that have a FMV that is lower than basis at the time of gift are subject to the double basis rule. The recipient gets the FMV basis for losses and the adjusted basis for gains. Thus, the current loss on the asset would be lost. If she wanted to gift this property she should sell it first for the loss, claim the loss deductible (subject to the applicable limits) herself and then gift the proceeds.

ITEM SET SOLUTION 36

Fundamentals—Statement of Financial Position

1. d

Stock	Number of Shares Owned on 12/31	Ending Price on 12/31 of Current Year	Total Value of Stock on Statement of Financial Position
ABC	200	$8	$1,600
XYZ	400 (split)	$15	$6,000
THE	200	$16	$3,200
			$10,800

The total value reported is $10,800.

Fundamentals—Statements of Cash Flows

2. b

Stock	Number of Shares Owned on 12/31	Dividends Paid per Share on 12/31	Total Dividend Paid
ABC	200	$0	$0
XYZ	400 (split)	$0.75	$300
THE	200	$1.00	$200
			$500

The total dividends received this year were $500, as computed above.

Stock	Number of Shares Purchased on Jan 1 of Current Year	Original Purchase Price per Share	Total Purchase Price
ABC	200	$16	$3,200
XYZ	200	$18	$3,600
THE	200	$14	$2,800
			$9,600

The total cash paid for the shares on January 1 was $9,600. Therefore, the net cash OUTFLOW was $9,100 ($9,600 − $500).

Investments—Ratio Analysis

3. e

The dividend payout ratio is the ratio of the stock's dividend to the company's earnings.

Based on the P/E ratio of 15, XYZ company's earnings are $1 per share. The P/E ratio is the price of the stock per share divided by the earnings per share ($15/$1 = 15).

Since the earnings are $1 per share, the dividend payout ratio is 75% (0.75/$1 = 75%).

ITEM SET SOLUTION 37

Tax—AGI

1. d

Description	Amount
Salary	$85,000
XYZ Company preferred stock dividend	$800
Interest income from corporate bond	$300
S Corporation loss	($2,000)
Adjusted Gross Income (AGI)	**$84,100**

The interest income from the private activity bond is not taxable (however, it will be subject to alternative minimum tax).

Since Tom is a limited partner in Realty Capital Partners, he is not a material participant, and therefore, his passive loss from this activity will not be deductible (Tom has no passive income).

Since Tom is not a material participant in ABC partnership, his passive loss from this activity will not be deductible (Tom has no passive income).

The mortgage interest expense and margin interest expense are itemized deductions, and are not deductible in arriving at adjusted gross income.

Tax—Itemized Deductions

2. b

Investment interest expense (margin interest) is only deductible to the extent of taxable investment income. Tom has taxable investment income of $300 taxable interest income). The $800 of dividends that are taxed at the 15% rate do not qualify when calculating taxable investment income for purposes of determining the investment interest expense. The private activity bond interest income is not taxable.

Retirement Planning—IRAs

3. c

Statement 1 is correct. Tom's AGI is less than $99,000 (the AGI phase-out for single taxpayers). Therefore, he can contribute to a Roth IRA.

Statement 2 is incorrect. Tom is an active participant in the 401(k). His AGI exceeds the phase-out limit, and therefore, he cannot deduct his contributions to a traditional IRA.

Statement 3 is correct. Tom could contribute to a nondeductible traditional IRA. Anyone with earned income can contribute to a nondeductible IRA.

Statement 4 is correct. Tom's AGI does not exceed $100,000, so he can convert an existing traditional IRA to a Roth IRA.

Tax—Passive Loss Activity

4.   d

The passive loss from the S corporation is deductible this year, because Tom is a material participant. The losses from Realty Capital Partners ($3,000) and ABC Partnership ($5,000) are disallowed this year and must be carried forward.

ITEM SET SOLUTION 38 CFP® Certification Examination, released 8/2004

Estates—Revocable Trusts

1. **b**

   Statement 1 is correct. The grantor is often the trustee of a revocable living trust.

   Statement 2 is incorrect. Assets in a revocable trust will be included in the decedent's gross estate. The assets will be excluded from the probate estate.

   Statement 3 is correct. The terms of the trust can provide for a successor trustee if Ana becomes incapacitated.

   Statement 4 is incorrect. The trust instrument will determine who will receive the assets.

Estates—Trusts

2. **e**

   This is a classic example of a spendthrift provision. A spendthrift provision prevents beneficiaries from transferring their interests in the trust property, and prevents the beneficiaries' creditors from seizing trust assets to satisfy their claims.

Estates—Revocable Trusts

3. **b**

   Statement 1 is incorrect. Transfer of an installment note receivable to a revocable trust will not require the immediate recognition of the deferred gain.

   Statement 2 is incorrect. This is an example of Section 1250 property. Section 1250 does not require depreciation recapture when an asset is transferred to a trust. Note: Depreciation recapture would be required when a depreciable asset is SOLD.

   Statement 3 is correct. A revocable living trust is a grantor trust for income tax purposes. Therefore, the grantor will be required to pay income tax on all income earned by the trust.

   Statement 4 is correct. The assets will receive a step-up in basis. The installment note will not receive a step-up because it is an income in respect of a decedent (IRD) asset.

Estates—Revocable Trusts

4. **d**

   The personal residence would be the most appropriate of the assets listed. All of the other assets could have named beneficiaries, thus avoiding probate, or cannot be transferred during the life of the settlor.

ITEM SET SOLUTION 39 CFP® CERTIFICATION EXAMINATION, Released 08/2004

Estates—Gift and Estate Taxation

1. **d**

A bypass trust would be appropriate to utilize the applicable credit of the first spouse to die. Since all assets are currently being left to the surviving spouse, the first spouse to die would waste his/her applicable credit. A bypass trust would solve this problem.

A is incorrect. Susan is already listed as the beneficiary of the policy. James would therefore be eligible for a marital deduction if the proceeds are paid to Susan. Transferring ownership of the policy will not result in any estate tax savings.

B is incorrect. Their current estate plan leaves all assets to the surviving spouse upon the first spouse's death. As a result, the first spouse to die will waste their applicable credit because of a full marital deduction. The best solution is to establish a bypass trust at the first spouse's death.

C is incorrect. Because of the applicable credit, James and Susan can avoid estate taxes at both of their deaths with proper planning. Giving gifts is not necessary. Of course, they may desire to give gifts, but the question asks for the best strategy for reducing transfer taxes.

Estates—Probate Estate

2. **a**

The stocks, valued at $300,000, would be the only asset included in James' probate estate.

The assets titled JTWROS would pass by operation of law, thus avoiding probate. The 401(k) and life insurance policies have named beneficiaries, thus avoiding probate.

Estates—Gross Estate

3. c

James' gross estate is $1,590,500 calculated as follows:

Asset	Value
Checking (50%)	$2,500
Savings (50%)	3,000
Certificates of Deposit (owned by Susan)	0
Home (50%)	140,000
Vehicles, furniture, and so forth (50%)	45,000
Stocks (owned by James)	300,000
Apartments (50%)	130,000
401(k) (owned by James)	600,000
Group term life insurance (owned by James)	120,000
Life insurance (owned by James)	250,000
Gross estate	$1,590,500

Estates—Life Insurance

4. a

Since Susan does not need the income from the policy upon James' death, the children should be named as the beneficiaries. By transferring the policy to a trust, the policy would be excluded from James' gross estate, provided James survives three years after the transfer.

B is incorrect. There is no need to surrender the policy, and if the policy was surrendered, the $10,000 gain would be taxable income.

C is incorrect. If Susan was the owner of the policy and the children were named beneficiaries, Susan will have made a $250,000 gift to the children upon James' death.

D is incorrect. If James' estate is named beneficiary of the policy, the proceeds will be included in his gross estate when he dies. This could be avoided using a trust.

Estates—Marital Deduction

5.   c

If Susan were to die, her marital deduction would be $680,500, calculated as follows:

Assets Left to James	Value
Checking (50%)	$2,500
Savings (50%)	3,000
Certificates of Deposit (left to James in Will)	380,000
Home (50%)	140,000
Vehicles, furniture, and so forth (50%)	45,000
Apartments (50%)	130,000
Life insurance (owned by Susan)	50,000
Liability on home (50%)	(25,000)
Liability on apartments (50%)	(45,000)
Marital deduction	$680,000

COGNITIVE CONNECTIONS
Problems

Cognitive Connections

1. Which of the following exchanges are not protected under IRC Section 1035?

    a. Exchange a universal life insurance policy for a variable life insurance policy.

    b. Exchange a variable annuity for a fixed annuity.

    c. Exchange a variable life insurance policy for a variable annuity.

    d. Exchange a variable annuity for a whole life insurance policy.

2. Which of the following would be the best suited for a zero-coupon Treasury bond?

    a. Joint brokerage account.

    b. Trust.

    c. IRA.

    d. Corporation.

3. If interest rates are low and expected to rise in the near future, what should you do?

    a. Sell long-term bonds.

    b. Buy intermediate bonds.

    c. Buy convertible bonds.

    d. Sell short-term bonds.

4. Mildred recently added her granddaughter's name to her $150,000 checking account as a JTWROS. Which of the following is true, assuming neither party has any additional accounts at this financial institution?

    a. A taxable gift occurred when the granddaughter's name was added.

    b. If Mildred died tomorrow, the entire balance of the checking account will be included in her gross estate.

    c. If Mildred writes a $15,000 check from the account to pay her granddaughter's credit card bills, there is no taxable gift.

    d. Only $100,000 of the checking account balance will be FDIC insured.

5. Marvin is 65 and has decided to surrender his Whole Life policy. As of this time:

- Cash Value—$85,000
- Existing Loan—$30,000
- Dividends Left in Policy—$10,000
- Premiums Paid—$60,000

How much cash will he get at surrender?

    a. $0.

    b. $20,000.

    c. $25,000.

    d. $55,000.

6. Marvin is 65 and has decided to surrender his Whole Life policy. As of this time:

- Cash Value—$85,000
- Existing Loan—$30,000
- Dividends Left in Policy—$10,000
- Premiums Billed—$60,000

How much is taxable to Marvin?

    a. $0.

    b. $20,000.

    c. $25,000.

    d. $55,000.

7. Ricky was in an accident this year and is now disabled. He is receiving disability benefits from a disability policy that was paid for by his employer. Which of the following is true regarding the disability benefits?

    a. The entire benefit will be tax-free.

    b. The entire benefit will be taxable.

    c. Only the benefit received over $50,000 will be taxable.

    d. The benefits received from his employer's policy will reduce the amount of social security disability benefits that he is eligible to receive.

8. In year 1, Paul receives stock worth $15,000 from Q Corporation as payment for services rendered. The stock is subject to substantial risk of forfeiture (if Paul leaves Q Corporation before year 3, he must forfeit the stock). Paul chooses to make a §83(b) election and include the $15,000 value of the stock in his gross income for year 1. In year 3, the risk of forfeiture lapses, the stock is worth $38,000. Which is true?

    a. Paul must include $23,000 in gross income in year 3.

    b. Paul has no gross income attributable to the property in year 3.

    c. Paul cannot recognize the gross income from the property in year 1.

    d. Paul will be taxed on the $15,000 value of the stock in year 1 regardless of the §83(b) election.

9. Ana Longoria is a shareholder and an employee of Powers Enterprises. Which of the following items is taxable to Ana, but tax-deductible by Powers?

    a. Group health insurance premiums paid by the employer.

    b. A reasonable salary paid to Ana.

    c. Powers cash dividends paid to Ana.

    d. Cost of employer paid group term life insurance benefits of $50,000.

10. Who should be the beneficiary of the life insurance under a cross-purchase agreement?

    a. The owner's surviving spouse.

    b. The owner's estate.

    c. The owner's business partners.

    d. The policyowner.

11. The reasonable compensation standards of the IRS apply to which of the following?

    a. Sole proprietorships.

    b. Partnerships.

    c. C corporations.

    d. All of the above.

12. Stacy had stock with a basis of $38,000 and a fair market value of $100,000. She sold the stock to her daughter in exchange for a private annuity. What are the consequences?

    a. The daughter can claim interest expense up to Stacy's imputed interest.

    b. Stacy can claim an interest expense deduction.

    c. The value of the stock will be included in Stacy's gross estate if she dies within three years.

    d. The interest expense cannot be deducted by Stacy or her daughter.

13. John is an employee of ABC company, where he earns a salary of $100,000. The company sponsors a defined benefit plan, with a unit-benefit formula that will pay John 2% of his final average compensation for each year of service with the company. The company also provides John with disability insurance that will replace 60% of John's income if he is disabled. ABC company pays the premiums on the disability policy.

If John is in the 25% income tax bracket, how much would John receive each month on an after-tax basis from his employer-paid disability policy were he to become disabled?

    a. $1,200.

    b. $1,400.

    c. $3,750.

    d. $5,000.

14. Debbie, age 38, is contemplating the purchase of her first home, a new home in a new housing development. The builder, Badman Development, has offered to sell her one of the new homes for $250,000, which includes the lot valued at $50,000. Debbie is self-employed, and has Schedule C income of $560,000. Three years ago she established a simplified employee pension (SEP), and has been making maximum contributions to the plan since its inception. Which of the following statements is/are true?

1. Debbie can withdraw up to $10,000 from her SEP for the purchase of the new home, without paying an early withdrawal penalty.

2. To cover full replacement of the home in the event of a loss, Debbie must purchase homeowner's insurance of $160,000.

3. Debbie's real estate taxes on the home will be fully deductible, if she itemizes her deductions on her income tax return this year.

4. The cost of title insurance paid by Debbie will not be deductible, but will be included in Debbie's basis in the home.

   a. 1 and 4.

   b. 2 and 3.

   c. 1, 2, and 3.

   d. 2, 3, and 4.

   e. 1, 3, and 4.

15. Your client recently purchased a 30-year, high-grade, municipal bond from the state of Louisiana. He paid $800 for the bond, which has a coupon rate of 5%. Which of the following is/are correct?

1. The bond will have high inflation risk.

2. Interest paid by the bond will not be subject to federal income taxation.

3. If your client sells the bond three years from now for $1,000, he will not be taxed on the gain.

4. The bond will have high default risk.

   a. 1 only.

   b. 1 and 2.

   c. 2 and 3.

   d. 2, 3, and 4.

   e. 1, 2, 3, and 4.

16. In November of the current year, Sara opened a bakery. For legal purposes, the bakery is owned and operated through the use of an LLC (calendar year) created by Sara and her husband. The LLC is taxed as a partnership for Federal income tax purposes. In the current year, Sara incurred legal fees of $10,000 to set up the LLC and provide the appropriate legal documents for the operation of the bakery. She also purchased $125,000 of bakery equipment. Because the bakery was only open two months during the current year, Sara will report a loss from operations. She expects the bakery to be profitable in three years.

    1. If Sara elects Section 179 to expense the equipment purchased, the deduction can be used to offset her husband's $200,000 salary.

    2. If Sara chooses to depreciate the equipment using MACRS, the half-year convention will apply to all business personal property purchased in the current year.

    3. If Sara establishes a profit-sharing plan for the business, she can exclude part-time employees from the plan, if the employees work less than 1,000 hours during the year.

    4. If Sara implements an entity buy-sell agreement, the LLC would own the policy on Sara's life and be allowed a deduction for premiums paid as long as Sara was an employee of the business.

        a. 1 only.

        b. 3 only.

        c. 1 and 3.

        d. 2 and 4.

        e. 2, 3, and 4.

17. Your client, John, is in the 25% income tax bracket. Assuming John works for a company that does not sponsor a retirement plan, which of the following would be the most beneficial in reducing John's income tax liability for the current year?

    a. Exchanging $10,000 of corporate bonds for municipal bonds, both with a 10% coupon.

    b. $1,000 mortgage interest deduction.

    c. $350 dependent care tax credit.

    d. $3,000 contribution to a Roth IRA.

18. Last year, Sally created and funded a 2503(b) trust, and named her son, Robbie, the beneficiary. The trust was funded with $60,000 in cash, which has subsequently been invested in various stocks, bonds, and mutual funds. Who will be responsible for paying the income tax on the interest and dividends earned within the trust?

    a. The trust will be liable for any tax due.

    b. Sally will be liable for any tax due.

    c. Robbie will be liable for any tax due.

    d. The trust is tax-exempt until Robbie reaches the age of majority.

19. Which of the following investments would be most appropriate for an emergency fund?

    a. Mortgage-backed security.

    b. Money market mutual fund.

    c. Exchange traded fund.

    d. All are equally appropriate.

20. Several years ago, David purchased a universal life insurance policy on the life of his wife, Michelle. The couple's 12-year-old son, Jonathan, is the named beneficiary. The policy has a death benefit of $500,000, and has a current cash value of $20,000. Which of the following would be true, if Michelle died?

    a. The $500,000 death benefit will be automatically paid to an irrevocable life insurance trust, because Jonathan is a minor.

    b. The $500,000 death benefit received by Jonathan will be subject to "kiddie" tax, because Jonathan is under age 18.

    c. The death benefit of the policy will be included in Michelle's gross estate.

    d. The death benefit of $500,000 will be considered a gift from David to Jonathan when paid.

    e. David will receive the cash value of the policy upon Michelle's death.

21. Roger Huley, age 29, is an administrator at the local hospital. His current salary is $30,000, and he expects his AGI this year to range from $35,000-$45,000. He is currently designing an education investment program to help fund the education for his 10-year-old son, Tom. Roger wants a portion of the investment portfolio to be invested in tax-exempt securities. Which of the following investments would produce interest or dividends that are free from federal income tax if proceeds are used to pay qualified higher education expenses?

    1. Zero-coupon Treasury bonds.

    2. State of Louisiana bonds with a 5% coupon rate.

    3. Zero-coupon corporate bond with a duration of 7.3 years.

    4. Series EE savings bonds.

        a. 1 and 3.

        b. 2 and 4.

        c. 1, 3, and 4.

        d. 2 and 3.

        e. 2, 3, and 4.

22. Which of the following employee fringe benefits would be taxable to the employee?

    a. A 5% employee discount on merchandise offered at a clothing store.

    b. Personal use of the company copy machine.

    c. Dinner provided to employees of a CPA firm during the busy tax season.

    d. Group term life insurance coverage of $35,000 provided to employees.

    e. Season tickets to basketball games.

23. Which of the following statements is/are true regarding a Charitable Remainder Unitrust (CRUT)?

    1. The grantor will receive an immediate income tax deduction when the assets are transferred to the trust.

    2. Income-producing assets are inappropriate investments for a CRUT.

    3. The charitable organization named as the beneficiary of the trust will be responsible for choosing the investments within the trust.

    4. The trust will pay the grantor a fixed percentage of the trust assets, valued annually.

        a. 1 and 2.

        b. 1 and 4.

        c. 2 and 3.

        d. 2, 3, and 4.

        e. 1, 3, and 4.

24. Which of the following is a correct statement regarding the tax characteristics of certain insurance products?

    1. Owners of single payment deferred annuity contracts may withdraw funds tax-free up to the basis in the contract, if the annuity was purchased before 1992.

    2. If the annuity is owned by a corporation, earnings within the contract are tax-deferred.

    3. In general, an individual can exchange a fixed annuity for a universal life insurance policy without any negative income tax ramifications.

    4. If a life insurance policy is classified as a modified endowment contract (MEC), the death benefit received by the beneficiary will be subject to federal income taxation.

    5. If an individual purchased a life and 15-year term-certain immediate annuity at age 52, the individual would not incur a 10% early withdrawal penalty.

        a. 5 only.

        b. 1 and 2.

        c. 3 and 4.

        d. 2, 3 and 4.

        e. 1, 2, 3, 4 and 5.

25. Which of the following statements is INCORRECT regarding the tax issues of nonqualified retirement plans?

    a. If there exists a substantial risk of forfeiture, then the deferred compensation will not be treated as constructively received and there will be no current taxable income.

    b. Funds that are deemed to be constructively received are required to be reported as taxable income by the executive.

    c. Since an unfunded promise to pay an executive has an element of risk, there is no current taxation to the executive.

    d. The deduction for the employer can occur at any time, regardless of when the inclusion of income occurs for the executive employee.

26. Todd and Diana Martin are establishing a college fund for their 14-year-old son, Mike. The Martins do not wish to invest aggressively, but are willing to take a reasonable and normal investment risk. Which of the following investments makes the most sense for the college fund and why?

    a. A series of taxable zero-coupon bonds owned by Todd, because they can provide appropriate funds at the correct times.

    b. A variable life insurance policy owned by Mike because it defers taxes, and it contains life insurance.

    c. Series EE Savings Bonds owned by Todd and Diana, because it provides tax-free interest income if used for college.

    d. A small-cap stock mutual fund owned by Mike, because it provides the best return at a modest level of risk consistent with the time horizon.

27. Your client, a conservative investor, is saving to build a new home in five years. Which of the following types of investment is the most appropriate for your client's goal?

    a. Science and technology mutual fund.

    b. S&P 500 Index fund.

    c. International stock mutual fund.

    d. Zero-coupon 5-year municipal bond.

28. Which of the following may be a shareholder of an S corporation?

    a. Grantor Retained Annuity Trust (GRAT).

    b. Nonresident alien.

    c. Partnership.

    d. Publicly-traded corporation.

29. Which of the following are true regarding a Health Savings Account?

    1. Health Savings Accounts are not available for self-employed individuals.

    2. Health Savings Accounts are used to pay unreimbursed health care expenses of the account holder, the account holder's spouse, or the account holder's dependents.

    3. Contributions to a Health Savings Account are subject to an annual limit.

    4. Distributions from a Health Savings Account that are not used for qualifying medical expenses are subject to income tax and a penalty, regardless of the account holder's age.

    a. 1 and 4 only.

    b. 2 and 3 only.

    c. 1, 2, and 3.

    d. 2, 3, and 4.

    e. 1, 3, and 4.

30. An individual received a 60% capital interest in a partnership by contributing the following:

    1. Land purchased for $70,000 and valued at $90,000.

    2. Services to the partnership valued at $5,000.

    3. Business inventory purchased for $10,000 and valued at $8,000.

    What is the partner's basis in the partnership interest?

    a. $0.

    b. $70,000.

    c. $83,000.

    d. $85,000.

    e. $103,000.

31. Bob is a cash-basis, calendar year, sole proprietor. It is now December of the current year, and Bob has come to you looking for a strategy that would help reduce his income tax liability for the current year. Which one of the following strategies would NOT help him reduce his tax liability for the current year?

    a. Buy office furniture.

    b. Distribute bonuses to employees.

    c. Deposit in January of next year a check that Bob received in December.

    d. Pay for small office equipment in December.

32. Which of the following is/are true statements regarding a Simplified Employee Pension (SEP)?

    1. With a SEP, the employer is not required to contribute each year.

    2. The employer will receive an income tax deduction for contributions made to the SEP.

    3. An employer can exclude part-time employees with less than 1,000 hours from participation in the SEP.

    4. Contributions to a SEP can be used to purchase universal life insurance.

    a. 1 and 2.

    b. 1 and 3.

    c. 2, 3, and 4.

    d. 1, 2, and 4.

    e. 2 and 3.

33. Which of the following is/are true with respect to a long-term care policy?

    1. Long-term care policies typically do not provide intermediate nursing care coverage.

    2. The COBRA continuation coverage requirements do not apply to long-term care plans.

    3. Long-term care insurance can be provided to employees in a cafeteria plan.

    4. If an employee pays the premiums on a qualified long-term care policy, the premiums are deductible as a medical expense itemized deduction, subject to the 7.5% of AGI floor.

       a. 1 and 2.

       b. 1 and 3.

       c. 2 and 4.

       d. 1, 3, and 4.

       e. 2, 3, and 4.

34. John is age 63 and single, and he began receiving social security retirement benefits at age 62. He was an employee for a manufacturing company for over 25 years, before retiring at age 55 due to a bad back. John's only other source of income for the current year is $80,000 of interest income received from State of New Jersey municipal bonds.

    John's wife, Stacy, died two years ago from leukemia. John owned a life insurance policy on Stacy's life with a $1,000,000 death benefit. The proceeds from the life insurance policy were used to purchase the municipal bonds. John had a son with Stacy. The son, Mark, is now 33-years old and is currently employed at a CPA firm.

    Which of the following is (are) true?

    1. John will lose some or all of his social security benefits because of his municipal bond income.

    2. The social security benefits will be income tax free to John, because the municipal bond interest income is tax-exempt.

    3. Mark will be eligible for a social security death benefit due to the death of his mother.

    4. Even though John's wife died, John will not be eligible for Medicare until age 65.

       a. 4 only.

       b. 1 and 4.

       c. 2 and 3.

       d. 1, 2, and 3.

       e. 2, 3, and 4.

35. Which of the following statements is (are) true regarding Medicare?

   1. Most persons age 65 and older who do not meet the eligibility requirements may voluntarily enroll in Medicare.

   2. Hospice benefits are covered under Medicare Part A.

   3. If an individual is eligible for Medicare and is still working for an employer that covers the individual under an employer-sponsored health plan, Medicare will be the primary payer of health expenses, and the employer-sponsored health plan will be the secondary payer.

   4. Medicare Part B is financed by payroll taxes.

      a. 1 only.

      b. 1 and 2.

      c. 2 and 3.

      d. 1, 3, and 4.

      e. 2, 3, and 4.

36. Which of the following statements is (are) correct with respect to a flexible spending account provided to an employee?

   1. Employee contributions to the account will not be subject to federal income taxes.

   2. Employee contributions to the account will not be subject to social security taxes.

   3. A flexible spending account is a cafeteria plan funded through employee salary reductions.

   4. Amounts in an employee's account can be used to make contributions to a Health Savings Account for the employee.

      a. 1 and 3.

      b. 1 and 4.

      c. 1, 2, and 3.

      d. 2, 3, and 4.

      e. 1, 2, 3, and 4.

37. Tina is a participant in her company's ESOP. The company transfers 1,000 shares at $5/share to her account. Several years later, when the stock is $11/share, Tina retires. If she elects to receive the stock at retirement and continues to hold the stock, what are the tax consequences, assuming the stock was worth $17,000 at her death?

      a. Tina will be taxed on $11,000 of ordinary income when she receives the stock at retirement.

      b. If Tina's son inherits the stock, and sells it for $17,000, he will not have a capital gain because the stock received a step-up in basis at Tina's death.

      c. Tina will include the entire $17,000 stock value in her gross estate at her death.

      d. If Tina's son inherits the stock, and sells it for $17,000, he will recognize ordinary income on the sale because the net unrealized appreciation on the stock does not receive a step-up in basis at Tina's death.

      e. If Tina sold the stock for $12,000 before her death, she would have recognized a capital gain of $1,000.

38. Bob and Mary Jane have three young children. They want to contribute to an education fund for their children. Assuming they have not given any gifts in the past, how much, in total, can Bob and Mary Jane contribute today to Section 529 plans for their children, without creating a taxable gift?

    a. $0.

    b. $60,000.

    c. $120,000.

    d. $360,000.

    e. $2,060,000.

39. Which of the following assets would be subject to capital gains tax, if sold at a gain?

    a. Accounts receivable.

    b. Clothing sold by a clothing store.

    c. A copyright.

    d. Land used in a business.

    e. Artwork sold by the artist.

40. Which of the following is (are) benefits of profit-sharing plans over a simplified employee pension?

    1. Profit-sharing plans allow in-service loans.

    2. Profit-sharing plans allow the participant to elect 5-year averaging on qualifying lump-sum distributions.

    3. A profit-sharing plan can be established after the close of the tax year.

    4. Profit-sharing plans can invest in life insurance.

    a. 1 and 3.

    b. 2 and 3.

    c. 2, 3, and 4.

    d. 1 and 4.

    e. 1, 2, and 3.

41. Bob and Mary Johnson are in the 15% income tax bracket. What is the best choice for their $20,000 emergency fund?

    a. GNMA fund.

    b. Money market fund.

    c. Exchange traded fund.

    d. Hedge fund.

42. Jay, a key employee, earns an annual salary of three million dollars. His employer is concerned with the reasonable compensation standards of the IRS. What is the most likely structure of this company?

    a. Sole proprietorship.

    b. Partnership.

    c. S Corporation.

    d. C Corporation.

43. If a bond is selling at a discount, which one of the following relationships is true?

    a. The yield to maturity is greater than the yield to call.

    b. The current yield is greater than the yield to maturity.

    c. The current yield is equal to the yield to maturity.

    d. The yield to maturity is greater than the current yield.

    e. The current yield is greater than the yield to call.

44. Which of the following is true regarding a Rabbi Trust?

    a. Employer contributions made to the trust will be subject to FICA.

    b. The amounts within the trust may be used to discharge the employer's obligation to creditors.

    c. Distributions from the Rabbi Trust will be tax free to the employee.

    d. If the company sponsoring the Rabbi trust has a change in control, the new owners can withdraw the assets from the Rabbi trust.

45. Susan was granted a nonqualified stock option that gives her the right to purchase 500 shares of employer stock at $10 per share. She exercises the option 6 months later when the market value of the stock is $40. What is her employer's deduction upon exercise?

    a. $0.

    b. $5,000.

    c. $15,000

    d. $20,000.

46. All of the following provisions should be included in a buy-sell agreement for a partnership EXCEPT:

    a. Purpose of the agreement.

    b. Parties to the agreement.

    c. Provisions allowing for Section 303 stock redemption.

    d. Funding.

47. Steve is age 75, and has withdrawn more than the required minimum distribution from his IRA over the last four years. Which is correct regarding minimum required distributions for the current year?

    a. Steve can defer the current year minimum distribution until next year.

    b. Steve is not required to take a distribution this year.

    c. Steve must receive the minimum distribution for the current year by December 31.

    d. Steve will be subject to the early withdrawal penalty.

48. Which of the following statements describes a disadvantage of a target-benefit plan as compared to a defined-benefit plan?

    a. For a given compensation level, a target-benefit plan requires the same contribution for all employees regardless of age.

    b. A target-benefit plan must cover all eligible employees, while a defined-benefit plan can exclude certain nonhighly compensated employees.

    c. A target-benefit plan has more stringent vesting requirements than a defined-benefit plan.

    d. Contributions to a target-benefit plan are subject to the annual additions limit of the Internal Revenue Code.

49. Kevin and Carol are married and live in Texas, a community property state. Which of the following assets listed below would NOT be considered community property?

    a. Their recently purchased home, financed using a variable rate mortgage.

    b. General Motors stock purchased during their marriage. Kevin purchased the stock out of his earned income.

    c. Municipal bonds inherited by Carol from her father.

    d. A life insurance policy of which Kevin is the beneficiary; premiums are paid from the dividends on the General Motors stock.

50. Which of the following statements is (are) true regarding a Simplified Employee Pension (SEP) plan?

    1. Distributions from a SEP will not be subject to the 10% early withdrawal penalty if the participant leaves the sponsoring company after attaining age 55.

    2. The plan can exclude all part-time employees working less than 1,000 hours per year.

    3. Contributions made to a SEP by the employer cannot be used to purchase life insurance.

    4. Distributions used to fund college education costs for the participant's daughter are not subject to the 10% early withdrawal penalty.

    a. 1 and 2.

    b. 3 and 4.

    c. 1, 2, and 3.

    d. 2, 3, and 4.

    e. 1, 2, 3, and 4.

51. Which of the following cannot be attached by creditors in the event of a client's bankruptcy?

    1. The client's 401(k) plan.

    2. Alimony owed to the bankrupt client.

    3. Section 1244 small business stock owned by the client.

    a. 1 only.

    b. 2 only.

    c. 1 and 2.

    d. 1, 2, and 3.

52. Linda, a New Jersey resident, just purchased a New Jersey municipal bond. The bond has a coupon rate of 5% and will mature in five years. Which of the following is (are) true with respect to the municipal bond?

    a. If the bond is a revenue bond, it will be secured by the taxing power of the State of New Jersey.

    b. If the bond is a private activity bond, the interest income will be a preference in calculating a client's alternative minimum tax.

    c. Linda will pay federal income tax on the municipal bond's interest.

    d. Municipal bonds are not subject to default risk.

53. Several years ago, Barbara purchased a rental condo for $50,000. The condo is now worth $85,000, and Barbara would like to exchange it for a duplex on the North side of town. The duplex is subject to a mortgage of $25,000. Barbara will not receive any cash in the transaction. Which of the following statements is true?

    a. If the duplex is owned by her son, Barbara's deferred gain must be recognized if the son sells the condo within two years of the exchange.

    b. If Barbara assumes the mortgage on the duplex, she may be required to recognize gain on the like-kind exchange.

    c. Barbara will be subject to Section 1245 depreciation recapture at the time of the exchange.

    d. If Barbara has a net operating loss carryforward that she would like to utilize, she can elect to immediately recognize the deferred gain on the like-kind exchange in the current tax year.

54. Bobby, a single taxpayer, purchased a 2,500 square foot home for $260,000. Six months later, he received a promotion at work that required him to relocate. He sold the home for $220,000. What are the tax ramifications of the sale, assuming Bobby had no other property transactions?

    a. Bobby can deduct $3,000 as a capital loss, and will have a $37,000 capital loss carryforward.

    b. Bobby can take a $40,000 ordinary loss deduction this year.

    c. Because the promotion forced him to sell the home, Bobby is entitled to a partial loss deduction of $31,250.

    d. Bobby's loss is nondeductible.

55. A life insurance agent had the following items of income for the current year:

Commissions	$30,000
Commissions assigned to son	$ 5,000
Salary	$40,000
Interest from a private activity bond	$ 3,000

    What is the agent's gross income for the current tax year?

    a. $45,000.

    b. $70,000.

    c. $75,000.

    d. $78,000.

56. In the current year, Della, a single mother, gifted stock with a basis of $1,800,000 and a fair market value of $1,010,000 to her grandson.

    a. If Della dies within three years, the entire date-of-death value of the stock will be included in her gross estate.

    b. Assuming Della had made no prior gifts, there would be no gift tax due on the gift of stock to her grandson.

    c. If Della paid $40,000 of gift tax on the gift, her grandson could allocate a portion of the gift tax paid to his adjusted tax basis in the stock.

    d. If the grandson subsequently sold the stock for $1,500,000, he would have a capital loss of $300,000.

57. Aaron, age 57, has worked at Tollisin Industries for 16 years. Tollisin sponsors a 5% money-purchase plan integrated with Social Security, as well as a profit-sharing plan. Aaron will earn $150,000 this year in his role as bank manager. Which of the following statements is correct regarding the retirement plans administered by Tollisin?

    a. If the bank decides to merge their money-purchase plan into the existing profit-sharing plan, this will be considered a "termination" of the money-purchase plan, and will cause all participants to become 100% vested in their existing money-purchase plan balance.

    b. The maximum permitted disparity for the money-purchase plan is 5.7%.

    c. Since Aaron is age 57, he will be entitled to an additional "catch-up" contribution to the money-purchase plan.

    d. The money-purchase plan can continue to be integrated with Social Security, even if the plan becomes top heavy.

58. Which of the following statements is (are) true regarding a Charitable Remainder Annuity Trust (CRAT)?

    1. If the grantor transfers $1,000,000 to the trust at inception, and the present value of the remainder interest is $88,000, the trust will qualify as a CRAT.

    2. If the grantor is concerned about the effects of inflation, a Charitable Remainder Unitrust (CRUT) may be more appropriate than a CRAT.

    3. The grantor can be the trustee of the CRAT and can make all investment decisions regarding the trust assets.

    4. The trust will pay the grantor a fixed percentage of the trust assets valued annually.

        a. 1 and 2

        b. 1 and 4

        c. 2 and 3

        d. 2, 3, and 4.

        e. 1, 3, and 4.

59. Which of the following powers of appointment would cause inclusion of the <u>full</u> trust assets in the beneficiary's gross estate?

    a. A limited or special power of appointment over the trust property.

    b. The power to use the trust property for the beneficiary's health or maintenance.

    c. A power limited to the greater of $5,000 or 5% of the value of the trust property.

    d. A testamentary power to dispose of the trust property for the beneficiary's creditors.

60. During his life, Tim gave his daughter his residence, retaining the right to live in the home for the rest of his life. He originally bought the home for $140,000. The home was worth $180,000 when he gifted it to her, and was worth $200,000 at his death. What is his daughter's gain if she sold the home for $200,000 after his death?

    a. $0

    b. $20,000

    c. $60,000

    d. $200,000

61. Joe recently died with an estate of $500,000,000. The gross estate consisted primarily of closely held stock in the family business. Preliminary estate tax calculations determined that his estate would owe approximately $250,000,000 in estate taxes. His executor has decided to make a Section 6166 election to help ease the estate tax burden. Which of the following items concerning the election is true?

    a. The Section 6166 election could help lower the overall estate tax due.

    b. Under Section 6166, estate tax is delayed for 10 years and then paid over 5 equal annual installments.

    c. Interest on any deferred estate tax is calculated based on the prime rate.

    d. If the decedent's family sells the business two years after Joe's death, the entire amount of deferred tax must be recognized immediately.

62. Thomas was considering an investment in a real estate limited partnership. He would contribute $20,000 to the partnership, which is raising capital for the development of a boat storage facility. Assuming he makes this investment, and his adjusted gross income was $160,000, which of the following statements is true?

    a. If the partnership has an operating loss for the year, Thomas can use his allocable share of the loss to offset any capital gains from the sale of his stocks.

    b. If the partnership has operating income for the year, the income will be taxed to the partnership, unless a cash distribution is made to the partners.

    c. If the partnership has an operating loss for the year, Thomas can use his allocable share of the loss to offset his interest and dividend income.

    d. If the partnership has an operating loss for the year, Thomas cannot deduct his allocable share of the loss, unless he has passive income from another activity.

63. Molly, a dermatologist, earns $500,000 per year. She wants to make a donation to her favorite charity, the Human Fund. She is willing to donate the following assets:

Description	FMV	Basis	Comments
Cash	$30,000	$30,000	Earns 3%
Utility Company stock	$29,000	$10,000	Pays 7% dividend; held long term
Municipal bond	$31,000	$33,000	Pays 4% interest; held short term
Growth Mutual Fund	$30,000	$27,000	Pays 5% dividend; held for five months

Which of the following assets would be the best from an income tax perspective for Molly to donate to charity?

    a. Cash

    b. Utility Company stock

    c. Municipal bond

    d. Growth Mutual Fund

64. Which is true regarding the kiddie tax?

    a. The kiddie tax applies only to income from assets purchased by the child.

    b. If the child is claimed as a dependent by his or her parents, the child will still be entitled to a personal exemption on his or her tax return.

    c. For a child under age 18, net unearned income above a certain level is taxed at the parent's marginal rate.

    d. For a child under age 18, net earned income above a certain level is taxed at the parent's marginal rate.

65. Val died during the current year. His estate consisted of the following assets:

1. Traditional IRA—invested in a global stock fund and a balanced mutual fund; Val's cousin, who died two years ago, was named the beneficiary. This beneficiary designation was never changed by Val.

2. Life Insurance policy—ash value of $55,000 and death benefit of $500,000; the policy is on the life of Val's sister who lives in Nevada. Val's daughter is the named beneficiary.

3. An installment note receivable, with a 9% interest rate and a remaining term of 7 years.

4. Land in Sandy, Utah—held as tenancy by the entirety with Val's wife.

Which assets listed above will be included in Val's probate estate?

    a.   1 and 2.

    b.   3 and 4.

    c.   1, 2, and 3.

    d.   1, 2, and 4.

    e.   1, 2, 3, and 4

66. Which of the following events will qualify for COBRA continuation coverage?

1. Divorce.

2. Termination of employment.

3. Death of the worker.

4. Resigning from a job.

    a.   1 and 4.

    b.   1, 2, and 3.

    c.   2 and 4.

    d.   1, 2, and 4.

    e.   1, 2, 3, and 4.

67. Which of the following are true statements regarding the capital asset pricing model?

1. Standard deviation is used as the measure of risk on the security market line.

2. The capital asset pricing model formula defines the security market line.

3. Superior performance exists if a fund's position is above the capital market line.

4. As investors substitute risky securities for risk-free assets, both risk and return of the portfolio decrease.

    a.   1 and 4.

    b.   2 and 3.

    c.   1, 2, and 4

    d.   2, 3, and 4.

    e.   1, 2, and 3.

68. Which of the following statements is (are) correct regarding bonds?

    1. If the maturities of a portfolio of bonds are equal, the zero-coupon bond must have the longest duration of all bonds in the portfolio.

    2. To immunize a bond portfolio over a specific investment horizon, an investor would match the average weighted maturity of the bond portfolio to the investment horizon.

    3. Duration of a bond is a function of the bond's yield to maturity.

    4. If a client has a cash need at the end of six years, a series of Treasury bills may be an appropriate investment to immunize a bond portfolio.

        a. 1 and 2.

        b. 1 and 3.

        c. 2 and 4.

        d. 1, 2, and 3.

        e. 2, 3, and 4.

69. Which of the following is not a type of unsystematic risk?

        a. Country Risk.

        b. Financial risk.

        c. Default risk.

        d. Foreign Currency Risk.

70. What mechanisms can the Federal Reserve use to help stimulate the economy?

    1. Purchase Treasury securities.

    2. Increase reserve requirements.

    3. Decrease marginal income tax rates.

    4. Increase the discount rate

        a. 1 only.

        b. 1 and 2.

        c. 2 and 3.

        d. 1, 2, and 4.

        e. 2, 3, and 4.

71. Several years ago, Stan purchased a $400,000 whole life insurance policy on his life. He has paid cumulative premiums over the years of $20,000, and has accumulated a cash value of $25,000. This year, he was diagnosed with a rare liver disease, and as a result his life expectancy is only six months. Due to his large medical costs, he is considering selling his policy to a viatical settlement company. They have offered him $250,000 for the policy. He would also like to explore other ways to generate cash from the policy. Which of the following statements is (are) true regarding Stan's situation?

    1.   If Stan sells his policy to the viatical settlement company, he will not be taxed on any gain from the sale if he dies within two years.

    2.   If the viatical company collects the death benefit as a result of Stan's death, the proceeds will be tax-free to the company.

    3.   If Stan sold the policy to his cousin for $250,000, Stan would not be taxed on the gain, but his cousin would be subject to ordinary income tax on a portion of the life insurance benefit when Stan dies.

    4.   If Stan takes a loan from the policy, some or all of the loan will be subject to ordinary income tax if the policy is classified as a modified endowment contract.

        a.   1 and 2.

        b.   2 and 3.

        c.   3 and 4.

        d.   1, 2, and 4.

        e.   3 only.

72. Your 49-year-old client, Rob, became disabled on February 20th of the current year due to a boating accident. He has a 48-year-old wife, Mary, and a 14-year-old daughter, Jean. Rob, who is fully insured, has met the Social Security definition of disability, and his primary insurance amount (PIA) is $1,000 per month. Which of the following statements is/are correct regarding the Social Security disability benefits for Rob and his family?

    1.   Rob will be entitled to begin receiving his Social Security disability benefit in March of the current year, even though he is only 49 years old.

    2.   When Rob reaches his Social Security normal retirement age, his Social Security disability benefit will automatically end.

    3.   Mary will be entitled to receive a Social Security benefit, even though she is only 48 years old.

    4.   If Jean earns $15,000 from a part-time job in the current year, she will lose some of her Social Security benefit.

        a.   1 and 4.

        b.   2 and 3.

        c.   1, 3, and 4.

        d.   1, 2, and 3.

        e.   2, 3, and 4.

73. In order to take an income tax deduction for premiums paid on a long-term care policy, the policy must be considered a "qualified" long-term care policy. Which one of the following is not a requirement for a "qualified" long-term care policy?

    a. The policy must not have a cash value.

    b. The policy must have an elimination period that does not exceed 60 days.

    c. The policy cannot pay for expenses reimbursable under Medicare.

    d. The policy must be guaranteed renewable.

74. Fred wants to transfer $50,000 of AAA-rated corporate bonds to his 9-year-old daughter, Sarah. The bonds have a coupon rate of 8% and will mature in 10 years. He is interested in using a Uniform Gifts to Minors Account (UGMA) to hold the bonds. If he transfers the bonds to the UGMA account, which is true?

    a. Since his daughter will not have control over the bonds until the age of majority, the transfer of the bonds to the UGMA account will be considered a future interest gift that is not entitled to an annual exclusion.

    b. The interest income earned by the bonds within the UGMA account will be taxed at trust income tax rates.

    c. A portion of the interest income earned by the bonds within the UGMA account will be taxed at Fred's marginal income tax rate.

    d. The interest income in the account will be income tax free if the account is used to fund Sarah's college education.

75. Which of the following risks is diversifiable?

    a. Default risk.

    b. Purchasing power risk.

    c. Interest rate risk.

    d. Market risk.

76. Stacey is covered under her own group medical insurance plan, which has a coordination of benefits (COB) provision, and also is covered as a dependent under her husband's individual health plan, which does not have a COB provision. If Stacey is hospitalized, which plan will pay, if any?

    a. Neither plan will pay.

    b. Stacey's plan is primary; her husband's plan is secondary.

    c. Stacey's plan is secondary; her husband's plan is primary.

    d. Both plans will pay and share expenses on a pro rata basis.

77. All of the following are characteristics of traditional split-dollar life insurance plans, EXCEPT:

    a. Allows discrimination in favor of certain classes of employees.

    b. At death, the corporation receives back its contributions.

    c. May be used to help fund a buy-sell agreement.

    d. The premiums paid by the corporation are tax deductible.

78. On November 15th of the current year, Aaron approaches you for some financial planning advice. He has owned and operated a profitable bakery for the last two years, and he would like to use some of the profits to save for retirement, while taking an income tax deduction in the current year. He has asked your advice with respect to establishing a retirement plan for the bakery. Aaron's salary is approximately $100,000 this year, and he would like a retirement plan that will allow employee contributions with a limited employer match. Recently, he met with his 15 full-time employees to discuss the idea of establishing a retirement plan, but none of the employees seemed interested in contributing. Nonetheless, Aaron would like to contribute to a retirement plan for himself and would like an income tax deduction on the bakery's income tax return this year. What would be the most appropriate retirement plan for the bakery?

    a. Profit-sharing 401(k).

    b. SEP.

    c. Safe harbor 401(k).

    d. SIMPLE 401(k).

    e. SIMPLE IRA.

79. Which of the following statements regarding characteristics of bonds is correct?

    1. Government National Mortgage Association (GNMA) securities are backed by the full faith and credit of the US Government.

    2. Federal National Mortgage Association (FNMA) securities are backed by the full faith and credit of the US Government.

    3. The Federal Insurance Guarantee Corporation is an insurer of municipal bonds.

    4. A high-quality, long-term municipal bond has low inflation risk and low default risk.

        a. 1 only.

        b. 4 only.

        c. 1 and 2.

        d. 1, 2, and 3.

80. John wants to purchase a life insurance policy on his own life. He is concerned that the policy may lapse if he inadvertently forgets to pay the premiums, and would like some protection. He recently heard about an Automatic Premium Loan provision that could provide protection for him in the event he forgets a premium payment. Under this provision, a loan would automatically be taken from the cash value of the policy to pay any premium due. If John is interested in including this provision in his policy, when could the election to include the Automatic Loan Premium provision be made?

    a. The election can be made anytime the amount of the premium due exceeds the cash value of the policy.

    b. The election must be made in the application for the policy.

    c. The election can be made at any time prior to the end of the grace period of any premium in default.

    d. The election can be made at any time during or after the grace period.

81. Steven is a sole proprietor. Three years ago, he purchased office equipment for $12,000. Over the years, he has taken depreciation deductions of $7,000. The equipment was depreciated for tax purposes using Modified Accelerated Cost Recovery System (MACRS) depreciation conventions. If the equipment was sold for $8,000 this year, what are the income tax consequences to Steven?

    a. $4,000 capital loss.

    b. $3,000 capital gain.

    c. $3,000 ordinary income.

    d. $5,000 capital gain.

82. Which of the following would be covered under Part B of an HO-3 policy?

    a. Dwelling.

    b. Attached garage.

    c. Detached garage.

    d. Dining room furniture.

83. Which of following statements regarding risk measures is (are) true?

    1. Standard deviation is equal to the variance squared.

    2. While beta measures only systematic risk, standard deviation measures unsystematic risk.

    3. Standard deviation is a measure of dispersion about the mean.

    4. Beta would be an appropriate measure of risk if the client has a portfolio consisting of three technology stocks.

    a. 1 and 2.

    b. 3 only.

    c. 2 and 3.

    d. 1 and 4.

    e. 1, 2, and 4.

84. David Johnson owns 40% of the stock of JohnCo, a closely held corporation. His son owns 35%, and the remaining 25% of the stock is divided equally among David's adult grandchildren. This year, David died after suffering from cancer for several years. His adjusted gross estate, including the stock, was valued at $10,000,000. Shortly before his death, the company was appraised at $5,000,000. The executor of David's estate has approached you regarding the Section 303 election, applicable to the estate of deceased business owners. Which of the following is a true statement regarding the use of the Section 303 election?

    a. Section 303 would be an appropriate election if a cross-purchase, buy-sell agreement was in place at the time of David's death.

    b. If Section 303 is elected by the executor, the estate tax can be paid over 10 equal annual installments.

    c. David's estate qualifies for the Section 303 election.

    d. If a Section 303 election is not made, stock redemptions by the estate may have unfavorable income tax treatment.

85. Which of the following gratuitous transfers would be considered a direct skip for purposes of the generation-skipping transfer tax (GSTT)?

    a. A transfer of assets to an irrevocable trust. The trust document stipulates that the donor's daughter will receive income for her life, with the remainder passing equally to the donor's grandchildren at the daughter's death.

    b. A transfer of assets to a Section 2503(c) trust for the benefit of the donor's grandson.

    c. A gift of $30,000 cash to the donor's grandson. The donor's only child passed away five years earlier.

    d. Payment of a grandchild's $25,000 tuition directly to the University of Akron.

Use the information below to answer questions 86 and 87:

Sara Sue, a 72-year-old widow, has an estate worth roughly $10,000,000. The estate is comprised of her principal residence, some stock investments, and a profit-sharing plan worth $4,000,000. Sara Sue has a 46-year-old son, Tom, and two grandsons. Although Tom is the principal beneficiary of her estate, she also has an interest in giving to various charitable organizations.

After reviewing the provisions of Sara Sue's profit-sharing plan, you determine that the only available distribution option for death benefits to a nonspouse beneficiary is a lump-sum cash distribution from the plan. In addition, the plan will not permit Sara Sue to take a distribution until she separates from service, which she plans to do at age 75.

Due to substantial gifts given in prior years, Sara Sue has used up her applicable credit as well as her full GST exemption amount.

86. Assuming Tom is named the beneficiary of the profit-sharing plan, and Sara Sue dies one year from today, which is true?

    a. Tom can take distributions from the qualified plan over his life expectancy.

    b. Tom could elect 10-year averaging on a lump-sum distribution from the profit-sharing plan, since Sara Sue was born before 1936.

    c. Tom would be subject to ordinary income tax on amounts distributed from the profit-sharing plan.

    d. The estate taxes on the retirement plan must be paid out of the distribution taken by Tom.

87. Assuming a Charitable Remainder Annuity Trust (CRAT) is named the beneficiary of the profit-sharing plan, and Sara Sue dies one year from today, which is true?

    a. The profit-sharing plan will be excluded from Sara Sue's gross estate.

    b. The profit-sharing plan will be included in Sara Sue's gross estate, but her estate will receive a charitable deduction equal to the date-of-death value of the profit-sharing plan.

    c. If Tom is named as the income beneficiary of the CRAT, he can receive an annuity for life, without paying income taxes on the amounts received.

    d. The CRAT payout rate should be set low enough so that the present value of the remainder interest in the trust will not be less than 10% of the initial amount transferred to the trust.

88. Which of the following is (are) correct regarding a Section 412(i) plan?

    1. A Section 412(i) plan is a defined-contribution plan that is funded exclusively by either life insurance or annuity contracts, or both.

    2. A Section 412(i) plan must comply with qualified plan nondiscrimination provisions of the Internal Revenue Code.

    3. If a Section 412(i) plan is funded with life insurance policies, participants in the plan may borrow from the cash value of the life insurance policies without immediate income tax ramifications.

    4. Although a Section 412(i) plan is a type of pension plan, it will not be subject to the minimum funding standards of the Internal Revenue Code.

        a. 1 and 3.

        b. 2 and 3.

        c. 2 and 4.

        d. 3 and 4

        e. 1, 2, and 4.

89. All of the following debt instruments have a fixed maturity date EXCEPT:

        a. Treasury bonds.

        b. General obligation bond.

        c. Subordinated debenture.

        d. Collateralized mortgage obligation.

90. All of the following statements regarding a real estate investment trust (REIT) are correct, EXCEPT:

        a. For tax purposes, REITs pass through both gains and losses to investors.

        b. Diversification and professional management are two advantages of REITs.

        c. REITs can be classified as Equity Trusts, Mortgage Trusts, or Hybrid Trusts.

        d. A REIT cannot elect a fiscal year for income tax purposes.

COGNITIVE CONNECTIONS

Solutions

Cognitive Connections

1. d	11. c	21. b	31. c	41. b	51. c	61. d	71. c	81. c
2. c	12. d	22. e	32. a	42. d	52. b	62. d	72. e	82. c
3. a	13. c	23. b	33. c	43. d	53. a	63. b	73. b	83. b
4. b	14. a	24. a	34. a	44. b	54. d	64. c	74. c	84. d
5. d	15. b	25. d	35. b	45. c	55. c	65. c	75. a	85. b
6. c	16. b	26. a	36. c	46. c	56. b	66. e	76. c	86. c
7. b	17. c	27. d	37. c	47. c	57. d	67. b	77. d	87. d
8. b	18. c	28. a	38. d	48. d	58. c	68. b	78. c	88. c
9. b	19. b	29. b	39. d	49. c	59. d	69. d	79. a	89. d
10. d	20. d	30. d	40. d	50. b	60. a	70. a	80. c	90. a

SOLUTIONS

Tax and Insurance

1. d

   Exchanging an annuity for a life insurance policy is not afforded protection under Section 1035. The exchange would be taxable.

Investments, Retirement and Tax

2. c

   An IRA would be the most appropriate. Zero coupon treasury bonds pay no interest income, yet are subject to income taxes on the ACCRUED interest. Therefore, since the investor will not receive any cash during the life of the bond, but will be subject to income tax, the best vehicle to own a zero coupon Treasury would be an IRA.

Investments and Fundamentals

3. a

   Sell long-term bonds.

   This question refers to a rate anticipation swap. When interest rates are expected to rise, an investor should sell long-term bonds and reinvest the proceeds at a higher coupon rate once interest rates rise.

Estates and Fundamentals

4. b

   If Mildred died tomorrow, the entire balance of the checking account will be included in her gross estate. JTWROS property is included in the gross estate based on the relative contributions by the tenants. Since Mildred contributed the entire balance to the checking account, the entire account would be included in her gross estate.

   Option (a) is incorrect. A taxable gift occurs when the granddaughter withdraws money.

   Option (c) is incorrect. The $15,000 gift exceeds the annual exclusion, and will therefore be a taxable gift.

   Option (d) is incorrect. Since this is a joint account, each party will be insured for $75,000 (one-half of the balance). Therefore, the entire account balance will be insured.

Tax and Insurance

5. d

   He will get $55,000.

   $85,000 cash value less $30,000 existing loan = $55,000.

Tax and Insurance

6. c

$25,000 is taxable.

$85,000 cash value less $60,000 premiums = $25,000.

When an insured surrenders a policy, any excess cash received over the net paid premiums is considered income and is taxable to the insured.

The dividends are either part of the cash value or were used to reduce premiums, so they are not applicable in the calculation of taxable income in this particular question.

Tax and Insurance

7. b

The entire benefit will be taxable. Since the employer paid the premiums, the entire amount of disability benefits received will be taxable to Ricky.

Option (d) is incorrect. The Social Security disability benefits will not be reduced by other disability benefits received. However, if Ricky is eligible to receive Social Security benefits, the disability benefits from his employer disability policy may be reduced.

Tax and Retirement

8. b

Since Paul made the election, he will be taxed on the $15,000 value of the stock immediately. When the risk of forfeiture lapses in two years, Paul will not be taxed. He will have capital gain when he subsequently sells the stock.

Tax and Employee Benefits

9. b

If the salary is reasonable, the company would receive a deduction, and Ana would be taxed.

Group health insurance would not be taxed to Ana.

Dividends paid would not be deductible.

$50,000 of group term insurance would not be taxable.

Insurance and Estates

10. d

The owner of the policy should also be the beneficiary of the policy. The insured are the owner's business partners.

Taxation and Fundamentals

11. c

Reasonable compensation standards apply to C corporations.

Reasonable compensation standards do not apply to sole proprietorships or partnerships, because there is no double taxation problem.

Estates and Tax

12. d

The interest expense cannot be deducted by Stacy or her daughter.

Option (a) is incorrect. The buyer cannot claim an interest expense deduction in a private annuity transaction.

Option (b) in incorrect. Stacy has no interest expense.

Option (c) is incorrect. The stock is excluded from Stacy's gross estate.

Insurance and Tax

13. c

Because the employer paid the premiums, the disability benefit received by John will be taxable at ordinary income tax rates.

Wages	$100,000
Disability Replacement Ratio	× 60%
Annual Disability Benefit	$60,000
Monthly Benefit	$5,000
1 – Tax Rate	× 75%
Monthly After-Tax Benefit	$3,750

Fundamentals, Tax and Retirement

14. a

Statement 1 is correct. The exception to the early withdrawal penalty for first-time home buyers applies to all IRAs. A SEP is an employer-funded IRA.

Statement 2 is incorrect. Although the minimum level of coverage to avoid a co-insurance situation is $160,000 (80% of the value of the home, excluding the lot), Debbie would be required to purchase $200,000 of coverage to cover a complete loss.

Statement 3 is incorrect. Although real estate taxes are deductible as itemized deductions, Debbie will not be entitled to a full deduction for the taxes, because her itemized deductions will be reduced as a result of her large adjusted gross income.

Statement 4 is correct. Title insurance paid by the purchaser is not deductible for tax purposes, but is included in the purchaser's basis in the home.

Investments, Insurance and Tax

15. b

Statement 1 is correct. A long-term bond is subject to more inflation risk.

Statement 2 is correct. Interest income from a municipal bond is not subject to federal income taxation.

Statement 3 is incorrect. The client would have a taxable capital gain resulting from the sale of the bond.

Statement 4 is incorrect. A high-grade bond has low default risk.

Insurance and Tax

16. b

Statement 1 is incorrect. Because the business will report an operating loss this year, the Section 179 expense deduction will not be allowed. It can be carried forward to future years.

Statement 2 is incorrect. Since Sara placed her equipment in service during the last quarter of the year, the mid-quarter convention will apply.

Statement 3 is correct. Part-time employees, working less than 1,000 hours, can be excluded from qualified plan participation.

Statement 4 is incorrect. The LLC would own the policy, but premiums are not deductible.

Retirement, Tax and Investments

17. c

A credit is a direct dollar-for-dollar reduction of the tax liability. Deductions only reduce the tax liability by the individual's marginal income tax rate.

Roth IRA contributions are not tax deductible.

Estates and Tax

18. c

A 2503(b) trust requires all income to be distributed to the beneficiary each year. Therefore, the income will be taxed to Robbie.

Investments and Fundamentals

19. b

Although not a cash equivalent a money market mutual fund is liquid and funds are invested in short-term notes. Neither the mortgage-backed security nor the exchange traded fund is invested in short-term funds.

Insurance, Tax and Estates

20. d

Since David owned the policy and named Jonathan the beneficiary, David has made a taxable gift to Jonathan.

Option (b) is incorrect because life insurance death benefits are income tax free.

Option (c) is incorrect because Michelle did not own the policy, nor was she the beneficiary.

Option (e) is incorrect. Jonathan is the beneficiary and will receive the entire death benefit.

Investments and Tax

21. b

Statement 1 is incorrect. Although the bonds are zero coupon bonds, the taxpayer is responsible for paying federal income tax on the accrued interest each year.

Statement 2 is correct. Interest on municipal bonds is not taxed at the federal level.

Statement 3 is incorrect. Although the bonds are zero coupon bonds, the taxpayer is responsible for paying federal income tax on the accrued interest each year.

Statement 4 is correct. Series EE bonds are not taxed, if the proceeds are used for education purposes. The tax benefit of Series EE bonds is phased out at certain AGI levels, however, Roger is well below those levels.

Employee Benefits and Tax

22. e

A 5% employee discount would be excluded because the amount does not exceed gross profit.

Personal use of the copy machine would be considered a de minimis fringe.

Dinner is excluded because it is furnished by the employer on the business premises for the employer's convenience.

Premiums paid on group term coverage up to $50,000 is excluded.

Season tickets provided by an employer to an employee would be taxable to the employee.

Estates, Investments and Tax

23. b

Statement 1 is correct. The grantor receives an immediate income tax deduction based on the present value of the remainder interest.

Statement 2 is incorrect. Income producing assets are appropriate, because the income could be used to satisfy the unitrust payment.

Statement 3 is incorrect. The grantor will choose the investments in the trust.

Statement 4 is correct. A unitrust payment is a fixed percentage of the trust assets, valued annually.

Insurance and Tax

24. a

Statement 1 is incorrect. FIFO basis recovery only applies to annuities purchased before 8/14/82.

Statement 2 is incorrect. If the annuity is owned by a non-natural person (such as a corporation), earnings within the contract are taxable each year.

Statement 3 is incorrect. Exchanging an annuity for a life insurance contract does not qualify for tax-free treatment under Section 1035.

Statement 4 is incorrect. Even if the policy is a MEC, the death benefit will be income tax free to the beneficiary.

Statement 5 is correct. An immediate annuity will not be subject to the early withdrawal penalty, because it will satisfy the "substantially equal periodic payments" exception to the penalty.

Retirement and Employee Benefits

25. d

The deduction for the employer can only follow the inclusion of income by the executive employee.

Fundamentals and Investments

26. a

Funds for education must meet the appropriate time horizon. Because small cap stocks are too risky of an investment for such a short period of time, Option (d) is incorrect. Options (b) and (c) do not match the investment vehicle to the time horizon of the investment. The Savings Bonds would need to be redeemed before they matured and would incur interest penalties The zero-coupon bond allows the Martins to match the time horizon of the investments to the duration of the bonds and avoid reinvestment risk.

Fundamentals and Investments

27. d

Because your client's goal is only five years away, equities would not be appropriate (Options (a), (b) and (c)). The best choice would be the zero-coupon municipal bond.

Estates, Tax and Fundamentals

28. a

A GRAT is a type of grantor trust. Grantor trusts are allowed to own stock in an S corporation. Grantors are treated as owners of GRATs for income tax purposes.

Nonresident aliens, partnerships, and corporations (other than Subchapter S subsidiary corporations) are prohibited from owning shares in an S corporation.

Tax and Retirement

29. b

Statement 1 is incorrect. HSAs are available for self-employed individuals.

Statements 2 and 3 are both correct.

Statements 4 is incorrect. Distributions not used for medical expenses are taxable and subject to a 10% penalty tax, unless made after the account beneficiary's death, disability or attaining age 65.

Fundamentals and Tax

30. d

When a partner contributes property to a partnership, there is no gain or loss recognized. The partner's basis in the partnership is equal to the basis of the property contributed.

If a partner contributes services to a partnership in exchange for a partnership interest, the partner must recognize compensation income equal to the value of the services. The amount of income recognized becomes the partner's basis.

Basis is calculated as follows:

Description	Basis
Land	$70,000
Services	$5,000
Inventory	$10,000
Total Basis	**$85,000**

Fundamentals and Tax

31. c

Even if Bob deposits the check in January of next year, he will be required to report the income in the current year because he has constructive receipt.

If Bob buys office furniture or equipment, he can take a depreciation deduction or take Section 179 expense this year.

Tax, Insurance and Retirement

32. a

Statement 1 is correct. The employer is not required to contribute to the SEP each year.

Statement 2 is correct. Contributions to a SEP are tax-deductible.

Statement 3 is incorrect. An employee must be included in a SEP if the employee meets all of the following requirements:

1. Age 21.
2. Worked for the employer 3 out of the last 5 years (one hour of service counts as a year of service).
3. $450 or more of compensation earned by the employee in the current year.

Statement 4 is incorrect. Life insurance is not allowed in a SEP.

Retirement, Insurance and Tax

33. c

Statement 1 is incorrect. Long-term care policies typically provide intermediate nursing care coverage.

Statement 2 is correct. COBRA continuation coverage requirements do not apply to long-term care plans.

Statement 3 is incorrect. Long-term care insurance cannot be provided in a cafeteria plan.

Statement 4 is correct. If the long-term care plan meets certain requirements (qualified long-term care), the premiums paid by an employee are deductible as a medical expense itemized deduction.

Insurance and Tax

34. a

Statement 1 is incorrect. Social Security benefits are only reduced if the recipient has earned income. Interest income is not considered earned income.

Statement 2 is incorrect. The benefits will be partially taxable to John. Even though municipal bond interest income is income tax-free, the municipal bond interest income will be included in John's Modified Adjusted Gross Income (MAGI). MAGI is used to determine the taxation of the Social Security benefits.

Statement 3 is incorrect. Only eligible children can receive Social Security death benefits upon the death of a parent. Mark is too old to receive Social Security death benefits.

Statement 4 is correct.

Insurance and Retirement

35. b

Statements 1 and 2 are correct.

Statement 3 is incorrect. Medicare will be the secondary payer.

Statement 4 is incorrect. Medicare Part A is financed by payroll taxes.

Employee Benefits and Tax

36. c

Statements 1 and 2 are both correct. Contributions are not subject to federal income tax or Social Security tax.

Statement 3 is correct. An FSA is a type of cafeteria plan.

Statement 4 is incorrect. Benefits under an FSA cannot be used for Health Savings Account contributions.

Retirement and Estates

37. c

Option (a) is incorrect. Tina will only be taxed on $5,000, the original cost of the stock when it was contributed to the plan. Net unrealized appreciation allows for recognition of only the value of the employer's contribution at the lump-sum distribution.

Option (b) is incorrect. Net unrealized appreciation of employer securities distributed from a qualified plan does not receive a step-up in basis at death.

Option (c) is correct. The entire value of the stock is included in the gross estate.

Option (d) is incorrect. The son will have a capital gain (not ordinary income) on the sale of the stock.

Option (e) is incorrect. Tina's basis in the stock is only $5,000, which is the amount she was taxed on when she received her distribution. Therefore, her capital gain will be $7,000 if she sells the stock for $12,000.

Fundamentals and Estates

38. d

A contribution made to a Section 529 plan will be considered a gift to the children. The 529 contribution can be treated as being made ratably over a 5-year period. Therefore, each spouse could contribute $60,000 ($12,000 annual exclusion × 5) for each child, without resulting in a taxable gift.

The total that can be contributed is $360,000 ($12,000 annual exclusion × 5 years × 3 children × 2 spouses). Any amount contributed in excess of the $360,000 will be considered a taxable gift, although there may be no gift tax due to the applicable credit.

Tax and Fundamentals

39. d

Land used in a business is a capital asset. Accounts receivable, inventory, copyrights, and creative works are all ordinary assets that would result in ordinary income tax (not capital gain) if sold at a gain.

Retirement and Employee Benefits

40. d

Statement 1 is correct. Profit sharing plans can have loan provisions. SEPs do not permit loans.

Statement 2 is incorrect. 5-year averaging is not available.

Statement 3 is incorrect. A profit-sharing plan must be established before the close of the tax year. Note: A SEP can be established by the tax return due date.

Statement 4 is correct. Qualified plans can invest in life insurance. SEPs do not permit life insurance.

Tax and Fundamentals

41. b

The money market fund would be the most appropriate investment for their emergency fund because it is the least risky of the choices given.

Tax and Fundamentals

42. d

Option (d) is correct. Only a C Corporation would be concerned with the reasonable compensation standards in this situation. Owners who take excessive salaries are attempting to bypass the double taxation of dividends. Owners of S Corporations are held to reasonable compensation standards as well; however, they would apply in the case of a key employee earning an unreasonably low salary.

Fundamentals and Investments

43. d

If Premium: Coupon Rate > Current Yield > Yield to Maturity.

If Par: Coupon Rate = Current Yield = Yield to Maturity.

If Discount: Coupon Rate < Current Yield < Yield to Maturity.

When a bond is selling at a discount, the yield to maturity is greater than the current yield.

Retirement and Employee Benefits

44. b

A is incorrect. Employer contributions are not subject to payroll taxes.

B is correct. Assets in a Rabbi trust are subject to the claims of the employer's creditors.

C in incorrect. Distributions from the trust are taxable as ordinary income.

D is incorrect. Assets in Rabbi trusts cannot be removed by new management.

Retirement and Employee Benefits

45. c

C is correct. When an employee exercises an NQSO, the employee will be taxed, and the employer will receive an income tax deduction for the same amount. The taxable amount to the employee and the deductible amount to the employer are based on the bargain element at exercise. The bargain element is the difference between the fair market value of the stock and the cost of the stock.

Therefore, the deduction would be $15,000 ($40 FMV − $10 Cost) × 500 Shares.

Fundamentals and Employee Benefits

46. c

C is incorrect. A Section 303 stock redemption is only available if the business entity is a corporation. All other items should be included in a buy-sell agreement.

Retirement and Employee Benefits

47. c

C is correct. Even though Steve has received more than the required minimum distributions over the last four years, he will still be required to take a minimum distribution for the current year.

Retirement and Employee Benefits

48. d

D is correct. Target-benefit plans are defined-contribution plans and are, therefore, subject to the annual additions limit per employee. Defined-benefit plans are not subject to this limit, and, therefore, employer contributions to defined-benefit plans can be much higher.

A is incorrect. Target-benefit plans favor older participants. Employer contributions are weighted according a participant's age.

B is incorrect. Both target-benefit plans and defined-benefit plans are qualified plans. Under ERISA, employers can exclude a certain percentage of nonhighly compensated employees from coverage under both the defined-benefit and target-benefit plans.

C is incorrect. Both target-benefit plans and defined-benefit plans have the same vesting requirements.

Fundamentals and Tax

49. c

C is correct. Gifts and inheritances received by one spouse are not considered community property.

A, B, and D are all examples of community property, because the assets were purchased with community property funds.

Retirement and Employee Benefits

50. b

Option 1 is incorrect. The exception to the early withdrawal penalty for those who leave the employer after attaining age 55 applies only to qualified plans and 403(b) plans. The exception would not apply to a SEP.

Option 2 is incorrect. A qualified plan can exclude employees working less than 1,000 hours. With a SEP, only one hour is necessary to accrue a year of service.

Options 3 and 4 are both correct.

Tax and Retirement

51. c

Option 1 is correct. Qualified plans have federal creditor protection.

Option 2 is correct. Alimony owed to a bankrupt person cannot be attached by creditors.

Option 3 is incorrect. Section 1244 stock can be attached by creditors in the event of bankruptcy.

Tax and Investments

52. b

B is correct. Interest income from private activity bonds are not subject to regular income tax. The interest income, however, is added back as a preference for alternative minimum tax.

A is incorrect. General obligation bonds are supported by the taxing power of the state. Revenue bonds are supported by the revenue from the specific project.

C is incorrect. Interest on municipal bonds is free from federal income tax.

D is incorrect. Municipal bonds are subject to default risk.

Fundamentals and Tax

53. a

A is correct. If the exchange occurs with a related party, both parties will be required to recognize any deferred gain if either party disposes of their property within two years of the exchange.

B is incorrect. If Barbara assumes the mortgage, she will in effect be paying boot to the other party. Gain is recognized only when boot is RECEIVED.

C is incorrect. Since this like-kind exchange will not be taxable to Barbara (she received no boot), she will not be required to recapture previous depreciation deductions taken.

D is incorrect. Deferral of gain on a like-kind exchange is mandatory. A taxpayer cannot elect to recognize the gain immediately.

Fundamentals and Tax

54. d

D is correct. The loss on the sale of a personal-use asset (personal residence, personal auto, etc.) is nondeductible.

Investments and Tax

55. c

C is correct. Under the Assignment of Income doctrine, a taxpayer is taxed on income assigned to another. Therefore, the agent would be taxed on commissions assigned to his son. All of the income would be included in gross income, except for the interest from the private activity bond. Therefore, gross income is $75,000 ($30,000 + $5,000 + $40,000).

Tax and Estates

56. b

B is correct. If Della had made no prior gifts, she would be able to use her full applicable credit of $345,800 for gift tax purposes. The credit will fully offset the gift tax on gifts of up to $1,000,000. Della's taxable gift would be $998,000 ($1,010,000 gift − $12,000 annual exclusion). The applicable credit would offset the tax on this gift.

A is incorrect. Gifts made within three years of death are not included in the gross estate unless the gifted property is life insurance.

C is incorrect. Gift tax paid can only be allocated to basis if the gifted property is appreciated property. Della has gifted "loss property."

D is incorrect. Because of the double-basis rule, loss property subsequently sold between its original basis and fair market value will recognize no gain or loss.

Retirement and Employee Benefits

57. d

D is correct. Although special minimum contribution rules apply to a top-heavy plan, the plan can continue to be integrated with Social Security.

A is incorrect. The merger of a money-purchase plan into a profit-sharing plan is not considered a plan termination.

Conversions:

Defined benefit to Defined benefit = Ok.

Defined contribution to Defined contribution = Ok.

Defined benefit to Defined contribution = No, plan must terminate.

Defined contribution to Defined benefit = No, plan must terminate.

B is incorrect. The maximum permitted disparity for a defined-contribution plan is the lesser of the base percentage (5% in this example) or 5.7%. Since the base percentage is 5%, the maximum permitted disparity would also be 5%.

C is incorrect. The additional catch-up contributions for participants age 50 or older only apply to employee-elective-deferral contributions, such as those found in a 401(k) plan.

Tax and Estates

58. c

C is correct.

Option 1 is incorrect. For a CRAT to be valid, the present value of the remainder interest must be at least 10% of the initial fair market value of the assets transferred to the trust.

Option 2 is correct. Payments to the grantor from a CRUT will increase each year if the assets in the trust are appreciating. This could provide a good inflation hedge.

Option 3 is correct. The grantor can be the trustee and make the investment decisions.

Option 4 is incorrect. Since the payment is based on the value of the trust assets valued annually, this statement describes a unitrust payment.

Estates and Tax

59. d

D is correct. If the beneficiary of a trust holds a general power of appointment over the trust property, the trust property will be included in the holder's gross estate at death. A general power of appointment is a power of appointment that can be exercised for the benefit of the holder, the holder's creditors, the holder's estate, or the creditors of the holder's estate.

A is incorrect. A limited power of appointment will not cause inclusion in the holder's estate.

B is incorrect. Powers that can be used for the holder's health, education, maintenance, and support (HEMS) are not considered general powers and do not cause inclusion in the gross estate.

C is incorrect. A 5-and-5 power is not considered a general power. However, a person who dies with the 5-and-5 power has the value of that power included in his gross estate.

Tax and Estates

60. a

A is correct. Since Tim retained a life estate in the residence, his gross estate will include the full value of the home ($200,000). His daughter will get a step-up in basis to $200,000, and therefore will have no gain.

Estates and Tax

61. d

D is correct. If the family disposes of the business during the deferral period, all deferred taxes must be recognized immediately.

A is incorrect. Section 6166 does not lower the estate tax. It allows the estate to defer the payment of estate taxes.

B is incorrect. The estate tax is delayed for five years, then paid over a 10-year installment period.

C is incorrect. Interest on the deferred tax is calculated based on IRS underpayment rates.

Tax and Investments

62. d

D is correct. Passive losses can only offset passive income.

A and C are incorrect. Passive losses cannot offset investment gains or income.

B is incorrect. Partnerships pass through their income to the partners, who report their share on their tax return.

Tax and Investments

63. b

B is correct. The utility company stock should be donated to charity. Since the stock was held long term, Molly will be entitled to a deduction equal to the fair market value of $29,000. This would be the most appropriate property to donate because of the low basis.

A is incorrect. Although cash is often an appropriate gift to donate to charity, highly appreciated assets are typically a preferable donation. If Molly were to donate the cash to charity and sell the stock, she would recognize a large capital gain.

C is incorrect. The municipal bond is worth less than what Molly paid. Her deduction would be limited to the lower fair market value. She would probably be better off selling the property and recognizing the loss, rather than donating this asset to charity.

D is incorrect. Since the growth mutual fund was held short term, Molly would only get a deduction for the basis in the property.

Tax and Investments

64. c

C is correct. Net unearned income of an individual under the age of 18 in excess of $1,700 will be taxed at the parent's marginal income tax rate.

A is incorrect. The assets do not have to be purchased by the child for the income to be subject to kiddie tax.

B is incorrect. A child claimed as a dependent is not entitled to a personal exemption on his/her own tax return.

D is incorrect. Earned income of the child is taxed at the child's tax rate.

Estates and Investments

65. c

C is correct.

The IRA will be included in his probate estate because the named beneficiary predeceased Val.

The life insurance policy will be subject to probate because the insured (Val's sister) is still alive. Therefore, the death benefit will not be paid out, and the insurance policy can be left to Val's heirs in his will.

The installment note receivable will be subject to probate.

The land will not be subject to probate because it is held as a tenancy by the entirety. Tenancy by the entirety passes by operation of law and avoids probate.

Employee Benefits and Insurance

66. e

E is correct.

All of the events are covered by COBRA continuation coverage.

Investments and Fundamentals

67. b

B is correct.

1 is incorrect. Beta is used as the measure of risk on the security market line.

2 and 3 are correct.

4 is incorrect. If risky securities are added to the portfolio, both risk and return will increase. The capital market line slopes upward indicating that as more risk is undertaken, more return will be achieved.

Investments and Fundamentals

68. b

B is correct.

Option 1 is correct. A zero-coupon bond has a duration equal to its maturity. Bonds with a coupon rate have a duration less than their maturity.

Option 2 is incorrect. To immunize a bond portfolio, an investor would match the average weighted duration (not maturity) of the bond portfolio to the investment horizon.

Option 3 is correct. To calculate duration of a bond, one must know the bond's yield to maturity.

Option 4 is incorrect. Treasury bills have durations of 1 year or less and therefore would not immunize a portfolio with a time horizon of six years.

Investments and Fundamentals

69. d

D is correct. Foreign currency risk is a type of systematic risk. Systematic risks are those risks that affect the entire market.

Systematic risks include market risk, interest rate risk, purchasing power risk, reinvestment rate risk, and foreign currency risk.

Fundamentals and Investments

70. a

A is correct.

Option 1 is correct. The Federal Reserve can purchase Treasury securities to stimulate the economy.

Option 2 is incorrect. If the Federal Reserve increased reserve requirements, banks would have less money to lend.

Option 3 is incorrect. The federal government is responsible for increasing or decreasing tax rates. Tax rate changes are a part of fiscal policy. The Federal Reserve only controls monetary policy.

Option 4 is incorrect. The Federal Reserve would decrease the discount rate if attempting to stimulate the economy.

Estates, Insurance and Tax

71. c

C is correct.

Option 1 is incorrect. Since Stan is terminally ill (expected to die within two years), he will not be taxed on the proceeds received from the viatical company even if he lives longer than two years.

Option 2 is incorrect. When the viatical company receives the death benefit, it will be subject to tax at ordinary income tax rates to the viatical company. The viatical company can reduce the taxable portion by the amount paid for the policy.

Option 3 is correct. The sale of the policy to Stan's cousin would be considered a transfer for value. Stan would not be taxed on the gain, because he is terminally ill. His cousin, however, would be taxed on the death benefit (less amounts paid) because the transfer for value rules cause the death benefit to become taxable.

Option 4 is correct. With an MEC, loans or distributions from the policy are taxed LIFO basis, meaning that any earnings in the policy are taxed first.

Insurance, Employee Benefits and Tax

72. e

E is correct.

Option 1 is incorrect. Rob will not be entitled to receive a Social Security disability benefit until a five-month waiting period has elapsed. He would not be entitled to a benefit until August (five full calendar months must pass). He will receive his first check in September (checks are paid one month after due).

Option 2 is correct. When Rob reaches his normal retirement age, his Social Security disability benefit automatically ends, and his Social Security retirement benefit begins.

Option 3 is correct. Normally, a spouse of a disabled worker is eligible to receive a Social Security benefit as early as age 62. A spouse of a disabled worker, however, can receive a benefit AT ANY AGE if the spouse is caring for a worker's child under the age of 16.

Option 4 is correct. Since Jean is under 18, she will be entitled to a dependent's benefit because her father is disabled. The earnings test would apply to Jean, however, because she has not attained normal retirement age. Under the earnings test, Social Security benefits are reduced $1 for every $2 of earned income above the threshold. For 2007, the threshold is $12,960. Therefore, Jean will lose a portion of her benefits.

Employee Benefits, Retirement and Insurance

73. b

B is correct. A 60-day maximum elimination period is not one of the requirements for deductibility.

Estate, Investments and Tax

74. c

C is correct. Since Sarah is under age 18, the kiddie tax rules would apply. Therefore, some of the interest income (amounts over $1,700 for 2007) would be taxed at the parent's (Fred's) income tax rate.

A is incorrect. Although the transfer to an UGMA is technically a future interest gift, the annual exclusion is allowed.

B is incorrect. The interest income would be taxed to Sarah and Fred based on the kiddie tax rules. The UGMA account is not a trust.

D is incorrect. The UGMA account is a taxable account.

Investments and Fundamentals

75. a

A is correct. Default risk is diversifiable (unsystematic) risk.

B, C, and D are examples of systematic risk, which is not diversifiable.

Insurance and Employee Benefits

76. c

C is correct. Stacey's group plan allows her to be covered by her husband's individual health plan because her plan has a coordination of benefits (COB) provision If her husband had a group health plan, then it would also have a COB provision and Stacey's plan would be her primary health plan.

Insurance, Employee Benefits and Tax

77. d

D is correct. The premiums on a split-dollar policy are not deductible.

Retirement and Tax

78. c

C is correct. A safe harbor 401(k) allows employee contributions and does not require an ADP test.

A is incorrect. A profit-sharing 401(k) plan requires ADP testing each year. Therefore, if Aaron's employees do not contribute, Aaron cannot contribute.

B is incorrect. A SEP does not allow employee contributions.

D and E are incorrect. Aaron wants a tax deduction for the current tax year. A SIMPLE 401(k) and SIMPLE IRA must be established by October 1 of the year of establishment. Since today is November 15, it is too late to establish a SIMPLE for the current year.

Fundamentals and Investments

79. a

Statement 1 is correct.

Statement 2 is incorrect. FNMAs are not backed by the US Government.

Statement 3 is incorrect. The Municipal Bond Insurance Association insures certain municipal bonds.

Statement 4 is incorrect. Long-term bonds typically have high inflation risk.

Insurance and Fundamentals

80. c

C is correct. The election can be made at the time of the application, but it can also be made at any time prior to the end of the grace period of any premium in default.

A is incorrect. The provision will not apply if the premium due exceeds the cash value of the policy.

B is incorrect. The election CAN be made with the application, but is not legally required to be made at that time.

D is incorrect. After the grace period, the policyowner cannot elect the automatic premium loan option. The policy will lapse at the end of the grace period, and it can only be reinstated if the insured provides evidence of insurability.

Tax and Fundamentals

81. c

C is correct.

Original cost	$12,000
Depreciation	$ 7,000
Adjusted Basis	$ 5,000

The gain on sale is $3,000 ($8,000 sales price less $5,000 adjusted basis).

Since this property is depreciable personal property, the property is classified as Section 1245 property. Gain on the sale of Section 1245 property will be treated as ORDINARY INCOME to the extent of depreciation taken. Since $7,000 of depreciation deductions have been taken, the entire $3,000 gain will be "recaptured" as ordinary income.

Insurance and Fundamentals

82. c

C is correct. Part B of an HO-3 policy covers structures other than the dwelling. A detached garage would be covered under Part B.

A and B are incorrect. An attached garage would be covered under Part A because it is considered part of the dwelling.

D is incorrect. Dining room furniture would be covered under Part C, personal property.

Investments and Fundamentals

83. b

B is correct.

Option 1 is incorrect. Standard deviation is the square root of the variance.

Option 2 is incorrect. Standard deviation measures total risk, which is comprised of both systematic and unsystematic risk.

Option 3 is correct.

Option 4 is incorrect. Beta is only an appropriate measure of risk if the client has a diversified portfolio.

Estates and Fundamentals

84. d

D is correct.

A is incorrect. With a cross-purchase, buy-sell agreement, the surviving shareholders would purchase the stock of a deceased shareholder. A stock redemption involves the sale of stock to the corporation. Therefore, Section 303 would not apply to a cross-purchase, buy-sell agreement.

B is incorrect. A Section 6166 election allows the payment of estate taxes, not Section 303.

C is incorrect. In order to make a Section 303 election, the value of the stock included in the gross estate must be more than 35% of the adjusted gross estate. David owns 40% of the stock of the company. Therefore, his stock is worth $2,000,000 (40% × $5,000,000). Since his adjusted gross estate is $10,000,000, his stock only comprises 20% of the adjusted gross estate. It should be noted that family attribution rules do not apply to Section 303 redemptions.

D is correct. Stock redemptions are generally treated as dividends for income tax purposes. Section 303 provides for favorable capital gain treatment of redemptions. Capital gain treatment is especially favorable in the case of Section 303 because the decedent's stock will receive a step-up in basis at the decedent's death resulting in little or no capital gain.

Estates and Tax

85. b

B is correct. Even though a trust is used, there are no nonskip beneficiaries. Therefore, this would be considered a direct skip.

A is incorrect. This trust would not qualify as a direct skip because there is a nonskip beneficiary (daughter) of the trust.

C is incorrect. Although a gift has been made directly to the grandchild, this would not be a direct skip due to the predeceased parent rule.

D is incorrect. Payment of college tuition directly to the school is not considered a gift.

Retirement and Estates

86. c

C is correct. A profit-sharing plan is a type of income in respect of a decedent (IRD) asset. IRD assets do not receive a step-up in basis at the owner's death. Therefore, Tom would be required to pay income tax on any lump-sum distribution.

A is incorrect. According to the information given, the employer requires a lump-sum distribution to the beneficiaries when the participant dies.

B is incorrect. Since Tom was born after 1936, he cannot elect 10-year averaging. The 10-year averaging election is only applicable to individuals born before 1936, as well as certain estates and trusts.

D is incorrect. Sara Sue's will can specify how estate taxes will be paid.

Estates and Retirement

87. d

D is correct. A CRAT is valid only if the present value of the remainder interest in the trust is at least 10% of the initial fair market value of the assets transferred to the trust. The higher the payout rate, the lower the present value of the remainder interest in the trust.

A is incorrect. The profit-sharing plan will be included in Sara Sue's gross estate.

B is incorrect. Sara Sue's estate will receive an estate tax charitable deduction, but only in an amount equal to the present value of the remainder interest in the trust. This deduction will be less than the full value of the profit-sharing plan.

C is incorrect. Tom could receive an annuity from the CRAT for life; however, he will be taxed on the annuity received.

Retirement and Insurance

88. c

C is correct.

1 is incorrect. A Section 412(i) plan is a defined-benefit plan that is funded exclusively by either life insurance or annuity contracts, or both.

2 is correct. A Section 412(i) plan is a qualified plan.

3 is incorrect. If a Section 412(i) plan is funded with life insurance policies, no policy loans may be outstanding at any time during the plan year.

4 is correct. If the plan qualifies under Section 412(i), it will not be subject to the minimum funding standards, even though it is a pension plan.

Investments and Fundamentals

89. d

D is correct. A CMO has an estimated, not fixed, maturity date.

Investments and Tax

90. a

A is correct. A REIT passes through gains, not losses, to investors.

APPENDIX

Appendix

■

* Denotes formula that will likely be provided on exam, without the variable definitions.
(See Appendix 2 for actual formulas provided on the exam.)

CAPITAL ASSET PRICING MODEL (CAPM)

---

* *Capital Market Line (CML)*

$$R_p = R_f + \left(\frac{R_m - R_f}{\sigma_m}\right)\sigma_p$$

R_p	=	The return of the portfolio.
R_f	=	The risk-free rate of return.
R_m	=	The return on the market.
$(R_m\text{-}R_f)$	=	The return from the market that exceeds the risk-free rate of return.
σ_m	=	The standard deviation of the market.
σ_p	=	The standard deviation of the portfolio.

* *Security Market Line (SML)*

$$R_s = R_f + \beta(R_m - R_f)$$

R_s	=	The return for a stock.
R_f	=	The risk-free rate of return.
β	=	Beta, which is a measure of the systematic risk associated with a particular stock.
$(R_m\text{-}R_f)$	=	The risk premium, which is the additional return of the market over the risk-free rate of return.

Characteristic Line (CL)

$$R_j = \alpha_j + \beta_j R_m + e$$

R_j	=	Return for asset j.
α_j	=	Y intercept or constant term.
β_j	=	The slope of the line (beta).
R_m	=	Rate of return for the market.
e	=	Error term from the analysis.

ARBITRAGE PRICING THEORY (APT)

* Arbitrage Pricing Theory (APT)

$$R = a_0 + b_1F_1 + b_2F_2 + \ldots + b_nF_n + e$$

R = The return from the security.

a_0 = The return that is expected for all securities when the value of all factors is zero. In some cases, this is called the expected return.

b_n = The sensitivity of the security to factor F_n.

F_n = The factor that affects the security, such as GNP of 3%.

e = The return that is unique to the security. It is also called an error term in some cases. **Note:** This error term should drop out if all relevant factors are captured by the equation.

MEASURES OF RISK

Beta

$$\beta_p = \left(\frac{\sigma_p}{\sigma_m}\right)(R_{pm})$$

β_p = Beta.

σ_p = Standard deviation of the portfolio.

σ_m = Standard deviation of the market.

R_{pm} = Correlation coefficient between the portfolio and the market.

Weighted-Average Beta

$$\beta_w = \sum_{i=1}^{N} (\beta_i \times \%_i)$$

β_w = Weighted-average Beta.

β_i = Beta return for security i.

$\%_i$ = Portion of security i to total portfolio.

N = Number of securities.

Expected Rate of Return

$$E(r) \ = \ P_1(R_1) + P_2(R_2) + \ldots + P_t(R_t)$$

$E(r)$ = The expected return.
P_1 = The probability assigned to the first rate of return.
R_1 = Rate of return for period 1.
t = The number of events that are being examined.

Standard Deviation of Forecasted Returns

$$\sigma \ = \ \text{Var.}(r)^{1/2} = [P_1[r_1 - E(r)]^2 + P_2[r_2 - E(r)]^2 + \ldots + P_t[r_t - E(r)]^2]^{\frac{1}{2}}$$

$E(r)$ = Expected return (calculated).
r_t = Forecasted return for outcome t.
P_t = Probability of outcome t.
σ = Standard deviation.

* Standard Deviation of Historical Returns

$$\sigma \ = \ \sqrt{\frac{\sum\limits_{i=1}^{n} (r_i - \bar{r})^2}{(n-1)}}$$

σ = Standard deviation.
n = Number of observations.
r_i = Actual return for period i.
$\bar{r}$ = Average return.

* Standard Deviation of a Two-Security Portfolio

$$\sigma \ = \ \sqrt{W_A^2 \sigma_A^2 + W_B^2 \sigma_B^2 + 2 W_A W_B [\sigma_A \sigma_B R_{AB}]}$$

σ^2 = Variance.
σ = Standard deviation.
W_A = The percent of the portfolio invested in security A.
W_B = The percent of the portfolio invested in security B.
$[\sigma_A \sigma_B R_{AB}]$ = Covariance between security A & B.
R_{AB} = Correlation coefficient.

Note: W_A and W_B must sum to 100%.

Duration (Example)

Bond:

PV   =   **$974.23**
N   =   3
i   =   8%
PMT =   70
FV   = $1,000.00

Duration Calculation			
Year	Cash Flow	Year × Cash Flow	PV @ 8%
1	70	70	64.81
2	70	140	120.03
3	1,070	3,210	2,548.20
	1,210	N/A	2,733.04

Duration = 2,733.04 ÷ 974.23 = 2.8 years

* Change in Price Using Duration

$$\frac{\Delta P}{P} = \frac{-D}{1 + Y} \ \times \ \Delta (1 + Y)$$

$\dfrac{\Delta P}{P}$ =   Percent change in price of a bond.

D   =   Duration.
Y   =   Yield to Maturity.

OR

$$\frac{\Delta P}{P} = -D\left[\frac{\Delta(1 + y)}{1 + y}\right], \ where$$

D   =   Duration.
Y   =   Yield to Maturity.

PERFORMANCE MEASURES

* The Sharpe Performance Index

$$S(p) = \frac{(R_p - R_f)}{\sigma}$$

$S(p)$ = Sharpe Performance Measure for portfolio p.
R_p = The average rate of return for a given time period.
R_f = The risk-free rate of return during the same time period.
σ = The standard deviation of the rate of return for portfolio p during the same time interval.

* The Treynor Performance Measure

$$T_p = \frac{(R_p - R_f)}{B_p}$$

T_p = Treynor Performance Measure for portfolio p.
R_p = The average rate of return for a given time period.
R_f = The risk-free rate of return during the same time period.
B_p = Beta for the same period or the slope of the portfolio's characteristic line during the period.

The Jensen Model

$$(R_p - R_f) = \alpha_p + \beta_p[R_m - R_f] + e$$

$(R_p - R_f)$ = The return that is earned solely for bearing risk.
α_p = Alpha, which represents the return that is able to be earned above or below an unmanaged portfolio with identical market risk.
β_p = Beta, which is the measure of systematic or market risk.
R_m = The return on the market.
R_f = The risk-free rate of return.
e = The error term.

* The Jensen Performance Index

$$\alpha_p = R_p - [R_f + \beta_p(R_m - R_f)]$$

α_p	=	Alpha, which represents the return that is able to be earned above or below an unmanaged portfolio with identical market risk.
R_p	=	The average rate of return for a given time period.
R_f	=	The risk-free rate of return.
β_p	=	Beta, which is the measure of systematic or market risk.
$(R_m - R_f)$	=	The risk premium, which is the additional return of the market over the risk-free rate of return.

RATES OF RETURN

Holding Period Return (HPR)

$$HPR = \frac{\text{Ending Value of Investment} - \text{Beginning Value of Investment} +/- \text{Cashflows}}{\text{Beginning Value of Investment}}$$

Internal Rate of Return (IRR)

$$P_0 = \frac{CF_1}{(1+k)^1} + \frac{CF_2}{(1+k)^2} + \ldots + \frac{CF_t}{(1+k)^t}$$

P_0	=	The value of the security today.
CF_t	=	The cash flow for period t.
k	=	The discount rate based on the security type.
t	=	The number of cash flows to be evaluated.

Yield To Maturity (YTM)

$$P_0 = \frac{CF_1}{(1+k)^1} + \frac{CF_2}{(1+k)^2} + \ldots + \frac{Par}{(1+k)^t}$$

P_0	=	The value of the security today.
CF_t	=	The cash flow for period t.
k	=	The discount rate based on the security type.
t	=	The number of cash flows to be evaluated.

Yield to Call (YTC)

$$P_0 = \frac{CF_1}{(1+k)^1} + \frac{CF_2}{(1+k)^2} + \ldots + \frac{\text{Call Price}}{(1+k)^t}$$

P_0	=	The value of the security today.
CF_t	=	The cash flow for period t.
k	=	The discount rate based on the security type.
t	=	The number of periods until the bonds may be called.

Arithmetic Mean

$$AM = \frac{\sum\limits_{t=1}^{n} HPR_t}{n}$$

Time-Weighted Return

$$P_0 = \frac{CF_1}{(1+k)^1} + \frac{CF_2}{(1+k)^2} + \ldots + \frac{CF_t}{(1+k)^t}$$

P_0	=	The value of the security today.
CF_t	=	The cash flow for period t.
k	=	The discount rate based on the security type.
t	=	The number of cash flows to be evaluated.

> **Note:** Time-weighted return considers cash flows of investment only. It does not consider cash flows of the investor.

Geometric Mean

$$GM = \sqrt[n]{(1 + R_1)(1 + R_2)\ldots(1 + R_n)} - 1$$

R_n	=	Return for each period.
n	=	Number of periods.

After-Tax Rate of Return

Tax-Adjusted Return = $R(1 - TR)$

R	=	Before-tax return or earnings rate.
TR	=	Tax rate.

Inflation-Adjusted Rate of Return

$$R_i = \left[\frac{(1 + R)}{(1 + IR)} - 1\right] \times 100$$

R_i	=	Inflation-adjusted return.
R	=	Earnings rate.
IR	=	Inflation rate.

Weighted-Average Return

$$\overline{x_w} = \sum_{i=1}^{N} [(R_i)(\%_i)]$$

$\overline{x_w}$	=	Weighted average.
R_i	=	Return for security i.
$\%_i$	=	Portion of security i to total portfolio.
N	=	Number of securities.

VALUATION MODELS

The Basic Present Value (Valuation) Model

$$P_0 = \frac{CF_1}{(1+k)^1} + \frac{CF_2}{(1+k)^2} + \ldots + \frac{CF_t}{(1+k)^t}$$

P_0	=	The value of the security today.
CF_t	=	The cash flow for period t.
k	=	The discount rate based on the type of security and risk level of the investment.
t	=	The number of cash flows to be evaluated.

* *Constant Dividend Growth Model*

$$P_0 = \frac{D_1}{k-g}$$

P_0	=	Price for the security.
D_1	=	The dividend paid at period 1.
k	=	The investor's required rate of return.
g	=	The growth rate of the dividends. The growth rate can be negative, positive or zero. See perpetuities for a zero growth rate.

Capitalized Earnings

$$V = \frac{E}{R_d}$$

V	=	The value of the company or firm.
E	=	The earnings used to value the firm.
R_d	=	The discount rate.

Perpetuity

$$P_0 \; = \; \frac{D}{k}$$

P_0	=	Price of the security.
D	=	The dividend paid per period.
k	=	Investor's required rate of return.

* Conversion Value

$$CV \; = \; \left(\frac{1,000}{CP}\right)(P_s)$$

CV	=	Conversion value.
CP	=	Conversion price of stock.
P_s	=	Current price of stock.

Note: Bond face = \$1,000.

APPENDIX 2: FORMULA PAGE PROVIDED ON CFP® CERTIFICATION EXAMINATION

$$V = \frac{D_1}{r - g}$$

$$r_i = r_f + (r_m - r_f)B_i$$

$$r = \frac{D_1}{P} + g$$

$$r_p = r_f + \sigma_p \left[\frac{r_m - r_f}{\sigma_m} \right]$$

$$COV_{ij} = \rho_{ij}\sigma_i\sigma_j$$

$$S_p = \frac{r_p - r_f}{\sigma_p}$$

$$\sigma_p = \sqrt{W_i^2\sigma_i^2 + W_j^2\sigma_j^2 + 2W_iW_jCOV_{ij}}$$

$$\alpha_p = r_p - [r_f + (r_m - r_f)\beta_p]$$

$$\beta_i = \frac{COV_{im}}{\sigma_m^2} = \frac{\rho_{im}\sigma_i}{\sigma_m}$$

$$T_p = \frac{r_p - r_f}{\beta_p}$$

$$\sigma_r = \sqrt{\frac{\sum_{t=1}^{n} (r_t - \bar{r})^2}{n}}$$

$$D = \frac{\sum_{t=1}^{n} \frac{C_t(t)}{(1+i)^t}}{\sum_{t=1}^{n} \frac{C_t}{(1+i)^t}}$$

$$S_r = \sqrt{\frac{\sum_{t=1}^{n} (r_t - \bar{r})^2}{n - 1}}$$

$$D = \frac{1+y}{y} - \frac{(1+y) + t(c-y)}{c[(1+y)^t - 1] + y}$$

$$CV = \frac{Par}{CP} \times P_s$$

$$\frac{\Delta P}{P} = -D\left[\frac{\Delta y}{1 + y} \right]$$

Reprinted, with permission, from the CFP Board of Standards Guide to CFP® Certification booklet.

APPENDIX 3: 2007 TAX RATES AND BRACKETS

Single – Schedule X

If taxable income is: Over --	But not over --	The tax is:	Of the amount over --
$0	$7,825	-------------- 10%	$0
7,825	31,850	$782.50 + 15%	7,825
31,850	77,100	4,386.25 + 25%	31,850
77,100	160,850	15,698.75 + 28%	77,100
160,850	349,700	39,148.75 + 33%	160,850
$349,700	------------	$101,469.25 + 35%	$349,700

Head of Household – Schedule Z

If taxable income is: Over --	But not over --	The tax is:	Of the amount over --
$0	$11,200	-------------- 10%	$0
11,200	42,650	$1,120.00 + 15%	11,200
42,650	110,100	5,837.50 + 25%	42,650
110,100	178,350	22,700.00 + 28%	110,100
178,350	349,700	41,810.00 + 33%	178,350
$349,700	------------	$98,355.50 + 35%	$349,700

Married Filing Jointly or Qualifying Widow(er) – Schedule Y-1

If taxable income is: Over --	But not over --	The tax is:	Of the amount over --
$0	$15,650	-------------- 10%	$0
15,650	63,700	$1,565.00 + 15%	15,650
63,700	128,500	8,772.50 + 25%	63,700
128,500	195,850	24,972.50 + 28%	128,500
195,850	349,700	43,830.50 + 33%	195,850
$349,700	------------	$94,601.00 + 35%	$349,700

Married Filing Separately – Schedule Y-2

If taxable income is: Over --	But not over --	The tax is:	Of the amount over --
$0	$7,825	-------------- 10%	$0
7,825	31,850	$7,825.50+ 15%	7,825
31,850	64,250	4,386.25 + 25%	31,850
64,250	97,925	12,486.25 + 28%	64,250
97,925	174,850	21,915.25 + 33%	97,925
$174,850	------------	$47,300.50 + 35%	$174,850

APPENDIX 4: TAX—STANDARD DEDUCTION AMOUNT AND ADDITIONAL DEDUCTION

STANDARD DEDUCTION

Filing Status	2006	2007
Single	$5,150	$5,350
Married, filing jointly/SS	$10,300	$10,700
Head of household	$7,550	$7,850
Married, filing separately	$5,150	$5,350

ADDITIONAL STANDARD DEDUCTION*

Filing Status	2006	2007
Single	$1,250	$1,300
Married, filing jointly/SS	$1,000	$1,050
Head of household	$1,250	$1,300
Married, filing separately	$1,000	$1,050

Aged (65 and older) or blind. Standard deduction for an individual claimed as a dependent by another taxpayer may not exceed the regular standard deduction and is limited to the greater of $850 or the sum of $300 plus the individual's earned income.

Other Deductions	2007
Standard deduction for one who may be claimed as a dependent of another (greater of $800 or earned income plus $250)	$850 (min)
Kiddie tax exemption	1,700
Personal and dependency exemptions	3,400

APPENDIX 5: THE TAX FORMULA FOR INDIVIDUALS

Income (broadly conceived)	$xx,xxx
Less: Exclusions	(x,xxx)
Gross Income	$xx,xxx
Less: Deductions for Adjusted Gross Income	(x,xxx)
Adjusted Gross Income (AGI)	$xx,xxx
Less: The Greater of:	
Total Itemized Deductions or Standard Deduction	(x,xxx)
Less: Personal and Dependency Exemptions	(x,xxx)
Taxable Income	$xx,xxx

APPENDIX 6: 2007 ESTATE AND GIFT TAX RATES

Over $0 but not over $10,000	**18%** of such amount
Over $10,000 but not over $20,000	$1,800 plus **20%** of the excess of such amount over $10,000
Over $20,000 but not over $40,000	$3,800 plus **22%** of the excess of such amount over $20,000
Over $40,000 but not over $60,000	$8,200 plus **24%** of the excess of such amount over $40,000
Over $60,000 but not over $80,000	$13,000 plus **26%** of the excess of such amount over $60,000
Over $80,000 but not over $100,000	$18,200 plus **28%** of the excess of such amount over $80,000
Over $100,000 but not over $150,000	$23,800 plus **30%** of the excess of such amount over $100,000
Over $150,000 but not over $250,000	$38,800 plus **32%** of the excess of such amount over $150,000
Over $250,000 but not over $500,000	$70,800 plus **34%** of the excess of such amount over $250,000
Over $500,000 but not over $750,000	$155,800 plus **37%** of the excess of such amount over $500,000
Over $750,000 but not over $1,000,000	$248,300 plus **39%** of the excess of such amount over $750,000
Over $1,000,000 but not over $1,250,000	$345,800 plus **41%** of the excess of such amount over $1,000,000
Over $1,250,000 but not over $1,500,000	$448,300 plus **43%** of the excess of such amount over $1,250,000
Over $1,500,000	$555,800 plus **45%**

APPENDIX 7: ESTATES—RATE AND CREDIT SUMMARY

Year of Death	Maximum Estate Tax Rate	Estate Tax Applicable Exclusion Amount	Estate Tax Credit
2007	45%	$2,000,000	$780,800
2008	45%	$2,000,000	$780,800
2009	45%	$3,500,000	$1,455,800
2010	Repealed	Repealed	Repealed